Remembered Words

Remembered Words

Essays on Genre, Realism, and Emblems

ALASTAIR FOWLER

OXFORD
UNIVERSITY PRESS

Great Clarendon Street, Oxford, OX2 6DP,
United Kingdom

Oxford University Press is a department of the University of Oxford.
It furthers the University's objective of excellence in research, scholarship,
and education by publishing worldwide. Oxford is a registered trade mark of
Oxford University Press in the UK and in certain other countries

© Alastair Fowler 2021. Chapter 4 © University of London 1984.
Chapter 10 © The British Academy 1996

The moral rights of the author have been asserted

First Edition published in 2021

Impression: 1

All rights reserved. No part of this publication may be reproduced, stored in
a retrieval system, or transmitted, in any form or by any means, without the
prior permission in writing of Oxford University Press, or as expressly permitted
by law, by licence or under terms agreed with the appropriate reprographics
rights organization. Enquiries concerning reproduction outside the scope of the
above should be sent to the Rights Department, Oxford University Press, at the
address above

You must not circulate this work in any other form
and you must impose this same condition on any acquirer

Published in the United States of America by Oxford University Press
198 Madison Avenue, New York, NY 10016, United States of America

British Library Cataloguing in Publication Data

Data available

Library of Congress Control Number: 2020946427

ISBN 978-0-19-885697-9

DOI: 10.1093/oso/9780198856979.001.0001

Printed and bound in the UK by
TJ Books Limited

Links to third party websites are provided by Oxford in good faith and
for information only. Oxford disclaims any responsibility for the materials
contained in any third party website referenced in this work.

Contents

Foreword	vii
Acknowledgements	xi
Introduction	1
1. Emblems of Temperance in *The Faerie Queene*, Book II	4
2. The Life and Death of Literary Forms	11
3. The 'Better Marks' of Jonson's *To Penshurst*	27
4. Pastoral Instruction in 'As You Like It'	44
5. 'Paradise Regained': Some Problems of Style	56
6. The Paradoxical Machinery of *The Rape of the Lock*	65
7. Georgic and Pastoral: Laws of Genre in the Seventeenth Century	84
8. *Twelfth Night* and Epiphany	92
9. 'Cut without hands': Herbert's Christian altar	105
10. Shakespeare's Renaissance Realism	116
11. Relevance	142
12. The Emblem as a Literary Genre	146
13. Lord's Space in Seventeenth-Century Britain	164
14. The Formation of Genres in the Renaissance and After	179
15. Gavin Douglas: Romantic Humanist	194
16. Anagrams	213
17. Ut Architectura Poesis	222
18. Perspective and Realism in the Renaissance	240
19. Penshurst Revisited	252
Bibliography	271
Index	275

Foreword

The publication of this volume of the essays of Alastair Fowler offers a remarkable opportunity both to explore the intellectual development of one of the finest scholars of the last half-century and more and also to encounter afresh some of the master-works of Renaissance literature in the company of a uniquely gifted guide.

There was, at the end of the last century, a brief craze for computer-generated visual puzzles that at first glance appeared to be sheets of merely abstract grey tessellation. If you knew how to look at them, however, and if you stared at them for long enough from just the right angle, gradually three-dimensional shapes seemingly hidden behind the opaque surfaces began to appear: balls, cubes, cylinders, and in the more advanced versions, animals, human faces, or birds in flight. The reward for the patient observer was thus the discovery of unexpected beauty and complexity behind a familiar façade, a discovery to which you alone seemed privy. Revisiting the classics of Renaissance literature alongside Alastair Fowler provides the same sense of uncovering hidden treasures in works whose riches had hitherto seemed long-exhausted. His impeccable reading of the emblems deployed in Book II of *The Faerie Queene* is a case in point, revealing unexpected patterns of fountains, lakes, and rivers, symbols of baptism, repentance, and regeneration, of cups and vessels, and finally of water poured into wine, all emblems related to the book's principal virtue, Temperance, and all evidencing a text startlingly rich in its conception and execution. Similarly, his virtuoso exposition of the symbolism of 'To Penshurst', drawing on points as diverse as the early-ripening of apricots and the numerologically significant placing of the word 'crown' and the first mention of King James in the poem, inspires a new appreciation of the geometric intricacies of Jonson's creative imagination.

Fowler is probably best known as the author of classic book-length studies such as *Kinds of Literature*, *Triumphal Forms*, and *Renaissance Realism*, and magisterial critical editions of Milton and Spenser, but in these essays he shows himself equally adept at delivering great reckonings in far smaller rooms. The collection offers a series of intellectually intense and deeply engaging lectures from a master of his craft who takes his readers deep into each carefully chosen text, pointing out a submerged classical allusion here, an echo of contemporary Neoplatonist thought there. Blink and you will miss an intellectual firework or a wry aside. A brilliant and paradigm-shifting reading of Shylock's devotion to his bond is offered almost in passing in a discussion of the multiplicity of

Shakespeare's plot-lines. A more sustained reading of *Hamlet* is exemplary both in its broadminded acknowledgement of the play's diversity (and why it matters) and in its command of fine, often seemingly arcane contextual detail. 'Hans Knieper's tapestry workshop at Elsinsore was famous,' he throws in, suggesting why Polonius was made to die behind an arras rather than under the rushes like his forebear in Saxo Grammaticus' narrative version, only then to show that this apparently incidental detail of local Danish colour is itself carefully woven into the play's wider fascination with 'words, words, words' (Francis Bacon among others having suggested a clear affinity between cloths of arras and spoken words 'opened and put abroad'). Discussing Shakespeare's comedies, Fowler is able to cast new light on the depth and prevalence of images of time passing and time measured and divided in *As You Like It* and on the deep layering of allusions to Epiphany in *Twelfth Night*. Turning to the literature of his native Scotland, he offers a sensitive reappraisal of the work of Gavin Douglas, making a compelling case for his election to the first rank of Renaissance linguists and translators.

Throughout his career Fowler has been in many respects the lone scholar par excellence, often ploughing a lonely furrow in pursuit of an idea thought unworthy of consideration or just too difficult a challenge by modish scholarship. And few modern critics are as well read or as erudite as he is. It might thus be wise to have a good dictionary to hand when reading further, unless 'immiscible', 'amphibolous', 'catoptric', or 'theriomorphic' are features of your familiar conversation. And perhaps just nod in agreement and hope for no further questions when he says of Malvolio that 'his comprehensively Saturnalian disposition will be obvious to anyone who recalls the *Tetrabiblios* and Ptolemy's description of Saturn's children…' But if Fowler's reputation for the rigour of his own mind and scholarship is fully exemplified here, that for the sharpness of his criticism of others less rigorous is effectively challenged. He is certainly more than willing to hand out low marks where he thinks them merited: witness the taking to task of Jacques Derrida for his 'poor grasp of Saussure' or of Stephen Greenblatt for the 'gross factual errors' in his *Will in The World*. And there is a particularly neat taking down of both W. H. Auden and A. D. Nutall with a single stone for each getting Shylock 'exactly wrong'. But the essays gathered here also allow us to appreciate Fowler's lifelong enjoyment of the pleasures of academic conviviality and companionable argument with other scholars from C. S. Lewis ('the first great critic I knew personally') through Barbara Lewalski and Christopher Ricks to 'Fred' Jamieson. Each of these essays was written in real or vicarious dialogue with other scholars, testing their hypotheses against the evidence of text and context, offering counter-proposals and alternative readings, and acting as enthusiastic advocate for Renaissance modes of thinking and writing that currently fashionable scholarship neglects. There is thus more than a grain of truth in his own self-deprecating suggestion, voiced in the Introduction, that 'I begin to see that my *raison d'être* lay in reminding critics about parts of literature they had forgotten'. The essays themselves, though, are anything but forgettable. By turns dazzling and inspirational, they are supreme examples of great scholarship motivated by the love of the works that form their subject and of the writers who produced them.

    Greg Walker,
    Regius Professor of Rhetoric and English Literature, University of Edinburgh

Acknowledgements

I am grateful for permission to re-use the following articles:

Fowler, A., 1988. The Paradoxical Machinery of *The Rape of the Lock*. In: C. Nicholson and A. Pope, ed., *Alexander Pope: Essays For The Tercentenary*. Elsevier. Reproduced with permission of Elsevier B.V. through PLSclear.

Fowler, A., 2008. Ut Architectura Poesis. In: C. Guest, ed., *Rhetoric, Theatre and the Arts of Design: Essays Presented to Roy Eriksen*. Novus Press.

Fowler, A., 1974. The Life and Death of Literary Forms. In: R. Cohen, ed., *Routledge Revivals: New Directions In Literary History*. Informa UK Limited. Reproduced with permission of Informa UK Limited through PLSclear.

Fowler, A., 2003. The Formation of Genres in the Renaissance and After. *New Literary History*, 34(2), 185–200. Reproduced with permission of the Johns Hopkins University Press via Copyright Clearance Center.

Fowler, A., 2010. Perspective and Realism in the Renaissance. In: K. Cartwright, ed., *A Companion To Tudor Literature*. Wiley-Blackwell. Reproduced with permission of John Wiley and Sons.

Fowler, A., 1984. *Paradise Regained*: Some Problems of Style. In: P. Boitani and A. Torti, ed., *Medieval And Pseudo-Medieval Literature: The J. A. W. Bennett Memorial Lectures, Perugia 1982–1983*. Boydell & Brewer.

Fowler, A., 1984. Pastoral Instruction In 'As You Like It': The John Coffin Memorial Lecture. University of London. Courtesy of Bloomsbury Publishing Plc. © University of London 1984.

Fowler, A., 2005. Gavin Douglas: Romantic Humanist. In: A. MacDonald, and K. Dekker, ed., *Rhetoric, Royalty, And Reality*. Peeters. Reproduced with permission of Peeters.

Fowler, A., 2008. Cut Without Hands: Herbert's Christian's Altar. In: Erskine-Hill, H., McCabe, R. and Jack, I., ed., *Presenting Poetry: Composition, Publication, Reception*. Cambridge University Press. Reproduced with permission of Cambridge University Press through PLSclear.

Fowler, A., 2007. Anagrams. *The Yale Review*, 95: 33–43. doi:10.1111/j.1467-9736.2007.00307.x. Reproduced with permission of John Wiley and Sons through PLSclear.

Fowler, A., 1992. Georgic and Pastoral: Laws of Genre in the 17th Century. In: M. Leslie, and T. Raylor, ed., *Culture And Cultivation In Early Modern England*. Continuum International Publishing. Used by permission of Bloomsbury Publishing Plc.

Fowler, A., 1996. *Shakespeare's Renaissance Realism, Proceedings of the British Academy 90.* Oxford University Press. © The British Academy 1996, pp. 29–64.

Fowler, A., 1995. Twelfth Night and Epiphany. In: S. Chaudhuri, and K. Datta, ed., *Renaissance Essays For Kitty Scoular Datta.* Calcutta: Oxford University Press. Reproduced with permission from Oxford University Press India.

Fowler, A., 1997. Relevance. *The English Review* 7.3. Reproduced by permission of Hodder Education.

Fowler, A., 1999. The Emblem as a Literary Genre. In: M. Bath and D. Russell, ed., Deviceful Settings: The English Renaissance Emblem and its Contexts. Selected Papers from the Third International Emblem Conference. New York: AMS.

Fowler, A., 2001. Lord's Space in 17th-Century Britain. In: R. Eriksen and M. Malmanger, eds, *Renaissance Representations of the Prince.* Edizioni Kappa Roma.

Introduction

From the beginning of my working life I had a sense that literature enjoys an unsearchable complexity. Working on Milton and Spenser did nothing to dispel this belief. Literature's complexity sometimes involves hidden anagrams or numerical patterns; but an education in mathematics, science, and medicine ensured that I had no fear of numbers. More than once, indeed, I made forays into numerology.

Being selected from the work of six or seven decades, these essays differ in the aims and assumptions they share with other criticism of their periods. At first, the New Criticism of I. A. Richards and William Empson, R. P. Blackmur and W. K. Wimsatt dominated. Largely displacing the biographical preoccupations of Lord David Cecil and others, this New Criticism counted as 'formalist' in the sense of focusing on formal relations between the parts of literary works—repetitions, for example, and such devices as irony. It necessarily cultivated 'close reading'. And it treated literary works as self-contained: independent of biographical context—independent, even, of other works. New Critics ignored the interrelations of literary history. In fact, T. S. Eliot was almost the only critic of his generation to write about tradition.

The early essays here share the assumptions of New Criticism. I was impatient with talk about the lives of writers, and wrote simply to bring out the coherence of literary works: to clarify their qualities. I aimed to explain, to remove difficulties—often by recovering half-forgotten conventions. Through the emblems in Essay 13, for example, Spenser displays the virtue of Temperance in *The Faerie Queene* Book II. I took for granted that criticism is subservient to literature, and that literature deserves favourable attention, even when it serves the values of a former age.

If the earliest essays suggest any influence, it is that of C. S. Lewis, the first great critic I knew personally. But soon the essays engaged with the ideas of later mentors: Don Hirsch, Ralph Cohen, and Frank Kermode. An intellectual watershed was the 1972 Bellagio conference organized by Cohen to assemble theorists from both sides of the iron curtain, who were to address the large question: Was it still realistic to attempt literary history? Between the participants—Hans Robert Jauss, Wolfgang Iser, Jean Starobinski, and the Marxist Fred Jameson—sharp differences emerged. The present essays suggest aversion from the Bellagio tribalisms, and a preference for exploring common ground where possible.

The next school, structuralism, had more repercussions on linguistics and anthropology than on literature. But the contexts of literature, slighted by the New Criticism, returned in New Historicism. This owed much to Fernand Braudel, the great historian of everyday life. Yet it found room too for the highly selective, ideologically slanted histories of such as Michel Foucault and Steven Greenblatt. The only completely negative review I had previously published was 'Enter Speed: A Feverish Life of Shakespeare, Like History on Amphetamines,' which identified many gross factual errors in Greenblatt's *Will in the World*. This review attracted a good deal of attention.[1] Nothing could show more clearly the prevailing disregard of historical contexts than the fact that Greenblatt's book continued to be cited favourably. 'Enter Speed: a Feverish Life of Shakespeare' was put down to personal animosity, despite my very different reviews of Greenblatt's other works.

Although not by any means a New Historicist, James Shapiro convincingly explored historical contexts in *A Year in the Life of William Shakespeare: 1599*, as did Stuart Gillespie in *Shakespeare's Books* (2001). Valuable studies of theatrical contexts include Bart van Es's *Shakespeare in Company* (2013) and Tom Rutter's *Shakespeare and the Admiral's Men* (2017).

Almost as influential in the seventies and eighties, deconstruction changed for many the procedures of criticism. This school of criticism, associated with Jacques Derrida in France and J. Hillis Miller in the USA, oddly claims allegiance to the great linguist Ferdinand Saussure. According to Derrida, all writing is ambiguous and crammed with irreconcilable contradictions. But in this he shows a poor grasp of Saussure. Any well-written text contains its own disambiguation.[2] Much of my criticism in those decades worked against the uncritical adulation of Derrida.

The successive schools—New Criticism, structuralism, deconstruction—should not be dismissed as mere fashions. They exposed serious concerns, emphasizing neglected aspects of literature. Deconstruction, for example, reacted against structuralism's fixed coding. But a sense of literature's unsearchable complexity made me averse from each school in turn. Each falsified literature by denying its true complexity. Biographical contexts, authorial intentions, readers' responses: each in turn was slighted. I begin to see that my *raison d'être* lay in reminding critics about parts of literature they had forgotten. But I must confess that something was also due to the aggressiveness I used to indulge.

The three divisions of this selection correspond to prevailing focuses in my work: genre, realism, and relations with visual art. The earlier essays on genre follow Hirsch; but the later take a less abstract approach, and depend more on

---

[1] See, e.g., John Sutherland, 'Where there's a Will there's a payday', *The Guardian*, 16 Feb. 2005.
[2] As Deirdre Wilson shows in *Meaning and Relevance* (Cambridge University Press, 2012).

Ludwig Wittgenstein's theory of family resemblance. (Instances of a genre being here the family.) Concepts of genre figure in any sound literary theory.

Essays on realism—or realisms in the plural—form a second grouping. For I see medieval and Renaissance realisms as distinct, just as both are distinct from the realism of pre-modern novels. The development of representation, far from being one of steadily improving verisimilitude, has gone through several distinct sorts of realism. Essays 10 and 12, for example, distinguish the participatory realism of the Renaissance from the spectator realism of nineteenth-century novels.

The old canon has rightly been replaced by one with a much larger proportion of women authors than before, including some previously passed over altogether. On this I count myself a feminist. I share, for example, Wallace Robson's view that Virginia Woolf was the best critic of her time. This must have widespread repercussions on the whole canon. It need not mean demoting every male author; but it surely involves giving less attention to the likes of Shakerly Marmion.

In a third grouping of the essays attention turns to the kinship of literature and art. Christopher Ricks has often told me I waste my time writing about the visual arts. But he has never convinced me. Conventions of visual art offer essential parallels with those of literature. The 'sister arts' display many family resemblances—obviously so in imagery, less obviously in their strategies of realism. Essay 14 explores imagery in a poem by Alexander Pope (himself an artist); Essay 15 studies an emblematic poem by George Herbert, in which he turns conventional features into expressions of personal devotion. Essay 16 considers emblems as themselves a genre. It was written for an emblem conference at Pittsburgh in 1993.[3]

Some of the essays have appeared in English or American journals such as *New Literary History* and *Review of English Studies*. Others are less accessible to American and British readers. Essay 3 was given as a lecture and printed only in a very small edition; Essay 15 was consigned to the comparative obscurity of a Festschrift; and Essay 8 receives here its first printing. Essays 6, 7, 9, and 11 were published in Italy or France. With the one exception, all are printed here as they first appeared, except for trivial changes in spelling and punctuation.

---

[3] The participants included Daniel Russell, Karl Joseph Höltgen, Peter Daly, Michel Bath, John Manning, and Alan R. Young, to whom I owe many additions and corrections.

Emblems of Temperance in *The Faerie Queene*, Book II

It was Spenser's invariable practice to build into the imagery of *The Faerie Queene*, at strategic points, the traditional emblems of the virtue whose legend he was writing. These emblems must once have helped to make at least the main drift of his allegory widely intelligible; but unfortunately it no longer works like that. In Book II, where emblems are heavily relied on for structure as well as for imagery, either their existence is now not even noticed, or else they are treated as mere surface decoration. Yet they are essential to Spenser's method, which is oblique, working indirectly through details. The golden set-square, the 'norm of temperance',[1] for instance, is only once mentioned explicitly, when Guyon says that 'with golden squire' the virtue 'can measure out a meane' between the fleshly death of Mordant and the self-accusing death of Amavia (II. i. 58). Because it is used in the geometrical construction of the mean proportional, the square is a symbol for the virtue by which Guyon will continually make the moral construction of the golden mean. The castles of Medina and Alma, however, are both founded on the same mathematical principle, and the set-square is a mason's instrument; so that from one point of view all the closely related architectural and geometrical images in the Book can be regarded as extensions of the emblem.[2] The bridle, a commoner emblem of temperance, is equally unobtrusive. Guyon has a horse with 'gorgeous barbes' (II. ii. 11) called Brigador (V. iii. 34)—a name which means Golden Bridle (*briglia d'oro*).[3] And this emblem, too, is functional; for it is Braggadocchio's theft of Brigador which precipitates Guyon into the pedestrian adventures which follow: that is to say, it is originally through pride (Braggadocchio) that the Platonic horse of man's desires ceases to be bridled by

---

[1] Achille Bocchi, *Symbolicarum quaestionum libri quinque* (Bologna, 1574), Embl. CXLIV, p. 145. in which the *norma temperantiae* is handed to a prince, is particularly apt as illustration. The square was as often an emblem of justice as of temperance; Spenser may have regarded the one virtue as essential to the other.

[2] Mean proportionals were actually used in Renaissance architecture: see R. W. Wittkower, *Architectural Principles in the Age of Humanism* (London, 1949), Pt. IV, 'The Problem of Harmonic Proportion in Architecture'.

[3] Yet Warton thought it merely a pompous name 'on the affectation so common in books of chivalry'. For the bridle emblem see Ripa, *Iconologia* (Padua, 1611), pp. 508 f.; and E. Male, *L'Art religieux de la fin du Moyen Âge* (Paris, 1925), pp. 313 ff. and figs. 168, 173, 175.

temperance.[4] I shall be solely concerned here, however, with a third emblem of temperance, which is perhaps the commonest of all—the pouring of water into wine.[5] This emblem makes the least obvious appearance, but only because it is developed on a scale we do not expect; it is hidden, only because most deeply structural.

The very first extended image in the Book is one of water: the nymph's fountain. This fountain of tears from the eyes of a petrified nymph not only occasions Mordant's death, but proves mysteriously immiscible with the blood of Amavia on Ruddymane's hands. The obscurity here, as so often in Spenser, is the result of compression: he has fused two emblematic fountains which apart would have been less difficult, if less original. We find them partly disengaged, as it happens, in a well-known emblem by Herman Hugo. Hugo portrays repentance as a seated female figure—Anima, the human soul—with a stream of tears issuing from her eyes and hair, as she faces a fountain in the form of a petrified nymph, from whose head and outstretched hands water flows into a large pool.[6] This is a visual rendering of Jer. ix. 1: 'Oh that my head were waters, and mine eyes a fountain of tears.' For epigram, Hugo gives Anima's prayer to be metamorphosed into a fountain, like Acis, Biblis, and Achelous; all of them mythological figures who, like Spenser's nymph, became rivers. (This allusion is reflected in the engraving by Boetius a Bolswert: the iconography of his petrified nymph, not to speak of the river-god in the background, is obviously influenced by illustrations of the *Metamorphoses*.) The streams of water from the nymph's outstretched hands, however, are neither from Jeremiah nor, solely, from the tradition of Ovidian illustration. They belong to another symbolic fountain, the Fountain of Life, as a glance at a later emblem of Hugo's will show (III. xli). In it, Christ-Eros is a fountain, with spouts issuing from his outstretched hands, side, and feet, and falling into a pool, the bath of salvation. The Fountain of Life—originally an expression of the cult of the Precious Blood—was a very popular motif in late medieval art; in the Reformation it persisted, though associated then with baptism rather than with the mass.[7] However disguised mythologically (as in the later

---

[4] At II. iv. 2 the 'rightfull owner' is described as able to 'menage...his pride'; at xii. 53 we find him 'Bridling his will'. Cf Rinaldo's stolen horse, which Harington interprets as 'fervent appetite' (notes to *Orlando Furioso*, Bks. I and II). On the horse as symbol for the wilful passions, see Valeriano, *Hieroglyphica* (Lyons, 1611), IV. xx–xxiii; as a special attribute of *superbia* in medieval graphic art, A. Katzenellenbogen, *Allegories of the Virtues and Vices in Medieval Art* (London, 1939), pp. 10, 79, and fig. 8a.

[5] For numerous examples of this emblem, see Mâle, pp. 321–3; Katzenellenbogen, pp. 55 f. *et passim*; and R. van Merle, *Iconographie de l'art profane* (La Haye, 1932), figs. 16, 22, &c.

[6] *Pia desideria* (Antwerp, 1624), I. viii, pp. 59–64; illustrated in M. Praz, *Studies in Seventeenth-Century Imagery*, i (London, 1939), p. 133 (fig. 56).

[7] See Mâle, pp. 110–18, and, for the earlier history of the motif, P. A. Underwood, 'The Fountain of Life in Manuscripts of the Gospels', *Dumbarton Oaks Papers*, v (1950), 43–138. The motif seems to have been introduced into emblem literature by Georgette de Montenay, in her *Emblemes ou devises chrestiennes* (Lyons, 1571), Embl. III, illus. Praz (fig. 9) from a later edition.

period it often was), it would be readily recognized, in the briefest allusion, by a contemporary reader. Thus Spenser's fountain, to which Mordant came when Amavia reclaimed him, is an extraordinarily complex symbol of the believer's identity with Christ; serving both as fountain of repentance and laver of regeneration, as *fons lachrymarum* and *balnea salutis*.

Closer examination would show that the early cantos form an allegory of baptismal regeneration. The rock of the fountain is Christ, the 'spiritual rock', from whom flows the water of baptism (1 Cor. x. 2–4). Mordant (the 'outer man') and Amavia (the 'inner man') of the old Adam die and are buried by the fountain, because baptism involves a sacramental death and burial with Christ (Rom. vi. 3–4). The Edward VI Form for Private Baptism contained a prayer 'that the old Adam in them that shall be baptized in this fountain, may be so buried, that the new man may be raised up again'. As for Guyon's new man, he is present too, in the shape of the laughing baby, Ruddymane. His 'guilty hands' are baptized simultaneously with Guyon's own; but even the water of life will not wash out the bloody stains, which derive ultimately (ii. 4) from the poison of Acrasia (concupiscence). As the Ninth of the XXXIX Articles warned, concupiscence, the cause of the death of the old Adam, is not effaced by baptism. Only the long process of mortification of the flesh—with which Book II deals—can do anything to arrest it. Some theologians, indeed, among them Calvin, held out little hope of concupiscence ever being eradicated in this life. 'This corruption', he says, 'never ceases in us, but constantly produces new fruits...just as...a fountain is ever pouring out water' *(Inst.,* IV. XV. 11, tr. Beveridge).

And this is how Spenser renders it, substantializing the traditional metaphor in the 'Infinit streames' of the fountain of Acrasia. With its erotic sculpture—profane Eroses bathing in the 'liquid ioyes' of love or playing 'wanton toyes' (xii, 60)—this fountain is so disturbingly matched against the earlier one that recollection is enforced. Guyon has bathed in tears under the streaming body of Christ; will he, then, bathe in the 'ample lauer' of Acrasia's fountain, under the ivy of Bacchus, whose 'lasciuious armes', creeping into the water, seem 'for wantones to weepe', in blasphemous parody alike of crucifixion and piety?[8] In grasping this opposition, Spenser's first readers would be assisted by their familiarity with the work he was emulating, Trissino's *L'Italia Liberata da Gotti*.[9] In Trissino the two fountains are more closely juxtaposed (IV. 873 and V. 152), their symbolism less complex. But in Spenser's Book II the whole action flows between the fountain of life and the fountain of death, which set, as it were, its alternative extremes. The contrast involves a paradox: those who drink Acrasia's fountain seem alive, but are virtually

---

[8] xii. 61; the parody is compressed into a pun: 'drops of Christ all seemed for wantons to weep'.
[9] Spenser's use of Trissino has been noticed by C. W. Lemmi, 'The Influence of Trissino on the *Faerie Queene*', *P.Q.*, vii (1928), 220–3.

dead—reduced, like Cymochles (v. 35), to a shade; while those who drink the nymph's fountain die, but only to rise to a new life.

This almost symmetrical opposition is far from being the only one of its kind; contrasted images of water are, indeed, the Book's leitmotif. Thus the dead lake of idleness is set against the lake of grace which swallows up the deathly Maleger in its life. Pyrocles is hotter than 'damned ghoste' in Phlegethon (vi. 50), a burning river answered by the nymph's *cold* fountain (ii. 9). Equally opposed, this time to its purity (ii. 9), is the black river Cocytus, those 'sad waues, which direfull deadly stanke' under the Cave of Mammon.[10] (The burning and the filthy rivers correspond to the two modes of corruption—ireful and appetitive, strong and weak—a dichotomy which runs throughout the Book.) Such contrasts, between good and bad fountains, rivers, lakes, not to speak of wands, nets, boats, pilots, &c., are no doubt in part a device of formal arrangement, in part expressions of the ambivalence of a natural order calling for constant discrimination. They may, however, carry the further implication that two entire ways of life, two complete mental landscapes, are being presented to our choice.

The Book has also its images of wine. Repeatedly the temptation of the Bower of Bliss is presented as a wine-cup, or is associated with symbols of Bacchus. This is a deliberate emphasis, and one which is not found in Spenser's models, Tasso's Bower of Armida or Trissino's Garden of Acratia.[11] First there is the 'mighty Mazer bowle of wine' of evil Genius; then the golden cup of Excess, with juice pressed from intoxicating grapes; and lastly the cup of Acrasia, the ample laver of her fountain, beneath the ivy of Bacchus. Acrasia's cup makes her lovers animals in the end; but for a time they become embodiments of the god Bacchus himself. Thus Mordant is actually called Bacchus in Acrasia's curse (i. 55); while Verdant, as his name suggests, enjoys that green age of youth which was the perpetual condition of the god.[12]

Into contact with these Bacchic images comes, at the moment of the mission's fulfilment, the principal water-image, Guyon, for the name Guyon derives from one of the four rivers of Paradise (Gen. ii. 10–14). These rivers were from patristic times identified with the four cardinal virtues, Pison usually being prudence, Tigris fortitude, Euphrates justice, and Gihon (Geon, Gaeon, Gyon, &c.) temperance. The Neoplatonist Philo probably invented the allegory; but it was Ambrose who developed it christologically. In Ambrose's interpretation, the single river from which the four river-virtues spring is Christ, the fountain of

---

[10] vii. 57. Such pairs of contrasted rivers were traditional: Bersuire contrasts the hot Egyptian fountain of avarice and worldly pleasure ('non est refrigeretiua, sed potius inflammatiua') with the waters of compassion and piety (*Dict.*, Pt. I, under *aqua*). Landino, the Neoplatonist, interprets the four rivers of Hell as the course of sin, flowing from man's concupiscence—'a concupiscentia nostra veluti a fonte manat aqua' (*Alleg. in Aen.*, Virgil, *Opera* (Basel, 1596), pp. 3038, 3044).

[11] Trissino has vines, but no cups of wine.

[12] For Bacchus as *semper iuvenis* and *puer aeternus*, see Conti, *Mytholog.*, v. xiii, and Alciati, *Emblemata cum comm. ampliss.* (Padua, 1621), p. 140a, on Embl, xxv, 'In statuam Bacchi'.

eternal life.¹³ The symbol was a familiar one in the Renaissance. To cite well-used reference works: Bersuire (*Comm. in Gen.*, ii, in *Reductorium morale*) traces the rivers back to the fountain of repentance which irrigates a righteous man's conscience; while Valeriano (*Hieroglyph.*, XXI. xiv) follows Ambrose and Philo, explaining that the Gaeon (Nile) signifies temperance because it washes Egypt (i.e. enticing pleasure) and Ethiopia, a land stained, like the human body, with a dark infection: 'it purges the vile body, and quenches the ardour of lust'.

The purpose of the four rivers allegory was to symbolize in a vivid way the absolute dependence of the virtues upon their source, the water of life. The same idea was expressed by a motif in late medieval graphic art, which associated human personifications of the virtues with the Fountain of Life. A Bellegambe painting at Lille, for example, depicts the faithful, assisted by female figures (the virtues), climbing into a large laver beneath the crucified Christ: signifying that men can only achieve virtues after bathing in the blood of salvation, each effusion of which washes out one deadly sin.[14] In a similar manner, and with similar meaning, Guyon the virtue of temperance helps Ruddymane to wash in the Fountain of Life.

Since Guyon's entry into the Bower of Bliss brings images of water and wine together, the missing emblem of temperance has been found. It remains to discover what symbolic force it exerts. Traditionally, temperance's pouring of water into wine had meant dilution: moderation in the indulgence of a burning desire. Such is the interpretation in Claude Mignault's Commentary on Alciati; somewhat disappointingly, he explains that when the Greek Anthology says that Bacchus delights to link with three nymphs, it only means that wine should be mixed with three parts water: unmixed, it causes fury and insanity. He quotes Plato's advice that 'the drunken god should be tempered with sober nymphs' (Alciati, 143b, 144b, and 146a). Sometimes, however, the two vessels of temperance carried another significance. Ripa tells us that temperance is portrayed with two vessels, one tilted into the other, 'because of the similarity between a mixture of two liquids, and that of two contrary extremes' (*Iconologia*, p. 508). The conception of temperance as the mixture or integration of extremes, as distinct from their avoidance, is clearly expressed in the triads of the Castle of Medina. But the mixture emblem is also worked up into a characteristic piece of poetic theology, more deeply hidden, which underlies the Bower of Bliss temptations, as well as Acrasia's curse upon Mordant.

Spenser seems to have taken a hint from Bersuire's allegorization of an account in Solinus of the marvellous river Diana, near Camerina. According to Solinus, if

---

[13] *De parad.*, iii. For further details about the history of this allegorization, see Underwood, pp. 47–9.

[14] See Mâle, p. 115 and fig. 62; it should be noted that the bath in this painting is an erotic bath, shared with the object of desire.

anyone of unchaste habits draws water from the Diana, it will not mix with the wine in his body (*Polyhistor,* xi). Bersuire takes this to mean that the unchastity of the drinker will be revealed. By water, he says, can be understood doctrine—especially by the water of the Diana, a name which means 'manifest' [*clara*]. But by wine can be understood the human will; for water (doctrine) cools, but the human will burns with desire. Therefore the water of good doctrine is applied to the wine of ardent will, so that the appetite may be tempered (*Reductorium morale,* VIII. Iii. 33).

By a common and obvious symbolism, intoxication and the consequent heating of the blood has throughout Christian literature been an image of sin. Thus, in Burnet's *Exposition of the Thirty-Nine Articles,* an extended speculation about how original sin altered the human constitution imagines the pathological effect as an inflammation of the blood (on Art. IX). More metaphysically, Neoplatonic writers used the intoxicating draught of Bacchus as a myth to describe the immersion of the mind in matter at birth, when 'the new drink of matter's impetuous flood' intoxicated the soul and brought oblivion. Augustinian theology, which took over the myth, also regarded the soul as overcome at birth; not, however, by matter, but by its failure to dominate the body's original sin, concupiscence.[15] Thus it is concupiscence (Acrasia) whose Bacchic draught brings Mordant such oblivion that he forgets Amavia. And having drunk the wine of wilfulness, he is confronted with his unfaithfulness by waters of doctrine from a fountain of Diana (revelation), so that he knows himself mortally guilty.

Since passions have the darkness of a Bacchic intoxication, the accomplishment of temperance must consist in remaining lucid amidst them, until their sources are understood. This is expressed allegorically by Guyon's refusal to bathe at the Bower of Bliss. Carrying with him on his course water from Diana's fountain, he enters the sphere of the natural, and *resists immersion in it.* For the temptation of the Bower would be underestimated if, with Bowra, we regarded it as 'sexual irregularity'.[16] It is nothing less than the primary temptation to relinquish the mind's dominion and succumb in animal wilfulness to the intoxication of the natural and the material: to succumb, that is, to concupiscence, 'the mind of the flesh', by wallowing in the desires of the heart. Nevertheless, the Bower is not simply to be avoided; to the passionate heart—the fountain of the will—Guyon must bring the water of doctrine and grace.[17] This allegory of a human conduit between fountains

---

[15] See Aquinas, *Disp.* IV *De malo,* 1, on the soul's contraction of original sin at its infusion. The Platonic myth can be traced from the *Phaedo* through Plotinus (*Enn.,* IV. iii. 2), Porphyry (*De antr. nymph.,* i. 88), and Macrobius (*In somn. Scip.,* I. xii) to Renaissance mythographers like Valeriano (*Collectanea,* II. ix).

[16] Lemmi, who notices much of the Bacchic imagery (*M.L.N.,* 1 (1935), 163-4, and *P.Q.,* viii (1929), 276-7), sees some of the symbolism, but makes it too narrowly sexual, treating Bacchus as the 'masculine principle' and Mordant as 'oversexed'.

[17] For the heart as the *fons voluntatis,* see Valeriano, XVIII. xiii, 'Concupiscentia'. N. S. Brooke, 'C. S. Lewis and Spenser', *Cambridge Journal,* ii (1949), 430, noticed that the fountain of Acrasia is the heart, but failed to make the connexion with the will.

was not entirely novel. In Trissino's *L'Italia Liberata,* water is carried in vessels from a fountain made by God from Virtue's tears, and is poured in literal fact into Acratia's fountain of concupiscence.[18] The difference, however, between this allegory and Spenser's is significant. Whereas Trissino automatically overcomes each obstacle by the same device, sprinkling with holy water, Spenser attempts to render the process of regeneration in greater detail, by the introduction of images with assignable psychological meaning, such as the Palmer's staff of concord and net of formal analysis. Characteristically, Trissino calls the water *acqua del sanajo*; while Spenser allows the theological meaning to remain implicit.

The symmetry of Book II now emerges, as we see Guyon on a massive scale bringing together, as temperance should, two vessels. He lives in no exclusively moral, natural world, as some critics have maintained; but in the full tension between spirit and rebellious flesh, between Fidelia's cup and Acrasia's.

---

[18] VI and V. Cf. also Goltzius's engraving 'Satisfactio Christi', where the Fountain of Life pours directly into a human heart opened like a box to receive it.

The Life and Death of Literary Forms

Forms and the Literary Model

The subject proposed is the 'life' and 'death' of literary forms, not of literary works (a different subject). We say that the mock epic form has died out but *The Rape of the Lock* in some sense lives on, that the sonnet continues viable though Constable's *Sonnets* are moribund, that pastoral persists in fresh guise, even if Googe's *Eclogues* do not. The historical duration of works need not coincide with the duration of the forms they use.

However, I must not take this as axiomatic, since for certain meanings of *form* it would be untrue. If forms meant personal configurations—as in Buffon's *le style est l'homme même*—they might be coterminous with individual literary works. And a Crocean idealist who thought of form as 'expression-intuition' would not even want to distinguish it from the internal event of the work;[1] for him, each work is formally unique, the diachronic propositions of literary history meaningless. Best begin, then, by specifying a literary model.

The theoretical model currently useful is likely to be based on recent ideas of the substrate, and consequently to draw on post-Saussurean linguistics and on information theory. Thus we may define a literary work as the record of a specialized speech act. An author makes and communicates it, much as speakers express themselves, through a system of shared grammatical rules—Saussure's *langue*—supplemented by other more specialized systems of conventions.[2] His individual speech act, however, is *parole*, a unique contingent communication, which, though it depends on previously shared conventions, may also modify them to initiate new conventions. These in turn become *langue* for subsequent *paroles*. As for the difference between everyday and literary communication, it seems to lie in the latter's more elaborate *langue*, which may include not only rules of spoken or written grammar but also many sorts of conventional types, such as modes, genres, motifs, topics, narrative devices, symmetries of structure, rhetoric, and meter. Literary forms, in short, are precisely what distinguish literature from ordinary communication.

---

[1] See René Wellek, *Concepts of Criticism*, ed. S. G. Nichols (New Haven and London, 1963), p. 56.
[2] Here I follow F. W. Bateson's extension of the concept *langue* in 'Modern Bibliography and the Literary Artifact,' *English Studies Today* (Bern, 1961); see esp. pp. 74-6. Cf. E. D. Hirsch, *Validity in Interpretation* (New Haven and London, 1967), p. 134.

Reflection finds a difficulty here, in that some literary forms occur in *paroles* outside decent literature, even outside writing altogether. Figures of speech may figure in speech, and verse was sometimes used for technical treatises during the Middle Ages. To account for this, one supplements the linguistic with the information theory model. In information theory, oral and written conventions work as signal systems, by which communications are constructed from series of signals. The signal system may work together to optimize construction of the correct message, through an arrangement of noise-combating codes called redundancy: "redundancy' may be said to be due to an additional set of rules, whereby it becomes increasingly difficult to make an undetectable mistake."[3] Now literary works, since they often deal with elusive or hard ideas, and since they communicate themselves across 'noncooperative links' (reception can't usually be checked by questioning an author) need a high degree of redundancy. Perhaps, then, what distinguishes literary communication is not any particular form or signal system, but rather the redundancy available. In short, the unity of mutually confirming structures. Thus, if ordinary speech achieves a high degree of redundant integration it may become memorable, pass into the literature, and be reckoned a 'saying.'

Redundancy of literary forms tends to prolong the possibility of constructing the work (or something like it) even after some of its many signal systems have fallen into oblivion. That is how literary works sometimes survive even their own genres. In a similar way redundancy makes it possible to construct very novel communications, such as *avant-garde* experiments. And it is the same all-important conception of information theory that guarantees validity of interpretation and determinacy of meaning.

Validity of interpretation in E. D. Hirsch's sense[4] can only be defended against subjectivism on the ground that a work remains inaccessible to interpretation, free or otherwise, until it is constructed. Since construction depends on identification of signals in terms of systems shared with the author, no reader can claim the freedom to interpret as he pleases. For signals themselves are meaningless. And if a reader identifies them according to inappropriate signal systems, or in disregard of redundancies, the communication he constructs is not the one to be interpreted.

As for determinacy of meaning, Hirsch's genre logic guarantees it *in potentia*. In practice, however, the generic rules which sharing of types depends on may remain inaccessible. Only by recourse to the conception of redundancy, can we understand how meaning continues determinate in practice in certain instances, even after some of the generic forms involved have long been smoked over by time's tenebrosity.

Still, 'genre ideas have a necessary heuristic function.'[5] Hirsch refers to his broad category of 'intrinsic genre,' but the same is true of genre in a more

---

[3] Colin Cherry, *On Human Communication* (New York, 1958), p. 185; see also Monroe C. Beardsley, *Aesthetics* (New York, 1958), pp. 215–17.
[4] *Validity in Interpretation*, pp. 3–6, 10.   [5] Ibid., p. 78.

conventional sense. Traditional genres and modes, far from being mere classificatory devices, serve primarily to enable the reader to share types of meaning economically. Moreover, his subsequent understanding is also genre-bound: he can only think sensibly of *Oedipus Tyrannus* as a tragedy, related to other tragedies. If he ignores or despises genre, or gets it wrong, misreading results. Johnson's blunder over *Lycidas* and the more recent and even more spectacular critical error of taking *Paradise Lost* as classical epic with Satan the hero are dreadful examples. Clearly, generic forms must rank among the most important of the signal systems that communicate a literary work.

By forms, then, I mean all the conventional elements of literature, from modes to metrical patterns. Archetypes, however, though closely associated with conventions by Northrop Frye,[6] and indirectly involved as we shall see in every full description of a genre, I exclude. For they appear just as much in other fields of discourse, so that they must be reckoned psychological rather than literary types. I also differ from Frye about the relative importance of forms. To 'commentary', or structural analysis of an individual work, he prefers 'identification', a superior kind of criticism that follows 'an inductive movement towards the archetype', away from verbal texture, through imagery and larger conventions, to mythic archetypes shared with other works.[7] I think that the *Hamlet* criticism of superior interest to all except theoreticians and anthropologists is likely to consist of statements about what is peculiar to Shakespeare's play, not what it shares with *Samson Agonistes* or ancient Greek myths. About intrinsic genres and individual *paroles*;[8] not archetypes, or even genres. Since, however, literary works can only be communicated through generic forms, these may be of great, though subsidiary, critical interest, according to the individual case. Historically, too, the interest of any form is liable to fluctuate over any considerable period. It may even lose significance altogether. Then either it will become a mere habit without value *qua* signal (as with some Romantic poets' use of stanza forms long after interest in their proportion had declined); or it will cease to be used altogether (pastoral eclogue, poulter's measure, epic). Of all literary forms the class whose continuance probably matters most is genre.

Interpretation and Genre

By genre I mean a better defined and more external type than mode. Genres each have their own formal structures, whereas modes depend less explicitly on stance,

---

[6] See, e.g., *Fables of Identity* (New York, 1963), p. 123, and cf. W. K. Wimsatt, 'Criticism as Myth', *Northrop Frye in Modern Criticism*, ed. Murray Krieger (New York and London, 1966), p. 87 n.

[7] *Fables*, p. 13; Wimsatt, p. 87.

[8] Hirsch (pp. 103, 111) defines intrinsic genre as between *parole* and *langue*.

motif, or occasional touches of rhetorical texturing. However, some types can function both as genre and as mode.[9] Thus epic (Dryden's *Aeneis*) is written side by side with heroic tragedy (*Aureng-Zebe*) and heroic satire (*Absalom and Achitophel*). Borderline cases inevitably occur: some critics have treated *Absalom and Achitophel* as satiric mock-epic. And mixtures abound: eclogues mingling pastoral and satire, epics embracing many modes or even containing inset passages in other genres. Nevertheless, we can usually identify broad generic and modal types with a fair degree of validity.

Recognition of genre depends on associating a complex of elements, which need not all appear in one work. But invariably external forms will be among the indicators: structure, or formal motif, or rhetorical proportion. We know epic by, among other things, its high style, formulae, episodes, and similes. And we know picaresque by its large-scale rhetorical proportions, such as the relative frequency of episodes and changes of scene, or the prominence of narrative and the relative unimportance of plot, character, and description. Motifs are particularly interesting as indicators, since they seem to reveal the ultimate relation of literary types to archetypes. And adequate description of pastoral eclogue—adequate enough, for example, to distinguish it from town eclogue and piscatory eclogue—is bound to deal with substantive motifs, such as climate and occupation, that can legitimately be related to Golden Age archetypes. However, it may be a mistake to identify genre primarily with thematic motifs,[10] since these often occur in more than one genre. Strictly speaking only motifs with a formal basis, such as the singing contest, are securely genre-linked. Usually there are so many indicators, organized into so familiar a unity, that we recognize the generic complex instantly. But recognition still depends on correlating individual signals, any of which is liable to change its value or cease to function. Conversely, if a genre becomes obsolete, its characteristic forms lose significance.

Some regard all genres as obsolete. They imagine them as sets of old rules, irrelevant to post-Romantic literature. But all literature may in fact be genre-bound, without this being consciously realized. Indeed, the operation of genre has always had a large unconscious element: no one could ever be simultaneously aware, for example, of all he meant by epic. But such scruples need not inhibit critical approximations. The first mock epicists might have been hard put to it to assign their poems to a genre now really obvious to us at a remove from the creative moment. And similarly modern fiction, itself not exactly uninstructed by

---

[9] Apparently only broad major genres have corresponding modes. Epithalamium, e.g., has none, unless one were to count such passages as Paradise Lost, VIII, 510–20. Puttenham is probably right in considering epithalamium a sub-genre of the triumphal: see *The Art of English Poesy*, ed. Gladys D. Willcock and Alice Walker (Cambridge, 1936), p. 46. Triumph itself, however, had a very flourishing equivalent mode in Elizabethan literature, of which a good example would be *The Faerie Queene*, III, xi–xii. See my *Triumphal Forms* (Cambridge, 1970), Ch. iii.

[10] As Frye tends to do: see, e.g., *Anatomy of Criticism* (Princeton, N.J., 1957), pp. 44–5.

critical precept, is necessarily communicated by modulation of at least potentially recognizable genres. (Even the novel is far from being the 'open' form, different from all others, that Alan Friedman calls it.) Thus Calder Willingham's *Eternal Fire* burlesques southern gothic; Thomas Mann's *Doktor Faustus* combines Bildungsroman with novel of ideas; and Pat Highsmith's *They Who Walk Away* departs from the crime in the direction of the psychological novel. Justifying any precise generic identification calls for lengthy critical demonstration; for it is naturally hard to define emergent sub-genres in explicit detail. But much contemporary criticism in effect attempts just this endeavour. Since new works often seem to mix existing types—successfully or unsuccessfully—many critical evaluations have to be in generic terms. We say that Burgess's *Tremor of Intent* vacillates uncomfortably between straight and burlesque espionage thriller; or that uncertainty of genre helps to account for the failure of Mailer's *Barbary Shore*.

It is not merely that old forms survive and new forms go on being generated. More fundamentally, genre operates in all interpretation, every meaning communicated being a type. The unique intrinsic type may be poles apart from such rigid extrinsic types as the traditional genres. Still, some sense of these must precede that grasp of the intrinsic type on which true reading depends. Hirsch's conception of generic types is more flexible and elusive than Rymer's; and no doubt only a very elastic conception indeed—stretching from types as broad as poetry and fiction down to minute variations of subgenres and even to grammatical forms—can accommodate the variety of actual literary communication. But to say this is not to abrogate conventional distinctions of genre, which continue to be of historical and heuristic value. Recognizing obvious epic forms in Joyce's *Ulysses* (e.g. formulae) sets the reader to noticing others more arcane (e.g. encyclopedic schemes).

However this may be, the obsolescence of a genre is certainly a critical event historically. For it alters the whole balance of significant forms, even making some of them insignificant; so that not only literary works embodying the generic form-complex, but also those in other genres may become more difficult. The discontinuation of the allegorical morality play, for example, has made obscure certain non-naturalistic passages in Shakespearean plays belonging to other kinds. In *Measure for Measure*, unfamiliarity with the Severine motif deprives many of the pleasures of surprise at Vincentio's clemency.[11] Changes of balance among significant forms affect readers' responses to constituents in a sweeping fashion comparable to that whereby colour in impressionist painting took the place of linear definition in the older schools. It is no exaggeration to assert that during the last two centuries interest in rhetorical schemes and in structural proportion

---

[11] On the motif of the disguised ruler, see Mary Lascelles, ed., *Shakespeare's Measure for Measure* (London, 1953), p. 101.

has almost completely given way in increased interest in rhetorical tropes and in tonal effects.

Obsolescence is the most noticeable change a genre may suffer. But really it is only one—and not necessarily the last—of a series of changes that generic forms continually pass through. This flux has somehow to be accommodated in any adequate theory of reading. For we must not think of extrinsic types as fixed and constantly available. On the contrary, valid interpretation will often involve laboriously chronicling a work's moment in its genre's history. Only relevant states of the form, not subsequent modifications or primitive antecedents, lead to the meaning; though a critic assessing significance may take the genre's whole time-worm into account. In other words, genre theory needs radical revision before it can be considered as providing a literary model with historical dimension. For example, it will not do to say, with Hirsch, that meaning remains the same, while its significance changes. This is true, so far as it goes. But meaning is genre-bound, and genres are themselves in a continual state of transmutation: epic was not the same before and after Homer, or Virgil, or Spenser, or Milton. Hence recognitive interpretation—that is, re-cognition of the author's meaning—demands recovery of appropriate phases of the genre concerned. Indeed, for distant historical periods it may necessitate reconstructing the then literary model.

Determinacy of meaning takes for granted the possibility of decoding signals that belong to determinate variable systems. This is obvious in practical contexts: a meaning can never be more than potentially determinate at any given time, in that readers may not discover enough about old forms to arrive at it precisely. But it is less obvious that in theory the mutability of genres presents an apparently insuperable obstacle to complete determinacy. For the genre that binds a reader's understanding is always the latest state of it that he knows, or at best the most inclusive conception he can realize. And since he cannot unknow these states of a form, he can never wholly recover earlier meanings. Familiarity with Virgil and later epicists makes it impossible quite to grasp the simplicities of Homer's epic.[12] Scholarship can mitigate but not remove this difficulty; because to explain a joke is to spoil it, to annotate an allusion to prevent the reader's ever recognizing it. We may suppose that the first mock epic was meant to elicit a response now unrecoverable unless by an eccentrically educated tyro. And the same no doubt applies to broad effects: how did novels strike readers for whom naturalism was a rare phenomenon? Evidently generic forms are bound up with criticism in a complex way.

---

[12] A separate problem from that presented by outmoded values, which Hirsch brilliantly treats in 'Privileged Criteria in Literary Evaluation,' *Problems of Literary Evaluation,* Yearbook of Comparative Criticism, Vol. II (State College, Pa., 1969), and in 'Literary Evaluation as Knowledge,' *Contemporary Literature,* IX (1968).

Death of Genres

Extinction will serve as the simplest instance of variation of genre. But even this change has its complications. As with biological organisms, the moment of 'death' is hard to fix. Does a genre die when it ceases to be used? Or when it is no longer regarded with interest? Or when readers become insensitive to its forms? Again, does a work's precarious survival, misinterpreted like *Gulliver's Travels*, ensure its genre's survival? Does the pastoral elegy live with *Lycidas*? Do genres 'die' at all?

Such terms as 'life,' 'death,' and 'extinction' imply a biological analogy. In its evolutionary form, this analogy has been attacked by René Wellek, with whose acute objections to importing specifically biological concepts many will feel inclined to agree. 'French tragedies were not born with Jodelle but just were not written before him.'[13] Plausible. But a weakness in Wellek's position is betrayed by the assertion that 'Darwinian or Spencerian evolutionism is false when applied to literature because there are no fixed genres comparable to biological species which can serve as substrata of evolution. There is no inevitable growth and decay, no transformation of one genre into another, no actual struggle for life among genres.'[14] This is true but irrelevant to the contemporary situation. Who now would wish to apply Darwinianism? Biologists no longer regard species as 'fixed' or entirely determined by genetic mechanisms.[15] As for transformations of literary forms, these are obvious enough if we imagine the generic type proposed earlier. Unfortunately Wellek understands genre as a single infinite set of works, whereas it should be understood as a whole series of form-complexes occurring as elements in a series of finite subsets of works. Loosely speaking, we say that the work 'belongs to' the genre or is a 'member' of it. But we should no more identify individual works with what constitutes genre in them, than regard men merely as biological entities. The literary genre does not define its members, only their forms.[16]

Hence Wellek's criticism of Brunetière, that Racine's *Phèdre* 'will strike us as young and fresh compared to the frigid Renaissance tragedies which, according to the scheme, represent the "youth" of French tragedy' lacks general force: it is scarcely works that evolve, but rather their genre.[17] Nor can he persuade by invoking the author's freedom of choice in 'reaching out into the past for models or stimuli' and by claiming that 'a work of art is not simply a member of a series, a

---

[13] Wellek, 'The Concept of Evolution in Literary History,' *Concepts*, p. 44.   [14] Ibid., p. 51.
[15] Cf. Eliseo Vivas, 'Literary Classes: Some Problems,' *Genre*, I (1968), 101.
[16] Cf. Hirsch, *Validity*, pp. 110-11: 'The only broad genre concept, then, which is by nature illegitimate is the one which pretends to be a species concept that somehow defines and equates the members it subsumes...If we believe they [classifications] are constitutive rather than arbitrary and heuristic, then we have made a serious mistake and have also set up a barrier to valid interpretation.'
[17] Wellek, *Concepts*, p. 44. In any case, is Eohippus 'young and fresh' compared to *Equus caballus*?

link in a chain. It may stand in relation to anything in the past.'[18] For only individual works reach out beyond temporal limitations, not the mutable type. Wellek is right to expose the limits of the biological analogy; but wrong to declare the analogy invalid. It would be strange if literature, life's image, contained no correlate of the evolution of biological forms. By organizing forms into complexes, a genre falls subject to such historical laws as govern all organizations in time. Like any other, it is bound to evolve.[19]

Genres, like biological species, have a relatively circumscribed existence in space and time. Individual works may elude locality and temporality; genres seldom to any extent. Though *Magister Ludi* intrigues a few British readers, the kind *Das Glasperlenspiel* belongs to finds little acceptance with us, the novel of ideas being construed here in terms of eccentricity or abortive naturalism. And cultural ethos similarly localizes other genres. The haiku is primarily Japanese; certain kinds of heroic fiction seem tolerable only to Chinese communists; and until recently France had no science fiction outside Verne. Or the geographical differentiation may be a little subtler, as between British detective story and American mystery—the latter merging easily into the thrillers of Chandler and Hammett, the former sharply distinct from the entertainments of Greene. In the seventeenth century the poem of locality begins in England rather late, whether because of national characteristics, social circumstances, or a time lag in fashion.[20]

The cultural matrix limits genre as strictly in time. Sir Kenneth Clark has observed that the use of the essay—a form reflecting the liberal attitude of uncommitted interest—began and ended with Humanism.[21] So too the hymn has been in abeyance since the recession of supernatural belief. And the pastoral eclogue could not survive changes in the relation of town and country that followed urban development.

These limitations apply to genre-linked structural forms in a quite pervasive way. Thus the use of sudden surprising turns of plot in the short story took for granted a universe of belief, within which *peripeteias* would disclose mysteries and prompt at least bafflement at the 'rumness of life.' Kipling is a transitional case: his stories still have plots and the plots still take odd turns (as in 'Without Benefit of Clergy'), but the metaphysical implication seems too explicitly realized for the device to hold much potential for future development in reserve. Or consider the sorts of allegorical images found in medieval genres. As many critics agree, 'the structure of images that C. S. Lewis in *The Discarded Image* calls 'the

---

[18] Ibid., p. 55.
[19] To do justice to Wellek's consistency, he considers the evolutionary character of history itself problematic: see ibid., p. 53 n.
[20] Charles Molesworth, 'Property and Virtue: The Genre of the Country-House Poem in the Seventeenth Century,' *Genre*, I (1968), admirably relates the house poem genre to political and sociohistorical changes, while wrongly identifying it with Puttenham's 'historical poesy' instead of with encomium. But I am more concerned with local descriptive landscape poetry.
[21] See Sir Kenneth Clark, *Civilization: A Personal View* (London, 1969), p. 163.

Model'... provided the main organization for literature down to the Renaissance: it modulated into less projected forms after Newton's time.'[22] Temporal limitations have even affected external structuring—notably numerical composition. The latter was almost completely abandoned in the early eighteenth century when cosmic proportion came to be imagined in a more impressionistically subjective way.[23] Indeed, we may say with only apparent paradox that the more formal the constituent, the more its significance depends on social context.

Genres are also limited by the intellectual capacities of readers. At least, no genre has ever been open to all social groups regardless of their level of education. Even great writers, not to speak of socialists intent on liberalizing conventions, seem to find it impossible to conceive of a universal reader. And when the education of their fit audience (few or many) ceases, the genre is in a sense finished. However, this limitation conceals a hope too. For, if a genre never was open to all men, may it not be enough that it should remain open to one or two? So long as a single scholar is fit to keep it alive, is any generic Tinkerbell quite dead?

The existence of genres is nevertheless thoroughly historical. In consequence, statements about them should always specify a chronological frame of reference. Thus a work's genre is the genre at composition, which relates to an antecedent genre, itself the cumulation of a series of earlier forms. But we are never aware of a first term of the series: we never witness the origin. Is Kipling's 'With the Night Mail' science fiction? Is Verne? Lucian? This is not because of any lack of antecedents, as Wellek would have it, but rather for an opposite reason, that every work of literature (as we know it) depends for intelligibility on a prior extrinsic type. Homer's *Odyssey*, for example, is partly unintelligible without an earlier genre of *nostoi* and an inherited convention of formulaic diction. Always the antecedent generic idea is subjective and cumulative, varying in response to literary and other experience, as Eliot described in *Tradition and the Individual Talent*; so that simplified synchronic analysis of genres meets with frequent pitfalls.[24] Invariable schematic classifications have often been devised, by writers as disparate as Aristotle and Scaliger, Hobbes and Frye. But all seem more or less simplistic and unconvincing.[25] Historically, it is just not the case that legends and romances

---

[22] Northrop Frye, 'Reflections in a Mirror,' in Krieger, p. 136. Many, however, will disagree with Frye's continuation: '... but it did not lose its central place in literature.'

[23] See my *Triumphal Forms*, p. 122.

[24] Angus Fletcher, 'Utopian History and the *Anatomy*,' in Krieger, pp. 34 ff., attempts a desperate defense of Frye against charges of unhistorical schematicism.

[25] Aristotle less, because some of his categories are logical (e.g. division of literature between narrative and dramatic forms) and because he takes evolution of genre into account to some extent, particularly in his description of tragedy. But he leaves to one side the question 'whether tragedy is now fully developed in all its species' (*Poetics*, IV, 13) and falls back instead on the assumption that 'after undergoing many changes it stopped when it had found its own natural form' (IV, 15). Scaliger introduced periodization, and was the first great exponent of the comparative method. But his famous comparison of Homer's and Virgil's epics (*Poetics* [Lyons, 1561], *lib*. V) only fumblingly begins to detect a difference between primary and secondary epic.

constitute variants of the same genre; or that literature comprises three modes and two manners of representation yielding 'neither more nor less than six sorts of poesy.'[26]

This is not to rule out the possibility of a few 'organic' forms determined by human rather than by cultural characteristics. The limits of short-term memory, for instance, may well have a bearing on the 'breath' of the verse paragraph. But organic characteristics perhaps change more than we realize. Thus memory can be cultivated or neglected. And allegory, though it probably corresponds to a mode of thought, undeniably suffered profound changes both in popularity and in use during the late antique period, and again in the seventeenth century. Even the elementary distinction between verse and prose, which many critics believe to have a permanent psychological basis, has undergone alteration, particularly at the time when typographic culture replaced oral and cheirographic. Broadly speaking, and discounting occasional gross features of scale, proportion, or diction governed by psycho-physiological laws, we may say that all generic forms are mutable.

Their death can be defined quite specifically. Pronounce a genre dead if works related to it directly are no longer widely read, so that its forms have become unintelligible without scholarly effort. Hence readership must be specified. For a genre may survive for one social group and lapse for others—like the tale of terror, which is little practiced as a literary form, but still vigorous in subliterary science fiction.

Hierarchic Mobility

This brings up one of the most fundamental changes a genre can go through: change of status in the generic hierarchy. *Anatomy of Criticism* systematizes such changes in a theory of five modes, ordered by the hero's calibre—supernatural myth; romance; high mimetic (epic and tragedy); low mimetic ('most comedy and realistic fiction'); and ironic. According to Frye, 'European fiction, during the last fifteen centuries, has steadily moved its centre of gravity down the list.'[27] The movement turns out to be cyclical, for as the ironic mode descends from the low mimetic, though 'it begins in realism and dispassionate observation...it moves steadily towards myth, and dim outlines of sacrificial rituals and dying gods begin to reappear in it. Our five modes evidently go around in a circle.'[28]

---

[26] *Anatomy*, pp. 33, 36; Thomas Hobbes, 'Answer to Davenant's Preface to *Gondibert*,' J. E. Spingarn, ed., *Critical Essays of the Seventeenth Century*, 3 vols. (Oxford, 1908–9), II, 55. Hobbes's six sorts are: epic, tragedy, satire, comedy, pastoral, and pastoral comedy.

[27] *Anatomy*, p. 34.   [28] Ibid., p. 42.

Frye's First Essay is impressively copious and contains many interesting incidental observations; but its argument seems no more likely to stand than any other simple cyclical theory.[29] For the literary corpus is more complex than Frye's dissection suggests. Not only does he ignore many elements of generic transformation altogether; but even the historical changes he does discuss have really had a more fluctuating tendency than he suggests. In actual fact there is nothing 'steady' about the movement of the hero down the modal scale and up again into myth. At the very time when the hero might plausibly be said to suffer eclipse in prose fiction, Shelley and Keats were raising his poetic status, even to the point of writing myths.[30] And Homer's epics, which ought to be 'lower' on the modal scale than the romantic *Chanson de Roland* and *Passing of Arthur*, really contain more supernatural and mythological action, not less. Many will agree with Angus Fletcher when he comments (in the ironic mode?): 'Another approach, perhaps more profitable, will be to see if the five modes could not occur in any order, without decline, ascent, or any other positive trend.'[31] Frye's mistake, we suspect, lies in supposing that hero and myth are 'fundamentals of an artistic process.'[32] In the *Anatomy* they have to be, however, to supply the need for unchanging archetypes.

It might be more empiric to begin with changes in the dignity of genres themselves, rather than of their heroes. The status of a genre—and hence the 'height' of what it communicates—depends on current evaluation of its whole conventional subject matter. (Compare generic hierarchy in the visual arts, which has been reordered to the disadvantage of religious and historical subjects and the advantage first of landscapes and still-lifes, then of abstracts.[33]) Describing the inquiry in these wide terms, however, shows what slender chance of success schematic speculation has. Indeed, one is first impressed by the abundance of paradoxes. Thus the same Christian faith that gave substance to mythic and 'romantic' forms (to use Frye's term) seems also to have increased respect for 'low mimetic' naturalism, as Auerbach's *Mimesis* convincingly shows.

And subject matter is only one of many factors determining dignity. Fashion plays a larger part than speculators care to allow; and so do contingencies such as the distribution and temperaments of great authors, and the environment of the practical or occasional functions of genre. Tudor sonnets circulating privately in manuscript could be relatively intimate, whereas letters in the vernacular often seem to us a bit formal. In the eighteenth century, however, letters might be more intimate even than visits: Smollett's Lady of Quality speaks of 'the increasing anxiety of Lord B—, who (though I still admitted his visits) plainly perceived that I

---

[29] Angus Fletcher reviews the shortcomings of cyclical theories of history in Krieger, pp. 51–2.
[30] A contradiction implicitly admitted by Frye: see *Anatomy*, p. 60.   [31] Krieger, p. 51.
[32] Fletcher's phrase, though he uses it without disapproval: see Krieger, p. 37.
[33] Max J. Friedländer, *Landscape: Portrait: Still-life* (New York, 1963), p. 11.

wanted to relinquish his correspondence';[34] and Richardson, used to communicating with his wife in writing while both were at home, easily turned the epistolary genre to fictional exploration of psychology. Such movements, which had widespread generic repercussions, appear not to have anything cyclic about them.

Changes in the canon and hierarchy of genres reflect the complexity of the historical process itself; so that it seems premature to attempt any comprehensive generalization. Speculative constructions may reveal patterns missed previously (including some that exist). But they are unlikely to lead to constitutive categories.

The Phases of Generic Development

A modest but in the long term necessary preliminary is to explore the limited range of formal processes by which any individual genre can change, when numberless historical factors and authorial decisions decree that it should do so. It turns out that genre proper develops through at least three principal phases. These are organic and invariable in sequence, though development need not go beyond the first or second.

During the first phase, the genre-complex assembles, until a formal type emerges. When poets first wrote dialogues between shepherds, or singing contests, these were probably independent motifs. It was only when they occurred regularly linked with other forms, that readers could respond to them as genre-sensitive characteristics of eclogue. In phase two, a 'secondary' version of genre develops: a form that the author consciously bases on the earlier primary version. He makes the latter an object of sophisticated imitation, in the Renaissance sense, varying its themes and motifs, perhaps adapting it to slightly different purposes, but retaining all its main features, including those of formal structure. The difference between primary and secondary versions stands out particularly clearly in epic, to which the terms 'primitive' and 'artificial' have been applied for some time. It was left to C. S. Lewis, however, to elaborate the distinction between primary epic (Homer, *Beowulf*) and secondary epic (Virgil).[35] Primary epic is heroic, festal, public in delivery and in subject, oral, formulaic; secondary epic civilized, literary, private in delivery, stylistically elevated or 'sublime'.

I believe that similar phases can be distinguished in other genres. Thus, the bucolics of Theocritus or his predecessors are really rural: singing matches no doubt took place in actual fact. But the shepherds in Virgil's *Eclogues* lie about a fictive landscape in literary guise. So with the novel of romantic adventure. A primary phase represented by eighteenth-century picaresque gives place to a more consciously conventional form in the nineteenth century. Stevenson's *Treasure*

---

[34] *Peregrine Pickle*, ed. James L. Clifford (London, 1964), p. 487.
[35] C. S. Lewis, *A Preface to Paradise Lost* (London, 1942), Chs. iii–vii.

Island and *Kidnapped*, with much of Scott, are examples of this secondary phase; while Dumas, Marryat, Reade, Ballantyne, and Taffrail produced the subliterary equivalent.

But it is also possible to distinguish a tertiary phase of development in many genres. This occurs when an author uses a secondary form in a radically new way. The tertiary form may be burlesque, or antithesis, or symbolic modulation of the secondary—*Lycidas* is tertiary pastoral elegy because its dead shepherd not only disguises an individual but also symbolizes a *pastor*; and because it implies a criticism of the values of ordinary pastoral elegy. And *Paradise Lost* is tertiary, in that it treats Virgilian motifs antiheroically: it incorporates them within a form of larger import, which reflects Christian values, achieving heroism and satisfying divine wrath differently from any pagan epic. Stevenson's *The Dynamiter* and *Ebb-Tide* belong to a corresponding phase of the adventure story; the one as burlesque, the other as symbolic. Tertiary development seems often to constitute an interiorizing. Thus *Paradise Lost*, like *The Faerie Queene*, has little wholly exterior action, while Golding's *Pincher Martin*, which begins as a tertiary version of Taffrail's *Pincher Martin*, has none at all. Or consider the single motif of mysterious ancestry: from a primary version in medieval romances we can trace a secondary sophisticated version in eighteenth-century romance and probably also in Jane Austen's *Emma* (unless there its ironic use verges on burlesque). But George Eliot, who uses the illegitimacy of Deronda symbolically, to represent an identity search,[36] has clearly taken the motif into a tertiary phase.

The three phases are not always very distinct. They may interpenetrate chronologically and even be in doubt within a single work. Theocritus and Homer, who had each some sophistication in grasping form, may be thought to produce secondary types. And an author might exceptionally press beyond a secondary to a tertiary version in a single leap—as Virgil's *Aeneid* may sometimes have done, if his Neoplatonic allegorists are to be believed. But in any case Virgil had the shoal of secondary models reviewed by Brooks Otis[37] behind him; and my point relates to the phases' qualities and sequence only.

Modal Transformation

Perhaps the sequence of phases is best described as a sequence of relations between genre, mode, and abstract formulation. At the primary stage, no equivalent mode or critical description of the genre as yet exists: following its requirements is a matter of unconscious obedience to the extrinsic type, or of imitation

---

[36] See esp. *Daniel Deronda*, Ch. xvi.
[37] *Virgil: A Study in Civilized Poetry* (Oxford, 1964), Ch. ii: 'From Homer to Virgil: The Obsolescence of Epic.'

in the common sense. With the secondary phase, criticism begins: the genre is labeled and its requirements are understood so abstractly that a modal form separates out. Secondary epic may therefore be defined as epic consciously in the heroic mode. During the tertiary stage, criticism may recognize variations of genre (Scaliger's comparison of Homer and Virgil; Tasso's defense of Ariosto's epic; Dryden's distinction between ancient and modern forms of drama). Now conscious modal innovations proliferate. We find not only tertiary epic, but also heroic tragedy and heroic satire: not only tertiary pastoral eclogue, but also pastoral drama, pastoral romance, and burlesque pastoral. It is a phase, too, of hybrid genres, such as Sidney's heroic pastoral romance *Arcadia*.

This restatement suggests a general hypothesis: namely that genre tends to mode. The genre, limited by its rigid structural carapace, eventually exhausts its evolutionary possibilities. But the equivalent mode, flexible, versatile, and susceptible to novel commixtures, may generate a compensating multitude of new generic forms. For the mode was abstracted from an existing concrete historical genre. The latter, closely linked to specific social forms, is apt to perish with them. But the mode corresponds to a somewhat more permanent poetic attitude or stance, independent of particular contingent embodiments of it. Pastoral eclogue is dead: long live pastoral. However, a mode too may pass, if its attitude becomes inappropriate. The heroic mode may be rendered obsolete by changed attitudes to war and aggression.

A surviving modal abstraction is capable of a variety of applications, which may result in new genres distant from their original both in quality and in degree of sophistication. The gothic novel or romance (*The Old English Baron*) yielded a gothic mode that outlasted it and was applied to forms as diverse as the maritime adventure (*The Narrative of A. Gordon Pym*), the psychological novel (*Titus Groan*), the short story (Isak Dinesen), and the detective story, not to mention various science fiction genres (not wholly unpredictable, these last, in view of Mary Shelley's *Frankenstein*). The later applications show more awareness of the mode's socio-political significance. Such a motif as the piercing eye, for example, seems to have been at first an uninterpreted symbol, deeply but not consciously related to the Renaissance eye of judgment. In gothic science fiction, however, the politics are often quite conscious. So too the mode abstracted from satire proper (Juvenal, Horace) was applied to other genres to generate the satiric mock-epic (*The Rape of the Lock*), the satiric travel-book (*Gulliver's Travels*), the satiric novel (*Catch-22*), and many other forms not easy to refer to their origin.

Needless to say, the process from genre to mode is usually so gradual and continual as to escape notice. New modal applications commonly make such modest departures that we can quite properly speak of 'slow, steady change on the analogy of animal growth' or at least, of animal evolution.[38] Only once in a while do bolder

---

[38] The analogy rejected by Wellek, pp. 40, 44–5.

departures show an appearance of complete originality. This is to be expected: generic variations have to proceed from recent or familiar genres, for readers to respond to them easily. One could trace an unbroken development from Chrétien's chivalric romance, through Le Sage's picaresque inset romance, Stevenson's semi-political *Prince Otto*, Buchan's exotic adventure stories, to the modern international thriller in its several varieties: sophisticated (Fleming), naturalistic (Le Carré), symbolic (Charles Williams), and burlesque (Anthony Burgess and John Gardner). This continuity of known types is an essential condition for the new statement. Without the romance, Stevenson's anti-hero would have made no point; without Buchan's gentlemanly fisticuffs and sympathy with the enemy, Fleming's ruthless violence and Le Carré's rejection of the concept enemy would have lacked force—if indeed they had been artistically practicable. *Natura non facit saltum.*[39]

Art may take the odd leap of originality; but far less often than the disappearance of subliterary precedents or the obscurity of latent characteristics in tradition may lead us to suppose. And the *Finnegans Wake* that does depart radically from prevailing forms is likely to prove unacceptable, until subsequent more dilute imitations provide the missing extrinsic type *ex post facto*. This is not just because of difficulty, but also because of deficiency in pleasure. Much of literature's proper enjoyment depends on interweaving the pleasurably familiar with the strangely novel.

I have argued that genres may directly generate modes and hence, indirectly, new genres. They may also die (or, as Wellek would say, not be written); in which case their components disintegrate. Subsequently, works lacking in modal invention or intelligence will be strewn with the detritus of old genres—as Whitfield observes with respect to Pulci and the epic.[40] More inventive works give worn forms new applications or new meanings, by a process whose creative power is difficult to exaggerate. This difficulty has sometimes been overcome, however, by some good critics too fond of life to admit the possibility of death. Empson finds some version of pastoral in every leaf of his favorite works, and Trilling applies the term 'idyll' to *Emma*.[41] Better to have accepted the irreversibility of historical change, and the limitations of genres and modes. This is not to deny that an author may imitate an old master and bring a discontinued form back to life. Epic almost returns in Joyce's *Ulysses*—in a hybrid form, to be sure; but more than a modal application. You can glimpse in it ghosts of the parts of epic: silent invocation, perhaps, in Mulligan's opening oblation of a bowl of lather as he intones

---

[39] See ibid., p. 39.
[40] J. H. Whitfield, *A Short History of Italian Literature* (Harmondsworth, 1960), pp. 127–78.
[41] William Empson, *Some Versions of Pastoral* (London, 1935); Lionel Trilling, '*Emma* and the Legend of Jane Austen,' *Jane Austen: 'Emma'* ed. David Lodge (London, 1968), pp. 163–5.

introibo ad altars Dei.[42] Scholarly resurrectionists dig up even forgotten ideas and forms: as Wellek shrewdly points out,[43] our intellectual life reaches far into the cultural past. But, just as in ordinary life we have to express our most primitive feelings in language that at least approximates to current idiom, so with literary atavism. There are limits, not only upon what we have access to, but also upon what we can assimilate and reintroduce into the cultural tradition by our own efforts. And when these succeed, the old form is not accepted without considerable modification. A genre revived is different from its first avatar, and different also from what it would be if works of its type 'just were not written' for a while.

---

[42] The prayer of invocation was said during the oblation, immediately after the raising of the chalice. Though the *introibo*, from the ordinary of the mass, is a comically wrong prayer to accompany the action, it adumbrates a telescoped liturgical contest. Soon after, Mulligan 'covered the bowl smartly' in travesty of the veiling of the oblations.

[43] *Concepts*, pp. 50–1.

The 'Better Marks' of Jonson's *To Penshurst*

'TO Penshurst' first appeared in print as the second poem of Ben Jonson's *The Forest*, in 1612. At that time the system of personal patronage, in spite of the increasing importance of monetary contracts and of public patronage, had still its full force,[1] and this older system, which could spur or check a poet's genius, threaten or sustain his integrity, brought out the best in Jonson. Indeed, addresses to patrons figure among his greatest poems. They have a judiciousness and independence that similar poems of Donne's, for example, arguably lack. A fine work in its own right, 'To Penshurst' also established an emergent English genre, the country-house poem, adumbrated only indistinctly in the Latin verses of Jonson's old schoolmaster Camden, or Spenser's emblematic houses and topographical passages, on the one hand, and Martial's epigrams, Horace's *Beatus ille*, or Ausonius' *De Mosella*, on the other.[2] The pattern of subsequent imitation shows that the kind is directly generated by 'To Penshurst' and 'Sir Robert Wroth' (*The Forest*, iii). It includes poems by sons of Ben—Thomas Carew's 'To Saxham' and 'To my friend G. N. from Wrest', Herrick's 'A country-life: to his brother Mr. Thomas Herrick' and 'A panegyric to Sir Lewis Pemberton'—and pretty well the last of the line is Marvell's 'Upon Appleton House'; except for a collateral descent through the topographical genre (Denham's *Cooper's Hill*; Pope's *Windsor Forest*).[3] Fittingly, Jonson's seminal exemplar was challenged by a great centre of patronage. For Penshurst's lord was Robert Sidney, who belonged to a family of brilliant literary patrons. We have to imagine the place as equally prominent on

---

[1] See Patricia Thomson, 'The Literature of Patronage, 1580–1630', *Essays in Criticism*, ii (1952), esp. 277, 280; qualified ibid., iii (1953), 109, 120; John Buxton, *Sir Philip Sidney and the English Renaissance* (London, 1954); Eleanor Rosenberg, *Leicester: Patron of Letters* (New York, 1955).

[2] G. R. Hibbard, 'The Country House Poem of the Seventeenth Century', *J.W.C.I.*, xix (1956), 159–77, outlines the genre, leaving historiographic interpretation to C. Molesworth, 'Property and Virtue: the Genre of the Country-House Poem in the Seventeenth Century', *Genre*, i (1968), 141–57. Paul M. Cubeta, 'A Jonsonian Ideal: "To Penshurst"' *PQ.*, xlii (1963), 14–24, discusses the ancient sources. Renaissance antecedents include the river epithalamia of Camden (1586), Vallans (1590), and Spenser (1595). Jonson addresses Camden—'to whom I owe | All that I am in arts'—in *Epig.*, xiv.

[3] Molesworth, loc. cit., pp. 155–6, rightly distinguishes the two genres (country-house poems scarcely touch the pastoral court–country polarity), but with difficulty in face of hybrid forms. Even 'Sir Robert Wroth' is a variant, since it verges on praise of retired life. On the problem of generic classification, see further J. W. Foster, 'A Redefinition of Topographical Poetry', *JEGP,* lxix (1970), 394–406. Raymond Williams, 'Pastoral and Counter-pastoral', *Critical Quarterly*, x (1968), 277–90, mistakenly treats the country-house poem as pastoral; but his account of 'To Penshurst', though ideological, contains interesting and serious comments. On Pope's imitation of the poem, see Maynard Mack, *The Garden and the City* (Toronto, Buffalo, N.Y., and London, 1960), Index, s.v. *Jonson*. Consult also John Chalker, *The English Georgic* (London, 1969).

28   REMEMBERED WORDS

the map of letters with any college. As Patricia Thomson remarks, 'the strength of the Sidneys and Herberts as patrons lay in a form of enlightened hospitality'.[4]

In 'To Penshurst', as in Jonson's poetry generally, many readers are aware of a special relation between the ideal and the real; and that is what I want to explore here.

II

Ideal and real seem already embattled in the initial opposition between an idealized Penshurst and a sort of Timon's villa: between the reverenced 'ancient pile' and ambitious houses built as show places. But Penshurst really was quite a modest building in actual fact, with a fourteenth-century hall small by Elizabethan standards. Far from being designed for 'show' it was scarcely architect-designed at all; having grown by accretion into a traditional, irregular, functional form.[5] By contrast, the pretentious palaces that Sir John Summerson has termed 'prodigy houses' were status symbols never meant for continuous occupation, but only for reception of the court during the sovereign's progresses: 'Sir Francis Willoughby built Wollaton purely and simply as an extravaganza'; 'Hatton hardly used his new house [Holdenby], nor did he build it for use.'[6] Designed for spectacular display and characterized by a conspicuously ostentatious extravagance that sometimes issued in quite astonishing vulgarity, these competitive palaces—

> prouder piles, where the vain builder spent
> More cost in outward gay embellishment
> Than real use[7]

as Carew says—were indeed 'built to envious show'. Burghley, for example, was criticized for building beyond his means or necessity, and in a letter of 1585 he deprecates the riches of a stateroom at Theobalds quite defensively. Its

---

[4] Op. cit., pp. 275–6. Sir Philip Sidney, his sister Mary Countess of Pembroke, his daughter Elizabeth Countess of Rutland (according to Jonson 'nothing inferior to her father in poetry'), his niece Lady Mary Wroth, and his nephew William Herbert Third Earl of Pembroke, were all both patrons and writers.

[5] On the type Penshurst belongs to, see Sir John Summerson, *Architecture in Britain 1530 to 1830* (Harmondsworth, 1953), pp. 62–3, and John Newman, *West Kent and the Weald* (Harmondsworth, 1969), pp. 438–9. At this date 'pile' meant a *small* castle, a peel (see *OED*, s.v. Pile sb.²); Burghley said that at first he meant Theobalds 'for a little pile'—Peck, *Desiderata curiosa* (1598), cit. J. Nichols, *The Progresses and Public Processions of Queen Elizabeth* (London, 1823), i. 309 n.

[6] Quoted Summerson, op. cit., pp. 30–3, 41; cf. Hibbard, op. cit., p. 160. Hibbard stresses (p. 161) the declining importance of the hall in the seventeenth century; but the houses of prodigy Jonson meant were Elizabethan in design.

[7] Thomas Carew, 'To my friend G. N. from Wrest', ll. 53–5 (*Poems*, ed. R. Dunlap (Oxford, 1957), p. 87).

magnificence (which appears to have run to imitation trees and an indoor waterfall) was exaggerated, he writes; it 'need not be envied'.[8]

Jonson's curiously negative stance—'Thou art not' this, 'nor canst boast' that; 'Thou hast no lantern, whereof tales are told'—seems contrived to specify particular features. Thus Herford and the Simpsons felt constrained to comment, with tedious brevity, 'There is a louvre at Penshurst Place, but Jonson's point, which we do not follow, appears to be that it has no special history.' And John Carey has most ingeniously discovered an allusion to Theobalds, over which a belfry lantern with a chiming clock and dials showing the zodiac and planets was prominent,[9] made, according to a seventeenth-century Parliamentary Survey, 'with timber of excellent workmanship curiously wrought standing a great height with divers pinnacles at each corner'.[10] Now, Jonson certainly had hard things to say in private about the Earl of Salisbury, Burghley's second son and owner of Theobalds until 1607. But he would scarcely have risked publishing such a slight unless it was at least concealed among the ambages of possible allusions to other palaces. And in fact the Theobalds lantern belonged to a tradition: the same tradition with the Hampton Court hall louvre and the Nonesuch clock tower.[11] As for the Earl of Shrewsbury's Worksop (before 1590), it sported no less than four prominent lanterns on corner towers.

Other architectural particulars in the opening lines similarly indicate characteristic features of contemporary houses in the grand style. 'Stair' is specially suggestive: Burghley had a magnificent stone-vaulted stair; and Knole in Kent, where Lord Treasurer Sackville around 1605 built staterooms of exceeding sumptuousness, could boast the first English staircase treated as an architectural spectacle (but one soon imitated at Hatfield, Blickling, and Aston Hall).[12] Penshurst lacks 'courts' because the court plan was designed to provide lodgings or suites for large-scale, and sometimes big-businesslike, entertaining.[13] Kirby and Burghley had one court each, Theobalds and Holdenby two, and Knole seven, possibly in accordance with a temporal symbolism. Again, 'touch', black granite or marble, was common, for example in the portentous mantelpieces then fashionable.[14] At Wrest Park, writes Carew, 'No sumptuous chimney piece of shining stone...coldly entertains' the visitor's sight.[15]

---

[8] *Victoria County History, Hertfordshire*, ed. W. Page (London, 1902), iii. 448; Nichols, op. cit., i. 205.
[9] Private communication.
[10] See Sir J. Summerson, 'The Building of Theobalds, 1564–1585', *Archaeologia*, xcvii (1959), 107–26, and Ian Dunlop, *Palaces and Progresses of Elizabeth I* (London, 1962), p. 175. Other relevant features of Theobalds include its notable dogleg stair (Summerson, 'Building of Theobalds', p. 122) and a fountain of white and black marble ('touch') (ibid., p. 119; *V.C.H. Herts.*, iii. 250).
[11] Summerson, 'Building of Theobalds', p. 118.
[12] Newman, op. cit., pp. 81, 347; Summerson, *Architecture in Britain*, pp. 39, 53.
[13] Ibid., p. 34.   [14] Newman, op. cit., pp. 345, 347–8.
[15] 'To my friend', ll. 25–7 (*Poems*, ed. cit., p. 87).

That Jonson intends a moral antitype rather than a lampoon of Salisbury finds support in Gayle Wilson's comparison with the idolatrous Solomon's Temple in 1 Kgs. 6–7.[16] That had prominent 'pillars of brass'; 'winding stairs'; an 'inner court'; and a 'great court'. Moreover, 'the whole house' was 'overlaid with gold'.[17] Wilson's argument is not unassailable: 'lights' (7:4) means windows, not lanterns. But Solomon's profane house may well form a wing of the anti-palace. If so, it is surely no coincidence that an entertainment of Jonson's, performed at Theobalds in 1606 for the visit of King James with the King of Denmark, contained a representation of Solomon's Temple.[18]

Besides prodigy houses and Solomon's Temple, this densely allusive passage may also suggest the pagan architectural wonders that Milton quarried for his Pandemonium and Spenser for his Panthea: namely, the Pantheon, Holovitreum, and Capitol of the medieval *Mirabilia urbis Romae*.[19] The last, used in Du Bellay's *Vision* as a symbol of Rome, is a 'stately frame' of gold and crystal

> With hundreth pillars fronting fair the same
> All wrought with diamond.

It in some sense resembles a lantern, having a wall of 'shining crystal'; and it has a roof of gold:

> Gold was the parget [ornament plasterwork] and the ceiling bright
> Did shine all scaly with great plates of gold.[20]

From such originals derive Spenser's proud House of Lucifera with its 'golden foil' and 'dial', as well as the houses Jonson contrasts with Durrants, 'free from proud porches, or their gilded roofs'.[21] But then, so does Spenser's good Panthea, about

---

[16] Gayle Edward Wilson, 'Jonson's Use of the Bible and the Great Chain of Being in "To Penshurst"', *Studies in English Literature*, viii (Houston, Texas, 1968), 79–81, 84, and 88, where he compares Vaughan, 'The Shepherds', ll. 17–26: 'Wretched Salem... Her stately piles with all their height and pride |... Her cedar, fir, hewed stones and gold were all | Polluted....'

[17] See 1 Kgs. 7:6, 15–22; 6:8; 6:36; 7:9, 12; 6:22.

[18] Letter from Sir John Harington, cit. Nichols, *Progresses of King James I* (1828), ii. 72. According to Harington, the English king became very drunk, and the performance went badly wrong with the Queen of Sheba tripping on the steps and emptying her gifts precipitately into the Danish king's lap.

[19] For accounts of this twelfth-century guide-book, see Margaret R. Scherer, *Marvels of Ancient Rome* (New York and London, 1955), p. 4, *et passim*; also Isabel E. Rathborne, *The Meaning of Spenser's Fairyland* (New York, 1937), p. 25.

[20] 'The Visions of Bellay', ii, in *Spenser: Poetical Works*, ed. J. C. Smith and E. de Selincourt (London, 1912), p. 523; for another version see ibid., p. 607.

[21] *Faerie Queene*, I. iv. iv. 'To Sir Robert Wroth', l. 14 (*Ben Jonson*, ed. C. H. Herford, Percy and Evelyn Simpson (Oxford, 1925–52), viii. 97).

which tales are quite literally told.[22] Thus, besides setting up an evil antitype in 'To Penshurst', Jonson may also be amplifying the greatness of the other houses, to show that Penshurst compares favourably even with kings' palaces. (This by no means disqualifies Theobalds, which was so ambitious a heap that in 1607 James I exchanged Hatfield for it, at a ceremony for which Jonson himself wrote a masque.) On the other hand, Jonson nowhere expresses Raymond Williams's opinion, that Sidney was a local exception to general corruption in landowners. He is careful to specify an antitype to a particular degree of wealth and pretension.

III

I have treated this architectural passage at length, because it has a bearing on the form of the whole poem. For a characteristic feature of prodigy houses was their elaborate planning. Meant as impressive spectacles, they were carefully proportioned and usually symmetrical. Moreover, many had an ideal form objectifying some political or philosophical idea. Theobalds, for example, besides the great chamber's zodiac ceiling, had twelve bells and a zodiac in its lantern, recalling the Mirabilian description of the Holovitreum: 'made of glass and gold by mathematical craft, where was an astronomy with all the signs of heaven'.[23] And Knole had 365 rooms, 52 staircases, and 7 courts. Indeed, Summerson distinguishes a category of houses with programmatic designs such as Thorpe's extravagant trinitarian conceit for Longford Castle (1580).[24] Now Penshurst, a house that had developed through the accretions of centuries, could offer no such ideal significances. And that is why Jonson credits it instead with 'better marks', or symbols.[25] These he finds in the beauties and advantages of its estate: most of the poem goes to show that the estate of Penshurst possesses as much order and symbolism as the prodigy houses, but in land and use rather than in architectural display; until Jonson is justly able to conclude

> Now Penshurst, they that will proportion thee
> With other edifices, when they see
> Those proud ambitious heaps, and nothing else,

May say, their lords have built, but thy lord dwells.

The 'better marks' of Penshurst include 'marks, of soil, of air, | Of wood, of water'. Here the ideal is microcosmic significance. Penshurst may not have the

---

[22] On the use of materials from the *Mirabilia* for Panthea (*Faerie Queene*, I. x. xlviii, II. x. lxxiii), see Rathborne, op. cit., pp. 25 ff. She rejects (p. 67) Warton's suggestion that the original is Windsor, regarding it rather as a symbol of Rome.
[23] Ibid., p. 26.   [24] *Architecture in Britain*, pp. 41–2.   [25] *OED*, s.v. *Mark*, sb., iii. 10.

elements of architecture, but it has the four elements Earth ('soil'), Air, Water, and Fire. The fourth resides potentially in the 'wood' used to make it: an association repeated in lines 15-16, where the 'writhed bark' of Sidney's Oak records the silvans 'taken with his flames'.[26] Such tropic flames of love, zeal, and hospitality flicker over Penshurst like a benign St. Elmo's fire. At line 73 fire warms the visiting poet's room without his asking: at lines 77 ff. fires of hospitality

> Shine bright on every hearth, as the desires
> Of thy Penates had been set on flame,

inviting the king to pay an impromptu visit. In its broadest application, fire symbolizes the warmth of the country's loyalty (80-1). The other elements also reappear: the Medway and the fishpond with their produce (22, 31-8), the 'lower land' and 'middle grounds' with theirs (22-30), and the 'fresh...air' (40). In this, as in much else, Carew's 'To Saxham' follows 'To Penshurst'; though with a simpler and more explicit manner:

> Water, earth, air, did all conspire,
> To pay their tributes to thy fire. (29-30)

Carew, like Jonson, distributes produce between the elements, and like Jonson gives honour of place to hospitable fire, highest of the elements.

This is the first way in which Jonson portrays a Penshurst endowed with cosmic proportions, as ideal as a work of architectural art. Like Ausonius,[27] he turns from marble splendours to discover Nature's artistry more intricate, consummate, and compressed than any human imitation. His inventory of the estate, for example, gives a strong sense of abundant plentitude. Yet this effect is at first unaccountable; for, though he mentions many items, it is to catalogue rather than describe or realize them. There is little sensuous particularity: even 'the painted partridge' (29) functions as an allusion, through Martial's *picta perdix*, to Faustinus' homely farm.[28] How, then, is the effect of fertile plenty sustained?

---

[26] Either 'his passion' or 'Sidney's passion: the same passion as Sidney's'. Cf. Waller, 'At Penshurst': ''When to the beeches I report my flame', 'all we can of love, or high desire, | Seems but the smoke of amorous Sidney's fire' (3, 13-14).

[27] *De Mosella*, ll. 48-52:

> I nunc, et Phrygiis sola levia consere crustis
> tendens marmoreum laqueata per atria campum.
> ast ego despectis, quae census opesque dederunt,
> naturae mirabor opus, non dira nepotum
> laetaque iacturis ubi luxuriatur egestas.

('Now go, and with Phrygian slabs lay smooth floors spreading an expanse of marble through your fretted halls. But I, despising what wealth and riches have conferred, will marvel at Nature's handiwork, not at the ruin of prodigals, at reckless extravagance where poverty wantons.')

[28] *Epig.* III. lviii. 15.

A clue may lie in the labyrinthine elaboration of Jonson's arrangement of the items in relation to one another. For the effects of Penshurst form highly ordered sets, which communicate an impression of inexhaustible complexity, and in which some of the poem's 'completeness' may reside.[29] Not only has Jonson ordered the poem's substantive catalogues and formal divisions, but he has ordered them according to several independent organizational ideas.

IV

First, there is spatial arrangement. Jonson divides the estate geographically into clearly distinct and exhaustively enumerated levels, through which his reader passes on separate 'walks' (9): 'Mount'; 'middle grounds'; 'lower land'; 'river'; 'banks'; 'tops'. One formal division follows a similar plan. As Paul Cubeta remarks, roughly the first half treats the exterior, and the second half the interior. The transition is at line 48, where 'all come in, the farmer, and the clown'. Outdoors offers the estate's teeming provision, indoors the cornucopia of hospitality and the inner magnificence of noble or spiritual fruitfulness.[30]

Secondly, there is temporal arrangement. Fruits come in emphatically seasonal schemes, besides being set in the flowering branches of a harmoniously balanced pre-Augustan rhetoric:

> Then hath thy orchard fruit, thy garden flowers,
> Fresh as the air, and new as are the hours.
> The early cherry, with the later plum,
> Fig, grape, and quince, each in his time doth come:
> The blushing apricot, and woolly peach
> Hang on thy walls, that every child may reach.[31]

Rhetorically, the catalogue divides 2 | 3 | 2, comprising two temporal opposites 'early...later'; then three 'each in his time'; then another two temporal opposites (the apricot took its name from the fact that it was early-ripe, sooner than other peaches), moderated, however, by the coy blushing of the precocious fruit. The three fruiting times realize the 'new...hours', that is, the Horae, divinities presiding over the three seasons of the ancient year. Other items similarly represent stages of growth harmoniously succeeding in the fullness of time.

---

[29] See Lester Beaurline, 'Ben Jonson and the Illusion of Completeness', *PMLA*, lxxxiv (1969), 51–9, for a study of structural completeness in Jonson's drama.

[30] See Cubeta, op. cit., p. 17. The most obvious sections are as follows: ll. 1–6 architectural; 7–8 elements; 9–48 provisions: outdoors; 49–88 hospitality: indoors; 89–98 virtues; 99–102 architectural, i.e. 6 | 2 | 40 | 40 | 10 | 4. In 'To Sir Robert Wroth' the indoors–outdoors division more simply bisects the poem.

[31] ll. 39–44; cf. Cubeta, p. 21.

'Mares, and horses breed': kine have calves: and 'bright [i.e. mature] eels', 'fat, aged carps', 'ripe daughters', and the 'fruitful' lady are all creatures who, in Spenser's words, 'by their change their being do dilate', working their perfection.[32] The natural achieves here an ideal season of fruition and oblation.

Temporal order also appears in the over-all structure. The largest movement is from Sidney's 'ancient' (5) inheritance from the past, his estate, through its present enjoyment and use in hospitality and loyal service, to provision for the future by the nurture of children in the poem's last third. This scheme of three parts of time relates Penshurst to the historical context, which Charles Molesworth has argued to be essential to the country-house poem.[33] For the time span implied is far longer than that of an individual life. The legacy of the past includes

> that taller tree, which of a nut was set,
> At his great birth, where all the Muses met

—that is, the Bear's Oak (so called after the badge of the Dudleys), said to have been planted at the birth of Sir Philip Sidney, Robert's brother.[34] It is a family tree, commemorating a heritage of greatness, a tradition of patronage. As Molesworth puts it, the country-house poem engages the 'life of memory', arousing a sense of the patron's virtuous forefathers.[35] More remotely, the oak's roots reach down, through mythology of feasting gods (10-12), to an earthly paradise of accessible fruit; to the golden age; to a cosmic past.

The present is time to spend and enjoy; so that the poem's second part treats the hospitality of Penshurst, which is given a focal prominence. The warmth of the 'liberal' (but not extravagant) hospitality is contrasted with the mingy parsimony of a disagreeable new type of 'great man'. The latter, however ostentatious his entertainment of V.I.P.s, doled out hospitality to others grudgingly, keeping a watchful eye on expense. Thus Jonson's praise of the 'high huswifery' at Penshurst gains historical perspective from his mingled complaint about a contemporary decline ('this day') in the traditional liberality of 'housekeeping', which had formerly made the great house an important cell of social organization. Like some other observers, Jonson deplores the tendency to move away from informal direct dealings to impersonality, contractuality, commercial system, and bureaucratic administration through intermediaries: to 'household economy put on a business footing'.[36] He sets 'this age' (92) of historically deteriorating manners against the ideal feast, the national golden age, still lingering, still celebrated, perpetuated in reality, at Penshurst.

---

[32] *Faerie Queene*, VII. vii. lviii. Cf. Wilson, op. cit., p. 81.   [33] Loc. cit., pp. 142-3.
[34] See Herford and Simpson, xi. 33.   [35] Jonson's phrase: see Molesworth, p. 144.
[36] R. H. Tawney, 'The Rise of the Gentry, 1558-1640', *Economic History Rev.* xi (1941), 5, 10, 33-8; quoted Molesworth, pp. 147-50, and Hibbard, pp. 159, 161.

The third part of time, approached in the last passage, deals with the upbringing of the new generation in 'manners, arms, and arts' by the example of their 'virtuous parents' (97–8). Penshurst's true estate, the 'fruit' (90) and 'fortune' (92) of human values he will leave to posterity, dwells in these children. To this explicitly Christian hope for the future—the children 'are, and have been taught religion'—Jonson leads up through a passage of implicit eschatology. For as Gayle Wilson has noted, King James's unexpected visit conforms to Biblical parables of the coming of the kingdom, when men are judged by their readiness for the master's sudden arrival.[37]

V

Another organizing principle is the hierarchical, early manifested in the catalogue of trees, where 'that taller tree' is the primate, oak (Bear's Oak, Lady's Oak). Critics have recognized several hints of the Great Chain of Being, in which the duty of lower ranks was to serve man. A chief end of the panegyric, as in other country-house poems, is to dignify the patron by showing creatures on Penshurst's estate fulfilling their subservient roles with enthusiasm; influenced to unusually willing sacrifice by love of an unusually virtuous lord. Thus the copse 'never fails to serve...deer', 'each bank doth yield' rabbits, the partridge 'is willing to be killed', pikes 'themselves betray', eels

> leap on land
> Before the fisher, or into his hand

and the apricot and peach so hang 'that every child may reach', Wilson aptly cites Genesis 9, where God, commanding fruitfulness, gives man (in the person of Noah) dominion over other creatures: '*into your hand* are they delivered'.[38] Yet he and Hibbard (p. 164) may be wrong to take the partridge's submission entirely at face value. 'Willing to be killed' surely recalls the *ipse capi voluit* of Juvenal's turbot (*Sat.*, iv. 69), in a context of 'gross flattery'. May not Jonson intend that playful panegyric tone which depends on openly hyperbolic excess of flattery?

The political links of the Great Chain appear more obviously in an ascending series of visitors: neighbours with their tribute of unnecessary gifts (49–60), the guest (61–2), the poet favoured with service fit for king or owner (74), and finally the king, to whom the Sidneys themselves offered tribute of hospitality and from

---

[37] e.g. Mark 13:32–7; see Wilson, op. cit. p. 86. With the bright fires that attract the king, cf. the lamps of Matt. 25.
[38] Gen. 9:2; see Wilson, pp. 82–3, who observes that Carew's 'To Saxham', ll. 21–8, clearly modelled on Jonson, makes the allusion to Noah explicit.

whom they 'reaped' in turn a harvest of praise. Characteristically, Jonson makes this series of stewardship relations lead up to a sudden enlargement in the eschatological symbol of a test of the house's readiness. As Sidney holds Penshurst in fee from James, so James is a steward, responsible for his kingdom to the divine lord, whose coming he expects.[39]

King James comes last and greatest of all the visitors, at the position of honour in ancient triumphal processions. But he may also be dignified numerologically, by the formal position of his name and first introduction 27 lines from the end, matching a mention of *crown* ('To crown thy open table') 27 lines from the beginning. For 27, the cube of the number of limitation, was sacred to Cybele, goddess of the natural law all landlords must obey; and Cybele's familiar attribute was a crown.[40]

VI

Yet another principle of organization is the numerical. Here I take leave of Professor Beaurline, who contrasts Jonson's completeness of treatment with an 'older more simply quantitative' copiousness through numerical schemes.[41] But the seventeenth-century poet's structural style seems to me no less numerological than before; though it may be more organic and internalized.

We notice that the 17 creatures yielding 'free provisions' fall into 3 groups: namely, animals or birds (produce of the various 'grounds'); fish; and fruit (produce of the orchard). These items are arranged as symmetrically as any palace façade—*deer | sheep | cows | horses | conies | pheasant | partridge || carp | pike | eel || cherry | plum | fig | grape | quince | apricot | peach*, or 7 | 3 | 7. It is possible that the heptads are meant to be subdivided. For the motif of 7 as the union of 4 and 3 was a common number symbol, signifying either the power of the creative *tetraktus* to form the cosmic heptad from its triad and tetrad, or else the sevenfold grace of the Trinity's triad and the Gospels' tetrad.[42] Penshurst's 7 land creatures may be divided into 4 domestic+3 wild species; just as the orchard, as we saw, yields (2+3+2) fruits. Similarly, the neighbours' 7 gifts comprise capons, cake,

---

[39] Cf. Cubeta, pp. 18, 22; Wilson, pp. 85–6. Raymond Williams finds the hierarchic element in the poem unpalatable, attacking Penshurst as a paradise of 'easy consumption', from which the curse of labour is extracted 'by a simple abstraction of the existence of labourers' (p. 288). But waiters and cheesemakers are not abstracted. Besides, 'To Penshurst' is not a 'work-song' like Herrick's 'The Hock-cart', with which Williams contrasts it.

[40] Vicenzo Cartari, *Imagini delli dei* (Venice, 1556), p. 207 (ed. W. Koschatzky from the 1647 Venice edn. (Graz, 1963), p. 112). According to Boccaccio, the crown symbolizes the earth's circlet, set with cities, castles, and villages. The pun on crown is noted by Cubeta, p. 19. I discuss a similar numerological use of 27 to symbolize Cybele in *Spenser and the Numbers of Time* (London, 1964), p. 186.

[41] Loc. cit., p. 55.

[42] Pietro Bongo, *Numerorum mysteria* (Bergamo, 1591), pp. 197, 287. Pico develops the idea of a threefold and fourfold universe in the most authoritative Renaissance work on the heptad; see *Heptaplus*, Second Proem, tr. D. Carmichael, ed. P. J. W. Miller (New York, 1965), pp. 78–9.

nuts, apples, together with 3 from the cheese producers (cheese itself, pears, plums).[43] More obviously, many of the poem's enumerations form triads. There are 3 kinds of trees (beech, chestnut, oak), 3 groups of mythological beings on the mount (dryads, satyrs, fauns), 3 copses (Gamage's, Ashore, Sidney's), 3 comforts bestowed on guests ('fire, or lights, or livery'). In the last part, the triads become more abstract: Lady Sidney is 'noble, fruitful, chaste'; the children learn mysteries of 'manners, arms, and arts'.

Formal divisions of the poem are also organized numerically. The dichotomy between outdoors and indoors draws some attention to the midpoint, where panegyrics commonly had a prominent mention of the person honoured. Here, Penshurst's 'lord, and lady' are first mentioned in the fiftieth of 102 lines. A modern reader might ask why Jonson made 'To Penshurst' in 51 couplets, rather than the obvious 50 or 52. But in fact 51 was a common compositional number, because of its structural use in the Psalms. Pietro Bongo, least original of Renaissance arithmologists, explains it as the product of 3 and 17, the latter symbolizing the decalogue together with the sevenfold gifts of the spirit. He further associates 17 with the miraculous draught of 153 fish (or species of fish) in St. John's Gospel, interpreted as the Elect and analysed as the triangular number on 17 as base.[44] Now Jonson, as we saw, makes 17 the number of species provisioning Penshurst estate—among which the fish form a prominent central group. It seems reasonable to inquire whether the poem's 51 couplets are divided into triadic parts of 17 couplets each. And sure enough, a division between the first two-thirds is wittily noticed in the lines that enclose it:

> pikes, now weary their own kind to eat,
> As loth, the second draught, or cast to stay,
> Officiously, at first, themselves betray.

For *draught*, primarily the drawing of a net (*O.E.D.* iii. 7), means also a passage of writing (*O.E.D.* xii. 38). In other words, the pikes are too eager to wait for Part 2, but press forward into the seventeenth couplet and hence scrape into Part 1; so that their dutifulness puts them in the sovereign central place of 17 species.[45] Wilson's view that the willing sacrifice expresses creaturely acceptance of the Chain of Being hardly does justice to the wit of Jonson's Biblical allusions. The third draught, beginning at line 69, is again signalled by a reference to counting:

---

[43] For precedents for the numerological organization of gifts, see my *Triumphal Forms* (Cambridge, 1970), p. 64.

[44] John 21:11; see *Triumphal Forms*, p. 189, citing Bongo, pp. 594–5. According to Gregory the Great and others, 17 signifies the decalogue with the sevenfold Spirit; this 17, multiplied by the divine triad, yields first 51, then 153.

[45] On the symbolism of the central place, see *Triumphal Forms*, chs. ii–v. Elizabeth McCutcheon, 'Jonson's "To Penshurst", 36', *Explicator*, xxv (1967), item 52, catches a pun in 'officiously'.

'Here no man tells [counts] my cups.' An inhospitable great man's waiter stands just at the division, to count draughts in another sense, the thirsty poet's drinks (*O.E.D.* v. 14), ordered in the first line of Part 3. In view of the prominence of architectural symbolism in the poem, a third pun on *draught* is not out of the question. It could mean 'a measure of sawyers' work' in stonemasonry (*O.E.D.* iv. 12): a use that would come naturally to Jonson, a former mason.[46] The poetic collation he adds to the Sidneys' feast may thus be edifying in more senses than one.

There remains the rhetorical division, in which we may distinguish an architectural introduction of 3 couplets, contrasting Penshurst with prodigy houses, and an architectural coda of 2 couplets. Thus the total 51 couplets divide 3 | 46 | 2. Now 46 traditionally symbolized 'edification', or the building of a regenerate human nature as a temple of the spirit (partly through association with the second Temple of Jerusalem, which took 46 years to build).[47] Moreover, the 10 lines of the framing passages symbolize the *tetraktus* of virtue that informs the building. Thus, from a numerological point of view, substantive mention of architecture in introduction and coda frames a formal symbol of building in a more organic manner. All accords with the affirmation 'their lords have built, but thy lord dwells': the other 'edifices' are built with hands and owned by absentee landlords, but Penshurst is the creaturely temple of a regenerate spirit who dwells in the house of the Lord. Hence the *prosopopeia* to Penshurst estate simultaneously addresses Penshurst the man. And to 'proportion' it (99) means not merely compare, but also shape and divide[48] in the fair proportions of Sidney's nature.

VII

The moral character of this well-ordered structure is displayed both in direct examples and in emblems. As Molesworth remarks (p. 145), country-house poem estates regularly 'reflect the virtue and character of the owner' by metonymy. From this point of view it is a brilliant stroke to delay the entry of the lord and lady, so that until the sudden salute in line 50 we learn of them only obliquely, through their estate.

Not that these 'creatures' of a patron all appear in an ideal light: the poem's supercharacter, it seems, generates not only good but also vicious subcharacters. Thus, Sidney's virtue is shown against foils of ambitious social climbing, which

---

[46] 'Measures of hewed stones' are mentioned in the description of Solomon's three-chambered temple (1 Kgs. 6:6, 7:9).

[47] The symbolism of 46 also depends on the numerical value of Adam's name; see Bongo, pp. 527–31. For examples in literature, see *Spenser and the Numbers of Time*, p. 54. The notion of spirit as an informing *tetraktus* is discussed ibid., pp. 275 ff.

[48] See *O.E.D.*, s.v. *Proportion* vb., 2, 4.

range in culpability from the grotesquely emulous eel (an overreacher who leaves his true element when he leaps on land) and the Medway sometimes too 'high-swollen'[49] to pay its tribute like the ponds, through tolerantly observed neighbours vying to marry their daughters well,[50] to the degree-conscious 'great man' satirized for inhospitality (65–73). Even the thirsty poet is presented critically, almost as an emblem of unruly excess, the opposite of the 'great man's' extreme of businesslike niggardliness. The poet is Sir Toby to the waiter's Malvolio, Sansloy to the bad host's Elissa. As the true mean there stands the Sidneys' liberal moderation, a 'taller tree' between ambitious Pan and lawless Bacchus. The Sidneys' 'freedom doth with degree dispense',[51] so that the poet is treated as if he 'reigned'; whereas duty to the real king is very fully acknowledged. True hospitality being a free and reciprocal communion, Wilson (p. 85) can intelligibly find a symbol of the Lord's Supper in 'the lord's own meat...and bread, and self-same wine' (62–3).

Jonson explicitly announces the emblematic mode where it is least obvious, in the 'ripe daughters'

> whose baskets bear
> An emblem of themselves in plum, or pear.

By doing so, he directs our attention beyond the prominent sensuousness of fruit offered by mature, ready girls[52] to the significance of the specific fruits selected. The pear was an emblem of accessibility ('The ripe pear falls even of its own freewill');[53] whereas the plum, as a 'later fruit', proverbial of difficulty ('The higher the plumtree the sweeter the plum'),[54] counterbalances its amenable suggestion.

---

[49] Cubeta (p. 19) finds in 'high-swollen Medway' a 'suggestion of luxuriant, almost overflowing abundance'. But in its moral sense the word was more dyslogistic, implying excess: see O.E.D., s.v. Swollen, 2. a; and cf. Milton, Samson Agonistes, 1. 532, 'swollen with pride'.

[50] A motif not in the source, Martial's description of the Baian villa. Cubeta's sense of 'sly poking of fun at motives of calculating farmers' (p. 22) seems surer than Wilson's notion (p. 84) of an allusion to Ruth.

[51] 'To Sir Robert Wroth', 1. 58; Herford and Simpson, viii. 98.

[52] Growth stages of fruit—whether ripe or, as in Ariosto's pome acerbe, unripe—were obvious metaphors for breast development (Orl. Fur., vii. 14; cf. Carew, 'A Rapture', 1.66).

[53] Jacob Cats, Proteus (Rotterdam, 1627), Embl. xi. x, 'Mite pyrum vel sponte fluit'. For a use of the pear as an attribute of Venus, see Guy de Tervarent, Attributs et symboles dans l'art profane 1450-1600, Travaux d'humanisme et renaissance, xxix (Geneva, 1958), col. 309.

[54] Proverbial: see M. P. Tilley, A Dictionary of the Proverbs in England in the Sixteenth and Seventeenth Centuries (Ann Arbor, 1950), Item P 441, citing John Clarke, Paroemiologia anglo-latina (1639), s.v. Difficultatis. For the plum as a symbol of fidelity, see G. Ferguson, Signs and Symbols in Christian Art (New York, 1961), p. 37.

VIII

The last part of 'To Penshurst' presents a more abstract generalization about the Sidneian way of life. Some of this has been implicit in the previous parts. For country-house poems view 'man's estate as the "effect" of his virtue'.[55] Thus Lady Sidney is 'fruitful' and 'reaps'; and her children learn mysteries embodied in their parents, as in the oak planted 'At his great birth, where all the Muses met'. The generalizations are idealistic. But then, idealism was obligatory in the panegyric mode, and was to become a general requirement of the country-house poem.[56]

This weakens Parfitt's objection, that the poem gives no total impression of life at Penshurst: that 'the only hints of anything non-ideal are there for contrast'.[57] He concludes Jonson's achievement to be 'one of exclusion', finding 'the account of the Sidneys' hospitality... clearly simplified'. But the Sidneys were after all remarkable patrons and hosts. Hibbard, more plausibly, contrasts Jonson, for whom Penshurst 'represents the norm, slightly idealized, perhaps, but still the norm', with Pope, for whom 'Timon's villa is the norm'.[58] Certainly the later poet wrote differently, for a very different society; but the difference hardly amounts to an absence of 'the values Pope believes in' from 'the great houses being built at the time'. Surely it must also have had much to do with attitudes to personal patronage. Pope, writing after the system had largely broken down, was more interested in general moral qualities than in styles of patronage. Jonson, addressing a good patron while the system still worked, might hope to influence by a specific portrayal of a noble life-style.

'To Penshurst', like other country-house poems, unquestioningly accepts 'the social value of real property', at least when well used.[59] But its praise of Sidney never really adopts the 'somewhat offensive panegyric tone' that John Wilson Foster hears.[60] Indeed, its tone seems characterized by detached alertness. It reflects unusual awareness of the civilized forms achieved by society at its best, and of the threat presented to them by excessive display. In fact, it observes what has been called the crisis of the aristocracy, in the perversion of 'housekeeping', the decline of property as a mark of virtue, and the spread of monetary contractually.[61] Moreover, far from having a servile relation to his patron, Jonson takes for granted an easy friendship and even an advisory responsibility. Through recommendatory panegyric he guides the aspirations of the ruling class.[62] Indeed,

---

[55] Molesworth, p. 145.
[56] Ibid.: 'The "outer form" of the country-house poem is structured by the description of the estate; the "inner form" is the tone of panegyrical praise for the purpose of establishing the owner's virtues as worthy of (indeed, demanding) emulation.'
[57] G. A. E. Parfitt, 'The Poetry of Ben Jonson', *Essays in Criticism*, xviii (1968), 29.
[58] Hibbard, pp. 159–60.   [59] Molesworth, p. 146; cf. pp. 142, 145.
[60] *J.E.G.P.*, lxix (1970), 396, 398.   [61] Molesworth, pp. 146–50.
[62] Cf. Hugh Maclean, 'Ben Jonson's Poems: Notes on the Ordered Society', *Essays in English Literature from the Renaissance to the Victorian Age Presented to A.S.P. Woodhouse 1964*, ed. Miliar MacLure and F. W. Watt (Toronto, 1964), p. 57; cf. Hibbard, p. 159.

when he writes on nurture, a hint of exhortation may be discerned. As for past actions, his praise is measured: the Sidneys welcomed King James promptly, not grandly; with '(great, I will not say, but) sudden cheer'. He feels no need to cover up or avoid the fact.

Nevertheless, as Parfitt says (p. 29), the poem's descriptions are 'miniatures of Elizabethan ideals', in active detail. And the relation between ideals and real details is unusually intricate. Cubeta (p. 14) cites Jonson's own view that a poet was responsible for having 'exact knowledge of all virtues, and their contraries; with ability to render the one loved, the other hated, by his proper embattling them'.[63] He shows that while 'To Penshurst' includes details of Faustinus' Baian villa, its ideal is radically different from Martial's. For it combines the rude fertility of Faustinus' villa with an artificial 'patterned, formal beauty' much like the 'farm' of Bassus, instead of contrasting these types.[64] The realistic details of the fertile pastoral scene, themselves partly literary, form so many patterns and are informed with so much meaning that they overwhelm the reader with the rich, highly civilized art of Sidney's client as much as with Nature's increase of his property.

'To Penshurst' interfuses art and nature, ideal and real in astonishing complexity. William V. Spanos ('The Real Toad in the Jonsonian Garden')[65] notices a characteristic 'transfiguration of the real' by introducing classical mythology into the English estate:

> Thy Mount, to which the dryads do resort,
> Where Pan, and Bacchus their high feasts have made,
> Beneath the broad beech, and the chest-nut shade;
> That taller tree, which of a nut was set,
> At his great birth, where all the Muses met. (10–14)

'The aesthetic pleasure', Spanos suggests, 'derives from the resonance generated by the fusion of the opposites.' However, Jonson presents Penshurst not only as *locus amoenus*—a necessary motif in the country-house poem—but also as an equivalent of the golden age. He does the same in 'To Sir Robert Wroth':

> Thus Pan, and Sylvane, having had their rites,
> Comus puts in, for new delights;
> And fills thy open hall with mirth, and cheer,
> As if in Saturn's reign it were. (47–50)

---

[63] *Discoveries, Works*, ed. Herford and Simpson, viii. 595.
[64] Ibid., pp. 16–17; cf. Hibbard, p. 163, and see Martial, *Epig.*, III. lviii.
[65] *J.E.G.P.*, lxviii (1969), 1–23.

Moreover, from the generalized neoclassical landscape of 'broad beech, and...chest-nut shade' with its mythological staffage there stands out one local detail: 'that taller tree' planted at Sir Philip Sidney's birth. At first this may seem natural detail in classical setting, a converse interplay of ideal and real also labelled by Spanos. But the case is more complex. The passage alludes to another Martial epigram, in which a tree planted by Caesar symbolizes his lasting memory and harmonious relation to the gods.[66] Thus Jonson opens a further reach of idealization, this time literary and historical, associating Philip Sidney with the divine Caesar. Molesworth sees this as a reference simply to poetic genius— 'Sidney, having conquered time by the enduring virtues of his poetry, assumes...his true mythological status' (p. 154). But I think Jonson must intend a more serious and Christian deification.

For the alfresco feast of the gods continues in Penshurst's indoor hospitality, adding yet another idealization. The poem here assimilates the Banquet of Immortals type, commoner in the visual arts,[67] but by no means devoid of literary exemplars (Catullus' nuptial feast of Peleus and Thetis; Apuleius' marriage of Cupid and Psyche; Spenser's spousal feast for Thames and Medway). With this generic identification several features of Jonson's poem agree, such as its images of plenty.[68] Wilson's identification of the feast as the Lord's Supper is also in accord: the latter is a banquet of immortals too, the communion of saints of which Philip Sidney partakes. From these high suggestions the poet's extensive drinking of untold cups brings us suddenly to earth. True, Jonson sometimes connected hard drinking with poetic inspiration, and 'when he was reconciled with the church and left off to be a recusant at his first communion in token of true reconciliation, he drank out all the full cup of wine'.[69] Still, we are bound to feel that Bacchus finds in the poet a palpable avatar, and that he suffers by contrast with Sidney's godly feast.[70] The classical ideal, which formerly elevated the real, is now dwarfed by it: the mythological turns out to have foreshadowed the Christian.

---

[66] lx, lxi; cf. Cubeta, p. 18.

[67] See E. Wind, *Bellini's Feast of the Gods* (Cambridge, Mass., 1948) and Henry Bardon, *Le Festin des dieux* (Paris, 1960).

[68] Cf. Carew, 'To my friend G. N. from Wrest', ll. 57–60: 'Amalthea's horn | Of plenty is not in effigy worn | Without the gate, but she within the door | Empties her free and unexhausted store.' Amalthea's abundant horn figured in the classical divine feast; see Ovid, *Met.*, ix. 85–96. Cf. also the flocks in Catullus, lxiv.

[69] *Conversations, Works*, ed. Herford and Simpson, i. 141.

[70] There may also be a lost local allusion in ll. 10–18. Cf. Carew's imitation (above, n. 3), praising the absence of statues of Amalthea, 'Ceres...in stone', and Bacchus 'on a marble tun'. Perhaps such statues were prominent at some prodigy house—not impossibly Theobalds, which boasted a Satyrs' walk and much statuary (see Summerson, 'Building of Theobalds', p. 116 n. 1).

IX

The interaction of real and ideal that characterizes 'To Penshurst' is typological, in a word, so that Molesworth's frequent emphasis of the historical element, though it generates very interesting criticism, must itself, in the last resort, be judged unhistorical. Molesworth attributes to Jonson a post-Romantic neo-Kantian emergent ideal, much like that of Cassirer, whom he cites at length. But Jonson's own ideal was much less historical. He was indeed concerned with '"lastingness", in terms of property, natural riches, and personal virtue'.[71] But this was less a matter of historical tendencies—though Jonson was not blind to those—than of moral choices. Virtue and vice were always embattled. There were good houses, bad houses, good stewards, bad stewards; and the difference was set eternally. The future to which he looked was the coming of a kingdom, which is always: the posterity for which the Sidneys were to train their children is not yet.

'To Penshurst' is a more religious poem than most critics have suggested. But it is also more complex and difficult. Its difficulty is concealed by an easy style, to give a satisfying harmony of soft and hard. This style, or diction, has been called *plain* style. But it is evident from the above that, at least in one poem, Jonson's plain style is not incompatible with rich allusion, delicate suggestion, and complex wit.

[71] Molesworth, p. 142.

Pastoral Instruction in 'As You Like It'

If critics of *As You Like It* agree on one thing, it is that the play is pastoral-romantic by genre. The plot, what there is of it, conforms to 'the standard dramatic pastoral pattern…of extrusion or exile, recreative sojourn in a natural setting, with ultimate return "homeward"…a return in moral strength reinforced by the country experience'.[1] The action actually introduces the keeping of sheep; which is more than pastoral dramas usually do. And life has a natural simplicity in Arden, which from a distance at least seems like life in the Golden Age: there the banished Duke Senior's followers 'fleet the time carelessly as they did in the golden world'. Then, many minor pastoral romance motifs are worked in, such as the carving of names on trees;[2] and many regular pastoral themes are developed, such as the contrast of court and country—not only in the conversation of Touchstone and Corin, but implicitly in the alternation of scenes between civil Arden and the cruel court.[3] After the usual manner of pastoral romance, court figures appear; but they lose their status through exile or voluntary rustication, or renounce their power (like Frederick), or (like Celia) hide their identity under disguise—'under the veil', in Puttenham's phrase, 'of homely persons'.[4] Such is Shakespeare's generic tact that one critic has spoken of the play as bearing 'brilliant witness to its author's capacious comprehension of the whole pastoral tradition'.[5] Steeply as that is put, I have no wish to disagree. Nevertheless, there are some problematic features of *As You Like It*, which have been called antipastoral.[6] And it is some of these that I want to consider now.

What I have in mind is not merely the satiric element—a common enough ingredient of pastoral romance.[7] Satire was even an acceptable admixture in pastoral eclogue itself. Mantuan and Spenser offered Shakespeare the most authoritative models for the type of pastoral with moral satire. Within this

---

[1] Rosalie L. Colie *Shakespeare's 'Living Art'* (Princeton 1974) 245.
[2] See Rensselaer W. Lee *Names on Trees: Ariosto into Art* (Princeton 1977) 5–7 et pass.
[3] See Harold Jenkins '*As You Like It*' in *Shakespeare: Modern Essays in Criticism* ed. Leonard F. Dean (New York 1957) 111.
[4] George Puttenham *The Art of English Poesie* ed. Gladys D. Willcock and Alice Walker (Cambridge 1936) 38.
[5] Eamon Grennan 'Telling the Trees from the Wood: Some Details of *As You Like It* Reexamined', *ELR* vii.2 (1977) 206.
[6] See, e.g., Colie 261, 266; Grennan 197. For a good attempt to treat the play as more or less pure pastoral romance, see Charles W. Hieatt 'The Quality of Pastoral in *As You Like It*', *Genre* vii.2 (1974) 164–82.
[7] See Eugene M. Waith *The Pattern of Tragicomedy in Beaumont and Fletcher* (New Haven 1952) 85.

tradition, for example, Jacques's biography can be located quite precisely. His melancholy satiric attitude is partly motivated by his experience as a traveller—just as Diggon's satire is, in *The Shepheardes Calender*.[8] By a convention that went back to Petrarch's *Eclogue* X, the returning traveller brings news of corruption outside the pastoral world.[9] Ecclesiastical satire, in particular, was a regular ingredient of medieval and Mantuanian pastoral; as Shakespeare surely knew when he introduced his village parson Sir Oliver Martext. Moral pastoral was so well established, in fact, that Puttenham could regard it as the distinctive modern form: 'The *Eglogues* came after to containe and enforme morall discipline, for the amendment of mans behaviour, as be those of Mantuan and other moderne Poets.'[10] But this is not the only way in which pastoral was susceptible to generic blending. Pastoral drama was very often combined with other kinds—romantic, comic, tragic; so that it became a key topic in Renaissance discussions of the theory of *genera mista*.

The Spenserian parallel is a good one, in that *The Shepheardes Calender* itself has problematic, unpastoral features. Developing Hesiodic elements in the pastoral of Mantuan, it portrays dialect-speaking rustics involved in actual work, as if in a georgic poem. Whether he learnt it from Spenser or from the old pastoral play *Sir Clyomon and Clamydes*, Shakespeare obviously took up this mode of impure or georgic pastoral, and in some ways carried its mixture of values further still. His Arden—as Dame Helen Gardner and other critics have noticed—is conspicuously unidealized. It threatens hunger, thirst and 'the seasons' difference'; while its fauna include the lion and snake of the romantic forest. It may be enchanting; but it is also an exhausting 'desert' in which Orlando expects to meet with 'savagery'. And the staffage of this desert landscape offers corresponding realism in an unexpected mixture of pastoral with its opposites. We have a touching sketch of the conventional shepherd in Silvius. But Audrey is a filthy goatherd, and Corin's master churlish and absentee. Old Corin himself, the chief embodiment of pastoral values of simplicity and stoicism, we may regard as one of nature's gentlemen—but of a type foreign to ordinary pastoral. For he is a real shepherd, and knows the practicalities of his occupation—the greasiness of fells—in a distinctly georgic way. And the very putting of virtue on the side of the old, of Corin and Adam, sticks out as extraneous to pastoral.[11] I need not say that in all this Shakespeare by no means flouts or satirizes pastoral convention, but merely selects a particular shade of mixed, realistic pastoral, in the interests of a particular strategy. Ordinary pastoral would have contrasted the best in nature with the worst at court. In Shakespeare's heightened contrast, even the worst in the wilderness of Arden

---

[8] See Grennan 200.
[9] In Virgil *Ecl.* i and Mantuan *Ecl.* ix, the traveller is told about the city by a better-informed local shepherd.
[10] Puttenham 38–9.
[11] See Thomas G. Rosenmeyer *The Green Cabinet: Theocritus and the European Pastoral Lyric* (Berkeley and Los Angeles 1969) 58; also Index s.v. *Hesiodic Tradition*.

makes an effective foil: when Duke Senior shrinks with cold he consoles himself that 'This is no flattery. These are counsellors/That feelingly persuade me what I am.' The outside world, it seems, is even worse than pastoral writers have made it.

A similarly complex departure from pastoral is made by the prominent introduction of hunting, not only in the scene introducing Jaques, but also in the short scene with the song 'What shall he have that killed the deer?' From Theocritus on, pastoralists had regarded hunting as an alien activity.[12] After the introduction of foresters in Queen Elizabeth's alfresco entertainments, however, hunting scenes became a popular if anomalous component in pastoral plays.[13] But now Shakespeare strikingly reactivates pure pastoral objections, and puts the decorum of hunting again in question. To raise the issue was not an eccentric thing. As Claus Uhlig has shown, Jaques's sentiment relates to a persistent humanistic tradition that represented hunting as mere slaughter—as the pastime of tyrants, an outrage against the original harmony of men and animals.[14] Shakespeare himself, however, can hardly be said to agree altogether with Jaques. For one thing, Duke Senior is somewhat exonerated, in that he feels compunction about hunting. It makes him uncomfortable that 'the poor dappled fools,/ Being native burghers of this desert city'—notice the aristocratic anthropomorphism—'Should in their own confines with forked heads / Have their round haunches gored.' True, exculpation is badly needed; for Shakespeare has made it comically evident that the duke still has the eagerness for hunting typical of his rank. When Amiens compliments him on his resignation, on translating 'the stubbornness of fortune / Into so quiet and so sweet a style', his brisk response will not strike everyone as exactly sweet; 'Come, shall we go and kill us venison?' Still, Duke Senior's hunting will surely seem an innocent response to fortune, if it is compared with, say, Duke Frederick's usurping? Not on Jaques's view. According to First Lord, he grieved at the duke's hunting, and swore, 'you do more usurp / Than doth your brother that hath banished you.' Here Jaques may be said to take up a rigorist pastoral stance. His position is undercut (as all are, in this subtle comedy); since he ignores the fact that the duke's followers hunt to eat—something that even John of Salisbury and Sir Thomas More and the other authorities countenanced. But does the humour of his extremity quite cancel out the pastoral view? Even outside Arden, after all, some men managed to survive without game forests. Shakespeare has readjusted the generic balance in such a way as to disallow the usual pastoral romance mixture, in which romantic aristocrats in their forest easily coexist with pastoral shepherds.

A fundamental characteristic of pastoral was its apparent artlessness: pastoralists went to great lengths to avoid the implication of knowledge in their

---

[12] *Ibid.* 135–6.   [13] *As You Like It* ed. Agnes Latham (1975) 102n.
[14] '"The Sobbing Deer": *As You Like It*, II. i. 21–66 and the Historical Context', *Ren. Drama* n.s. iii (1970) 79–109.

shepherds.[15] Shakespeare uses this convention to amusing effect when he makes the ultrapastoralist Jaques pretend that he is innocent of even the most ordinary technical terms of poetry ('Call you 'em stanzos?'). In the mixed pastoral romance, a very limited instructional element entered, in that the temporary shepherds were initiated into the value of stoicism (and the faults of the court), and heard idealistic speeches about love. But in *As You Like It* the educational element bulks so large as to become the main activity. Many critics have commented on the play's lack of action, which to some has seemed a fault.[16] But once we think of the action as instruction, we see that there is a great deal of it. Indeed, the play's very style suggests the classroom. Its frequent logical debates, catechisms and enumerative schemes belong to that milieu; and Jaques even goes through the form of construing, in his intimidation of William.

Most of the main characters are shown learning. With Duke Senior, the chief instructor is nature. Nature in Arden teaches hard facts; but the duke finds edification in affliction nonetheless. 'Sweet are the uses of adversity,' he tells Amiens:

> And this our life, exempt from public haunt,
> Finds tongues in trees, books in the running brooks.
> Sermons in stones, and good in everything.

Besides his not caring about power and security, it is this contemplativeness that sets Duke Senior off from his usurping brother. (The pattern will be repeated in Prospero and Antonio.) But Duke Senior also learns through disputation, particularly with Jaques: 'I love to cope him in these sullen fits, / For then he's full of matter.' Jaques, for his part, professes to avoid Duke Senior, telling Amiens, 'He is too disputable [disputacious] for my company. I think of as many matters as he, but I give heaven thanks and make no boast of them.' But if Jaques prefers teaching to learning, he nevertheless likes to hear the 'deep-contemplative' fool Touchstone moralizing 'in good terms, / In good set terms', and laughs to 'hear / The motley fool thus moral on the time.' He may well learn from Touchstone, for Touchstone is Shakespeare's most erudite and Latinate fool—one who has in his brain 'strange places crammed / With observation'. Ever restless for novelty, Jaques is determined to become a fool. And at the end he is still seeking new instruction: he goes to join the reformed Duke Frederick, who has 'put on a religious life'. 'Out of these convertites', says Jaques, 'there is much matter to be heard and learned.' Jaques's extremist enthusiasms are a source of comedy throughout. But when he finally stops railing and expresses approbation of Duke Senior, we are encouraged to hope that he may have entered on some deeper process of learning. It is never *too*

---

[15] See Rosenmeyer 54–5.   [16] See Jenkins 109, Latham lxxx.

late, it seems. Duke Frederick learns about the good life so belatedly that he only just arrives in time to give the political story its hurried flimsy denouement. Critics sometimes say that he is converted supernaturally, by the mere action of entering the forest's magic circle.[17] Certainly Shakespeare makes full use of romantic convention at this point. But Frederick's conversion is in fact explained. On the way to make his state secure by fratricide, he no sooner comes 'to the skirts of this wild wood' than he receives *instruction*. Not until 'after some question [i.e. disputation]' with 'an old religious man' is he converted. Others too engage in the georgic but unpastoral activity of teaching and learning. Silvius and Phebe learn about love; Touchstone is instructed about marriage by Jaques; and even Celia, when she pretends to forget the marriage service, is taken through the words by Rosalind-Ganymede.

I have not yet mentioned Orlando; but his instruction may be the most significant of all. The opening scene's very first words are his complaint that Oliver broke faith and deprived him of the formal education promised in Sir Roland's will. And the play's most prominent educational process of all, forming one of the main connecting strands, is Orlando's instruction by Ganymede—a plot Shakespeare did not find in Lodge's *Rosalynde*. If Orlando will woo her every day, Ganymede undertakes to cure him of the 'madness' of love. (The well-named Orlando has comically demonstrated this madness earlier in the scene, in a brief *furioso* appearance.) She will pretend to be his mistress—'proud, fantastical, apish, shallow, inconstant, full of tears, full of smiles...as boys and women are for the most part cattle of this colour'. This drove a previous patient 'from his mad humour of love to a living humour of madness...to live in a nook merely monastic'. She promises to daunt Orlando's love: to test its seriousness. Unlike the usual pastoral 'instruction' in love—a business of sentimental disquisitions—this is to be practical learning and discipline. Elizabethan audiences would have recognized it as a class in the School of Love: the same school attended by that unruly pupil Astrophil.[18] Ganymede's curriculum seems very little different from what Rosalind herself might have taught in her own person. Indeed, she herself attends school too; suffering when Orlando seems light in love, learning patience when he fails to keep appointments. We can choose to regard this as a trivial story. But then we stay with the superficial symbols, instead of moving to the deeper allegory that Shakespeare makes it shadow forth.

What does Ganymede, the mysterious androgyne, actually teach? The topic appears in her very first speech to Orlando in the forest—'What is't o'clock?' Much of her instruction, similarly, seems to concern time rather than love.

---

[17] See Latham lxx.
[18] See *Astrophil and Stella* Sonnets xix, xlii, xlvi, lvi, lxxiii, lxxix, etc. On discipline for purification of love as a Renaissance mystery, see Edgar Wind, *Pagan Mysteries in the Renaissance* (Faber rev. edn 1958) 145–7.

Indeed, the main vicissitudes in the story arise from Orlando's failure to keep the appointments that test his constancy. When he is late, Rosalind weeps, and feels Orlando to be as false as Judas. When he turns up 'within an hour of [his] promise', she lectures him on punctuality, as Ganymede, in a way that she might only have longed to, in her own person. He cannot be in love if he is not punctual. 'Nay, and you be so tardy, come no more in my sight. I had as lief be wooed of a snail.' The denouement of their story comes with another broken appointment—this time, however, occasioned by wounds incurred during the compassionate rescue of Oliver. Now Orlando can leave school, for he has disciplined his irresponsibility. He has been tested and found acceptable—a 'gentleman of good conceit' as Ganymede now calls him.

And the subject of time comes up elsewhere. Ganymede's first lesson is in the form of a catechism about it. Orlando asks in turn who Time trots, ambles, gallops and stays still withal; and Ganymede makes witty answers proving that 'Time travels in diverse paces with divers persons'. On Jaques's first meeting with Rosalind's companion Touchstone, the moralizing similarly concerns Time's pace. Touchstone draws out a pocket sundial, and

> Says, very wisely, 'It is ten o'clock...
> And after one hour more 'twill be eleven;
> And so from hour to hour, we ripe, and ripe,
> And then from hour to hour, we rot, and rot...'

At these bawdy puns Jaques, always immoderate, laughs for an hour's measure of his own rotting. But Shakespeare's audience may also have noticed that time and clocks were being made much of.—Or, indeed, that they were mentioned at all. Did not pastoral normally unfold its green thought within a timeless stasis? Here, again, the parallel with *The Shepheardes Calender* may help; for Spenser's most remarkable innovation was to add the seasonal structure that gives his work its name. Drawing attention to this, Alexander Pope wrote: 'The addition he has made of a Calendar to his Eclogues is very beautiful.'[19] But that is a little too bland; making the timeless pastoral world seasonal was no mere addition, but a profound departure from classical values.[20] Spenser's audacious innovation not only put pastoral into confrontation with the opposing georgic mode and its contrasting topics of seasons and their labours, but also implied the Christian calendar with its consequent associations.[21] Shakespeare, I believe, saw the dramatic possibilities of a similar generic mixture.

---

[19] *The Prose Works of Alexander Pope...1711-1720* ed. Norman Ault (Oxford 1936) 301.
[20] It was not without partial anticipation in the vernacular, however: on the *Kalendrier des Bergeres* tradition, see Helen Cooper *Pastoral: Medieval into Renaissance* (Ipswich and Totowa, N.J. 1977) 78.
[21] See Robert Allen Durr 'Spenser's Calendar of Christian Time', *ELH* xxiv (1957) 269-95 and Maren-Sofie Røstvig '*The Shepheardes Calender*—a Structural Analysis', *Ren. and Mod. Studies* xiii (1969) 49-75.

There is no need to argue that Shakespeare introduces time into his pastoral world, for several critics have already done so—Rosalie Colie, for example: 'we are endlessly made aware, both in earnest and in jest, of the passage of time: in the confrontation of generations (Silvius and Corin, dukes and daughters, Sir Rowland's sons and his aged servant Adam)';[22] in Orlando's unpunctuality and Jaques's oration about the ages of man. She concludes: 'In other words, this forest is at once ideal and real.' It is less widely recognized, however, that besides the idea of time Shakespeare introduces time's various measures. Moreover, he does so far more often than he need have, merely to establish Arden's reality. It is not just that the mentions of time indicate a georgic admixture, but that time pertains to the substance of the georgic instruction.

Besides the subjective paces of time, *As You Like It* contains many references to its objective measures. The numerous mentions of hours and times of day arise naturally from the action, but are remarkable for their frequency in a pastoral play. More striking are the references to Ages of the World. Charles speaks of Duke Senior's followers' fleeting the time 'as they did in the golden world'; and Duke Senior himself refers to the Christian version of this golden age, and to the age of Adam, when he mentions 'The penalty of Adam, /The seasons' difference.' A later age, the age of the Giants, is implied when Celia says, 'You must borrow me Gargantua's mouth first. 'Tis a word too great for any mouth of this age's size.' Then, Jaques likens the lovers' pairing off to that of the animals 'coming to the ark'—in the age, that is, of the Flood. And Rosalind thinks along the same lines when she says, 'The poor world is almost six thousand years old.' It was commonly believed that the six Augustinian Ages of the World would be completed in no more than six thousand years (less, if human sin was sufficiently outrageous); so that Rosalind's speech has an apocalyptic overtone.[23] Together, these references to Ages of the World work to establish the scale of existence and the world-scheme of redemptive history. They are anti-pastoral, but not specially calculated to evoke a realistic world.

Shakespeare's intention in assembling the measures of time comes out clearly in Jaques's famous oration on the ages of man—yet another measure of time—

> All the world's a stage,
> And all the men and women merely players.
> They have their exits and their entrances,
> And one man in his time plays many parts,
> His acts being seven ages.

---

[22] Colie 258; cf. Jay L. Halio '"No Clock in the Forest": Time in *As You Like It*', *SEL* ii (1962) 197–207; Frederick Turner *Shakespeare and the Nature of Time* (Oxford 1971) 28–44.

[23] See C.A. Patrides *Milton and the Christian Tradition* (Oxford 1966) 271 and chs. viii and ix *pass.*

The last line gave a great deal of trouble to Warburton and Malone, who actually conducted a search for plays with seven acts. But by now we can see that Jaques is merely being pastoral again, and pretending to be simple about technical terms. Just as he was not sure about 'stanzos', so now he does not know about acts and scenes. ('His *scenes* being seven ages' would have lost a pun, but would otherwise have fitted in well—not least with the number of the scene Jaques is speaking in.) His oration gains effectiveness from its visible context: the entrance of Orlando bowed under the weight of Old Adam. Here Orlando enacts an emblem of the physical decline that Jaques describes; but in his Aeneas-like *pietas* he also compassionately takes up the burden of the first Adam's penalty of mortal nature, in a way that transforms it.[24] Jaques's speech may not exactly be refuted.[25] Nevertheless, the contrast is forcible: Jaques rails at man's frailty; Orlando cares for it. The full dramatic context of the speech only emerges, however, when its 'painted cloth' commonplace is examined more closely.

Jaques begins by following the Ptolemaic variant of the Ages of Man scheme, with each age showing the expected planetary influence, except that his cynical emphasis has the moistly Lunar infant 'mewling and puking', while his 'schoolboy', engaged as a child of Mercury in education, creeps 'like snail / Unwillingly to school', imperfectly influenced by the fastest of the planets.[26] (The audience may recall this when Orlando is late for the school of love, and Rosalind compares him to a snail.) In age three, Jaques's lover duly expresses the influence of Venus, next in Ptolemaic order. But what is this? Where is the fourth, Solar age, the prime of life, the best of all the seven ages? Jaques omits it altogether; replacing it, at the end, by a second Saturnian age of ultimate decrepitude, 'sans teeth, sans eyes, sans taste, sans everything'. This dark view of life is obviously distorted. But we can scarcely see how distorted Shakespeare means it to be, until we reflect that, out of all the deities, Jaques has chosen to omit the *declarator temporum*, the indicator of time, the centre and heart of the planetary cosmos, Sol himself. Melancholy was endemic in British pastoral.[27] But in Shakespeare the melancholy of Jaques meets with decisive rejection. 'Monsieur Melancholy' is shown to play false when he exaggerates the domain of the melancholy god. At the centre of his life Jaques has enthroned, instead of the sun, Mars and enthusiasm and anger. His conception of life is hollow and disorientated: no wonder he is a restless figure who 'in his time

---

[24] For the *pietas* emblem, see Nancy R. Lindheim, cit. Colie 258; for the theological allegory, see Alastair Fowler 'The Image of Mortality: *Faerie Queene* ii.i–ii' in *Essential Articles for the Study of Edmund Spenser* ed. A.C. Hamilton (Hamden, Conn. 1972), esp. 147.

[25] See Jenkins 124: 'Shakespeare seeks no cheap antithesis.'

[26] On the scheme associating planetary deities and ages of man, see F. Boll 'Die Lebensalter' in *Neue Jahrbucher fur das klassische Altertum* xvi (1913) 117ff. and Raymond Klibansky, Erwin Panofsky and Fritz Saxl *Saturn and Melancholy* (1964) 149n. Boll loses his way in the Shakespearean passage; Klibansky *et al*. detect Jaques's omission of Sol but fail to grasp its reason, suggesting implausibly that 'the age corresponding to the sun is omitted as too similar to the "jovial"'.

[27] See Rosenmeyer 227.

plays many parts'. Lacking a centre, and lacking the Solar gift of steadfastness,[28] he moves on changeably from libertine to outlaw, outlaw to recluse, recluse to fool—and from fool, perhaps, to religious. In *As You Like It*, it seems, attitudes to time may offer a useful index to character.

Other measures of time are also prominent. The theme of the 'seasons' difference' is developed both by Duke Senior and in the play's many songs. These not only serve practically to mark the passage of time, but also interiorize its measure. By a very ancient tradition (and one followed in the popular non-fictional *Kalender of Shepherdes*), seasons were correlated with Ages of Man—this time the Four Ages.[29] Thus, in 'Under the greenwood tree' the enemy is winter, the season that feeds Jaques's humour: 'It will make you melancholy,' Amiens warns. 'Blow, blow, thou winter wind' links the same season with man's ingratitude. And the pages' song is of 'spring-time, the only pretty ring-time'. Lovers naturally 'love the spring', because it correlates with Age I, youth and the sanguine humour.

Why should Shakespeare have assembled so many measures of time in *As You Like It*? Doubtless he partly means to offset the pastoral elements. The play's finest critic, Harold Jenkins, has seen in it a pervasive effort to bring characters and positions into encounter with their opposites, leaving none unadjusted.[30] No doubt the generic contradictions are in part instances of this. Unpastoral features function as ironic comment on the pastoral; just as unromantic features—Rosalind's matter-of-factness or impatience to marry—provide a counterstatement to the romantic. But the georgic admixture, the temporal element, is too elaborate and coherent to be accounted for as a balancing adjustment, still less as realistic shading. It seems rather to amount to thematic content. This content is of course mediated dramatically—and sometimes heavily disguised, as in Jaques's Ages of Man oration. Yet its implications are not wholly undercut or counter-pointed. Shakespeare himself, in fact, seems to imply the view that life is comprehensively subject to mutability, yet divinely ordered. Orlando's bad poem implies a similar view: 'how brief the life of man / Runs his erring pilgrimage'. And so do various passages introducing the idea of measure in the ordering of experience—particularly the enumerative schemes based on the mutable seven, such as Touchstone's set piece on the protocol of quarrelling. Shakespeare makes it clear enough that this mutability and mortality should not lead to Jaques's melancholy. Indeed, Jaques is in a way answered as well as replaced by his studious namesake Jaques de Boys, when the latter brings news about mankind as good as Jaques's was bad.

---

[28] On fortitude as the central gift of the Holy Spirit, see Rosemond Tuve *Allegorical Imagery: Some Medieval Books and their Posterity* (Princeton 1966) 96 and Index s.v. *Fortitude*; on the correlation of planets and gifts, see Klibansky *et al.* 166n.

[29] See Cooper 78; Klibansky *et al.* 291–6 *et pass.*   [30] Jenkins 124–5; cf. Latham lxxxiv.

Even Touchstone's view is wiser, in its foolishness, than Jaques's. For Touchstone, time measures, hour by hour, human ripening and rotting—a view neatly confirmed by the application elsewhere of the epithet 'ripe' to Ganymede and William, and 'rotten' to Touchstone himself. To this mortality Touchstone makes the base but not life-denying response of lechery. He 'speak'st wiser than [he] is ware of' and can tell that 'as all is mortal in nature, so is all nature in love mortal in folly'. On the scale of human life, it behoves us to remember 'that a life [is] but a flower'—whether this leads us to seize the ring-time, or to prepare like Duke Frederick for eternity.

One normal response to human mortality was supposed to lie in generation; so that the main denouement of the play aptly takes the form of a masque of Hymen, a piece of romantic magic that resolves the emotional tangles by transcending them. The masque, like the immediately preceding compact, has a highly formalized pattern of repeated speeches in the Lylyan rhetorical manner. Here, at last, the measure is not a temporal one. As Hymen draws to our notice—'Here's eight that must take hands'—it is based on the number of eternity, the number that goes beyond the seven of mutability, and symbolizes repentance, harmony and justice.[31] In this as in every way the masque makes an almost shocking contrast with Touchstone's preceding exposition of the literature of quarrelling. The seven stages of giving the lie, and the eight plighting their troth; the masque's magic liturgy of reconciliation, and the books that set out civil arrangements for murder.

The number eight was apt not only because it signified the eternal. It also carried an ancient symbolism, often alluded to in Elizabethan wedding masques, whereby the mystery of Juno, the goddess of marriage, was unfolded into eight subordinate powers, one of them Hymen.[32] Moreover, Juno herself was associated with the dyad or first even number; so that the marriage union (*unio*) under her auspices could foreshadow the Christian idea of marriage as a mystery of two in one flesh. Thus, in *As You Like It*, Hymen sings: 'Then is there mirth in heaven, / When earthly things made even / Atone together.'

Rosalind herself, who arranges the masque, thereby assumes the role of Juno. Of this mythological involvement we have had anticipatory hints in her earlier invocations of Jupiter, in her assumed name Ganymede ('no worse a name than Jove's own page') and in her connection of Orlando with Jupiter (when Celia reports finding him under an oak, Rosalind says, 'It may well be called Jove's tree, when it drops such fruit.'). Yet the emancipated Rosalind also plays the part of a

---

[31] On these meanings, see Alastair Fowler *Spenser and the Numbers of Time* (1964) 35n., 53f., 285. All were standard: they occurred in authorities such as Macrobius and St Augustine, as well as in handbooks such as Pietro Bongo *Mysticae numerorum significationis liber* (Bergamo 1585).

[32] Sometimes, too, the dancers were made to number eight. See D.J. Gordon '*Hymenaei*: Ben Jonson's Masque of union' in *The Renaissance Imagination* ed. Stephen Orgel (Berkeley, etc. 1975) 157–84; Alastair Fowler *Triumphal Forms* (Cambridge 1970) 151–4.

priest of Jupiter, Providence the giver of all good things,[33] when she distributes destinies:

> I have promised to make all this matter even.
> Keep you your word, O Duke, to give your daughter,
> You yours, Orlando, to receive his daughter;
> Keep you your word Phebe, that you'll marry me,
> Or else refusing me to wed this shepherd...
> from hence I go
> To make these doubts all even.

Notice how the reiterated promise of an even (just) outcome is made to depend on other promises: specifically, on the keeping of faith. If promises are kept, hopes will be fulfilled—if in rather unexpected ways. That, in a sense, is the theme of *As You Like It*.

And this is where time comes in. One might have looked to the pastoral stasis for a symbol of time transcended and hopes fulfilled. And indeed Orlando raises a suggestion that time in Arden is somehow clockless and different. But the possibility is broached only to be summarily dismissed. When Orlando says 'there's no clock in the forest,' Rosalind firmly replies 'Then there is no true lover in the forest, else sighing every minute and groaning every hour would detect the lazy foot of Time.' Time here is not so much a mutability, to be escaped if possible, as an opportunity for faithfulness and love, to be seized by the forelock. When Orlando arrives late for an appointment and rather casually says he comes 'within an hour of [his] promise', Rosalind tells him that no one can be in love if he 'divide a minute into a thousand parts, and break but a part of the thousand part of a minute [of his promise] in the affairs of love.' A far cry, this, from the heedlessness of pastoralists, who 'Lose and neglect the creeping hours of time.'—Or from the lawyers, insensitive to time's scale, who 'sleep between term and term, and...perceive not how Time moves.' Rosalind comes a good deal closer, in fact, to the Christian view of time as something to be redeemed by zealous activity, than to ancient pastoral's ideal of a static *Otium*. She teaches, in a word, the *urgency* of love. Time, for her, is a brief opportunity to keep faith.

Even by comparison with the other non-naturalistic comedies, *As You Like It* stands out as a consistently moral play, although its morality is treated with conspicuous lightness. Again and again it teaches, in its mocking way, that time moves on; that opportunities to keep faith should be grasped; that only the faithful truly love. In short, it enjoins zealous faith. Now, this is so simple a Christian message that some may call it none at all. That is as you like it.

---

[33] For Jupiter as Providence and *dator omnium bonorum*, see Natale Conti *Mythologiae* I.viii and II.i. Besides being Jove's tree, the oak was a georgic plant and topic.

Certainly the play would not be Christian, if that meant division of its characters into elect and reprobate. Shakespeare is remorseless in exempting no one from criticism. Even Rosalind may not preach without the suggestion that her sense of urgency is partly inspired by the foolishness of love—a maid's sense that Time's pace is hard. But then, all are foolish in one way or another. And Shakespeare never allows us to doubt that it is better to be foolish in love like Rosalind, or to be called a fool for faithfulness, as Celia is by Frederick. Ultimately, such as they seem foolish only to undiscerning Greeks—'the natural man receiveth not the things of the Spirit of God: for they are foolishness unto him'. The presence of this spiritual content, simple as it is, has a complex bearing on much of the play, articulating and informing its details. It validates, for example, the belated conversions of Frederick and Oliver. These crises are not convincingly realized in such a way as to encourage us to take them seriously for their own sake. But on the view I have tried to advance, the play has a persistent allegory concerned with keeping faith; and allegorically it makes quite good sense to have a Frederick or an Oliver receive a heavenly reward he does not deserve—and that he has not striven for through convincing emotional ordeals.

In such symbolic terms, *As You Like It* makes a coherent appeal for a society based, both privately and publicly, on love. We have only to be faithful to our professions and love our enemies, it seems to say, for society to be restored. But alas, that 'only'! It has not often happened in six thousand years, and is not likely to happen in the years to come. Part of the play's poignancy comes from this: from the very sketchiness of its optimistic conclusion. How sadly improbable the ending seems.

'Paradise Regained': Some Problems of Style

Evaluation of Milton's *Paradise Regained* presents unusual problems. The work was begun and energetically carried through to an early conclusion, immediately after *Paradise Lost* was finished—that is, about 1667. It could be said, then, to have been written at the height of the poet's powers. And Milton himself, we are told, thought it not inferior to the longer epic. Yet it has but a low standing, on the whole, not only among Milton's detractors—those who from time to time have tried to 'dislodge' him—but even among his supporters. John Dennis thought him 'by no means so happy in the choice of *Paradise Regained*, a subject that could supply him neither with the ideas nor with the spirit'. Elijah Fenton pitches it more steeply, exclaiming: '"Oh, what a falling off was there!"... there is scarcely a more remarkable instance of the frailty of human reason than our author gave, in preferring this poem to *Paradise Lost*...'. Landor imagines himself saying to Southey about *Paradise Regained* that 'invention, energy, and grandeur of design, the three great requisites to constitute a great poet,... are wanting here'. And even Mark Pattison is drawn to 'the usual explanation of the frigidity' of *Paradise Regained*, that it 'betrays the feebleness of senility'. I may close the list with my redoubtable colleague Wallace Robson, with whom I hesitate to disagree: he writes of 'work which considered by the standards of [Milton's] own best writing is inert, jejune, and dull'.

In part, these adverse views relate to the fact that *Paradise Regained* belongs to a different genre from *Paradise Lost*. It is 'brief epic', the genre Milton refers to in *The Reason of Church-government*, where he speaks of 'that Epic form whereof the two poems of Homer... are a diffuse, and the book of Job a brief model'. Brief epics do not just have fewer words than diffuse ones. And much of the criticism favourable to *Paradise Regained* has rightly dealt with its membership of a kind quite distinct from that of Homer or Virgil: a form altogether more didactic and with far less room for episodes, ornaments, or the 'expansions' Robson regrets. A book particularly influential in this way is Barbara Lewalski's *Milton's Brief Epic*, which provides the modern reader with perhaps his first introduction to the form; including a history and some account of the congeners of *Paradise Regained*. So decisive has her contribution been that I need not go further into this matter of fact—although, if I were to do so, I might wish to say rather more about the important element of dialogue in brief epic, a matter to which she does not quite do justice.

Paradise Regained belongs, in fact, to a genre otherwise dead, a genre of which no other examples have survived in the canon of works that are still read. (This is by no means true of *Paradise Lost*: several diffuse epics have survived; and in any case the genre itself has prolonged its existence to some extent, if in a modulated form, in the novel.) And demise of a genre is very often a reason for adverse value judgements upon its exceptional survivors. But is this to say any more than that there are other works as dull as *Paradise Regained*, and in a similar way? I do not think so. My point is rather that when we lack congeners, when we are ignorant therefore of a work's generic conventions, we tend to falsify its proportions in our criticism—even when we are trying to find emphases that will bring it closer to our modern formal interests. And this means that we do not view the work itself fairly.

Yet somehow Lewalski's book, powerful as it is, has not succeeded in persuading the generality of critics as to the worth of *Paradise Regained*; and we may perhaps begin to suspect that that work's involvement in the broad conventions of a dead genre is not the whole story of its dislike. This suspicion is confirmed when we notice that many of the adverse voices address themselves to alleged defects in the style of *Paradise Regained*. Symonds is not unrepresentative: he speaks of the poet of *Paradise Lost* as one in whom 'the fancy has not yet grown chill or lost luxuriance': 'it is hardly to be denied', he says, 'that, in comparison with the *Paradise Lost*, much of richness, variety, sonorousness, and liquid melody has been sacrificed' in *Paradise Regained*.

Several critics have spoken of a barer Miltonic style, found in *Paradise Regained* and in some other of his works, which contrasts with the grand style of *Paradise Lost*. This barer style is deliberately plain, and on principle avoids the ornate epic magniloquence of 'swelling epithets thick-laid'. Thus, the bare style of *Paradise Regained* is defended by F.W. Bateson as a 'triumph of the middle or pastoral style'. And Robson, too, dwells on the bareness, although he scarcely approves it. Others have seen Milton as pursuing a biblical ideal: D.L. Clark cites *Of Reformation*, where there is appreciation of 'the sober plain and unaffected style' of the bible. On this view, the poet of *Paradise Regained* has so to say preferred Christ's own style, in contrast to Satan's—which consequently stands out as relatively 'rich'. But if the bare style is biblical, why do we not get it *in Paradise Lost*, which as W. Kerrigan says is Milton's fullest imitation of the bible? Clark also argues that *Paradise Regained* belongs stylistically to the division known as 'low style'—*stilus humilis* or *subtilis*—traditionally regarded as suitable for the conduct of argument. This may have some truth: *Paradise Regained* exhibits some low-style features, such as laconism—it was not immune to the widespread plain-style transformation of the seventeenth century. But it has far more middle-style features. And in any case, these are too general categories to take us very far.

Another approach has been to see *Paradise Regained* as reflecting a new personal phase, not necessarily quite decrepit, in Milton's development. Not a few great artists, after all, have found a late style characterized by simplicity—and sometimes a harsh simplicity at that. As Symonds put it, 'the master has grown older, and his taste is more severe'. Discounting ideas of senility or lassitude, some critics have affirmed the qualities of what they see as a late phase of Milton's art. To Walter Raleigh, 'the enhanced severity of a style which rejects almost all ornament' seems partly due 'to a gradual change in Milton's temper and attitude'. John Carey is scrupulous in avoiding biographical speculation; but he may be talking about the same phenomenon, and appreciating the same astringency, when he writes that if the style of *Paradise Regained* is 'flatter and drier...it is also terser and tenser'. To take Milton's advancing age into account is only common sense. But it must be faced that he could manage all styles in every period of his life: parts of *Paradise Lost* XI and XII are plain, parts of *Paradise Regained* IV relatively sensuous and rich in simile. In any case, as Dunster already saw, 'with a fancy, such as Milton's, it must have been more difficult to forbear poetic decorations, than to furnish them; and a glaring profusion of ornament would, I conceive, have more decidedly betrayed the *poeta senescens*, than a want of it'.

It is Dunster's appreciation of 1795 that points the way to a true understanding of the style of *Paradise Regained*: 'They who talk of our author's genius being in the decline when he wrote his second poem, and who therefore turn from it, as from a dry prosaic composition, are, I will venture to say, no judges of poetry.' We note that Dunster did not find it a dry or prosaic poem. Whereas appreciation of *Paradise Regained* was fairly widespread in the eighteenth century, when it first appeared this was by no means the case. Writing in 1694, Milton's nephew Edward Phillips tells us that *Paradise Regained* 'is generally censured to be much inferior to the other, though he could not hear with patience any such thing when related to him; possibly the subject may not afford such variety of invention, but it is thought by the most judicious to be little or nothing inferior to the other for style and decorum'. There are two things to be observed here; first, Phillips's contrast between the judgement of the generality and of the most judicious; and second, that whereas he concedes a possible lack of variety in invention, on the other hand he affirms the poem's style and decorum—qualities that the general censure had missed. Does it not begin to look as if *Paradise Regained* may have had unobvious qualities of style: may, perhaps, have been written in a new style, for which the public were unprepared? That is what I shall argue to have been the case. The style of *Paradise Regained* was, I believe, innovative.

What was this new style? Milton seems to have been pressing beyond the style of *Paradise Lost* to one in some ways subtler. It is, indeed, a little elusive at first. But once we see how much is going on in the poem stylistically, it gives a great deal of pleasure: it will then seem to us, too, far from dry or prosaic. To discover what the characteristics of the new style may be, let us begin by looking at one of John Carey's objections to it. He points to a lack of solid realization in the description of Satan's 'spectacular visual aids', such as the banquet in the wilderness: 'It is in part the generous concessiveness of the description which dissipates its actuality: "beasts of chase, *or* fowl of game, / In pastry built, *or* from the spit *or* boiled",... The repetition, or... or, leaves us to make up our own minds, so that instead of forming a defined image we remain in doubt about what was actually seen and heard. Similarly total inclusiveness lands us back at the generality of the generic: "*all* fish from sea or shore, / Freshet, or purling brook, of shell or fin", cannot be grasped like "cod" or "oyster", but retain the mistiness of mere "fish", like the later "fruits and flowers."' One might argue, I suppose, that incomplete solidity is exactly calculated to realize the phenomenon of materialization that Milton is writing about. After all, the banquet is more than a visual aid: it is a temptation, and must therefore, from Milton's point of view, give an impression of illusory physical existence. But we have to admit that similar alternatives—what Carey refers to as 'concessiveness'—are a feature of the poem that is widely, though not ubiquitously, distributed. To take an instance at random: the same phenomenon occurs at I, 303-7:

> Full forty days he passed, whether on hill
> Sometimes, anon in shady vale, each night
> Under the covert of some ancient oak,
> Or cedar, to defend him from the dew,
> Or harboured in one cave, is not revealed...

Why should Milton subvert his own effects like this?—For that is what he seems to be doing.

There are two answers, one general and the other more particular. From one point of view, the alternatives can be thought of as part of a general ground style. Looked at in this way, they may represent a way of getting as much as possible into the poem—by getting in as many things as possible, even mutually exclusive possibilities. And we have to concede that it works, in the sense that although it is far shorter than *Paradise Lost*, *Paradise Regained* seems almost to cover as much ground. Its inclusiveness, which sweeps over the whole gamut of human history and experience, is largely achieved by swift accumulation of alternatives. We seem to receive an angel's vista of things. And it may well be that the difficulty of the poem—and the reason why some dislike it—has something to do with this demandingly high degree of compression. In a way we come back, here, though from a different angle, to the idea of the style's being appropriate to brief epic. As we saw, decoration would be out of place in a brief epic. To look for it here is like expecting fish scales on a nightingale, or solidity in an eggshell. But this is to speak in terms of privation and restriction. Milton finds how to make the requirements of brief epic a positive matter stylistically. For him the genre style is not merely bare, but actively compressed. Compression becomes its ideal. 'How much', the poet seems to ask himself, 'how much can I get in?'—And he achieves what may have seemed, at least to the more sophisticated taste of his time, a miracle of baroque packing.

But the alternatives may also work in a more particular way. It will not have escaped you that alternatives are specially apt to this particular epic, in that its subject is temptation, moral choice, choosing between alternatives. So the accumulated alternatives in *Paradise Regained* may sometimes render mimetically the action of choosing; so that we are given not just the labels of temptations, but something of the very experience of being tempted—of the uncertainty between options. Thus, at IV, 368 ff., Satan summarizes the temptations themselves with many alternatives:

> Since neither wealth, nor honour, arms nor arts,
> Kingdom nor empire pleases thee, nor aught
> By me proposed in life contemplative,
> Or active, tended on by glory, or fame,
> What dost thou in this world?

From the beginning of the poem, indeed, grouped alternatives have been almost the signature of Satan. His disguise as 'an aged man in rural weeds' is of no avail when he speaks like this:

> Sir, what ill chance hath brought thee to this place
> So far from path or road of men, who pass
> In troop or caravan...

At I, 381 he talks about his ability to admire 'What I see excellent in good, or fair, / Or virtuous'; and at II, 182 ff., arguing with Belial, Satan gets the better of him with a positive flurry of alternatives:

> Have we not seen, or by relation heard,
> In courts and regal chambers how thou lurk'st,
> In wood or grove by mossy fountain-side,
> In valley or green meadow to waylay
> Some beauty rare...

In all these passages, it seems to me, Milton's point depends on the Renaissance doctrine that whereas truth is single, things multifarious, duplicitous, or changeable are evil. Alternatives are therefore doubly apt to Satan, since they mime his duplicity. They can even serve as a signal to alert us to the presence of evil; as at I, 314 ff., where Satan first appears as

> an aged man in rural weeds,
> Following, as seemed, the quest of some stray ewe,
> Or withered sticks to gather...

As Carey observes, 'Satan's apparent occupations relate to his usual occupation, looking for lost souls (strayed sheep) to burn.' The withered sticks are St John's metaphor for the reprobate.

A similar point is made when Satan is given speeches containing duplicitous double entendres. At I, 383 he claims still to be able to admire goodness: 'What can be then less in me than desire / To see thee...' Ostensibly he means that this is the least response he can make to Christ's virtue. But, as Lewalski has seen, 'the word arrangement ironically suggests the opposite and truer meaning, that there can be nothing Satan desires less than thus to confront and listen to Christ'. In reply, Christ speaks of Satan's utterances through the oracles as 'dark / Ambiguous and with double sense deluding' and 'not well understood as good not known'—itself a speech that can be construed in different ways, according to whether a pause is put after 'dark', and whether 'good' is taken as noun or adverb. This may seem to endanger my point about duplicitousness. But Christ's speeches are describing evil; and in any case his alternatives, unlike Satan's, are mutually confirmatory.

I have dwelt on the poem's alternative patterns. But they compose only one of a various repertoire of similar effects. For we are talking about nothing less than an entire style, in which meaning is continually acted out, by way of local variations in the proportions of syntax and diction. Another frequent effect of this kind is appositional sequence, or apparent reiteration—in its simplest form, strings of near synonyms, as at I, 24 ff., where Jesus comes to Jordan

> as then obscure,
> Unmarked, unknown; but him the Baptist soon
> Descried, divinely warned, and witness bore
> As to his worthier...

Such passages have been censured as carelessly prolix, and by Christopher Ricks as overemphatic. But in fact they are almost exactly the opposite. They imitate the tentative, diffident, exploratory movement of thought as it keeps revising itself. Milton is simulating the mind's error correction as it arrives at the exact word or covers omitted nuances. So at II, 225–7, where Satan proposes to try Christ with 'manlier objects...such as have more show / Of worth, of honour, glory, and popular praise'. Or, at II, 464, where Christ defines 'the office of a king, / His honour, virtue, merit, and chief praise'. We get a slightly different effect in the lines immediately following, where he asserts that 'he who reigns within himself, and rules / Passions, desires, and fears, is more a king'. Here 'desires, and fears' are grammatically in apposition to 'passions'; but they are not mere synonyms. Rather do they give the categories into which the Stoic in control of himself knows how to subdivide his passions. Thus the sequence enacts the subdivision. Milton uses apposition as the briefest and most concise form; but also as one that allows formal arrangement such as I have described. The phrase communicates, in fact, by extra-grammatical means, through poetic shaping. Milton means to mime the shape of his character's thought. Elsewhere, he mimes actions; as at II, 427, where Satan advises Christ, 'Get riches first, get wealth, and treasure heap'; the heaped synonyms imitating the accumulation of treasure. The style of *Paradise Regained* may be bare by some criteria; but it is incomparably rich in such mimetic effects—richer, indeed, than most of *Paradise Lost*.

But you may be wondering what the fuss is about. For I have been discussing a type of local mimesis that some people take for granted today. Particularly if they write poetry themselves, they expect any good poet to provide this felicity, as a matter of course. Maybe so. But it was a rare sort of effect in English poetry before Spenser and Shakespeare and Milton—if, indeed, it occurred at all. Where then did it come from? To Milton, obviously, it came in part from Spenser, his acknowledged model. But in part, I think, it came from an ancient source, Virgil's *Georgics*. In this respect it is significant that Louis Martz has for quite independent reasons connected the style of *Paradise Regained* with that of the *Georgics*. Martz argues that *Paradise Regained* is in a middle style and a georgic mode; and concludes that it is 'not an epic'. This is a challenging idea. But Martz may not have got the nature of generic modulation quite right. After all, parts of *Paradise Lost* itself are in a similar georgic mode; notably the instructional Books VII and VIII, where many local mimetic decorums, such as I have been tracing, are to be found. Everyone must have noticed such effects there, in the description of the great sea creatures 'Wallowing unwieldy, enormous in their gait (VII, 411)—where the big words are themselves unwieldy on the tongue—although hardly so much so as the 'promontory' to which Leviathan is compared. Yet we do not say that *Paradise Lost* is not an epic. True, *Paradise Regained* modulates out of epic quite frequently; and such passages as the evocations of exotic cultures are highly characteristic of one mood of georgic. Nevertheless, the poem has many sublime passages, and is unquestionably epic in overall form and scope.

Beyond describing it as a 'frugal ground style', and identifying it as middle on the scale of three style heights, Martz does not characterize the style of *Paradise Regained*. But a description along the lines I have proposed would I believe amply confirm his connection of the poem with Virgil's *Georgics*. For Virgil's didactic masterpiece was regarded in the late seventeenth century as the poem with most exquisite decorums. The ground style of georgic, being at the middle height of the poet's own voice, is such as most readily to allow decorous variation. A full characterization, certainly, would require me to treat many other features of the style: I have only touched on one or two. But the local expressive decorums I have illustrated constituted a striking feature, which was to have a far-reaching influence on Pope and the Augustans. Milton, in fact, far from being exhausted or senile, was exploring a new world of stylistic possibility: one that would be exploited fully (and, as some think, too fully) in the century to come. For in eighteenth-century georgic and georgic-related poetry, largely under Milton's influence, the accommodation of sound to sense became a main objective.

But to associate the style of *Paradise Regained* with Augustan local expressiveness is to link it with a style whose own value has been called in question. Pope's mimetic effects, for example, have always been subject to disputed valuations. Dr Johnson himself, in a famous passage in his Life of Pope heaps scorn and scepticism on the idea that 'the sound should seem an echo to the sense': 'This notion of representative metre, and the desire of discovering frequent adaptations of the sound to the sense, have produced, in my opinion, many wild conceits and imaginary beauties... Beauties of this kind are commonly fancied; and when real are technical and nugatory, not to be rejected and not to be solicited.' And in the ninety-fourth *Rambler* he says severely of Milton that 'he had, indeed, a greater and a nobler work to perform; a single sentiment of moral or religious truth, a single image of life or nature, would have been cheaply lost for a thousand echoes of the cadence to the sense; and he who had undertaken to "vindicate the ways of God to man," might have been accused of neglecting his cause, had he lavished much of his attention upon syllables and sounds'. Recently, Irvin Ehrenpreis has written at length against local expressiveness in Pope, on the similar ground that such 'tricks' (and for him they are little else) distract the poet from more important matters—from larger decorums, perhaps, or from the conduct of the argument itself.[1] Whatever may be true of Pope, Milton at least can hardly be said to neglect the argument of *Paradise Regained*. And effects of 'general decorum or propriety of style' are not neglected either, as could easily be shown. (Think, for example, of Christ's response to Satan when he flies his true colours and asks to be worshipped: how Christ's style becomes abrupt, harsh, laconic; as if there were no more to be said.) Nevertheless, I believe that the different valuations of *Paradise Regained* may in part be related to these wider differences and controversies about local expressive decorum. Some critics respond to mimetic effects and value the

---

[1] 'The Style of Sound: The Literary Value of Pope's Versification', in *The Augustan milieu: Essays Presented to Louis A. Landa*, ed. Henry Knight Miller et al. (Oxford, 1970), 232–46.

poem's style highly in consequence; others, like Johnson, do not notice the subtler of the effects, and despise the more obvious.

Such differences are not to be easily reconciled. The question of the value of the style of *Paradise Regained* is not one that we can expect to settle quickly. But something may have been done to change its terms. At least we know that it is not a matter of how much sympathy we are to extend to a senile Milton whose energies were exhausted; but rather to an adventurous experimenting Milton, who was still calling for our closest attention and keenest efforts of understanding, as he introduced a style that would be taken up by a whole literature of subsequent poets. We may not like the style of local decorum. But we do well to admit that it was of strategic importance. It led, eventually, by continuous filiations, not only to the style of Augustan georgic but to the idea of expressive process that underlies much modern poetry in Britain and (even more) in the U.S.A.

The Paradoxical Machinery of *The Rape of the Lock*

The two-canto *The Rape of the Locke* of 1712 had mythological machinery of an ordinary epic (or mock-heroic) sort—'Now Jove suspends his Golden Scales in Air'.[1] But in the five-canto 1714 version Pope greatly enlarged and individualized the machinery. Indeed, much of the poem's effect is due to its Rosicrucian mythology. Yet John Dennis, the Critic himself, called it contemptible, in his *Remarks on Mr Pope's The Rape of the Lock*, the final dud missile of his poetomachia. As often with Dennis's admirably detailed criticism, even his formidable failures, compounded as they are by irascibility, help more than many other critics' successes to define the context of Pope's intentions.

All machineries and none

Dennis objects that Pope's machines

> are not taken from one System, but are double, nay treble or quadruple. In the first Canto we hear of nothing but Sylphs, and Gnomes, and Salamanders, which are Rosycrucian Visions. In the second we meet with Fairies, Genii, and Daemons...Spleen and the Phantoms about, arc deriv'd from the Powers of Nature, and are of a separate System. And Fate and Jove...in the fifth Canto, belong to the Heathen Religion.[2]

What Dennis took for indecorum is a complexity that eluded his inelegant mind. For Pope's machinery stylishly subsumes a whole library of Renaissance and seventeenth-century controversies about Christian epic. These debated whether epic should have a Christian machinery of angels, like the *Gerusalemme Liberata*; or Olympian deities; or allegorical powers like Discord, whose employment 'always excites conviction of its own absurdity';[3] or All of these, like *The Faerie*

---

[1] 2.126. Significantly romance *cantos, pace* Laura Brown, who writes [*Alexander Pope* (Oxford, Blackwell, 1985)] that the poem 'was published first in three books'.
[2] John Dennis, *Remarks on 'The Rape of the Lock'*. In *The Critical Works of John Dennis*, Edward Niles Hooker (ed), vol 2:1711–1729 (Baltimore, Johns Hopkins, 1943), p. 339.
[3] Samuel Johnson, *Lives of the English Poets*, George Birkbeck Hill (ed), vol 3 (Oxford, Clarendon), p. 233.

Queene; or none.[4] Pope has represented all these possibilities—and the whole pre-Enlightenment pneumatology—within his elegant miniature epic. Already 1712 hints at something more than poetic religion in 'So when bold Homer makes the Gods engage, /And heav'nly Breasts with human Passions rage' (2.104–5), where the Olympians with their destructive rages are contained in a simile and effectively euhemerized. But the 1714 *The Rape of the Lock* is far more complex, assimilating as it does 'Fays, Fairies, Genii, Elves and Daemons' (2.74) reminiscent of Spenser;[5] allegorical powers of nature; guardian angels and devilish *succubi* hidden under the Sylphs; and the 'Rosicrucian' spirits themselves, suggested by *The Count of Gabalis,* but as Johnson says, original with Pope—'A race of aerial people never heard of before...presented to us in a manner so clear and easy, that the reader seeks for no further information' (3.233).

Could the sylphs be taken seriously enough to work as real machinery? The serious Dennis thought not, since Pope 'has not taken his Machines...from any Religion, nor from Morality' (p. 337). Dennis is not blinkered by a circumscribed idea of mock-heroic: as his objection shows, he senses that more than mock-heroic has been attempted. Indeed, Pope himself evidently feels the need to defend a machinery incredible to 'Learned Pride' (1.37). Ariel solicits belief in what the superstitious instruction of nurse and priest instil (visions of 'airy Elves' or 'Angel-Pow'rs') almost as audiences of *Peter Pan* will be asked to remain immature and save Tinker Bell. Pope's admission that his 'unnumber'd Spirits' are beneath the credit of 'doubting Wits', and such as 'Fair and Innocent' young girls believe despite them, may seem to discount in advance Dennis's objection (p. 339). Society gets the machinery it deserves.

But this is not to say that Pope shared Dennis's and Butler's contempt for the Rosicrucians, 'the most ridiculous Sots of all Mankind'.[6] The sylphs had once been part of a serious philosophical magic, hardly to be judged by the popularizations of *The Count of Gabalis. The Rape of the Lock* accurately reflects this decline of the spirits: although Ariel still relates them to the spirits moving the planets,[7] their circumstances are clearly much reduced. Dennis finds inconsistency in Ariel's choosing to be 'Guard of Shock' (2.116): the leader of the aerial spirits is only 'Keeper of a vile Iseland Cur' (338), while Crispissa, presumably his junior, tends

---

[4] See, e.g., Bernard Weinberg, *A History of Literary Criticism in the Italian Renaissance,* 2 vols (Univ of Chicago, 1961), Index, s.v. *Gods;* Gerald Wester Chapman (ed), *Literary Criticism in England: 1660–1800* (New York, Knopf, 1966), Index, s.v. *Mythology;* H James Jensen, *A Glossary of John Dryden's Critical Terms* (Minneapolis, Univ of Minnesota, 1969), s.v. *Machine.*

[5] As Tillotson notes, the elves are not in *Gabalis.*

[6] *Hudibras,* 1.1.539, 2.3.613–34.

[7] Dennis objects that this is rather the office of intelligences, and asks, 'Did you ever hear before that the Planets were roll'd by the aerial Kind?' But Pope may have had in mind the old tradition correlating planets with elements: see Raymond Klibansky *et al., Saturn and Melancholy* (London, Nelson, 1964), p. 129 *et passim.* Venus and Juno associated with air, Mars with fire, Saturn with earth, Luna with water.

the fatal lock (2.80). Earl Wasserman explains that Ariel observes in this the right order of importance (lock—Shock—petticoat); since Belinda's lapdog is a theriomorphic husband-substitute. Pope makes here through machinery the same point about disordered values as he makes through zeugma in 'When Husbands or when Lap-dogs breathe their last'. However, the name Shock was generic for lapdogs (originally for Icelandic 'shock-dogs') because they consisted mainly of a 'shock of hair'.[8] Shock is not only a husband-substitute but a symbol of Belinda's own pudendal 'Hairs less in sight'. Ariel is himself a former coquette, and the libido 'he' encourages need not be orientated to anything outside Belinda's narcissism.

Pope's machinery has the originality of being thoroughly interiorized. His spirits are not supernatural at all, but natural female types after death, or abstraction. Dr Johnson has no answer (p. 235) to Dennis's objections that 'There is no Opposition of the Machines to one another' (p. 337), and that the machinery does not work, 'that by all the bustle of preternatural operation the main event is neither hastened nor retarded'. Both critics conceived the action in so rationalistic and external a way that they failed to see how Pope's spirits exerted a continual leverage psychologically. For, in his attempt to capture the elusive, Pope had fallen back on an older set of thought forms. His machinery does not belong entirely to Dennis's Enlightenment world of conscious decisions and mechanical operation, but in part to an older, more animistic one, operating as a drama of spirits.[9] Emrys Jones hints at something like this when he writes:

> 'Melting Maids' are not held in check by anything corresponding to sound moral principles; they are checked only by something as insubstantial, or as unreal, as their 'Sylph'. Mere female caprice or whim prevents a young girl from surrendering her honour to the importunity of rakes. Pope is working on a double standard: as readers of the poem we enjoy the fiction of the sylphs, but the satire can only work if we are also men and women of good sense who do not confuse fiction with fact—so that we do not 'believe in' the sylphs any more than we 'believe in' fairies.[10]

The principles of female conduct were not rational, but 'mystic' or psychological. And Pope extends the same treatment to all his machines. Dennis (p. 340) ridicules the opening because the Muse is replaced by Belinda herself—'If she

---

[8] As Earl R Wasserman notes, 'The Limits of Allusion in *The Rape of the Lock*', *JEGP* 65 (1966), p. 430. See examples in *OED* s.v. *Shock*, sb.: *Shock-dog*; *Shough*. Add John Gay, 'The Toilette', 9–10: 'Around her wait Shocks, monkeys and mockaws,/To fill the place of Fops, and perjur'd Beaus.'

[9] Cf. Frances A Yates, *Giordano Bruno and the Hermetic Tradition* (London, Routledge and Kegan Paul, 1964), p.452.

[10] 'Pope and Dulness', *Proceedings of the British. Academy* 54 (1968), 241.

inspire'.[11] He is determined not to see the decorum whereby Pope methodically replaces supernatural machinery by internal 'spirits'—not Dennisian allegorical 'powers of nature', but ones rather more elusive. Even the Cave of Spleen, that hell of nightmare disorders, is presided over not by a supernatural being, but by a psychological power.

The Olympian machinery is comparably interiorized, as the gods engage 'with human Passions' (5.45). Most obviously, Apollo is humanized in Belinda, 'Rival of his Beams' (2.3). But she manifests other Olympians too: just after Jove's judgement, there is 'Lightning in her eyes' (5.76); and at 5.82 the 'wily Virgin' is probably Athene, when, in a Homeric strife of the gods ("Gainst Pallas, Mars', 5.47) she encounters the Baron. And, of course, she is (or ought to be) a Venus all the time.

Rather less obviously, Sir Plume naturalizes the messenger god, when he is sent (not by Jupiter but by the fulminating Thalestris) to moderate the dispute and request the return of the lock.[12] His name comes from the feathers of Mercury's *petasus* or winged cap;[13] and for caduceus he has a 'clouded Cane'. This richly condensed but beautifully natural image refers to a fashionable type of cane, variegated with dark veins. But 'clouded' glances, in a general way, at the god's power to control clouds by the conduct of his magic staff; while, more particularly, variegated colours were assigned to Mercury as planetary deity.[14] The feathers of the *petasus* and the *talaria* were to show the speed of the god's words;[15] and we are soon given a specimen of Sir Plume's swift eloquence: 'My Lord, why, what the Devil? Is...' (4.127–30). Even the Baron acknowledges the power of this brilliant rhetoric—'It grieves me much...Who speaks so well shou'd ever speak in vain' (131–2). How little has Pope's Renaissance reading been allowed for, when a joke so good as the 'unthinking' Sir Plume's miscasting as Mercury could be missed.

---

[11] Cf. 5.123–4, where the Muse becomes Pope himself.

[12] See Joseph Spence, *Polymetis* (London, 1747), p. 104: 'his character of being sent always on the particular commission of Jupiter.' On Hermes as the master of concord, see Edgar Wind, *Pagan Mysteries in the Renaissance* (2nd edn, London, Faber and Faber, 1967), 100n. *et passim*.

[13] See Spence, p. 104: 'This cap of his has generally two little wings attached to it...tho' in some of the very oldest works, you see him sometimes only with two feathers stuck in it.'

[14] Wind, p. 122; HC Agrippa, *De Occulta Philosophia* (Cologne, 1533), p. 35: 'lapides...qui sunt diversorum colourum et quibus figurae variae a natura insitae, aut qui ab arte factitii sunt, ut vitrum, et quae croceum cum viridi miscent.' If Sir Plume's cane is of wood, cf. Pope's *Odyssey* 5, 302, 'Wrought of the clouded olive's easy grain' (Johnson defines Cloud v.a.4 as 'To variegate with dark veins'). For the caduceus as a 'rod of peace', cf., e.g., Spenser, *The Faerie Queene* 4.3.42. Even the amber of Sir Plume's snuff-box may be mercurial. For 'amber' could mean white electrum or *marcasita argentea*, which was assigned to Mercury: see Paracelsus, *The Hermetic and Alchemical Writings*, A E Waite (ed), 2 vols (London, 1894), 2.103; HC Agrippa, *Opera Omnia* (Cologne, 1533), p. 35.

[15] See, e.g., Cesare Ripa, *Iconologia* (Padua, 1611), p. 58.

Psychological machinery

Without making Pope into a post-Jungian and Ariel into an *animus* figure, one can regard *The Rape of the Lock* as working out ideas of feminine psychology in terms of 'irrational' mythologies. Dennis calls *The Count of Gabalis* 'fantastick' (p. 328), and Locke treats all talk of aerial vehicles as 'gibberish';[16] Pope's interiorizing of machinery might suggest he agreed. But the matter is not so simple—any more than it would be, to decide how far Pope embraced Enlightenment ideals. After all, the Rosicrucian movement was itself an enlightenment, in its reformism and insistence on new illumination.[17] As a moderate Catholic and a Freemason, Pope would find the ecumenical ideals of the Rosicrucians congenial—indeed, the Freemasons traced their origins to the Rosicrucian Fraternity.[18] The doubtfully rational, 'fantastic' character of the Rosicrucian system—by turns above and below reason—would be attractive to any poet who felt Enlightenment rationalism constricting. Its alchemic element retained lingering associations with philosophical magic, while having become a psychological discipline of inner illumination.[19]

Even aerial spirits and fairies could be seriously credited in Pope's time. (One might compare attitudes to spiritualism around 1900.) Shaftesbury, in his 'Letter Concerning Enthusiasm', wrote of 'an Eminent, Learned, and truly Christian Prelate' who was 'so great a Volunteer in Faith, as beyond the ordinary Prescription of the Catholick Church, to believe in *Fairys*';[20] and the life of Goodwin Wharton shows that a Restoration courtier might be prepared to stake good money—repeatedly—on their existence.[21] For the more sophisticated, fairy lore, half-real and potentially meaningful, offered a convenient non-moralistic language for broaching unconventional matters. Political and sexual taboos in particular were addressed in this way, as the long tradition of fairy poetry strikingly demonstrates. To this tradition Pope's sylphs stand in some close relation still to be determined. But the answer to Ariel's question 'What guards the purity of melting Maids?' may be a little more than the 'Nothing' Emrys Jones proposes.

If the machinery has psychological functions, what are they? A widely accepted view is outlined in Maynard Mack's Life of Pope.[22] The sylphs ('maidenly

---

[16] See Tillotson, p. 149.
[17] See Frances A Yates, *The Rosicrucian Enlightenment* (London, Routledge and Kegan Paul, 1972), p. 232; also p. 230, on its relation to the Jesuit movement, parallel but opposed.
[18] See ibid., pp. 206–19.
[19] See CG Jung, *Psychology and Alchemy*, trans RFC Hull (London, Routledge and Kegan Paul, 1953), *passim*.
[20] *Characteristicks* (London, 1711), p. 6.
[21] See J Kent Clark, *Goodwin Wharton* (Oxford UP, 1984). On the strength of magic in the seventeenth century, see Keith Thomas, *Religion and the Decline of Magic* (London, Weidenfeld and Nicolson, 1971).
[22] *Alexander Pope: A Life* (New Haven and London, Yale UP, 1985), pp. 253–7.

coquetries') guard Belinda, until she falls in love and Ariel leaves her; whereupon 'the lock of maidenliness is forfeit'. (Here the account becomes a little unclear.) Belinda objects, a little prudishly; being afflicted by Umbriel's furies of affectation. She then learns from Thalestris to confuse the name and reality of honour; 'Honour forbid! at whose unrival'd shrine/Ease, Pleasure, Virtue, All, our Sex resign' (4.105-6). The account is well enough; but its narrative leaves the problematic side of Belinda's character alone. Yet it seems a little bland about the Baron's enormity too: is it mere affectation to be affronted at losing half one's hair style?[23]

On a different tack, Gary Boire valuably relates the poem to Burton's *The Anatomy of Melancholy*, and sees Belinda's experience in terms of seventeenth-century medical concepts.[24] On Boire's view, she suffers throughout from 'maid's melancholy', a splenetic disorder. Love melancholy underlies her initial changeableness no less than her 'dotage' on the 'light' occasion of losing a lock of hair. Developing an emphasis of Wasserman's, Boire sees Ariel as a Burtonian *incubus* desiring aery copulation with Belinda, and therefore encouraging her in 'an unnatural, aggressive virginity' (p. 13). Belinda becomes a love melancholic in the special sense that she takes pride in making men enamoured only to scorn them. At the crisis, Boire's Ariel leaves in melancholic depression, while Belinda herself suffers melancholy with an equally sexual basis, as the description of forms of spleen indicates (4.54: 'Maids turned Bottels, call aloud for Corks').

There can be no doubt of Pope's interest in the medical tradition, or of the intertextuality with Burtonian subtexts. Yet melancholy can hardly be sole mover of the action—even taking into account the many varieties of it distinguished by seventeenth-century psychologists (some of them could write in all seriousness of 'sanguine melancholy'), as well as Burton's generalization of the disease into *la condition humaine*.[25] For *The Rape of the Lock* is solidly built on a scheme of four complexions, all of them functional:

Element	temperament	spirit	Character
fire	choleric	salamander	Thalestris
air	sanguine	Sylph	Ariel
water	phlegmatic	nymph	
earth	melancholic	gnome	Umbriel

[23] Critics are evasive about the quantity of hair cut off: e.g. Rebecca Parkin vacillates between 'a curl' and 'a ringlet' in *The Poetic Workmanship of Alexander Pope* (Minneapolis, Univ of Minnesota, 1955), p. 114, etc. But Pope himself encourages this uncertainty—perhaps to allow relativity of viewpoint: see *The Rape of the Lock*, 4.116, 138, 148, but 168.
[24] See Gary A Boire, 'An Arrant Ramp and a Tomrigg: Pope's Belinda', *English Studies in Canada* 8.1 (1982), 9-22.
[25] On mixtures of melancholy, see Klibansky *et al.*, p. 115 n.

Besides using the four elements implicitly throughout as a rhetorical topos,[26] Pope makes the scheme explicit:

> For when the Fair in all their Pride expire,
> To their first Elements their Souls retire:
> The Sprights of fiery Termagants in Flame
> Mount up, and take a Salamander's Name.
> Soft yielding Minds to Water glide away,
> And sip with Nymphs, their Elemental Tea.
> The graver Prude sinks downward to a Gnome,
> In search of Mischief still on Earth to roam.
> The light Coquettes in Sylphs aloft repair,
> And sport and flutter in the Fields of Air.
>
> (1.57–66)

The various individual nymphs exemplify the same typology. Thus 'fierce' Thalestris, who 'fans the rising Fire' of Belinda's anger (4.99)—'raging' (4.121), 'enrag'd Thalestris' (5.57), the 'fierce Virago' (5.37)—displays the influence of choleric salamanders, spirits of 'fiery Termagants'. And 'grave' Clarissa (5.7), whom 'Thalestris call'd...Prude' (5.36), is melancholic, influenced by an erstwhile 'graver Prude' and given to gnomic speeches.

Moral machinery

Clarissa carries great authority, as most agree. Her important speech (5.7–36), added for the first time in 1717, seems to represent the poet's own moral. Indeed, Pope's annotation in his copy of Dennis's *Remarks* has been taken to imply as much.[27] Are we, then, to prefer the melancholic perspective? Is that what the poem's machinery implies? For, as Dennis says (p. 337), it would be a fault if the machinery were to 'give no instruction'.

Here again it may help to glance at the older moral psychologies Pope inherited. In medieval thought, pervasively imbued as it was by Christian ideals, cheerful sanguine was regarded as the best complexion, melancholy as the worst. Gradually, however, and especially after the Florentine Renaissance, an alternative tradition developed: melancholy came to be thought of as a creative mood rather than merely a disease. Despite its pathological tendencies, it came to be valued as the source of contemplation and imagination—none other than Spleen, in fact,

---

[26] See GFC Plowden, *Pope on Classic Ground* (Athens, Ohio, Ohio Univ, 1983), pp. 84–5.
[27] Where Dennis speaks of Boileau's superiority in giving 'broad Hints as to what was his real Meaning', Pope writes 'Clarissa's Speach': see Mack 1982, p. 407.

gave the 'poetic Fit' (4.60).[28] These two opposed traditions coexisted up to Pope's time; so that occasions would easily arise for choice—or ambivalence—between a sanguine ethic and a melancholic. Given the age's rationalism, the choice might present itself as one between a cheerful, reasonable, sanguine ideal ('Sense') and a gloomy, fantastic melancholy ('Sensibility').—Or, of course, as between a serious, imaginative, reasonable melancholy, and a frivolous, fantastic, sanguine vanity. Some such intellectual history as this appears to underlie Pope's contrast of sylphs and gnomes. It is one reason why his sylphs and gnomes bulk larger than the salamanders and nymphs.

As Johnson says, the reader seeks no further information about the Rosicrucian spirits, 'but immediately mingles with his new acquaintance, adopts their interests and attends their pursuits, loves a sylph and detests a gnome' (pp. 233–4). Nonetheless, the perspicacious Dennis—who like most critics takes the side of gravity and the gnomes—detects ambivalence in Pope's machinery:

> The Spirits, which he intends for benign ones, are malignant, and those, which he designs for malignant, are beneficent to Mankind. The Gnomes he intends for malignant, and the Sylphs for beneficent Spirits. Now the Sylphs in this Poem promote that Female Vanity which the Gnomes mortify. And Vanity is...the Cause of most of the Misfortunes which are incident to Humanity.
>
> (p. 339)

It will not do to suppose that Dennis missed all the ironies criticizing Belinda, any more than Johnson did. Nor can it be said that Pope has done much to make the gnomes attractive. It almost looks as if the confusion Dennis seized on was real— and as if Pope, when he added Clarissa's mortifying speech, was trying to correct a partiality for the sylphs. Had he been drawn to the old sanguine ideal of the gothick world? Beyond question he gave the aerial spirits by far the best press. They displace the others to such an extent that many write 'sylphs' when they mean 'spirits'.[29] If Pope's ironies take a 'melancholic' stance, his primary meanings are mostly sanguine.

Critics have taken over Dennis's perception of the sylphs as malignant; although they are not anxious to acknowledge *that* debt. Tillotson, Wasserman, Boire, Grove: all expose Ariel's dishonourable motive for being in Belinda's lap, and trace his evil influence on her character. On Dennis's assumptions, this should mean approval of Umbriel and the darker view. However, it is striking that no active opposition of sylphs and gnomes actually occurs. (Dennis in fact censures this.) For of course all four spirit categories are on the side of evil. Indeed, Pope's note to 1.145 half-encourages one to think of them in terms of

---

[28] See Klibansky *et al., passim.*
[29] See, e.g., Tillotson, p. 123: 'Pope...makes some of his sylphs "bad".'

fallen angels, subjects of 'the prince of the power of the air' of Ephesians 2.2. (Doubtless he had in view *Paradise Regained*, where Milton identifies the devils with 'Powers of Fire, Air, Water, and Earth beneath'.[30]) But this solemn viewpoint cannot be Pope's either: he has taken too much care to interiorize his spirits. As Thomas Parnell writes, 'The Sylphs and Gnomes are but a woman's heart.'[31] Besides, if it is true that 'unless the sylphs could gain an earthly lover they never achieved immortality',[32] was their aspiration so very evil?—or different from that of most earthly maidens? Coquetry is as reprehensible as Wasserman says. And Belinda's dream indeed resembles that of Milton's Eve. But to call Ariel's influence *demonic* seems a bit gnomelike, or superstitious.

And the moralists cannot claim that Belinda improves when Ariel abandons his guardianship and leaves her to other spirits, so that, after Umbriel's prayer, she falls into a melancholy, and much of the Fourth Canto is devoted to a hell of spleen. And these are not the only female disorders. Earlier, at the crisis of the ombre game (and the exact midpoint of 1714) 'Blood the Virgin's Cheek forsook' (3.89). Her 'livid Paleness' shows she has become as 'distemper'd' as the political state she is likened to. Already at 3.25, indeed, she burns with a Martian 'Thirst of Fame'.[33] Pope gives a crucial role to 'Rage, Resentment and Despair' (4.9): to the choleric promptings of the fierce termagant Thalestris. This Amazon is neither the (sanguine) 'resolute coquette' Wasserman would have her (p. 434), nor the mere phase of melancholy detected by Boire. Anger might be thought of as 'preparing the body to melancholy, and madness itself'.[34] But to make Belinda's anger a feature of her melancholy is to give her too individualized a personality. There is no evidence that Pope knew Arabella Fermor.

Belinda doubtless suffers from love melancholy, in the general sense that most girls do. But she can also be choleric: after the 'rape' she 'burns with more than mortal Ire' (4.89), and is an 'incens'd Virago' (5.87). Tillotson (p. 396) thinks she is virago-like merely in order to resemble a Homeric hero. But Dennis significantly thinks her 'a terrible Termagant' (p. 335); thus connecting her with the salamander type. At a turning point of the tragic action—her triumph at ombre—she is guilty of the *hubris* of a bad winner: 'The Nymph exulting fills with Shouts the Sky/The Walls, the Woods, and long Canals reply' (3.99–100). To Dennis, Belinda appears 'an arrant Ramp and a Tomrigg…Must not this be the legitimate Offspring of Stentor, to make such a Noise as that? The Nymph was within Doors, and she must set up her Throat at a hellish Rate, to make the Woods (where, by the by, there are none) and the Canals reply to it' (p. 334).

---

[30] 2.124; cf. 4.201: 'Tetrarchs of fire, air, flood, and on the earth.'
[31] 'To Mr Pope', cit. Wasserman, p. 441.   [32] Tillotson, p. 143, n.32.
[33] On her Martian boldness at this stage, see Plowden, p. 83.
[34] *The Anatomy of Melancholy*, 1.2.3.9.

Critics, ever protective of their author, have proved there *were* woods at Hampton Court, without attending to Dennis's point. Belinda is not being a light coquette, but a bold hoyden. (A ramp was a bold, ill-behaved woman, a tom-rig a 'strumpet, romping girl, a tomboy'.[35]) Indeed, the entire ombre game arises from a dangerous boldness on her part: she 'Burns to encounter two adventrous Knights,/At Ombre singly to decide their Doom' (3.26–7). Again the salamandrian 'burns'. This is not sylphlike.

From one point of view, Belinda is going too far. In playing men at their own game (*ombre* = man), and 'singly' at that, she ignores gender differences, and endangers her reputation. (Although the game is probably played in company, it symbolizes another that need not be.) Her behaviour has something of the dangerous 'innocence' described in *Spectator* 198 (17 October 1711), in a passage that has oddly remained unconnected with *The Rape of the Lock*. Although not itself Rosicrucian, Addison's essay may well have suggested to Pope his interiorization of the spirits:

> There is a Species of Women, whom I shall distinguish by the Name of Salamanders...a kind of Heroine in Chastity, that treads upon Fire, and lives in the Midst of Flames without being hurt. A Salamander *knows no Distinction of Sex in those she converses with*... She admits a Male Visitant to her Bed-side, *plays with him a whole Afternoon at Pickette*, walks with him two or three Hours by Moon-light; and is extreamly Scandalized at...the severity of a Parent, that would debar the Sex from such innocent Liberties. Your Salamander is therefore a[n]...admirer of the French Good-breeding, and *a great Stickler for freedom in Conversation*. In short, the Salamander lives in an invincible State of Simplicity and Innocence: Her Constitution is preserv'd in a kind of natural Frost: She wonders what People mean by Temptations; and defies Mankind to do their worst. Her Chastity is engaged in a constant Ordeal, or fiery Tryal...[36]

Belinda does not altogether escape the dangers of such boldness. When she comes to ask 'What mov'd my Mind with youthful Lords to rome?' (4.159), the answer might be a salamander almost as much as a sylph.

Belinda's boldness also appears in her solar role. Like a Stuart monarch, 'Bright as the Sun, her Eyes the Gazers strike,/And, like the Sun, they shine on all alike'.[37] So firmly is the role established that 'Belinda smil'd, and all the World was gay'

---

[35] See *OED* s.v. 'Ramp' sb., 'Tom' sb., 7a.

[36] Donald F Bond (ed), 5 vols (Oxford, 1965), 2.275–6 (my itals). Tillotson has compared *Spectator* 282, but unaccountably not this more relevant paper.

[37] 2.13–14. See Rebecca Parkin, 'Mythopoeic Activity in *The Rape of the Lock*', *ELH* 21 (1954), 30–8. In addition to her other instances, she might have mentioned the clipping of the sacred lock; since the sun's rays were often mythologized as hair, and his lessening power in winter as their cutting. Cf. Charles Cotton, 'Her Hair', st.5: 'Shee's now a Nazarite/Robb'd of her vigorous light,/For her resisting strength is gone.'

(2.52) seems to follow naturally from the 'Sun-beams trembling on the floating Tydes' a few lines earlier. However, to take the role for granted as no more than Belinda's due hardly does justice to Pope's subtlety. She makes a rather dubious *Sol iustitiae*—'declining from the Noon' of justice, in fact: 'The Sun obliquely shoots his burning Ray' (3.20) as hungry judges hurry their sentencing. This is not a matter of contrast with a 'larger, more disturbing world' outside, as Grove has it (p. 72): Belinda herself participates in the disorder actively. In her cosmic sovereignty she is something of an overreacher, like Spenser's Dame Mutabilitie.

Pope suggests as much, by insinuating suggestions of a better alternative to solar aspiring. So he associates Belinda with silver: the 'silver Sound' of her watch (1.18); her 'silver Token' (1.32); her 'Silver Vase in mystic Order laid' (1.122); 'the Bosom of the Silver Thames' (2.3–4) reflecting the true sun. And her petticoat, cardinal emblem of her chastity, has a 'Silver Bound' (2.121); conspicuously avoiding the subtext's gold.[38] It was a commonplace of the older world picture that silver belonged to Diana, Luna, or Venus, not to golden Sol.[39] Thus Belinda's solar role is made to conflict with her nature either as a Diana or a chaste Venus (Venus-virgo).

Perhaps the second of these mythological colorations better suited a fashionable sex-goddess like Arabella Fermor. Pope may not have known his patroness personally; but it seems he could count on her salamandrian 'innocence' in the face of some fairly gross sexual innuendos. True, he went a little warily at first: in 1712 the notorious speech wishing the youth had been 'content to seize/Hairs less in sight—or any Hairs but these!' was given to Thalestris. (Perhaps Pope felt surer of Mrs Morley.) But in 1714 it is spoken by Belinda herself, at an extremely prominent Canto end. It is hard to assess coarseness over a gap of centuries. Grove is not unpersuasive when he finds in Belinda's 'half innocent heroics' a passionately indignant appeal '*just* polite enough to lie within [her] range' (p. 82). But we have contemporary testimony. The invaluable Dennis writes that Pope 'could not forbear putting Bawdy into the Mouth of his own Patroness' (p. 130). He complains that Belinda 'talks like an errant Suburbian [whore]' (p. 335): Pope gives her 'Breeding, Modesty and Virtue in Words, but has in Reality and in Fact made her an artificial dawbing Jilt; a Tomrig, a Virago, and a Lady of the Lake [kept woman]'. And Charles Gildon makes a similar point.[40]

Other passages present much the same problem. In Ariel's order for Belinda's petticoat, as Dennis again objects (p. 342), the verse 'Oft have we known that sev'nfold Fence to fail' (2.199) can ludicrously be taken to mean that this

---

[38] The Homeric and Vergilian 'stiff with gold' is replaced, as Tillotson notes, by 'stiff with Hoops'.
[39] See, e.g., John Maplet, *The Dial of Destiny* (1581), in *The Frame of Order*, James Winny (ed) (London, Allen and Unwin, 1957), p. 187. There were a very few exceptions, as notably *Iliad* 20.91 in Pope's 1714 note. But in his own *Iliad* Pope actually mistranslates to keep the connection of silver with Diana.
[40] *A New Rehearsal* (1714), p. 43.

particular petticoat has often failed to protect its wearer's chastity. Indeed, sexual *doubles entendres* (like that at 2.106, 'frail China Jar') abound throughout, making *The Rape of the Lock* one of the most erotic works in the canon. Even the stellification that gives the poem its exquisite closure makes another instance. Many will have felt Pope's subject here to be poetic idealization itself—'The elevated lock is, in a sense, the poem' (Price p. 242). 'Who made a lampe of Berenices hayre?' asks Jonson; and the answer is 'Poets, rapt with rage divine'.[41] The lock of hair sacred as a nuptial sacrifice or token of love is one of the great poetic subjects.[42] Yet in linking Belinda's lock with the 'dishevel'd Light' of 'Berenice's Locks', Pope also associated it with a constellation whose vulgar name was 'Berenice's Bush'.[43] Again and again the poem recurs to its sustained juxtaposition—an oxymoron not unknown elsewhere in Pope—of the low and the ideal in woman.

How could innuendo have been thought calculated to reconcile the families, to 'laugh them together'?[44] Part of Pope's strategy may have been to make Belinda's world so erotic that the Baron's action came to seem almost natural. By tender ridicule of the way Belinda's heroics exaggerate the incident into a rape, he makes it seem a mere romp outwardly—while still sympathizing with its subjective apprehension as an outrage. And by the lurking lover at 3.144 he hints that Belinda's heavy reaction may be due to her having formed a serious attachment. Wasserman (pp. 428–9, 435, 442) rightly draws attention to the antique symbolism whereby clipping a lock was a ritual preparation for marriage: Catullus makes tears for the lock ambivalent. Indeed, a 'glittering Forfex' such as that used to cut Belinda's hair—'The scissors double shaft,/Useless apart, in social union joined'— is regarded by Richard Jago as an 'Emblem how beautiful/Of happy nuptial leagues'.[45] Pope's innuendos, then, were perhaps not so counterproductively unsuitable as they may now seem. But in any case the mock-heroic occasional poem was soon left behind (by 1713 Baron Petre was dead); as Pope consciously recognized, his subject became nothing less than 'female sex'.[46]

In his treatment of women, Pope departed radically from the hostility of his satiric models. Thus, his finely poised description of Belinda's toilet is only from one point of view censure of those who 'dress all day'. Belinda is obviously

---

[41] 'To Elizabeth Countess of Rutland', 60–3.
[42] Wasserman 428–9 cites many ancient examples. Callimachus's poem, on Berenice's lock lost from the temple, was itself lost so far as Pope was concerned; but Catullus's translation of it survived. The later tradition includes Drayton's *Egl.* 9.216–22; Lovelace's 'On Sannazar'; Butler's *Hudibras* 2.3.844; and Cotton's 'Her Hair'.
[43] R H Allen, *Star-Names and their Meanings* (New York, 1963), 170, citing Thomas Hill, *Schoole of Skil* (1599), etc.
[44] Pope's own account of his brief: see Joseph Spence, *Anecdotes,* James M Osborn (ed), 2 vols (Oxford, Clarendon, 1966), no. 104.
[45] *Edge-Hill* (1767), 3.545–8.
[46] Marginalium to Dennis's *Remarks,* Mack 1982, p. 407. Pope implies that this subject is comparable with the important ecclesiastical one of the *Lutrin*.

vain—idolatrous, even, in her self-love—as our modern Umbriels have explained in detail. But to dwell exclusively on this 'moral' is to prefer gnomic heaviness to the poetic effect of erotic warmth. For, throughout the description, the poetry's own 'busy Sylphs surround their darling Care', like *putti* round a Renaissance Venus. Erotic nuances of language are here particularly marked. 'The Fair each moment *rises* in her Charms' (140); 'Arabia *breathes*' (134); and when the maid ('Th' inferior Priestess') 'begins the sacred Rites of Pride' she is 'Trembling',[47] Wasserman legitimately spells out the 'Rites of Pride', reminding us how bad is Ariel's advice to know 'thy own Importance'; and that 'The mirror in which Belinda sees herself as a goddess is, of course, the traditional emblem of Pride' (pp. 431–2). Pride is certainly a strong moral card, and Pope's readers would expect it to be played against Belinda. But we have not responded to the passage unless we also see the cosmetic rites as beautiful. The mirror is also, we recall, a traditional emblem of Venus.[48] Pope's description of the *garniture de toilette* is less a conventional *Vanitas* still life than a *Vénus à sa toilette*.[49]

To Parkin, 'the whole point of the metaphor' of worship is 'the actual disparity between the realms of make-up and religion'.[50] Certainly the metaphors are disjunctive morally. But it would be simplistic to take the 'heav'nly Image in the Glass' merely as Belinda's own reflection.[51] As Cleanth Brooks already recognized, Belinda also serves, paradoxically, as priestess in a religion of beauty.[52] To grave moralists, Venus is, of course, an idol—perhaps like Addison's coquette, 'An Idol...wholly taken up in the Adoring of her Person'.[53] But Venus could be a little more. The magic of female beauty, which everywhere enchants in *The Rape of the Lock*, was a serious interest for Pope in a way it never was for Addison.[54] It is the poem's concern with this magic, indeed, that makes its Rosicrucian machinery exquisitely appropriate.

In a Rosicrucian poem, Belinda's toilet can be the rite of a magical 'Art' (3.143), a purification of the quintessence of Venus. In this art, alchemic apparatus and symbols are evident. What is Belinda's glass but a magic mirror of intellectual

---

[47] Cf. Robin Grove, 'Uniting Airy Substance: *The Rape of the Lock* 1712–1736', in *The Art of Alexander Pope*, Howard Erskine-Hill and Anne Smith (eds) (London, Vision, 1979), p. 68.
[48] See, e.g., Guy de Tervarent, *Attributs et symboles dans l'art profane 1450–1600* (Geneva, Droz, 1958), col 274.
[49] Iconographically the sylph-putti are decisive against the harsher interpretation; cf., e.g., Oliver Millar, *Dutch Pictures from the Royal Collection* (London, The Queen's Gallery, 1971), p. 85, on the putto in a *toilette* by Steen.
[50] Parkin 1955, p. 103.
[51] As Hugo M Reichard, 'The Love Affair in Pope's *The Rape of the Lock*', PMLA 69. I (1954), 894; Parkin 1955, p. 107; Grove, pp. 64–5.
[52] Cleanth Brooks, 'The Case of Miss Arabella Fermor: A Re-examination', reprinted in *The Well Wrought Urn* (London, Dobson, 1949), p. 77.
[53] *Spectator* 73, cit. Reichard, p. 889.
[54] It is seen also, for example, in the echo of The Song of Solomon, on beauty's power to draw with a single hair.

reflection? or 'Each Silver Vase in mystic Order laid' but an alchemic vessel?⁵⁵ Indeed, the line (like several in the poem) has an explicitly alchemic subtext.⁵⁶ To Wasserman (p. 434), 'The Tortoise here and Elephant unite' alludes to 'the Hindu emblem of the world' because the proud Belinda pretends to govern the universe. But Grove (p. 64) notices that 'the verse...catches Tortoise and Elephant coupled in love-play, before the prudent explanation ("combs") returns the stage to rights'. The point of the Hindu world image for Pope probably lay in Locke's prominent use of it to destroy the illusion that qualities are supported by substance. (What supports the tortoise?) And Pope, too, has used the image for a metaphysic of perception—perception of beauty. For the union of elephant and tortoise is an alchemic *coniunctio* of opposites—strength and weakness, superhuman intellectual power and Venerean emotion.⁵⁷ The beauty that results from the Art, then, could truly be called a 'heav'nly Image'. It is hardly surprising that the Baron follows Prometheus in stealing its illumination:

> Sure shee is Heaven it self, and I
> In fervent zeal This lock did steal,
> And each life-giving thread,
> Snatcht from her beamy head,
> As once Prometheus from the skie.⁵⁸

Burton, writing of love-melancholics who 'prank up themselves to make young men enamoured', asks 'why do they make such glorious shows with...whatsoever Africa, Asia, America, sea, land, art and industry of man can afford?'⁵⁹ But his elephantine attitude (which rests on the porcupine of misogynistic satire) is far from Pope's.

Similarly with Pope's famous asyndetic couplet—

> Here Files of Pins extend their shining Rows,
> Puffs, Powders, Patches, Bibles, Billet-doux.

(1.137–8)

---

⁵⁵ On the mirror, see Herbert Grabes, *The Mutable Glass*, trans Gordon Collier (Cambridge UP, 1982), pp. 336–7; Jung, p. 111; on the vessel, which was of central importance in alchemic thought, see ibid., s.v. *Vas*. Paracelsus (e.g. 1.14) has much to say about the 'silver pixis' or receptacle; see also ibid., 1.298, on the 'vase of the philosophers', quicksilver, or Mercury.

⁵⁶ *Gondibert* 2.7.17. Cf. the notorious line 'Nor bound thy narrow Views to Things below', which echoes a central alchemic symbolon, 'As above, so below': see Stanislas Klossowski de Rola, *Alchemy: The Secret Art* (London, Thames and Hudson, 1973), p. 15.

⁵⁷ As it happens, Pope's knowledge of the Renaissance elephant and tortoise can partly be documented, since he annotated Montaigne's account of the elephant's powers extensively: see Mack 1982, p. 427.

⁵⁸ Charles Cotton, 'Her Hair', st.3.

⁵⁹ *The Anatomy of Melancholy* 3.2.5.5; 3.2.2.3, cit. Tillotson, Boire.

Morally, it betrays Belinda's notorious confusion of values. But its diminutive organization also delights, by enhancing a scene of delicate activity, thronged with 'busy Sylphs'. Pope the satirist is bound to censure the spending of resources on mere beauty—as Clarissa would say, it is not a 'Thing of Use' (5.22). Yet Pope the artist knows that beauty may be higher than use; and so he makes Belinda's rituals the mysteries of a separate world, with its own *magnum opus*. Gnomes compare the couplet with one of Halifax's (which is perhaps the origin of one used by Richard Steele on Philauthia's closet): 'Prayer-book, patch-boxes, sermon-notes and paint,/ At once t'improve the sinner and the saint.'[60] But Pope's lines are as close to Cowley's 'The Chronicle':

> But should I now to you relate,
> The strength and riches of their state,
> The Powder, Patches, and the Pins,
> The Ribbans, Jewels, and the Rings,
> The Lace, the Paint, and warlike things
> That make up all their Magazins:
> If I should tell the politick Arts
> To take and keep mens hearts,
> The Letters, Embassies, and Spies,
> The Frowns, and Smiles, and Flatteries,
> The Quarrels, Tears, and Perjuries,
> Numberless, Nameless Mysteries![61]

—a poem whose tone is not at all misogynistic.

Political machinery

The chief of the aerial spirits who preside over the human race, as Ariel's Thames speech explains, 'guard with Arms Divine the British Throne' (2.89–90). Is, then, *The Rape of the Lock* a political poem?

A loosely politicized interpretation of the poem has become fairly common—as in discussions of Belinda's toilet articles in terms of 'commodity fetishism'.[62] This is perfectly legitimate, whenever a specifically political perspective is appropriate. Everything in literature can be seen in political and economic terms: every mention of every object. When Lear says 'undo this button', his speech

---

[60] Tillotson, n. to 1.138; cf. Reichard, p. 894, referring to *Spectator* 79.
[61] *Poems*, A R Waller (ed) (Cambridge 1905), p. 41.
[62] Brown, pp. 12–24; C E Nicholson, 'A World of Artefacts: *The Rape of the Lock* as Social History', *Literature and History* 5 (1979), 183–93; Robert Casillo, 'Dirty Gondola: The Image of Italy in American Advertisements', *Word and Image* 1.4 (1985), 344.

reflects technological developments whereby buttons replaced points. But the decision how far to trace such reflections must depend on the pragmatic context. Doubtless Belinda's world could be described so as to seem one in which 'objects have taken over all meaning', by exclusion of human values and of 'the actual production of the commodities'.[63] But would this help us to appreciate what is specific to Pope's poem? Is it true that 'of all the major works of its period, *The Rape of the Lock* does the most to match imperialism and commodity fetishism, and the most to place the commodification of English culture in the context of imperial violence' (Brown p. 22)? Is it true, even, that the poem's highly charged objects reflect the structural economic facts of Pope's time in a new way? After all, poems full of things that constitute the main repositories of value were hardly new. One thinks of Elizabethan satires, or of medieval romances with their overdetermined objects.[64] Pope may have given prominence to charming objects—cosmetic articles, and to tea and coffee—because they bulked distinctively large in female life. (They were also important in Pope's own, in ways that have little to do with his anti-mercantilism: he used to relieve his frequent headaches 'by inhaling the steam of coffee'—a surprising light on Ariel's threat that the punished spirit 'In Fumes of burning Chocolate shall glow,/And tremble at the Sea that froaths below!'[65])

If *The Rape of the Lock* was a political poem, why are politics never mentioned in Dennis's *Remarks*? True, Pope himself pseudonymously proposed a political allegory (concerning the Barrier Treaty). But if its logic is considered, *A Key to the Lock* will be seen to point another way. When Esdras Barnivelt discloses that Roman Catholics claimed to be the original of Sir Plume so as to disguise an anti-government allegory in the poem, Pope surely means the fantastic argument to imply that detailed political allegorization lets real Sir Plumes evade moral satire. Politics is not of course to be excluded from *The Rape of the Lock*; but its place there is for most purposes very subsidiary.

Howard Erskine-Hill's account of the ombre game finds some probable political allusions, like the ones to 'The Queen of Hearts', and to Marlborough in 'mighty Pam that...mow'd down Armies in the Fights of Lu' (another card-game; William III's palace in Holland).[66] But when all is said, Erskine-Hill concludes that 'no tidy political allegory is revealed'. Political allusions are to be expected in a mock-epic; but they need not be systematic, or very frequent. For example, the suits—'Sable Matadores,/In Show like Leaders of the swarthy Moors' (3.46–7); 'Club's black

---

[63] Brown, pp. 13–14.
[64] See, e.g., Sir John Davies, 'In Claium', or his Gulling Sonnet 6: *The Poems*, Robert Krueger (ed) (Oxford, Clarendon, 1975), pp. 158–9, 166.
[65] 2.133–6. See *Gent. Mag.* (1775) 435, cit. Johnson, p. 197.
[66] Howard Erskine-Hill, 'The Satirical Game at Cards in Pope and Wordsworth', in *English Satire and the Satiric Tradition*, Claude Rawson (ed) (Oxford, Blackwell, 1984), p. 190.

Tyrant' (3.69)—conceivably refer to political orientations.[67] But the imagery may be sufficiently accounted for by the physical appearance of the cards, by epic precedents for allusions to Africa, and by the erotic associations of moors (Belinda plays, symbolically, to avoid a jealous tyrannical husband).[68] It is noteworthy, moreover, that a tyrannical moor plays a prominent part in the Rosicrucian *Chemical Wedding*.[69]

Political allusions are fatally easy to discover. And, after all, the sylphs who perch on Belinda's cards (3.31–6) are Ariel and his inferiors: those limited to 'humbler' private duties, explicitly not the cadre who guard thrones.[70] However, there might be an analogy (without resemblance) between Belinda's sovereignty over hearts, and the political Queen of Hearts.[71] Queen Anne, too, was playing a man's game; and the sylphs may be meant to revive 'memory of the magical power of monarchs'.[72] Douglas Brooks-Davies finds reflections of Pope's Stuart or Jacobite views of monarchy—by no means a far-fetched idea.[73] The loss of Belinda's lock may well hint at Anne's loss of prerogative through recent constitutional changes. It is certainly suggestive that the poem's numerology alludes to Anne's sovereignty, in such a way as to connect her with Belinda. For each canto of 1712 has an Anna at or next to its numerical centre.[74]

Doubtless *The Rape of the Lock* does reflect Pope's dislike of the unnecessary War of the Spanish Succession. But this reflection cannot be said to throw a very discriminating light on the poem. The ombre game is better approached along the lines sketched in W K Wimsatt's fine 'Belinda Ludens'.[75] It is at once a crucial stage of the action and a model of the whole. The sylphs are involved because it is both part and symbol of Belinda's coquetry, her engagement with a plurality of men. (Even her choice of spades ('swords') as trumps, for example, signifies her combative boldness.[76]) Indeed, Wimsatt's interpretation could be further developed, into a parallel of game and poem. Thus, Belinda at first wins at cards, then nearly loses, and finally is victorious; while in the poem at large her hubristic triumph is similarly followed by near-catastrophe, when the Baron rapes the lock and nearly scores. (His possession of a 'favour' would have ruined her

---

[67] See ibid., p. 186. [68] The 'bawdy intimations' of the game are well described in Grove, p. 75.
[69] Yates 1972, p. 63.
[70] Cf. 2.73–100: Ariel distinguishes aetherial spirits with translunary offices, and others 'less refin'd' with sublunary macrocosmic or national affairs. A third, yet lower, grade ('Our humble province') is Ariel's own sort. Pope's marginalium in Dennis underlines this subdivision: see Mack 1982, pp. 408–9.
[71] *A Key to the Lock*, p. 189 might be taken to hint that characters can have dual roles.
[72] See Douglas Brooks-Davies, *The Mercurian Monarch* (Manchester UP, 1983), p. 193.
[73] See Howard Erskine-Hill, 'Literature and the Jacobite Cause: Was There a Rhetoric of Jacobitism?', in *Ideology and Conspiracy: Aspects of Jacobitism, 1689–1739*, Eveline Cruickshanks (ed) (Edinburgh, Edinburgh UP, 1982); Douglas Brooks-Davies, *Pope's Dunciad and the Queen of Night: A Study in Emotional Jacobitism* (Manchester UP, 1985).
[74] Alastair Fowler, *Triumphal Forms* (Cambridge UP, 1970), p. 120.
[75] W K Wimsatt, 'Belinda Ludens: Strife and Play in *The Rape of the Lock*', *NLH* 4.2 (1973), 357–74.
[76] Cf. Plowden, p. 87.

reputation.[77]) Finally, armed struggle leads to a victory of sorts—although its hollowness is only transcended by the poet's apotheosis of the lock.

The poem, then, has large implications. Its artistic principle, brilliantly elucidated by Wimsatt, is enlargement, whereby a trivial quarrel is related to all human and cosmic strife. Just as the private is enlarged to the political in 'Dost sometimes Counsel take—and sometimes Tea' (3.8), so Pope allows himself soft focus of 'aerial', using the word now for the sylphs specifically, now for spirits generally. By this frail means he connects the sylphs with the quite different spirits who 'roll the Planets'.[78] It is a characteristic instance of his love of blurred categories that leave one momentarily uncertain whether to see confusion of thought, political allegory, a mere pun, or a deliberate aesthetic strategy.

But the most interesting politics in *The Rape of the Lock* are sexual politics. Here we need to glance at a machine so far neglected; the nymphs. Just as Pope plays on senses of 'aerial', so he uses 'nymph' in a swerving way. According to Ariel, nymphs are one of four subcategories of elemental spirits or types: 'Soft yielding Minds to Water glide away,/And sip with Nymphs, their Elemental tea.' Yet all the female characters are called nymphs—Belinda, Clarissa, even the termagant Thalestris (5.61). Is this another piece of interiorized machinery? Or an implication that submissive 'yielding' nymphishness is the natural, general state of woman? Does Pope mean that Belinda should be a bit more yielding, less of a scornful beauty?[79] While this may be Pope's official intention, it is by no means his only one. Tradition pressed him to approve submissiveness; nevertheless he shows an undeniable partiality for sylphs. His preference, indeed, is a very large fact still calling for interpretation. So much do the sylphs dominate the poem that some have written as if the other spirits did not exist.

For generations, male chauvinist criticism has dwelt on Pope's satire of female vanity, and obscured his fondness for women. Critics rightly use *Spectator* papers to illustrate the poem. But it has an airy warmth quite unlike the misogynistic pruderies of Addison. For an originality of *The Rape of the Lock* is that it addresses 'the matter of woman' with genuine interest. And in treating it, Pope identifies with women to an unusual extent. His feminine world is not only one of fairies and sylphs and superstition, but also of imagination—including poetic imagination. (And male imagination too: the fantasy whereby 'Men prove with Child' (4.53) is not a female one.) Significantly, the character Pope gives an 'unthinking Face' is Sir Plume, not a woman. Pope is not to be read as a wholehearted satirist when he speaks of female beauty as sacred.

---

[77] On the compromising significance of the lock in contemporary convention, see Reichard, pp. 891, 900, 902.

[78] 2.80. On the confusion of 'aerial', see Tillotson, pp. 118, 397.

[79] Cf. Wasserman, p. 435 *ad fin.*, on 1.12.

What then of Clarissa's speech? Although it invokes Popeian values (use, sense), we should not assume too easily that it contains Pope's only moral. It was Clarissa, after all, who 'with tempting Grace' drew her scissors and armed the Baron. She figures in the Dryden subtext as a 'careful Devil', and is on the side of man. Surely Grove (p. 83) is right to find 'unctuous advice' in her counsel that Belinda should prevail through (submissive) good humour. Pope's deeper sympathy—and Jupiter's scales—speak for Belinda's bold anger. Above all, the poem communicates conspiratorial fellow-feeling for the poignantly mutable beauty—for one who aspires to airy lightness in a world of heavy prudes.

Although Pope's poem had models in Cowley and others, it effectively initiated a new attitude to the feminine world. Johnson is a good guide:

> The subject of the poem is an event below the common incidents of common life; nothing real is introduced that is not seen so often as to be no longer regarded, yet the whole detail of a female-day is here brought before us invested with so much art of decoration that, though nothing is disguised, every thing is striking, and we feel all the appetite of curiosity for that from which we have a thousand times turned fastidiously away.
>
> (p. 234)

Here Johnson writes about defamiliarization; but incidentally he makes a moral point: that Pope was not too 'fastidious' to write about female trivia. For Dennis 'nothing can be more...contemptible' (p. 338) than the 'vile functions' of the sylphs, as they 'save the Powder from too rude a Gale,/Nor let th'imprison'd Essences exhale' (2.93-4). But to Pope they were not contemptible—delicate, rather, and beautiful. The diminutive machinery provided a language whereby to begin to alter the evaluation of the feminine world as 'vile' (lowly), and to portray it as it was—as the tortoise that supported the elephant. *The Rape of the Lock* may be said to have performed a not unimportant rite in the *Magnum Opus* of revaluing woman.

Georgic and Pastoral:
Laws Of Genre in The Seventeenth Century

I fully expect some anti-genre reader, some Benedetto Croce *de nos jours*, to rebut my title by rejecting the whole notion of genres being governed by laws—if indeed the genres themselves can be said to exist at all. Surely no writer worth his salt (I almost put, no epigrammatist worth his *sal*) ever conformed to laws? With such an objector I should have much sympathy. We tend to make our literary histories—not to say our literary theories—altogether too neat, too orderly, indeed, too abstractly remote from literature itself. In the real seventeenth century, ideas of genre were not very tidy. Consider for a moment an ordinary seventeenth-century critic listing the main genres: one J. D., whose 'Short Institution of English Poesy' was prefaced to the posthumous 1677 edition of Joshua Poole's *The English Parnassus*, an invaluable *gradus* and thesaurus drawn from the works of some sixty contemporary writers. J. D.'s Preface lists eight 'species' (or as we should say, modes): heroic, lyric, elegiac, dramatic, epigrammatic, didactic, epistolary, historical. Interesting, if not very logical. But J. D.'s vagueness about contemporary genres fully emerges only when he lists the hyponymic subspecies into which these modal groupings are divided. Under dramatic, for example, he lists not merely tragedies, comedies, interludes, masques, and entertainments, but also dialogues, satires, frolics,[1] memorials, georgics, pastorals, piscatories, and nauticals—'which three last pass commonly under the name of eclogues'. In view of such type-fallacies, it seems quite likely that if strict laws of genre operated in seventeenth-century England, they were not within the consciousness of critics like J. D.

At any rate, what I shall mean by laws is not a system of conscious, prescriptive rules, but rather tendencies or patterns of regularity, perceived, it may be, only in retrospect. The idea of laws of genre, at least in their modern form, was imported into literary theory from linguistics, and specifically from a linguistics based on Saussure's old semantic model of communication. At a time when literary conventions were thought of as supplementary language rules, genres understandably came to be regarded as coding systems. But more recently, in the light of modern pragmatics, the limitations of Saussure's semantic model coding

---

[1] The 'frolic' was a set of verses corporately composed at a feast by passing them round from guest to guest.

as only a part of what goes on in communication—Dan Sperber and Deirdre Wilson would say, a small part[2]—so in literary criticism and theory we need to acknowledge how little literature can be understood apart from its contexts, both external and literary. In other words, we need to restore the genres to their settings in history and literary tradition, and to see them once more as diachronic existences.

In 1982, in *Kinds of Literature*,[3] I treated genres mainly as coding systems—constantly changing languages for communication—rather than as fixed categories for classification. And I still regard this conception as part of the truth. But I am more inclined now to conceive genres also as spheres of interest, of knowledge, of association—in fact, to relate them to what Sperber and Wilson call 'domains of assumption'. Certainly genres assist literary communication; but they do so not merely by acting as systems of coding rules. (Insofar as they work in that way, they remain very general, of limited use to the reader.) Rather do they function quasi-pragmatically, as a literary surrogate for real-life situations of utterance. Acting as substitutes for context in this way, the genres supply shared guides to relevance. Individual works in a genre communicate—and have literary point—by virtue of their relevance to the genre's current domains of assumption, from which they depart in some more or less novel way.

This makes interpretation sound easier than it is; for the hermeneutic problem remains, of returning behind our own genres, and our own domains of assumption, to those of, say, seventeenth-century writers and readers. How are we to recover the simplicity of their comparative confusion? The simplicity of a world without benefit of neoclassicism, for example? This is not to say there were no laws of genre in the seventeenth century. But sometimes the 'laws' may have been dimly apprehended patterns, or dawning discoveries—and discoveries about life, as much as about art. At other times, laws of genre may have been like psychological laws of association and memory. For example, one notices that the maximum number of items in short-term memory, namely seven, is about the same as the number of items in many seventeenth-century schemes or hierarchies of canonical genres.

Among the strongest claims for the status of law is surely the arrangement of genres in pairs: epigram and lyric; pastoral and georgic; novel and romance. Between such paired genres there seem to obtain relations both of similarity and

---

[2] See Dan Sperber and Deirdre Wilson, *Relevance: Communication and Cognition* (Cambridge, Mass., 1986); also 'Mood and the Analysis of Non-declarative Sentences', in *Human Agency*, eds J. Dancy, J.M.E. Moravcsik, and C.C.W. Taylor (Stanford, 1988), pp. 77–104.

[3] In the case of epigram and lyric, similarly, there was a *tertium quid* or intermediate stage in the shape of sweet epigram. This helps to explain why the increased accessibility of the Greek Anthology shortly after 1600 had so decisive an effect on the development of the epigram. In short, the parasitic mixtures of genre that Gilbert Highet traces in *The Anatomy of Satire* (1962) may not be a feature altogether peculiar to that genre. It may, indeed, belong to the large general process whereby genres readjust their canonic relations, and form new hierarchies of values.

of contrast. This may be only a matter of the genres' relative position on some more or less arbitrarily chosen axis, formal or substantive; as when we say that satire's sour note contrasts with the sweet harmony of celebratory lyric. Certain generic relations, however, like those of epigram and lyric, seem closer; suggesting the exclusivity of the antonym relation in semantics.[4] As Ann Coiro has recently shown, Robert Herrick's *Hesperides* achieves many of its finest effects through sustained juxtaposition of the seemingly immiscible elements of lyric and epigrammatic: a confrontation whereby he pushes epigram *sylva* or miscellany, *The Forest* (1616), but also of *Idea's Mirror*, where as early as 1599 Drayton was combining sonnets and epigrams in such a way as to interweave their generic features.[5] The rhetorically improper intimacy of Sidney's middle-style diction in *Astrophil and Stella*; the epigrammatic closures of Shakespeare's sonnets; the plain-style sour sonnets of Sir John Davies: all these are instances of a vogue for playing off sonnet against epigram, in such a way as to exploit their differences.

Such phenomena can be seen in two ways, according to whether one stresses internal or external aspects of literature. (1) One may regard the fusion of epigram and lyric as the overwhelming of the latter by the former—part of the imperialistic aggrandizement whereby epigram came to dominate other forms in the seventeenth century. As epigram rose in the hierarchy of genres, other genres tended either to be discarded, or reinterpreted as epigram. Epigrams were everywhere: 'public favour so increased their pride, / They overwhelmed Parnassus with their tide'—as Boileau put it (with Dryden's help).[6] By aggregation, the epigram might even conquer the long poem: in 1659 the anthologist Thomas Pecke wrote that 'if a poem be good, it consists of nothing else, but various epigrams, cemented by a dextrous sagacity'.[7] Similarly, the epigram vogue (or 'mode') dictated that neo-Platonic love lyrics should be answered by anti-Neoplatonic epigrams of cynical lust, and eventually replaced by the plain-style Restoration love 'lyric' (as we still call it). (2) Alternatively, one can see the fusion of genres as an effort towards realism. For every genre sets a lattice of convention as well as a window of mediation between writer and reality. But the lattice, or filter, is different in each case, so that by mixing genres, writers sometimes feel, you can get more of reality in.

A similarly close link connects seventeenth-century pastoral and georgic. It would be easy to characterize these two genres, at least in their purer forms, as contrasting in every way. Pastoral is spoken dramatically by shepherds, and in consequence must use simple diction that avoids any hint of precise knowledge: a

---

[4] See Karen Sparck Jones, *Synonymy and Semantic Classification* (Edinburgh, 1986), p. 106; John Lyons, *Introduction to Theoretical Linguistics* (Cambridge, 1968), pp. 460–9.

[5] See Ann Baynes Coiro, *Robert Herrick's 'Hesperides' and the Epigram Book Tradition* (Baltimore, 1988), pp. 104–8 *et passim*.

[6] *The Art of Poetry*, lines 329–46; in John Dryden, II, 134–5.

[7] Thomas Pecke, *Parnassi Puerperium* (London, 1659), sig. A3.

language of feeling incapable of particularization or detailed description. Georgic, on the contrary, is spoken in the poet's own voice, and far from avoiding knowledgeability seeks to inculcate it through didacticism, albeit didacticism concealed by implicitness and sweetened by delightful details—description of landscape particulars, perhaps (a common *topos*), or sensuous representation of seasonal change. For georgic continually changes in its calendrical variety, whereas pastoral is immutably fixed in a stasis of unchanging spring. Even the values of the genres seem opposed: the simplifying abstraction of the one, against the specificity and sensuousness, fertility and richness of the other. The fact that both are concerned with the country: does it not serve to define their relation as one of antonymic contrast? I want to suggest that in fact we can carry analysis further if we think of the two genres, instead, as corresponding to alternative but overlapping domains of assumption about a similar field of interests.

The contrast of pastoral and georgic would have been counted elementary in the Augustan period. But now it has largely been forgotten, so that the label 'pastoral' tends to be attached to both genres, as if georgic were merely another of Empson's versions of pastoral. This recent blurring of pastoral and georgic does not exactly help us to understand the history of English literature in the seventeenth century. For one of the largest and most significant changes during that period was the displacement of pastoral by georgic. Here I need only mention a few token instances and aspects of that dislodgement: namely, the growth of didactic literature; the proliferation of essays and essay-like poems, such as Cowley's *Sylva* (1637) and *Essays in Verse and in Prose* (1668); and the many literary 'arts', from angling and cookery to the art of poetry itself; to say nothing of the formal georgic of husbandry. 'The sway of georgic in the *Essays [of Cowley]* is so strong that it all but subsumes the heterogeneity of sylva into the even temper of the middle style.'[8] Georgic digression and indirection became respectable; and seasonal literature of all kinds abounded, from Breton's 'Months' in *Fantastics* (1626) to Gay's times of day in *Trivia* (1716). Over little more than a century, georgic climbed in esteem, from being only doubtfully regarded as poetry at all by Sir Philip Sidney, to being at or near the top of the hierarchy of genres. In 1697, Joseph Addison, in his Preface to Dryden's important translation of the *Georgics*, could discuss whether it was not Virgil's greatest poem; calling it 'the most Compleat, Elaborate, and finisht Piece of all Antiquity'.[9]

Meanwhile pastoral was demoted. It continued to be often used, but attracted fewer and fewer serious creative efforts, as if only waiting the *coup de grâce* of Dr Johnson's famous attack. Does the descent of pastoral and the ascent of georgic not exactly parallel the descent of lyric and ascent of epigram? And is it not, in

---

[8] David Hill Radcliffe, 'Sylvan States: Social and Literary Formations in Sylvae by Jonson and Cowley', *Journal of English Literary History*, 55 (1988), 802.
[9] Dryden, V, 153.

each case, displacement of a genre by its nearest neighbour? It seems as if there is a limit to the number of genres that can be appreciated during any particular literary period. (Indeed, in our own period many people enjoy only the novel.) If one of a pair of genres rises, must not the other fall? It may not, however, be quite so simple as that. Changes in the generic hierarchy do not take place in a vacuum; they need to be related to the historical setting—to shifts in domains of assumption, both literary and extraliterary. The information explosion of the seventeenth century, for example, was a large circumstance favourable to the miscellaneous variety of georgic and to its appetite for factual details. When such contexts are taken into account, the laws of genre become less obviously a matter of binary oppositions.

When the relations of pastoral and georgic are put into their historical and comparative literature contexts, two features stand out. First, English pastoral has to be related to the consequential fact that from an early date England was Europe's major wool producer (the quality of its wool being so fine as to make it a 'veritable golden fleece', as Girolamo Lando called it).[10] The English were then not yet a nation of shopkeepers, but of shepherds, woolcarders, dyers, weavers, fullers, and other of the sixteen occupations assignable to the wool trade. Not surprisingly. English pastoral tended in consequence to be somewhat more realistic, its shepherds a little less implausibly innocent of all knowledge about the trade they practised so effectively. Accordingly, alongside 'correct' pastoral, there developed a less idealized type taking in rather more detail of the phenomenal world. Already the fifteenth-century Wakefield Second Shepherds' pageant opens with the complaint 'Lord, what these weders are cold'; and in Spenser's *The Shepheardes Calender* (1579), Cuddie in February can actually complain, 'Ah for pity, will rank winter's rage / These bitter blasts never gin to assuage!' True, the realism in Spenser's version of pastoral may have had a particular ideological motivation, like that inspiring Petrarch's allegorical imitation of Virgil's *Eclogues*. But, in the seventeenth century, some of the loveliest and least ideological passages in Michael Drayton's and William Browne's pastorals similarly introduce a sensuous rustic *vrai-semblance* quite improper to the kind in its classical form—and consistently avoided by Alexander Pope in his correct Virgilian *Pastorals* of 1709. Here is Browne's description of morning in *Britannia's Pastorals* (1613–16):

> The Muses' friend, gray-eyed Aurora, yet
> Held all the meadows in a cooling sweat,
> The milk-white gossamers not upwards snowed,
> Nor was the sharp and useful steering goad
> Laid on the strong-necked ox; no gentle bud

---

[10] *CSPVen 1621–23*, p. 431.

> The sun had dried; the cattle chewed the cud
> Low levelled on the grass; no fly's quick sting
> Enforced the stonehorse in a furious ring
> To tear the passive earth nor lash his tail
> About his buttocks broad; the slimy snail
> Might on the wainscot (by his many mazes'
> Winding meanders and self-knitting traces)
> Be followed, where he stuck his glittering slime,
> Not yet wiped off. It was so early time
> The careful smith had in his sooty forge
> Kindled no coal; nor did his hammers urge
> His neighbours' patience: owls abroad did fly,
> And day as then might plead his infancy.[11]

In short, English pastoral is specially characterized by mixture with georgic—as Pope was well aware when in another mood he noticed Spenser's 'beautiful addition' of seasonality to the pastoral genre in *The Shepheardes Calender*.[12]

Secondly, there is the remarkable belatedness, or apparent belatedness, of georgic in English. Italy had its fourteenth-century *Sonneti di mesi*, its fifteenth-century *Rusticus*, and many sixteenth-century works by Alamanni and Vida and others. But English georgic is not supposed to have appeared until after Addison's Preface to Dryden's translation of Virgil's *Georgics* in 1697. Then, indeed, a flood of georgics and mock-georgics followed, from Philips and Gay to Smart.[13]

Anthony Low explains this lateness as due to the English aristocracy's contempt for the georgic value of labour—their preferred pastoral, despite its ostensible simplicity, being secretly more refined.[14] Now we may indeed find a preference for contemplative aristocratic pastoral, as against sweaty plebeian georgic, in Sir Philip Sidney; but no more, surely, than in many Continental aristocrats. Mainly he gave georgic a low place for quite another reason: because it lacked fictionality—the 'feigning' he wanted to establish as the prime *differentia* of 'poesy', or literature. So much is shown by his classing of astronomical and other scientific works as georgic. Besides, as Annabel Patterson has shown, even Virgil's pastoral, let alone Mantuanus's, could be a rallying-point against the establishment.[15]

Low also goes wrong in supposing that the movements associated with the Civil War had the effect of mitigating aristocratic contempt for rural labour; as if the revolution's 'underlying causes' were somehow ameliorated by the achievement

---

[11] Part II, Song ii, lines 1–18.
[12] 'A Discourse on Pastoral Poetry', *The Prose Works of Alexander Pope*, vol. I, *The Earlier Works, 1711–1720*, ed. Norman Ault (Oxford, 1936), p. 301.
[13] See John Chalker, *The English Georgic* (London, 1969).   [14] *TGR*, pp. 13–34.
[15] Annabel Patterson, *Pastoral and Ideology: Virgil to Valéry* (Oxford, 1988).

of English georgic. It is not just that this notion disregards royal patronage of agricultural science, or the fact that (as Low admits) the early georgic poets were as often Royalists, like Robert Herrick, as Commonwealth men, like George Wither. It is also an unnecessary explanation; because English georgic was not late at all, or at least, no later than other genres in a country afflicted by a cold northern air that retarded most cultural developments.[16]

English georgic seems late only on an Augustan understanding of the genre, which is to say, a Virgilian understanding. Around 1600, however, a much looser conception of georgic obtained, based as much on Hesiod, whose *Works and Days* were translated by George Chapman as the *Georgics* of 1618. We have got so used now to Virgilian georgic, through Augustan imitations of it, that we find the earlier idea hard to envisage. By the cruellest law of genre, recent forms obliterate earlier forms.

Hesiodic georgic shared many topics with Virgilian, such as labour, the seasons, and landscape description. But it had others of its own, notably hospitality, hunting, and the happy life of retirement. And with these in view it becomes possible to recognize many previously unidentified or supposedly new types of seventeenth-century poems. I have in mind such types as the poem of country life; the poem of happy life (like William Strode's 'Melancholy' and 'Opposite to Melancholy', or Milton's *L'Allegro* and *Il Penseroso*); and particularly the so-called country-house poem. All these are in the georgic mode, if not actually ur-georgics.[17] However, georgic itself changed a good deal during the century. The 1600 domain of assumptions was of Grecian, small-scale domesticity; unpretentious estates; and local aspirations to recover the Golden Age: the 1700 associative domain assumed ambitiously large estates (the economic norm had changed), and ideas of national reform.

The changes in georgic's hierarchic relation to pastoral are well brought out by setting them against the grid of triple style heights. In the sixteenth century, when georgic was excluded as unfictional, lowly pastoral was free to take over responsibility for rustic matters, and so rise in status. In the Elizabethan understanding of pastoral, it was regarded as an allegorical form, high masked as low. During the seventeenth century, however, as classical forms became less medievalized, less overtly ideological, this allegorical dimension vanished. In consequence, georgic was reconfirmed as higher than lowly pastoral. (Whether Virgil's *Eclogues* are 'really' allegorical is a separate issue.) Georgic's reestablished mediocrity, accordant not only with the mean position of its style height but also with the mid-century ideal of retirement, is particularly clear in Cowley's *Sylva* and *Essays*.[18] Finally, with the larger norm for estates, georgic claimed a more

---

[16] *TGR*, pp. 221–95. See Alastair Fowler, 'The Beginnings of English Georgic', in *Renaissance Genres*, ed. Barbara Kiefer Lewalski (Cambridge, Mass., 1986), pp. 105–25.
[17] *Ibid.*, p. 122.   [18] See Radcliffe, 'Sylvan States'.

important national role; and the chivalric hero was replaced by a new civil ideal, the 'gentleman'. In the absence of credible epic values, georgic could fill the gap and become one of the highest genres.

All these changes were necessarily very gradual, coming as they did in response to complex and slowly perceived changes in social conditions. Probably literature in general responds to social change as much through incremental alteration in domains of assumption as by dramatic innovation. Perhaps only our ignorance of intercalary gradations makes genres seem discontinuous. But overall syntheses (and formal revisions of the hierarchy) come slowly; so that genres mediate between external history and literature, filtering out purely ephemeral political 'reality', or volatility, and bringing to bear values of longer validity.

The processes whereby generic hierarchies change are complexly interwoven. Nevertheless, I venture to suggest that in hierarchic inversions such as we have been looking at, a certain broad pattern can be guessed at: namely, that a halfway stage intervenes, precluding any dramatic displacement of one genre by another. This intermediate stage is one of mixture and confusion; reflecting uncertainty of values on the writers' part. Consequently it may not find much theoretical expression. Yet it is precisely through fusion and confusion of genres that the canonic system achieves each new fixity. Thus, before georgic could ascend the hierarchy, it had to undergo a phase of mixture with pastoral. As we have seen, the impurity of English pastoral, gradually established over centuries, facilitated this temporary mixture: georgic was able to enter mixtures, change places, and within the space of less than a century achieve its exalted Augustan status.[19]

[19] Addison already noticed the confusion of georgic and pastoral: see Dryden, V, 145.

Twelfth Night and Epiphany

WHEN THE medieval element in Elizabethan drama is discussed, tropes of survival or degeneracy tend to predominate. Older forms are said to show 'dissolution' or 'decay'. So Bernard Spivack writes of 'naturalistic disintegration' of the homiletic pattern in *Othello*: the devil's hatred of good 'survives like a trunk stripped of its leaves': in Iago the image's 'verbal structure has crumbled'. Such imagery betrays a progressivist model: in actuality, older literary material seldom remains as mere detritus, without being freshly utilized. And certainly in Shakespeare's case, one should allow for the possibility of consciously retrospective art. Like Spenser in *The Faerie Queene*, he was quite capable of reviving medieval kinds for new purposes. Then it is more appropriate to speak of neo-Gothic construction than of dissolution.

Alternatively, older genres might not only 'survive', but enjoy vigorous health. For Shakespeare's world, which is sometimes thought of as uniformly Renaissance, was Renaissance only by innovation: whatever was not innovative remained early Tudor, or medieval, or older still. And much of this inherited world continued to function: not only buildings—like the Bodleian Library at Oxford or the Gothic pigsties that Miège noticed in late-seventeenth-century Lincoln—but books, and customs, and allegorical psychology, and plays for festive occasions. The occasional orientation of drama, which concerns us here, continued viable throughout Shakespeare's career.

Saints of the Season

It is not known just how many of Shakespeare's plays address a specific occasion; but the number keeps on growing. J. M. Nosworthy and Suzanne Westfall have studied their auspices and other circumstances of performance; Chris Hassel, their relation to Church festivals; and Emrys Jones, their inner calendricality (as in the All Souls' allusions in *Richard III*).[1] Such enquiries have had wide-ranging implications. No longer can it be assumed that Renaissance plays are

---

[1] J. M. Nosworthy, *Shakespeare's Occasional Plays: Their Origin and Transmission* (London, 1965); R. Chris Hassel Jr, *Renaissance Drama and the English Church Year* (Lincoln, Neb., 1979); Suzanne R. Westfall, *Patrons and Performance: Early Tudor Household Revels* (Oxford, 1990); E. L. Jones, 'Bosworth Eve', *Essays in Criticism* 25 (1975), pp. 38–54. Several occasions have been suggested also for *A Midsummer Night's Dream*.

self-explanatory, autonomous fictions. That assumption once allowed critics to treat Shakespearean comedies much like modern novels. They expected action to emerge from character naturalistically, with a psychological realism directly accessible to anyone educated by life and by Freud. Suppose, instead, that Shakespeare's comic actions emerge from the associations of Church feasts, and a somewhat different approach is called for.[2]

In *Twelfth Night*, some of the occasionality is obvious enough. C. L. Barber and Leslie Hotson have easily related certain of the play's topics to Elizabethan Twelfth Night customs.[3] There are riddles (Feste's and Maria's); practical jokes against a butt (Malvolio); saturnalian excesses (nocturnal revelry); and formal praise of folly (Feste's catechism of Olivia)—all suggesting an Epiphany occasion.[4] Hotson went further, however, and argued—rather unconvincingly—that *Twelfth Night* was first acted before Don Virgilio Orsino on 6 January (Epiphany) 1601. Opposition to this hypothesis was so violent as to deny the play's occasionality *per se*. 'It seems to me', writes Professor T. W. Craik, 'that for a Twelfth Night play there could be no title more barren than *Twelfth Night*.'[5]

Recent scholarship, however, has confirmed the play's appropriateness to the Epiphany season, although not necessarily to Twelfth Night itself. To this may now be added the evidence of naming. For almost all its characters are named in a way covertly apt to the season. Toby, Titus, Cesario, Curio, Antonio, Feste, Orsino, Olivia, Andrew, Valentine, Fabian, Sebastian, and Maria all have a feature in common; each is named after a saint whose day falls in the festive season or just after. St Tobia's day is 2 January; St Titus' (V.i.61), 4 January; St Cyrus', 8 January; St Caesaria's, 12 January; St Antony Abbot's, 17 January; St Festus', 27 January; St Ursinus', 31 January; St Oliva's, 3 February; St Andrew Corsini's, 4 February; and St Valentine's, 14 February.[6] As for Maria, Candlemas (2 February) is the

---

[2] For a classic discussion of the problems of motivation in Shakespeare, see C. S. Lewis, 'Hamlet; the Prince or the Poem?' in W. Hooper (ed.), *Selected Literary Essays* (Cambridge, 1969).

[3] Cesar Lombardi Barber, *Shakespeare's Festive Comedy: A Study of Dramatic Form and Its Relation to Social Custom* (Princeton, 1959); Leslie Hotson, *The First Night of Twelfth Night* (London, 1954).

[4] One might add, the three gifts of the Magi, alluded to in the play's three gifts: the ring sent by Olivia to Cesario (I.v.305, etc.); the pearl she gives to Sebastian (IV.iii.2); and the purse Antonio gives to Sebastian (III.iii.38). All references to the New Arden edition of *Twelfth Night*, ed. J. M. Lothian and T. W. Craik (London, 1975).

[5] Actually, the title is in line with the subtitle 'What You Will' in this respect: both seem at first to be non-titles. 'What You Will' has an obvious thematic relevance to festive wish-fulfilment; but to educated members of Shakespeare's audience it would certainly also suggest *quodlibet*, an academic term meaning a topic for scholastic disputation, or an interpretation of Scripture. (It probably also had its later genre sense of medley or fantasia, as in nineteenth-century music and still-life painting titles: Cf. Robert Hayman, *Quodlibets, Lately Come over from New Britaniola, Epigrams and Other Small Parcels* (London, 1628).) Shakespeare's title thus covertly announces the play's religious content. See Barbara Everett, 'Or What You Will', *Essays in Criticism* 35 (1985), pp. 294–314; especially p. 304, arguing that 'the "subtitle" is really no subtitle, but a generic, perhaps primary, and certainly important part of the title'.

[6] See Christopher Robert Cheney, *Handbook of Dates for Students of English History* (London, 1970); H. Pomeroy Brewster, *Saints and Festivals of the Christian Church* (1906; rpt. Detroit, 1974). Saints Antony, Andrew, Valentine, Fabian and Sebastian, and Maria were all familiar from common

Feast of the Purification of the Virgin Mary. The familiar Saints Fabian and Sebastian, moreover, have the same feast day, 20 January: a twinning that is profoundly thematic, and that appears again in the plot structure.[7]

To object that the naming may have been prompted by unconscious associations would concede the occasionality in another form. Besides, since the saints in question were not all familiar, or even listed in common calendars, the naming must have been intentional. The names have, of course, other aptnesses— the name of the naming game is polysemousness. But their hagiographic sources lend no little support to religious interpretations of the play such as Barbara Kiefer Lewalski's. Beyond any reasonable doubt, *Twelfth Night* is pervasively an Epiphany play. It calls for a set positively festooned with holly.

Twelfth Night marks the end of a festive season in which there were other occasions alluded to by Shakespeare, notably the *Festum Stultorum* or Feast of Fools, sometimes celebrated on St Stephen's Day (26 December) or New Year's Day, rather than Twelfth Night. But the correlations with Twelfth Night itself are salient: its customary activities provide plot material, and its emotional tone, as the last of festivity, can be sensed in the melancholy atmosphere of transience. Yuletide feasting ended officially on Twelfth Night, although popularly it might continue until Candlemas. Sir Toby's late revelling is thus doubly protracted. It puts off the return to normality supposed to mark the day after Twelfth Night, St Distaff's Day:

> Partly worke and partly play
> Ye must on S. Distaffs day:...

---

calendars. For the less familiar saints, I have consulted Joannes Bollandus and Godefridus Henschenius, *Acta sanctorum*, 58 vols, (Antwerp, 1643–1867), as ed, Joannes Carnandet *et al.*, 69 vols. (Paris, 1863–). Shakespeare could not have known the Bollandists' great work; but he might have used Aloysius Lipomanus, *Sanctorum priscorum patrum vitae*, 8 vols. (Venice and Rome, 1551–60); Lawrence Surius, *De probatis sanctorum historiis* (Cologne, 1570–5); the *Roman Martyrology* of 1584, 1586, etc.; or one of many earlier martyrologies. For St Tobia, one of the martyrs of Sirmium, see *Acta sanctorum* vol. 1, p. 80; for Titus Episcopus, ibid. p. 163; for St Caesaria, ibid. p. 729; for St Cyrus, ibid. p. 531; for St Festus Martyr, ibid. vol. 2, p. 769; for St Ursinus Martyr, ibid. p. 1080. There was also a St C. Caesarius (d. 369), brother of Gregory Theologus, student of mathematics and Quaestor of Bithynia, who remained faithful during Julian's apostasy: see ibid., vol. 3, pp. 496–502. For St Oliveria or Oliva, Virgin, see ibid. p. 361; for St Antonius Martyr, see ibid. p. 490. To gender theorists, Cesario is an exquisite choice of name since it derives from a female saint, yet has a masculine inflection. Shakespeare, however, has a different matter in view. Hagiographic reference is not the only association of 'Orsino' and 'Viola'. Both were flower names: see Pliny, *Hist. Nat.* XXI.xxxviii.64 and xxxix.67, where they appear in proximity.

[7] In a sense Viola-Cesario's saint's day is also twinned, since 25 February is the day not only of another St Caesarius but of St Antonius Martyr. The father of Sebastian and Viola is another Sebastian: see Anne Barton, *The Names of Comedy* (Oxford, 1990), p. 144; Murray J. Levith, *What's in Shakespeare's Names* (London, 1978). Professor Barton's, the best account of Shakespeare's naming, does not discuss seasonal decorums. The choice of Sebastian may have been influenced by the strange contemporary cult of the Portuguese king Sebastian, who was expected to return from the dead, much like Shakespeare's Sebastian. Sebastianism attracted many literary treatments: see *The Works of John Dryden*, ed. Edward Niles *et al.*, (Berkeley, 1976), vol. 15, p. 384; C. R. Boxer, *The Portuguese Seaborne Empire 1415–1825* (London, 1977).

> Give S. Distaffe all the right,
> Then bid Christmas sport good-night.
> And next morrow, every one
> To his own vocation.[8]

Robert Herrick's poem is much in the vein of Shakespeare's play, whose denouement puts so decided an end to Sir Toby's revelling that he reprehends Dick Surgeon as a 'drunken rogue'. And his turning from bachelor pleasures to the quotidian obligations of a workaday world is but one instance of a larger movement. Other characters, too, move from subjective volitions to public responsibilities. Their love, self-love, mourning—their 'What you will'—gives way before deeper purposes. Viola's adopted name may have been chosen as appropriate to this theme: in 1601 St Caesaria's day, 12 January, coincided with Plough Monday, when ceremonies in disguise marked the resumption of work.

Recent scholarship has related several themes of *Twelfth Night* to meanings of the feast it was written for. Most notably, Epiphany celebrates Christ's manifestation, to shepherds and Magi, in shockingly humble circumstances. Barbara Kiefer Lewalski and Marion Bodwell Smith focus on Epiphany's revelation, correlating this with the play's 'clarification' of the dual nature of Cesario-Viola, a type of selfless love. To this, Hassel adds the theme of humbling: Orsino, Olivia, and Malvolio all make humiliating discoveries of love's nature. Hassel also persuasively connects the darkness of Malvolio's prison with the imagery of the First Lesson for Epiphany, Isaiah 60: 'Arise, be enlightened...'.[9] To these correlations others may now be added.

The Ancient Theology

Consider, first, Feste's ministry of enlightenment. When Malvolio complains of incarceration in a dark house, Sir Topas replies, 'Madman, thou errest. I say there is no darkness but ignorance, in which thou art more puzzled than the Egyptians in their fog' (IV.ii.43–5). Sir Topas refers to the plague of darkness in Exodus, generally interpreted as a type of sin, or benighted ignorance of the gospel. Doubtless the palpable darkness of Exodus 10:21 comes to mind because of its association with Epiphany. For such imagery was ubiquitous in sermons for this season. Lancelot Andrewes's Sermon for Christmas Day 1612, for example, calls

---

[8] Robert Herrick, 'Saint Distaffs Day, or the Morrow after Twelfth Day', lines 1–2, 11–14: *Complete Poetry*, ed. J. Max Patrick (New York, 1963), p. 416. On St Distaff's Day, spinning was resumed; cf. the reference to spinning at *Twelfth Night* I.iii.108.
[9] See Hassel pp. 77–85; Barbara Kiefer Lewalski, 'Thematic Patterns in *Twelfth Night*', *Shakespeare Studies* 1 (1965), pp. 168–81, especially pp. 176–7; Marion Bodwell Smith, *Dualities in Shakespeare* (Toronto, 1966), especially p. 112.

Christ 'the Brightness': there is 'no clear light of knowledge, nothing but mists and darkness, but by Him'.[10]

When Malvolio insists that his prison is 'as dark as ignorance', a catechism follows that seems complete nonsense. This passes in performance: the fun of the scene, after all, depends precisely on the despised clown's arbitrary power to drag Malvolio behind whatever train of thought he pleases. With another dramatist, indeed, this might be enough to account for the *non sequiturs*. But in Shakespeare's case, while scouting Coleridge's assumption of his infallibility, one must surely explore further. Why does Sir Topas harp on Pythagoras? Why this particular preoccupation?—'remain thou still in darkness. Thou shalt hold th'opinion of Pythagoras ere I will allow of thy wits' (IV.ii.58–60).

Even this detail belongs to the occasion. While the major Epiphany was Christ's appearance to all mankind as the child Jesus, in the so-called minor Epiphany he appeared specifically to the gentiles. And the journey of the Magi to the Nativity was interpreted as a spiritual journey through the *preparatio evangelii* of whatever was best in pagan wisdom. That might be a great deal: Lancelot Andrewes, in his 1620 Christmas Day Sermon, goes so far as to assert, 'There is no star or beam of it; there is no truth at all in human learning or philosophy, that thwarteth any truth in divinity.'[11] According to the doctrine of Ancient Theology, wise pagans learnt the preambles of faith from Moses' writings.[12] In another Christmas sermon, Andrewes discusses how much of prophecy paganism may have had access to, instancing Virgil's Sixth Eclogue.[13]

As Shakespeare (if not Feste) would know, syncretists speculated on an oral tradition through Orpheus, Pythagoras, and Plato. Pico della Mirandola writes: 'That divine philosophy of Pythagoras, which they called Magic, belonged to a great extent to the Mosaic tradition; since Pythagoras had managed to reach the Jews and their doctrines in Egypt, and knowledge of many of their sacred mysteries.'[14] According to this line of thought, Pythagoras, Orpheus, and Plato were the philosophers principally associated with the Magi, and so with Epiphany. The Platonic and Pythagorean content of *Twelfth Night* has recently been explored by Anthony Gash, although not in relation to Epiphany.[15] As Gash persuasively shows, Plato's fable of the cave is enacted in Malvolio's imprisonment (p. 647), while Pythagorean philosophy underlies marriages and groupings in the recognition scene (pp. 655–6). Perhaps something remains to be said, however, on the Pythagorean content.

---

[10] Lancelot Andrewes, *Seventeen Sermons on the Nativity* (London, 1890), p. 106; cf. the 1616 Christmas Sermon, ibid. p. 186.

[11] *Seventeen Sermons* p. 242.

[12] See Daniel Pickering Walker, *The Ancient Theology: Studies in Christian Platonism from the Fifteenth to the Eighteenth Century* (London, 1972); Index, *s.v.* 'Moses'.

[13] *Seventeen Sermons* pp. 252ff. [14] See Walker p. 50.

[15] Anthony Gash, 'Shakespeare's Comedies of Shadow and Substance: Word and Image in *Henry IV* and *Twelfth Night*', *Word and Image* 4 (1988), pp. 626–62.

Pythagoras and the Elements

The focus on Pythagoras doubtless has several aspects.[16] There may be a ludicrous association of Twelfth Night Bean Kings and bean pies with the Pythagorean diet of beans. And surely another idea is to satirize the vogue for neo-Pythagoreanism at Court, as Sir John Harington does about this time in his epigram 'Of One that Seeks to be Stellified Being no Pythagorean'.[17] Pythagoras' most familiar doctrine was that of the *tetraktys* and its related tetradic categories, from which evolved schemes of four elements, four humours, and the like. Accordingly, *Twelfth Night* has a recurrent joke, as critics have remarked, satirizing the overuse of the term 'element' by Jonson and others. Most explicit is Feste's gibe: 'Who you are and what you would are out of my welkin. I might say "element", but the word is overworn.' (Naturally Malvolio is insensitive to such a nuance: he uses the overworn word quite obliviously: 'You are idle, shallow things, I am not of your element.'[18]) The wit even of the revellers has a Pythagorean tinge:

SIR TOBY:...Does not our life consist of the four elements?
SIR ANDREW: Faith, so they say, but I think it rather consists of eating and drinking.

(II.iii.9–12)

Sir Andrew may be aware (Shakespeare surely was) that in Pythagorean metaphysics the grosser elements feed on the finer.[19]

The doctrine of the tetrad seems also to underlie the structure of *Twelfth Night* in a deeper way. Shakespeare might satirize fashionable Pythagoreanism, but he

---

[16] For an interesting exploration of Pythagorean musical theory in relation to *Twelfth Night*, see John Hollander, '*Musica Mundana* and *Twelfth Night*' in Northrop Frye (ed.), *Sound and Poetry*, English Institute Essays (New York, 1957), pp. 58–9.

[17] *Epigrams* i. 68; *The Epigrams of Sir John Harington*, ed. Norman Egbert McClure (rev. edn: Oxford, 1930), no. 69, p. 174. First printed in 1615 and 1618, Harington's epigrams were in many instances written a good deal earlier.

[18] There may be a topical reference here, to the peer reported by Sir Robert Naunton, who famously said (and it did him no good), 'That he was none of the *Reptilia*, intimating that he could not creep on the ground, and that the Court was not his element': *Fragmenta regalia*, 1641; *Harleian Miscellany*, 12 vols. (1811), vol. 5, pp. 137, 140.

[19] See Pythagoras' account of the transmutation of elements in Ovid, *Metam.* XV. Cf. *Timon* IV. iii. 445; Milton, *Paradise Lost* V.415ff.: 'of elements/The grosser feeds the purer, earth the sea/Earth and the sea feed air, the air those fires/Ethereal...'. See E. M. W. Tillyard, *The Elizabethan World Picture* (London, 1943), p. 64; also John Hollander, '*Twelfth Night* and the Morality of Indulgence' in Walter N. King (ed.), *Twentieth Century Interpretations of 'Twelfth Night'* (Englewood Cliffs, 1968), p. 84 : 'the essence of our lives lies in a movement from hunger to satiety that we share with all of nature.' Hotson's solution to Maria's riddle of M.A.O.I. (Mare, Aer, Orbis, Ignis) would fit in neatly here. But unfortunately it was not a recognizable acronym. For other solutions, none satisfactory, see *Connotations* 1 (1991). The riddle is probably in fact an anagram for 'Omnia [vanitas est]'. The abbreviation OMIA can be paralleled in a Bodleian copy of Pierre de La Primaudaye's *The French Academy* (Shelfmark: Antiq. e. E. 67), where a fly-leaf inscription in an early hand reads 'OAI Vanitas'. See Alastair Fowler, 'Maria's Riddle', in *Connotations*.

took its profounder doctrines of substance and of cosmic unity very seriously indeed. In one of the most influential passages in any of the *auctores*, Macrobius interprets Pythagoras' tetrad, in the light of the *Timaeus*, as the basis of stability in the cosmos. With two elements, Macrobius says, its bonds would have lacked tenacity, but with four they are unbreakable. For the two extremes are held together by two interlocking mean terms: 'Earth is dry and cold, and water cold and moist; but although these two elements are opposed, the dry to the wet, they have a common bond in their coldness.'[20] Macrobius allegorized the elemental system, finding patterns of Necessity, Harmony, and Obedience. And allegorical conceptions of the elements continued into the seventeenth century: for example, Lancelot Andrewes's analogy of the four elements and the four Daughters of God, in another Nativity sermon.[21] In *Twelfth Night*, however, the tetrad seems less abstractly realized.

Shakespeare may have found a model for this in *The Faerie Queene*, Book IV, where Spenser groups characters in elemental fours embodying moral types.[22] Not dissimilarly, Orsino, Viola, Sebastian, and Olivia form a human tetrad connected by emotional bonds that are at first chaotically tangled ('time, thou must untangle this': II.11.39) but later harmonious. In their conflicting affinities of love, friendship, and kinship, they offer a good analogy of the four elements. Like these, they are variously attracted, repelled, and eventually held in harmonious tension, by the bonding of their qualities. Orsino, at first, embodies sexual appetite or affinity; whereas at an opposite extreme Olivia, held by a strong familial bond with the dead, renounces sexual affinity altogether. Harmony is arrived at through Cesario and Sebastian, twin mediating elements who combine likeness of appearance with difference of gender.

By virtue of this double nature, Viola–Sebastian bring about transferences that in the end link all four in interlocking relations. Orsino says then of his marriage:

> A solemn combination shall be made,
> Of our dear souls. Meantime, sweet *sister*
> We will not part from hence.   (V.i.382–4; italics mine)

Affectionate bonding of Orsino and Olivia has become possible, thanks to Cesario. She is the principal mediator or mean, composing all affinities. She attracts Olivia's love and Orsino's friendship; yet, when her true nature and name

---

[20] Macrobius, *Commentary on the Dream of Scipio*, I.vi.23; trans. and ed. William Harris Stahl (New York, 1952), p. 104.
[21] Christmas 1616: *Seventeen Sermons* p. 190; *Sermons*, ed. G. M. Story (Oxford, 1967), p. 72: 'Truth as the earth, which is not moved at any time...Peace as a water-streame, the quills whereof make glad the citie of God. Mercie, we breath and live by, no lesse than we doe by aire: and Righteousnesse, she *ventura est judicare saeculum per ignem*, in that element.'
[22] See Alastair Fowler, *Spenser and the Numbers of Time* (London, 1964), pp. 24–33.

come out, she engages different, previously latent, desires. Then Orsino's friendly love transposes to married love, and the misplaced attachment of Olivia (sister-in-law twice over) changes to sisterly feeling. So completely transformed are their relations that Olivia can say to Orsino: 'My lord, so please you, these things further thought on,/To think me as well a sister, as a wife.' (V.i.315–16).

Such abstract formulations may seem dryly schematic. But Renaissance comedy, even Shakespeare's, was still close to the Moralities—too allegorical for a modern interpreter to assume post-Cartesian, continuously unified characterization. Learn to expect discontinuous, allegorical representation, however, and many difficulties resolve themselves that have arisen from inappropriate expectation of modern fictive modes. Only by the standards of Enlightenment and Victorian realism does Orsino transfer his love to Viola with puzzling abruptness, or Sebastian seem strangely prompt in marrying Olivia (an implausibility that troubled Dr Johnson).

Similarly, *Twelfth Night* has little naturalistic development of character. Even Orsino remains a self-absorbed melancholic lover, with few signs of alteration. Cesario anxiously questions Valentine about Orsino's constancy, and Feste compares him to the variegated opal (perhaps implying lunar immaturity). But one cannot say that Orsino is first inconstant and later constant. His constancy continues to the end untried: he has not *served*. Fortunately, the mysterious love revealed in Cesario does not demand works of constancy, but gives itself freely. Of such selfless love, *Twelfth Night* offers a symbolic exposition.

The main plot nevertheless sets out stages in Orsino's love. At first, he talks wonderfully about it, but is content to woo by proxy, after the correct, indirect manner of noble courtship. Gervinus' shibboleth about Orsino's being 'in love with love' is misquoted: the subtler German actually wrote that Orsino seems 'almost more in love with love than with his mistress'.[23] Even so, to call him sentimental would introduce a post-Goethean irrelevance; Orsino must, after all, seem a fit spouse for Viola. And in fact his feelings are discreditable only to an ordinary human degree. The love he knows at first is immature, narcissistic, intellectualized: love *in potentia*, love at a safe distance. But with Cesario he learns a love more firmly based on familiarity. The generalizing habit of the Renaissance would ensure that these stances were interpreted both as contrasting styles of courtship, and as phases of a single courtship.[24]

Similarly with Olivia's exclusive attachment to her dead brother, which gives place first to an ambiguous desire for Cesario and then to married love for Sebastian. Here again, love for a spouse is prepared for by an amphibolous relation with a disguised likeness. The two loves, Orsino's and Olivia's, may be

---

[23] Georg Gottfried Gervinus, *Shakespeare Commentaries*, trans. Fanny Elizabeth Bunnett (rev. edn., London, 1892), p. 430.

[24] See Barber pp. 279–80 on styles of courtship in *Twelfth Night*.

regarded as illustrating complementary aspects of courtship. In Olivia's story, family attachment is transformed to love; in Orsino's, romantic desire.

Viola, too, illustrates increasingly committed love. Initially, she wishes to join Olivia in renouncing the world, but is easily put off when she hears that Olivia 'will admit no kind of suit'. Taking an epicene rôle instead, she joins Orsino's household. With him she is tongue-tied, like an uncertain adolescent—and like Orsino himself (who, if not tongue-tied, has also been put off by Olivia). Soon, however, sacrificing her own happiness, Cesario continues Orsino's courtship of Olivia with a new directness. This certainly amounts to a challenging commitment: a duel with a 'rival', Andrew, occasions apprehension as real as it is comic. And this in turn brings out a more forceful version of herself—her twin Sebastian—to win the duel and Olivia. Literally, Olivia's husband has done nothing to win her. But allegorically, as Cesario, he has run the gamut of patient service and known a love that made him nearly pine to death.[25] One may say that Cesario's love symbolizes Sebastian's as it does Orsino's—or rather, the love of the supercharacter they are generated from.

Emblems of Love

In Shakespeare's unfolding of true love, narrative motifs are not the only resource. Others range from implicit emblem to rhetorical explication. What could be more explicit than the play's opening *propositio* and invocation of love?

> O spirit of love, how quick and fresh art thou,
> That notwithstanding thy capacity
> Receiveth as the sea, nought enters there,
> Of what validity and pitch soe'er,
> But falls into abatement and low price,
> Even in a minute!
>
> (I.i.9–14)

This magnificent speech, however exaggerated its eloquence, is hardly motivated as the expression of an immature youth 'in love with love'. Here, at the very outset, Orsino recognizes love's demanding exclusivity. He may be only on the shore of its ocean, but already he imagines its engulfing totality and alarming capacity to annihilate other values.

---

[25] Cf. Hollander, '*Twelfth Night* and the morality of Indulgence' p. 85: 'Viola and Sebastian are really the same'.

At the implicit extreme are love emblems, mostly associated with Viola. She first enters as an Anadyomene emerging from a sea of passion, whose love is fixed, beyond it, on the image of her reborn twin Sebastian riding the sea by harmonious magic, 'like Arion on the dolphin's back' (I.ii.15).[26] Twins may have suggested the astronomical Gemini, Castor and Pollux, interpreted by Renaissance mythographers in terms of shared immortality. Twins of different sexes, however, would also be associated with another representation of the Gemini: the androgyne. For C. L. Barber, the play gives a sense of how much the sexes have in common ('everyone who is fully alive has qualities of both'). An amused Sebastian observes to Olivia, 'You are betroth'd both to a maid and man' (V.i.261); Barber comments, 'The countess marries the man in this composite, and the count marries the maid.'[27] In all this Stephen Greenblatt, anachronistically concerned to 'unsettle the secure relation between the normal and the aberrant' in differentiation of the genders and sexes, finds instability of gender. But Shakespeare seems to have been more interested in the philosophy of love: as Frank Romany remarks, *Twelfth Night* is conspicuously unconcerned with sex, by comparison with its sources.[28] It is more relevant that Viola and Sebastian together compose the androgyne emblem, an archetype often pictured as male–female twins.[29] Cesario's banter hints at her own symbolism when she demands privacy for her wooing: 'What I am, and what I would, are as secret as maidenhead: to your ears, divinity; to any other's, profanation' (I.v.218–20). In human terms, her nature is a secret 'divinity' (religious mystery), because *henosis* (the one-flesh relation) is reserved for private initiation. Symbolically, however, Cesario-Sebastian's androgyne identity embodies the larger significance of the *mysterium coniunctionis*. Signifying, as it does, the meeting of revealed and non-revealed worlds, this is the aptest possible symbol for an Epiphany play. Epiphany is precisely the feast of mysteries revealed. Philosophically, moreover, the androgyne was associated with Ancient Theology. As Barbara Everett and Anthony Gash have explained, androgyny would have evoked Plato's *Symposium* and neo-Pythagorean ideas of cosmic unity.[30]

Cesario speaks of herself as an emblem in a different way when she tells Orsino the story of her father's daughter, who 'loved a man,/As it might be perhaps, were I a woman,/I should your lordship' (II.iv.108–10). Barber thinks that this

---

[26] For Arion on the dolphin's back, see Lawrence Otto Goedde, *Tempest and Shipwreck in Dutch and Flemish Art: Convention, Rhetoric, and Interpretation* (University Park, Penn., 1989), fig. 33; and, for the erotic symbolism of the sea, cf. Jan Krul, cit. ibid. p. 135.

[27] Barber p. 247.

[28] Stephen Greenblatt, *Shakespearean Negotiations* (Berkeley, 1988), p. 72; Frank Romany, 'Shakespeare and the New Historicism', *Essays in Criticism* 39 (1989), p. 277.

[29] Most familiarly in medieval and Renaissance calendar representations of the Gemini as erotic twins.

[30] Everett p. 314, referring to Mircea Eliade, *The Two and the One*, trans. J. M. Cohen (New York, 1965), p. 107 *et passim*; Gash p. 656.

allegorical woman, 'this supremely feminine damsel, who "sat like patience on a monument" is not Viola', but rather a 'polarity within Viola, realized all the more fully because the other, active side...does not pine in thought at all'.[31] Cesario's *fictio*, however, does not merely pine. The sister-self 'sat like Patience...Smiling at grief' (II.iv.115-16). Like Cesario herself, the *fictio* emblematizes a 'love indeed' that continues to serve cheerfully, silently, in the face of neglect or loss. The inset tale confesses Viola's own love; but it is also the description of an emblem of faithful love itself, the love that resolves the impasse of the play. From Orsino's failure to apply Cesario's anecdote, it may thus be inferred that at this stage he is unready to grasp love's commitment.

Saturn and Melancholy

If *Twelfth Night* presents a philosophy of love, and traces the moderating of various erotic passions, there is nevertheless a focus on one excess in particular: love melancholy. Many have commented on the melancholy atmosphere of the main plot—a mood already established in the opening scene of Orsino's attempt to purge himself from languorous melancholy by surfeit. Saturn's influence is explicitly diagnosed: Feste prays, 'Now the melancholy god protect thee' (II.iv.73). But Orsino is not the only sufferer. Cesario's *alter ego* pines 'in thought...with a green and yellow melancholy' (II.iv.113-14), while Olivia is confidently expected to dislike Malvolio's grins, 'being addicted to a melancholy as she is' (II.v.202-3).[32] As for Malvolio, his comprehensively Saturnian disposition will be obvious to anyone who recalls the *Tetrabiblos* and Ptolemy's description of Saturn's children as selfish, petty, churlish, and tyrannic. This pervasive influence of the melancholy god reflects the then current psychology. Timothy Bright and others were attempting to rethink the passions in terms of various mixtures of the melancholic complexion: much as, in the 1930s, they were to be rethought in Freudian terms.[33] The play's ubiquitous melancholy can also be seen, however, as yet another seasonal decorum. For it was none other than Saturnus who presided over the Epiphany season as lord of Capricorn and Aquarius. And from Saturn, too, enlightenment rose, according to alchemic thought.[34]

---

[31] Barber p. 274. Patience as a monumental sculpture is inconclusively discussed in William S. Heckscher, 'Shakespeare and the Visual Arts', *Research Opportunities in Renaissance Drama* 13-14 (1970-1), pp. 5-71, especially pp. 35-6.

[32] Cf. II.v.25-6, where Olivia is quoted as having said, 'should she fancy, it should be one of my complexion'—that is, Malvolio's Saturnian complexion.

[33] Timothy Bright, *A Treatise of Melancholie* (1586; rpt. Amsterdam, 1969). See J. B. Bamborough, *The Little World of Man* (London, 1952), p. 102, etc.; and, for the Galenic background, Raymond Klibansky *et al.*, *Saturn and Melancholy* (London, 1964), pp. 64, 100.

[34] See C. G. Jung, *Collected Works*, vol. 13: *Alchemic Studies*, trans. R. F. C. Hull (Princeton, 1967), p. 126.

The god of melancholy further possessed the dark power of imprisonment: 'Myne is the prison in the derke cote', says Chaucer's Saturn. (This astrological commonplace, going back ultimately to Ptolemy's *Tetrabiblos*, would be familiar to many in Shakespeare's audience.) In *Twelfth Night*, Saturn exercises his penal capability with striking frequency. Viola's sea captain is imprisoned 'upon some action' of Malvolio's. And Sebastian's captain Antonio is arrested after a farcical scene in which, taking Cesario for Sebastian, he thinks his trust repaid with lies about the purse he lent. The repetition is emphasized by plot symmetry: each twin trusts or is trusted by a sea captain; each captain is arrested; each must be freed by the magnate of like gender with the twin concerned. (Viola's captain is freed by Olivia, Sebastian's by Orsino.) More prominently still, the melancholy god imprisons Malvolio on account of his 'madness', in a 'derke cote' indeed. And the prisoner is only released because Olivia remembers him in connection with Viola's clothes. Viola's captain 'is now in durance, at Malvolio's suit':

> OLIVIA: He shall enlarge him: fetch Malvolio hither.
> And yet alas! now I remember me,
> They say, poor gentleman, he's much distract.   (V.i.276–8)

Apparently Viola's 'maid's clothes'—her sexual identity and chance of fulfilment—depend upon Malvolio's mental condition. When he is freed but exits in dudgeon, Orsino anxiously sends Fabian after him: 'He hath not told us of the captain yet' (V.i.380).

All this imprisoning is appropriate enough to Saturn's season; but what, if anything, does it signify? Perhaps it is to be referred to a widely distributed erotic motif of the Middle Ages and Renaissance: namely, the Prison of Love. Among many instances, perhaps the most familiar are Diego de San Pedro's popular *Carcel de Amor* (1492), and the lovers' prisons in Boccaccio's *Il Teseide* and Chaucer's 'The Knight's Tale'. In *Twelfth Night*, Antonio's imprisonment is possibly to be thought of as a limitation or channeling—a cathexis, as it were—of same-sex love. The imprisonment of Viola's captain, however, is linked with that of Malvolio, the prisoner of self-love.

Here, our elusive assumptions about the undivided self are likely to impede interpretation. Modern audiences take for granted that Olivia, Viola, and Malvolio, who are distinct characters, must represent completely separate people. Elizabethan audiences, however, were readier to imagine that the three were *fictions*—perhaps moral entities, perhaps aspects of a single character (as, indeed, their orthographically related names might suggest).[35] In particular, Elizabethans often thought of a noble household as representing the character of

---

[35] On this point, see Barton p. 122; Carl Dennis, 'The Vision of *Twelfth Night*', *Tennessee Studies in Literature* 18 (1973), p. 67.

its lord or lady.³⁶ Both in real life and in fiction, servants were easily regarded as components or variant samples of their household's collective personality.³⁷ From this viewpoint, Malvolio may not only exhibit and represent self-love, but also present an implication about Olivia's tendency to narcissistic self-sufficiency ('She will admit no kind of suit').³⁸ Olivia's outcry 'Oh, you are sick of self-love' amounts, allegorically, to self-realization. Like Malvolio, she is forbidding to all who seek entry. Both are in darkness; both need, and both receive, Feste's catechism. And just as Olivia is freed from self-love by Sebastian, so is Malvolio freed by Fabian, Sebastian's twin saint (V.i.314).

All this has a bearing on the question whether *Twelfth Night* ends ominously. Does it project cosmic peace and harmonious closure, or foreshadow the closure of the theatres? For a character with a subsequent life of revenge, there is no room in the *Twelfth Night* Shakespeare wrote, the last word of which is reconciliation: 'entreat him to a peace' (V.i.379). For peace, after all, is the mystery disclosed at Epiphany. In the context of Epiphany, Malvolio is likely to represent a more extensive depravity, more in need of enlightenment, than mere disapproval of the theatre. Divine comedy, however, holds out hope even for self-love and self-importance.

Viewed as a seasonal mélange, the themes of *Twelfth Night* fall into place and gain coherence. And in the context of medieval Mystery traditions, its philosophical themes and hints of resurrection aptly belong. What is new and impressively Shakespearean is the relentlessness of the sceptical and psychological explorations, and the hilarity of the comedy that makes them tolerable, even invisible.

---

[36] See Kate Mertes, *The English Noble Household, 1250 to 1600: Good Governance and Politic Rule* (Oxford, 1988), p. 177 *et passim*.

[37] A good example of such thinking is Thomas Randolph's 'On the Inestimable Content he Injoyes in the Muses, To Those of His Friends that Dehort Him from Poetry', where the offices of a household are internalized as agencies of the poet's mind. See *The Poems of Thomas Randolph*, ed. G. Thom Drury (London, 1929), p. 23.

[38] Cf. iv.254, where Olivia is 'too proud'.

'Cut without hands':
Herbert's Christian altar

So far as the seventeenth century is concerned, numerical composition is often thought of as a medieval inheritance: a survival, or perhaps a hangover that the aspirins of the Enlightenment were soon to dispel. That is very far from true. Numerology seems in fact to have been more widely practised than ever in the Renaissance—certainly more assiduously elaborated. In the seventeenth century, particularly, a new excitement burned for everything mathematical. Mathematics seemed to hold the key to nature's mysteries. But science was not the only new excitement with a bearing on literary form. Writers were also greatly excited by the new medium of print. It now began—in Britain only just began—to displace script as the preferred medium for serious writing. These two excitements combined to affect the forms of poetry profoundly. It was not just that reading print had become easier than reading script, so that more pondering beyond surface meanings was in order. (For early blackletter could actually be less legible than a good scribal italic.) Nor was it merely that texts, and the positions of individual passages within them, had become relatively stable. (For in the cheirographic tradition, a standard modulus of thirty lines per page often allowed fairly easy line-counting and finding.) It was rather that print had a property of self-resembling lastingness that for want of a better word may be called monumentality. Poetry was now often described, significantly, as 'framed', 'raised', 'built'—'he knew / Himself to sing, and build the lofty rhyme'. Ut architectura poesis. For this and other reasons, the visual appearance of writing was more considered. The written (and printed) word was often visually emblematic, in one way or another, of the meaning it communicated.

The early effects of print on literature were in some ways quite surprising. One might have expected writing to become steadily more like our own—or, at least, more like Victorian writing—to be, as it were, 'forward-looking'. Specifically, one might have expected the written word, as it donned the decent uniform of print, to become less noticeable. Surely it would seem more transparent, so that readers would read more directly for the content, as we tend to do. But not a bit of it. By the seventeenth century, typographers were using a thick impasto of italics and full capitals, to say nothing of hands, rules, fleurons, and pilcrows, in such a way as to make the printed page a thoroughly opaque medium. The poem on the page now looked less like a modern poem than early Tudor scribal scribbles had ever done. Professor Donald McKenzie suggests that the early ostentatiousness of 'setting forth' was an attempt to limit the difference of print from script.[1] But that does not explain the increased opacity in the seventeenth century. Rather should one think in terms of aesthetic preferences.

The repercussions of print on memory art seem to have been equally contrary to expectation. The assumption has been that as the printed word came in, the need to memorize declined, and the arts of memory went out. But, as Frances Yates, Mary Carruthers, and others have shown, memory art thrived into the late seventeenth century and beyond. In so far as texts were used primarily as memory prompts, print may positively have assisted memorizing, since it facilitated rapid skimming to supply forgotten details. For memory art worked chiefly with res rather than verba. When Richard Baxter speaks, as he often does, of his congregations 'repeating' sermons, he hardly means learning them by heart, word for word.[2] On the other hand, Milton had reasons for using memory art to keep the words of *Paradise Lost* in mind, in their proper locations.

I am not thinking, here, only of Milton's blindness. There is also the reason that *Paradise Lost* was to be organized numerologically. Notoriously, when Messiah ascends the throne of his cosmic chariot to begin the triumphal alchemic work of creation, he does so at the numerical centre of the poem's 10,550 lines (1667 edition): 'He ... Ascended, at his right hand Victory / Sat, eagle-winged' (VI. 760–3). (Recently, a confirming intertextuality has been found, with Michael Maier's seminal alchemic treatise *Atalanta Fugiens* (1618), where Jupiter sends eagles east and west to 'establish Earth's centre'—medium explorare locum.)[3] Numerology was closely bound up with memory art; since, at the simplest level, verse was memorized in relation to a numerical grid.[4] Symbolic associations of a line-number, moreover, could often supply a useful additional link to fix an elusive passage.[5] It is not very surprising, therefore, to find that in *Paradise Lost* the content of a verse sometimes agrees quite strikingly with the symbolic value of its line number.

A glance at the opening of the *principium*, book one, lines 1–5, may make clear what I mean:

> Of man's first disobedience, and the fruit
> Of that forbidden tree, whose mortal taste

---

[1] Donald F. McKenzie, 'Speech–Manuscript–Print', in *New Directions in Textual Studies*, edited by D. Oliphant and R. Bradford (Austin, 1990), p. 101.

[2] See *OED*: Repeat vb 2 'to recount': e.g. Shakespeare, II Henry IV, IV.i.201–4: 'therefore will hee...keepe no Tell-tale to his Memorie, / That may repeat and Historic his losse, / To new remembrance'; and 2b 'to hear lessons': 'to repeit with the studentis' (1579).

[3] Epig. xlvi. I am indebted for this reference to Paul Cheshire.

[4] See Mary Carruthers, *The Book of Memory: A Study of Memory in Medieval Culture* (Cambridge, 1990). Index: *Numbers, Numerology*.

[5] *Ibid.*

Brought death into the world, and all our woe,
With loss of Eden, till one greater man
Restore us, and regain the blissful seat...

One, the monad, was a form of the Pythagorean sacred tetraktys, the fountain of all creation, and by a universally understood syncretism identified with God and Christ.[6] In the 'fruit' of the forbidden tree, Milton refers to the evil consequences of disobedience, further described in the lines that immediately follow. But he also refers to the felix fruit of that culpa, in Christ's incarnation. Before even the consequences are spelt out, Christ is preveniently present in the poem, metaphorically, to redeem them. The first line also contains the word first itself; and Milton places other occurrences of 'first' with similar appropriateness, for the word occurs again in line 8 ('That shepherd who first taught the chosen seed') and line 27 ('Say first, for heaven hides nothing from thy view'); 8 being 2^3, the first cube of a female number, and 27 being 3^3, the first male cube.[7] In the same way, 'one' occurs in line 4 because 4 is the first square number. In line 2, 'mortal taste' introduces the earliest suggestion of death, which in number symbolism was regarded as a manifestation of the evil dyad, interrupting the unity of life.[8] Line 4 aptly has 'Eden' and 'one greater man', for the four rivers of paradise (Genesis 2:10) were the basis of a strong association of paradise with this number.[9] The tetrad was also the number of the human body with its four humours and complexions.[10] 'One' may pointedly recur in this line because in Pythagorean and Christian number symbolism tetrad and monad were both forms of the tetraktys, besides being identified with Christ, the 'greater man', vinculum of matter and spirit, and the 'unknown god'.[11] Finally, the 'blissful seat' or throne occurs aptly in line 5, because five occupied the central place of sovereignty among the nine digits, and hence symbolized triumph or sovereignty.

The opening lines thus suggest, through their number-symbolic associations, many of the themes of the poem at large. Of course, not every image and word is apt in this way—that would be insufferable dirigisme. But other striking examples come to mind, such as the traditionally nine 'heavens' in line 9, and the 'sea-beast'

---

[6] Pietro Bongo, *Numerorum Mysteria* (Bergamo, 1591) pp. 13–61 (p. 18). For convenience I give references to this authoritative work, but most of the symbolisms can be found in the Venetian Francesco Giorgio's *Harmonia Totius Mundi* (Paris, 1545), in biblical commentaries, or in popular writers such as Thomas Lodge and John Taylor the Water Poet. Among a great many scholarly and critical works on the application of number symbolism to poetical composition, there is room only to mention two of general application—Vincent Foster Hopper, *Medieval Number Symbolism* (New York, 1938: rpt Norwood, Pa., 1977); Ernst Robert Curtius, *European Literature and the Latin Middle Ages*, translated by Willard Trask (London, 1948)—and two primers—I. Christopher Butler, *Number Symbolism* (London, 1970); John MacQueen, *Numerology: Theory and Outline History of a Literary Mode* (Edinburgh, 1985).
[7] See Bongo, pp. 322, 355.
[8] See *ibid.*, p. 49: 'regnum mortis, in odio, quae divisio...vita praesens est unio: mors, divisio.'
[9] See *ibid.*, 244–5.   [10] *Ibid.*, p. 193.   [11] *Ibid.*, p. 235.

Leviathan in line 200.[12] The point may seem sufficiently obvious. It is not exactly an obvious one, either, though. For not every such instance can be taken as proving Milton's conscious intention. Some may wish to suppose that we have stumbled, here, on the mechanics—or merely the scaffolding—of composition. But in my own view these are not real alternatives. Conscious or not at the time of publication, the numerical associations had been in Milton's mind and would be in the minds of some of his fit readers. They are meanings of what he has written. Besides, against the 'unconscious' theory may be set the many instances, studied by Gunnar Qvarnström and others, of verse-paragraphs in the poem with symbolic line-totals.

Fewer problems of intentionality arise with figure- or pattern-poems. These too were a new, or renewed, phenomenon. Certainly there are many striking examples from the Carolingian period and earlier, such as the astronomical manuscripts of Julius Hyginus, in which painted heads or limbs emerge out of bodies shaped from sprinkled letters; or the pious grids of Hraban Maur, who deploys every cheirographic resource of coloured ink and outline drawing, to signalize multiple acrostics and complex hypograms.[13] But figure-poems were actually far more popular in the late Renaissance than in the Middle Ages.[14] The rediscovered Greek Anthology, which in this as in other ways profoundly influenced the development of Renaissance lyric throughout Europe, offered, in its many technopaegnia or art-games the principal models for figure-poetry.[15] A neglected subsidiary factor, here, is the simultaneous development of print as a medium of communication. The new possibilities are visibly played with in the forms given to colophon and bastard titles. There is a striking transition from the simple colophons of early incunabula, through centred inverted cones (as in the bastard title to the Venice 1502 Statius) to more elaborate forms like the lozenge or diamond in Guyart's *Compendium* (Bordeaux, 1524), and the drinking-glass in J. Schoeffer's edition of Trithemius (Mainz, 1515). Italy is in the forefront of this particular avant-garde: there was already a drinking-glass in a Paduan edition of Petrarch in 1472.[16]

---

[12] *Ibid.*, p. 595: the number is often taken 'in malam partem'.

[13] See Massin, *Letter and Image*, translated by Caroline Hillier and Vivienne Menkes (London, 1970), with many illustrations.

[14] For figure-poetry treated as a Renaissance phenomenon, see Margaret Church, 'The First English Pattern Poems', *PMLA*, 61 (1946), 636–50; Bart Westerweel, *Patterns and Patterning: a Study of Four Poems by George Hebert* (Amsterdam, 1983); Ian D. McFarlane, 'The Renaissance Epitaph'. Presidential address of the MHRA. *MLR*, 81 (1986), 1–11.

[15] See Westerweel, *Patterns and Patterning*, Index: *Greek Anthology*.

[16] These and other examples are illustrated in Theodore Low de Vinne, *A Treatise on Title-Pages*...(New York, 1902); cf. Alfred W. Pollard, *An Essay on Colophons with Specimens and Translations* (Chicago, 1905; rpt New York: Franklin n.d.), pp. 103–5 (inverted cone from Gasparo Visconti, *Rithmi* (Milan, 1493) and verse in the form of a rhombus displayed, or hourglass, from *journal Spirituel* (Paris, 1505)).

It is no exaggeration to say that the emblem vogue and the figure-poetry vogue had a common origin in printers' devices, among which almost all their components are to be found, decades before Andrea Alciatio's *Emblemata* (1531)—although not, to be sure, assembled in quite the same constellation.[17] The new medium was regarded, in fact, as a form of graphic art: the art of print was not unlike the art of prints. About the same time, for reasons that also had to do with the Greek Anthology, the emblem was establishing itself as a dominant form, again throughout Europe. *Ut pictura poesis*: it was almost inevitable that the emblem should colonize poetry, and that poets should take up the device of printed shapes. The extent of the figure-poetry vogue is nonetheless remarkable. There were editions of the Greek Anthology pattern-poems by Crispinus, Henricus Stephanus, J. C. Scaliger, and Fortunio Liceti;[18] they reappeared in arts of poetry; and virtually every early seventeenth-century poet attempted one or two. Poets seem to have taken a special pleasure in the visual aesthetics of print. As John Kerrigan has remarked of Carew, the seventeenth-century poet 'seems to welcome print—its definite, almost emblematic disposition, but also leaden-type fixedness'.[19] George Herbert seems to feel this delight in printedness when he adds letters in 'Iesu', rearranges them in 'Ana-{MARY/ARMY}-gram', or prunes them one by one in 'Paradise', from GROW through ROW to OW. The erstwhile University Orator was naturally au fait with the vogue for emblems and figure-poems. But I should not like to give the impression he was merely in the grip of a fashionable craze. As the work of George Wither and Francis Quarles shows, emblems could also be conceived as sincere, naive, even demotic. And for Herbert himself, as we shall see, the figure-poem was anything but a toy—or, at least, anything but a trivial toy.

In the revived Hellenistic tradition, several set shapes reliably recur, such as wings, the pyramid, Simias' egg, and the column. Neo-Latin arts of poetry from J. C. Scaliger's and Richard Willes's to Dionysius Ronsfertus', and arts in the vernacular like George Puttenham's *The Arte of English Poesie* and King James's *Essayes of a Prentise* give more or less detailed specifications for constructing some of the shapes (not usually all).[20] In a chapter (II. xii) on 'Ocular Representation', Puttenham includes the lozenge, rhombus, triangle, square, egg, sphere or roundel, pilaster or column, and pyramid, together with the same forms 'reversed' and 'displayed'. It may seem an otiose business for poets to have reproduced set forms like these; but of course all depended on the relation of

---

[17] For a definition of the primer's device, and many illustrations, see Hugh William Davies, *Devices of the Early Printers 1457-1560: Their History and Development*...(London, 1935).
[18] See Westerweel, *Patterns and Patterning*, p. 67.   [19] 'Thomas Carew', *PBA*, 74 (1989), 346.
[20] J. C. Scaliger, *Poetices Libri Septem* (Lyons, 1561), facsimile ed. August Buck (Stuttgart, 1964); Dionysius Ronsfertus, Notes to Fr. Mario Bettini's *Rubenus* (Parma, 1614); Richard Willes, *Poetum Liber* (London, 1573); *The Arte of English Poesie*, edited by Gladys Doidge Willcock and Alice Walker (Cambridge, 1936), p. 97; James VI and I, *The Essayes of a Prentise in the Divine Art of Poesie* (1584).

content to form, on details, and on modulations of the tradition. Thus, the altar poems of Dosiadas (*c*.150 BC) and Vestinus (*c*.100 AD) in the Greek Anthology have the shape of pagan altars, complete with sacrificial slabs on top.²¹ Absence of this slab in the altar poems of most Christian poets may be taken to mean that Christ's crucifixion has done away with sacrifice; a point neglected by Westerweel when he speaks of Herbert's slabless altar as the Mosaic altar of Exodus 20:25.

Without the sacrificial slab, however, the akar shape becomes indistinguishable from a column:

5 Templates for shaped poems: Dosiadas (*left*) and Davison (*right*).

Such columns (sometimes called altars, as by Francis Davison and Herbert)²² are very common, in sacred and secular poetry alike. Undoubtedly the form implies an architectural analogy to poetry. This is particularly clear where several columns are used liminally, as a kind of porch (as in Joshua Sylvester's 1605 Du Bartas), or as division markers (as by Robert Herrick, to mark the division between *Hesperides* and *Noble Numbers*)—a well-known convention that may be compared to the metae or turning-posts of the ancient Roman circus, or the limiting pillars of Hercules in Charles V's PLUS ULTRA impresa. The substitution of column for altar—indeed, their virtual identification—may be puzzling at first. But it is illuminated by John Onions in *Bearers of Meaning*, where he explains how columns (sometimes used as altars in the early Christian church) came to be seen as

---

[21] For illustrations see Westerweel, *Patterns and Patterning*, p. 69.
[22] Richard Willes, 'Ara'; Francis Davison, 'An Altare and Sacrifice to Disdaine, for freeing him from Love'.

symbolizing Christ and his apostles.[23] Particularly when forming a sequence of eleven or twelve (as in the Sainte Chapelle), columns were taken to allude to the apostles. The same probably applies to Sylvester's twelve column-poems, which Westerweel (p. 79) calls altars of praise, but which might be described more precisely as the columns of virtue on which crowns or wreaths were hung in triumph. Herbert's altar-column, assimilating all these traditions, performs a liminal function, coming at the beginning of The Temple proper, immediately after 'The Church-porch' and 'Superliminare':[24]

The Altar

A broken ALTAR, Lord, thy servant reares,
Made of a heart, and cemented with teares:
  Whose parts are as thy hand did frame;
  No workmans tool hath touch'd the same.
     A HEART alone
     Is such a stone,
     As nothing but
     Thy pow'r doth cut.
     Wherefore each part
     Of my hard heart
     Meets In this frame,
     To praise thy name.
  That if I chance to hold my peace,
  These stones to praise thee may not cease.
O let thy blessed SACRIFICE BE mine,
And sanctifie this ALTAR to be thine.

Herbert's poem has rightly been discussed in relation to emblems in Daniel Cramer's *Emblemata Sacra* and Benedict van Haeften's *Schola Cordis*, and others by their English imitators Christopher Harvey and Patrick Carey. In all these the contrite heart is laid for sacrifice on an altar;[25] Herbert, however, unites heart and altar into a single image.[26] The stony heart has been broken by attrition, it is implied; contrite, its parts can be framed by God into an altar for the offering and

---

[23] John Onions, *Bearers of Meaning: The Classical Orders in Antiquity, the Middle Ages, and the Renaissance* (Princeton, 1988), pp. 70, 75, 79, 88, etc.

[24] On the position in the volume, see Westerweel, *Patterns and Patterning*, pp. 58–9, 66, 138; on Herbert's use of Sylvester, ibid., pp. 79–82.

[25] See Westerweel, *Patterns and Patterning*, p. 89 with illustrations; Rosalie L. Colie, *The Resources of Kind: Genre-Theory in the Renaissance*, edited by Barbara Kiefer Lewalski (Berkeley, 1973), pp. 58ff. See also Hans Sebald Beham's two emblems, of a flaming heart upon a pagan and on a squared altar, illustrated in Albert F. Butsch, *Handbook of Renaissance Ornament...*, edited by Alfred Werner (New York, 1969), p. 154.

[26] See Westerweel, *Patterns and Patterning*, p. 111.

sacrifice. It might be wrong to assume that this change is made simply in the interest of compression, or unity, or economy; for such differences often had a theological value. Joseph Summers comments:

> Herbert's conceptions that the broken and purged heart is the proper basis for the sacrifice *of* praise and that even stones may participate in and continue that praise were firmly biblical. In his psalm of repentance (Ps. 51) David had stated that the true sacrifices of God are 'a broken and a contrite heart'; Christ had promised that 'the stones' would cry out to testify to Him (Luke 19:40); and Paul had stated that 'Ye also, as lively stones, are built up a spiritual house...to offer up spiritual sacrifices.' (I Peter 2:5)[27]

But Herbert, a Protestant, would be very careful with the term 'sacrifice', and may have wished to convey the inherence of the believer in the once-only sacrifice of Christ. Perhaps for that reason he makes the heart itself the altar, for an inner sacrifice that is Christ's alone, although appropriated by the believer's true repentance.

If this point has been approached often enough in recent criticism, there has not been any recognition at all of the brilliant numerological content of Herbert's poem, which applies its metaphors so fitly as to make them movingly immediate. To the broad notion of the column in such as Puttenham (In architecture he is considered 'with two accessarie parts, a pedestall or base, and a chapter or head, the body is the shaft')[28] Herbert adds a more detailed prosodic proportioning that eloquently accompanies the sense. Verbal resemblances suggest that Herbert may have taken a hint, in this, from the 'Ara' of Publius Optatianus Porfirius, a celebration of his own poetic art. Porfirius minutely describes his slabbed altar as shaped by significant variations of metre: 'I force each edge to be drawn in, line by line, by tiny steps, in lines turning in...regulated everywhere by the measure.'[29] Possibly Herbert may have noticed an 'Ara' by the Jesuit Richard Willes, with a body of 8 lines.[30] However that may be, Herbert's poem is numerologically articulated to a far greater extent.

Metrically, first, it comprises: 2 pentameters | 2 tetrameters | 8 dimeters | 2 tetrameters | 2 pentameters. That is,

$$
\begin{array}{c}
2 \times 5 \\
2 \times 4 \\
8 \times 2 \\
2 \times 4 \\
2 \times 5
\end{array}
$$

---

[27] Joseph H. Summers, *George Herbert: His Religion and Art* (Cambridge, Mass., 1968), p. 142. Cf. the imagery of Henry Vaughan, 'Regeneration', lines 55–6, also drawing in I Peter 2:5.
[28] *The Art of English Poesie*, p. 97.
[29] Translated by Westerweel, *Patterns and Patterning*, p. 71.
[30] *Poematum Liber* (1573), No. 4. The altar is slabbed: presumably Willes keeps the pagan form out of decorum, since his poem refers to the slaying of Troilus at the altar of Apollo.

—altogether 16 lines, or 4^2. This is in consonance with the human referent; for, as Puttenham says, 'so is the square for his inconcussable steadinesse likened to the earth, which perchaunce might be the reason that the Prince of Philosophers in his first booke of the Ethics, termeth a constant minded man, even egal [equal] and direct on all sides, and not easily overthrowne by every litle adversitie, hominem quadratum, a square man.'[31] (One might contrast Davison's 20-line altar, with its probable allusion to the twenty of woe.)[32] More specifically, Herbert's 16 refers to the double octave of passions that in an integrated soul sounds as the music of a harmonious diapason. Then its 'parts are as thy hand did frame' (line 3).[33] 'This frame' (line 11) of the heart, moreover, belongs to an architectural allegoria ('mixed' or discontinuous), in which 'stone', 'parts', and 'cemented' besides 'frame' itself, figure as vehicle items, all being terms of art in building. And the general sense of all this is visibly confirmed by the contrast of the 8 very short lines of the column shaft and the 4 longer lines of capital and base. For the 4 | 8 | 4 pattern repeats the 1:2 ratio of the diapason, a ratio held to signify harmonious control of passion.[34] The shaft or body has 8 lines, as in Willes and Samuel Speed, for the same reason as baptismal fonts commonly had 8 sides: because 8 was the number of regeneration.[35]

Not only has Herbert ordered the metrical parts of his poem eloquently, but also the very distribution of its words. For, in the column shaft, the numbers of words per distich are: 7 | 7 | 7 | 8. Thus, the stoniness and hardness of the heart is the burden of distichs with 7 words each. But when its parts 'Meet in this frame / To praise thy name', this seven of mutability is raised to the eight of regeneration.

Herbert's interest in the aesthetics of print shows also in his use of capitalized words. In 'The Altar' four words are printed in full capitals: ALTAR, HEART, SACRIFICE, and ALTAR, in that order. They number four, clearly, because four is the sacred tetraktys. As we saw, this was the number of virtuous man, and identified by Christian authors with Christ as *vinculum*.[36] The sequence of Herbert's four capitalized words forms a chiasmic pattern—itself often symbolic of reconciliation—that closely links the two middle terms 'HEART' and 'SACRIFICE'. Most eloquent of all, though least obvious, is the decorum of the capitalized words' placement in their respective lines. 'ALTAR' comes in third place, and

---

[31] Puttenham, *The Arte of English Poesie*, p. 100. Cf. Bongo, *Numerorum Mysteria*, pp. 413–14: the number 16 is 'quadratus quadrati quaternary, quattuor in lateribus conrinens unitates'.

[32] See Bongo, *Numerorum Mysteria*, pp. 424–6 with many classical examples.

[33] See Alastair Fowler and Douglas Brooks (now Brooks-Davies), 'The Structure of Dryden's Song for St Cecilia's Day, 1687' in *Silent Poetry*, edited by Alastair Fowler (Routledge, 1971), p. 196; cf. Spenser's 'goodly frame of Temperaunce', *The Faerie Queene*, 11.12.1.

[34] Pico della Mirandola, *Opera Omnia*, 2 vols. (Basle, 1573), 1, 79.

[35] See Hopper, *Medieval Number Symbolism*; MacQueen, *Numerology: Theory and Outline History*, p. 80; Bongo, *Numerorum Mysteria*.

[36] For documentation see Alastair Fowler, *Spenser and the Numbers of Time* (London, 1964), pp. 275–8.

again in fourth; 'SACRIFICE' comes in fifth place; but the stony 'HEART' in second place. The praise this silently offers, through the disposition of the poem's physical members—'these stones'—is celebration of Christ's triumph over the hard heart. For 'a HEART alone' is in the second position of the evil dyad; but when the broken heart becomes a broken altar, it moves to fourth place, the position of the tetraktys. The third, fourth, and fifth places of the 'good' capitalized words indicate the Pythagorean 3-4-5 triangle of moral proportion. (Herbert elsewhere uses this as the main structural motif of another poem of regeneration and sanctification, 'Aaron'.)[37] Finally, in the first line of 'The Altar', the word standing fourth of seven, in the sovereign central place, is 'Lord'. Christ thus rules the apostolic column as its head or capital. And, in a visible imitatio Christi, the regenerate 'HEART' occupies an answering central position in the base. It, too, occupies the fourth place, that of the tetraktys, and so is en khristo.

If this is more or less on the right lines, it creates something of a critical problem. It is a problem of alterity, or distance. Herbert's consonant form is not quite that of a modernist process-poem; still less can it be called an 'organic' form, like that sometimes attributed to Romantic poems. Again, how serious is one to think of a figure-poem as being? Some have regarded Herbert's patterns as pious trifling. But in view of the above, many will surely now recognize that precipitate dismissal as having proceeded from ignorance—certainly that was true in my own case—of how much art was devoted to framing such devices. Perhaps we can now begin to glimpse how comprehensively Herbert strove to offer to God his poetic gift. The visual pattern was for him an opportunity for further and further restatements, ever more intimately close to God and his reader.[38] 'The Altar' is in this way not far removed from Gabriel Rollenhagen's altar with a laurel wreath of praise, in *Nucleus Emblematum* (1611).[39] Herbert wanted his whole art to be an offering.

In 'The Altar', Herbert represents his art through the metaphor of architecture. And naturally he conceives architecture according to its Renaissance understanding—as an art not of masonry but of geometry and number, 'all material stuff being excluded'.[40] It is this concept that allows Herbert's architectural pattern-poem to convey with touching aptness his sense of the altar prophesied by Daniel: 'a stone...cut without hands'.[41] The poem is all heart—contrite, unstony. There is to be nothing merely artificial about it: 'no workman's tool hath touched the same' (line 4).

---

[37] For the symbolism of the Pythagorean triangle, see ibid., Index; Zoogonic Triangle.

[38] The logical sequel was realization in print. But Herbert's pattern-poems were never printed in his lifetime.

[39] Emblem II. 1. Cf. *The Poems of Patrick Carey*, ed. Sister Veronica Delany (Oxford, 1978), p. 103, citing also Camerarius. Rollingen's emblem is modified by Wither (illustrated in Westerweel, *Patterns and Patterning*, Fig. 19) who has a burning heart on the altar.

[40] John Dee, Preface to *The Elements of Geometrie*..., translated H. Billingsley (1570).

[41] Daniel 2:34 and 45; cf Mark 14:58.

In describing 'The Altar' objectively, I have left aside a question as to how Herbert intends its pronouns. Whose heart is hard? Clearly 'The Altar' is not a confessional poem: no poem so full of art could be that. Nevertheless I do not think it merely dramatizes the thought-processes of some hard-hearted, recently repentant, new believer. In fact, it seems closer to figuring an act of repentance of just such a sinner as Herbert himself, renewing his vocation and confessing the incompleteness of previous repentances. To all except antinomian Calvinists, a believer's heart was always relatively or potentially hard. Thus, the poem's shaping may be thought of as shadowing Herbert's shaping of his own nature, as he puts on Christ. That is to say, it figures his sanctification, a constructive process commonly formulated by the architectural metaphor of 'edification'. Herbert was so far from being antinomian, indeed, that for him edification would certainly have involved frequent attempts to be virtuously four-square. At the same time, the poem also concerns processes of craftmanship; so that it may reasonably be seen as figuring Herbert's renewal of his art's dedication. Perhaps one may even see a new dedication, to the degree that he may have looked towards a printed version of his poems, and with that a new phase of his art. From this point of view, it is striking that in the Williams Manuscript version of 'The Altar' the four words full-capitalized in the print are not yet distinguished as such. Preparation for print appears to have occasioned a reconsideration of the poem's numerological structure.

Shakespeare's Renaissance Realism

I

AFTER DECADES OF EXPERIMENTAL THEATRE, no one now supposes that the realism of fifty years ago is the only realistic mode.[1] Several realisms are recognized, each with its own conventions; although realism can sometimes be thoughtlessly contrasted with 'convention'. But mind-sets change slowly, so that the realism of William Archer is still taken as normative for Elizabethan drama, much as single-point perspective is, for Renaissance art. Undeniable 'exceptions'—like Holbein's *The Ambassadors* with its amorphic skull, or the *Unton Memorial* with its differently scaled spatio-temporal insets—are commonly treated as oddities. Yet the possibility of multiple perspective and temporal viewpoints continued, well into the seventeenth century.[2] And Elizabethan drama was similarly free to move among spatial discontinuities on the 'imagined wing' of its 'swift scene'.[3] Time and place could be left unspecified, or have mainly symbolic import.[4] Indeed, scenery came to the British stage only during the 1630s;[5] and, even in Italy, architectural stages might exhibit incompatible perspective recessions.[6] Despite this, a continuous, single-point perspective—what I shall call 'spectator realism' —tends to be read back into drama innocent of its assumptions. Traditional and postmodern critics alike assume that by Shakespeare's time discontinuous, allegorical representation was more or less replaced by modern realism, with its post-Cartesian continuum of cause–effect sequences, inviting speculative extrapolation to supply

---

Read at the Academy 26 April 1995, © The British Academy 1996.

[1] There is a large literature on mimesis and on realism in its various senses; see, e,g., Auerbach (1953); Stern (1973); Lyons and Nichols (1982), especially Beaujour; Nuttall (1983) 56–7, etc. Ermarth (1983) valuably traces the development of realism away from the spatial and temporal discontinuities of medieval art; relating this to the introduction of single-point perspective (albeit with some confusion between viewpoints and vanishing points). Hagen (1986) is useful on different perspective systems. And, for those who speak the language of poststructuralism, there is an interesting theory of meta-representational discourse in Weimann (1985).

[2] For Unton, see Llewellyn (1991) Figure 28; for Rubens, Vergara (1982) 48. Many Elizabethan portraits contain additional scenes or *parergies*, often removed in place or time: see, e.g., Strong (1987). Study of Renaissance perspective needs to begin with White (1987); Kemp (1990); Elkins (1994). See also Aipers (1983), e.g. 64–9; Bunim (1970).

[3] *Henry V* III Chorus.   [4] Dessen (1984); Kernodle (1944).

[5] In a production of William Strode's *The Floating Island* (1638). Self-referring dialogue in J. Shirley, *The Triumph of Peace* (1633) 295–315, seems to imply the novelty of scenery; but this may need to be qualified for private theatres and great house venues, if the speculations in Mowl (1993) 150 are right.

[6] e.g. G. B. Albanese's drawing of the proscenium of Palladio's Teatro Olympico, Vicenza: Puppi (1989) 281.

missing details.[7] But there is a distinct Renaissance realism, an intermediate mode between medieval and modern. Locally, this may imitate reality naturalistically; but in its larger coherence it adopts multiple-perspective viewpoints that are often related morally or psychologically rather than causally.

Shakespeare's comedies even combine allegory with illusionistic representation. Instead of forcing them into a teleologically naturalistic strait-jacket, we should accept their own terms of realism. It is futile, for example, to demand a unified plot. Despite classicizing theorists, Renaissance drama at its best often implies a romance poetic of interlaced, separate viewpoints and multiple plots.[8] Some of the more honest cinquecento theorists even doubted whether a single plot could hold an audience.[9] Yet nowadays directors mostly rationalize Shakespeare's interwoven structures to a single sequence, or at least to a 'main plot' and 'sub-plot'. Elizabethan comedy was structured by scenes, not acts, however: by ideas, as much as plots.[10] Suspend belief in plot unity, and Shakespeare's comedies turn out to have plot multiplicity.

Twelfth Night has something like eight stories.[11] Yet we conspire to discuss a main plot, with Orsino, Viola, and Olivia as 'protagonists'—the solecistic plural gives all away—and a subplot, with Sir Toby, Feste, and the rest. Malvolio's confinement in 'hideous darkness' (IV. ii. 30), when Sir Topas catechizes him in Pythagorean doctrine, is treated as peripheral 'fooling'. Yet the play's occasion was Epiphany, and the Lesson for Epiphany concerned the palpable Egyptian darkness of sin. The Magi seeking the light were interpreted as the *praeparatio evangelii* of pagan wisdom, specifically including Pythagoras's.[12] Malvolio's instruction in ancient theology is thus anything but peripheral.

The Merchant of Venice, too, has many independent (although allegorically connected) plot strands. Among these is Shylock's plot of revenge on Antonio, which has proved hard to motivate without resorting to the soft focus of Heinrich Heine and Graham Midgeley, or (like Lancelot Gobbo and Barbara Lewalski[13]) identifying him with the devil. As recipient of the ring of Leah (allegorized by St Paul himself as the Law[14]), Shylock symbolizes legalistic belief in the Old Covenant, or its Christian equivalent, justification by works. He may be related to

---

[7] Auerbach (1953) and Ermarth (1983) contrast the two mimetic methods.
[8] See, e.g., Pettet (1949). On *entrelacement*, see Vinaver (1971); Bloomfield (1986). Illustration of *Orlando Furioso* is an obvious instance of the interaction of polyphonic romance and compressed-narrative, multi-perspective picturing; see Falaschi (1975).
[9] Also, whether the 'other perfection' of romance was not preferable. See, e.g., Bernardo Tasso; Weinberg (1961) 1010; cf. Camillo Pellegrino, and especially Gioseppe Malatesta: ibid. 1020, 1061.
[10] Forgotten until recently. See Jewkes (1958); Jones (1971).
[11] e.g. Orsino's, Cesario's, Andrew's, and Malvolio's suits to Olivia; Viola's love for Orsino; the intrigue of Maria's riddle; Antonio's love and imprisonment; Cesario's and Andrew's duel. Draper (1950); Hollander (1961).
[12] Gash (1988); Lewalski (1965); Fowler (1995) 120–6. [13] Lewalski (1962) 339.
[14] Gal. 4:22, a key passage in this context.

the intense seventeenth-century interest in the relation of Law and Gospel.[15] Yet of course no allegorical interpretation can adequately address the play's complex treatment of the ethics of lending, venture capital, and contracts. Its profusion of stories, vignettes, cases enacted, and cases alluded to constitutes a realism as multifarious as that of, say, Dos Passos' *USA*. It may include, for example, the unanticipated moral circumstance that in standing surety for Bassanio, Antonio was culpable.[16] Again, Shylock perhaps calls Antonio a 'fawning publican' because he is like those Biblical publicans (Matthew 5:47) who salute only their own friends.[17] Shylock is usually discussed in relation to Antonio's sacrifice. But Shylock has a sacrifice, and a plot, of his own. He could be seen as a sharp businessman enforcing a bond that, allowing for metaphor, is only a little more rigorous than some Elizabethans would have approved.[18] His revenge gets as far as it does because the authorities worry about Venice's credit, if the bond is not honoured. They can find no way of saving Antonio, since in effect Shylock's law is theirs too.[19] He comes close to being a revenge hero. He might have exposed the horrors of the new business world of unregulated contracts[20] more heroically, however, if he had kept his 'oath in heaven' (IV. i. 228). What if he had taken, as we say, his pound of flesh? In a good production, much will hang in the balance as Shylock hesitates—'Why doth the Jew pause?' But in the event he breaks his oath. Unable to cut Antonio's flesh without spilling blood and so incurring the death penalty, he shrinks from performance of his covenant, which is impossible without self-sacrifice.[21] W. H. Auden, in what A. D. Nuttall calls 'one of the most brilliant critical remarks of the century', gets it exactly wrong when he writes that Shylock 'did, in fact, hazard all for the sake of destroying the enemy he hated'.[22] Shylock is not prepared to sacrifice his life, as Antonio is.

Michael Ferber is right, then, to reject Terry Eagleton's idea of a Shylock with more respect for the law than Portia, and impelled to expose Venetian law as a

---

[15] As witness, e.g., Rembrandt's Hebraism, and Milton's: see, e.g., Schwartz (1993). Portia's important speech on 'the quality of mercy' is based on Isa. 55, then commonly interpreted as an invitation to the New Covenant.

[16] Nelson (1969) 153 cites Luther's condemnation of suretyship as un-Christian. The economic history is complex. Luther at first condemned usury, but later altered his position. Shakespeare's choice of *mise en scène* is pertinent: Venetian fraternities made free lending a condition of membership, only introducing usury (at low interest) in the sixteenth century. See Bossy (1985) 61, 77 ff; Ferber (1990) 461, 459–62; Braudel (1982) 438.

[17] Lewalski (1962) 330–1.

[18] On possible English referents for Shylock, see Ferber (1990), esp. 444–5.

[19] *Pace* Eagleton (1986) 37, Venice to preserve its credit is quite prepared to sacrifice Antonio.

[20] Ferber (1990) 457–8.

[21] Leviticus 17:10–16 requires separation of flesh and blood in sacrifice: Ferber (1990) 463.

[22] Auden (1963) 235; Nuttall (1983) 127: 'W. H. Auden in one of the most brilliant critical remarks of the century observed that this requirement [to give and hazard all] is met by two people in the play, neither of whom is Bassanio.' In fact only Antonio hazards his life.

sham.²³ But it will not do to rule out Eagleton's view on the ground that it does not fit with the overall meaning of the play's unified plot—its 'sequence of virtual actions unfolding in time before a real audience'.²⁴ Elizabethans were used to multiple plots with multiple meanings, and would have been quite prepared to consider Shylock's perspective. It may well have had for them, however, a more religious point: namely, the impossibility of satisfying the law, and the need for grace. 'Is this the law?' exclaims Shylock. When the Duke forces Shylock to give away all he has (in literal enactment of Luke 18:22), he makes the Jew a fuller practitioner of the New Covenant than the Venetian Christians themselves—a characteristically Shakespearean outcome, barbed and thought-provoking.

In such ways, Shakespearean comedy is a mosaic of parts, realistic or romantic, which may have tenuous motivational or causal connection at a narrative level. The overall coherence lies in a pattern of ideas, rather than in naturalistic realism.

II

Perhaps true of the comedies, it may be argued; but some of the major tragedies are more naturalistic. In *Macbeth*, or *Othello*, all plots are tributaries of the main stream; 'causes are all contained';²⁵ and the protagonist's motivation is continuous and detailed. Already in the cinquecento, theorists focused on tragedy their calls for unified mimesis. Even in England, continuity was obligatory by the end of the seventeenth century, just as artists (in Shaftesbury's view) were 'debarred the taking advantage from any other action than what is immediately present'.²⁶ From chronological continuity, it is a short journey to novelistic motivation—which more distinctly originates in the tragic art of Richardson than in the comic art of Fielding. The route is a familiar one: from Romantic subjectifying of *Hamlet* (in 1713 William Guthrie thought Hamlet spoke the language 'of the human heart'²⁷), to A. C. Bradley's separation of character from plot, to Freud and Ernest Jones. Hamlet's delays must have psychological causes, discoverable through sufficiently minute analysis.²⁸ This is far from ridiculous. Hamlet displays simulated or actual symptoms of melancholy, or depression, as identified by Renaissance authorities. His vituperation, his histrionism, his seeing of ghosts: all these were melancholy symptoms.²⁹ He displays enough symptoms, indeed, to suggest 'anatomy', or

---

²³ Ferber (1990) 461. On Marxist interpretations by Nerlich, Eagleton, Greenblatt, and others, see ibid. 457 ff.
²⁴ Ferber (1990) 462.
²⁵ Kastan (1982) 26.
²⁶ Cooper (1713): reprinted Holt (1958) 2. 246.
²⁷ e.g. Wiggins (1994) 209.
²⁸ ibid. 213.
²⁹ Colie (1974) 211. For ghosts as a melancholic symptom, see R. Burton, *Anatomy of Melancholy* I. ii. 1. ii, cit. Dodsworth (1985) 50; Aubrey (1898) ii. 266; (1972) 460.

epitome, rather than case study: some of his complexity comes from Shakespeare's amalgamating distinct melancholic types (or else from Hamlet's indiscriminate drawing on his reading of psychology).[30] And it is true that motivation abounds in *Hamlet*. That is not quite the same, though, as continuous motivation throughout the play. The Renaissance theatre had no continuity girl. Psychological motivation was less relentlessly expected, when actions could be moral or spiritual.

Romantic focus on expressive language was succeeded by two centuries of criticism devoted to construing psychological motives, sometimes for moral actions that had none. Well may Howard Felperin say, 'we half-perceive and half-create Falstaff'.[31] For we invent streams of consciousness like our own—or like those in novels. So Felperin, Graham Bradshaw, and others have done a service by showing that Shakespeare constructs characters on archaic armatures, or as types, and afterwards plasters them with complications and deviations—as if Hamlet were not so much like a real-life revenger as unlike the revenger of the ur-*Hamlet*.[32] Nevertheless A. D. Nuttall's view, or Arthur Kirsch's, seems preferable: that Hamlet is drawn from life. Only, to appreciate Shakespeare's realism, one needs perpetually to adjust to his assumptive world (to use the psychologists' convenient term). Modern assumptions are so strong as to be easily confused with nature herself. And when that happens, any departure from the uniformity of 'nature' (like the double time-scheme in *Othello*) is so disconcerting that it calls all in doubt.[33]

Yet such anomalies are the rule, not the exception. *Hamlet*, too, has multiple time-schemes, as one can find by asking, with Barbara Everett, how young the young prince is. Hamlet changes, without corresponding lapse of fictive time, from the undergraduate age (somewhere between sixteen and twenty-three) to the politically dangerous near-maturity of thirty. (The gravedigger entered his trade 'that very day that young Hamlet was born...thirty years'.)[34] Hamlet's age is not ambiguous; rather does he age during his sea voyage in a quantum leap— 'jumping o'er times'[35] or stages of life. The representation comprises two 'takes', from distinct chronological viewpoints, which are juxtaposed without any attempt to reconcile them within a single temporal frame. (One might compare the compressed narrative of many Renaissance pictures.) We are given two perspectives of Hamlet, or two Hamlets, one young and another mature. In the second perspective, the Ghost—already silenced by the oaths of Act I—has

---

[30] As Colie (1974) 210 suggests.
[31] Felperin (1977) 66.   [32] See Felperin (1977) *passim*; Empson (1986) 86, etc.
[33] On this so-called double time-scheme, see Ridley (1958) lxvii–lxx.
[34] V. i. 143, 157. Throughout, *Hamlet* references are to the text in Jenkins (1982). Questions of textual revision are largely passed over, since they do not alter the fact that multiple perspectives were allowed to remain in late versions of the play. See Everett (1989) 19–20. For documentation, see Jenkins's Long Note to V. i. 139–57. Jones (1971) 80 ff proposes a two-part structure, corresponding to the two temporal phases.
[35] Shakespeare, *Henry V*, Prol. 29.

disappeared altogether as a public, debatable phenomenon. Deutero-Hamlet may be said to have introjected the Ghost, abandoning scepticism and suspicion.[36] He is now hardened to honourable revenge, unlike the hesitant, perplexed young Hamlet.[37] Such multiple perspectives must surely figure in a critical account, even if they usually pass unnoticed in the theatre.

It seems appropriate to broach the subject of mimesis on this occasion, since Shakespearean tragedy early achieved great triumphs of realism. In *Hamlet*, as early critics observed, we seem to see nature herself.[38] The speeches, movingly natural, appear to voice a human consciousness directly. And Hamlet's censorious advice to the players—surely it is a manifesto of naturalism, the basis of Shakespeare's own art?—except that that would put it under the head of art rather than nature. 'Hold, as 'twere the mirror up to nature': surely the actors are to make themselves virtual images of life? But the Elizabethans had no large mirrors like ours; and Hamlet tells the actors to hold the mirror, not appear in it.[39] He means, in short, a moral mirror, in which audiences may see themselves—a mirror 'To show Virtue her feature, Scorn her own image'. This verse, by the way, invites a *distinctio*.[40] Virtue and Scorn are now rightly regarded as opposites; but the aristocratic Hamlet (though not Shakespeare) may well mean them as synonyms. Virtue may be *virtus*, valour or the inward aspect of honour; Scorn may be *sdegno*, noble disdain for everything base. Hamlet clearly conceives honour as requiring disdain. He scorns his servants ('I am most dreadfully attended': II. ii. 369), he scorns the courtier Osric ("Tis a chuff [churl]': V. ii. 88–9); he scorns Polonius; he scorns Rosencrantz and Guildenstern ('baser natures': V. ii. 60); he scorns the players; and he scorns Ophelia, Gertrude, and women generally. He even scorns those who write legibly (another 'baseness': V. ii. 34).[41]

If the speeches in *Hamlet* are natural, the soliloquies are positive touchstones of the natural, direct expressions of Hamlet s thoughts. Of the fourth soliloquy ('To be or not to be': III. i. 56–88) Harry Levin writes, 'we are permitted to share the stream of [Hamlet's] consciousness.'[42] Yet, marvellously eloquent as the speech

---

[36] Cf. Alexander (1971) 50.

[37] See Dodsworth (1985) 236, 252, 264 against the notion that the deutero-Hamlet is regenerate or superior.

[38] Although there would soon be more methodically uniform examples in Beaumont and Fletcher; cf. Felperin (1977) 60. On eighteenth-century appreciation of the natural in Shakespeare, see Nuttall (1983) 99–100.

[39] Frye (1984) 5. On the implications of the mirror, see Grabes (1982) 102–3. Felperin (1977) 45–6 transfers the demand for 'lifelike illusion' to the passage following ('the very age and body of the time his form and pressure'), which however will not bear that sense.

[40] On this strategic figure, see Skinner (1994).

[41] *Scorn* can be taken as 'objects of scorn': Jenkins (1982). For disdain as a basis for moral action, cf. Bruno's *Degli Eroici Furori* (1570), cit. Alexander (1971) 65, and see Fowler (1964) 108, 110, 112–13. On Hamlet's standing on rank, dispensing with degree only when it suits, see Dodsworth (1985) 105–6, 154, *et passim*. For a good guide on the honour code, see Dodsworth (1985), esp. ch. 1, with refs.; also Empson (1986) 118 ff; Quint (1992*b*).

[42] Levin (1959) 68.

is, it lacks immediate motivation. The audience last saw Hamlet eagerly planning to put on *The Murder of Gonzago*, the mousetrap catch Claudius's soul; they have no reason to expect thoughts of suicide.[43] Among attempts to supply motives, Levin, working on old Freudian assumptions, diagnoses a 'death-wish'; Philip Edwards finds a pessimistic sense of the impossibility of reform; Harold Jenkins, a vision of total depravity, Kay Stanton, improbably, a 'performance' by Hamlet (to divert the eavesdroppers' attention from his *Gonzago* plan).[44] Others cut the Gordian knot by moving the soliloquy elsewhere.[45] It is not felt to belong to the same cause–effect sequence with the scene before and after.[46]

Many feel it as direct address (a more common form of dramatic discourse before proscenium arches framed off the fictive world[47]): a *parados* speech in the dramatist's own person: an archaic convention: an example of what Levin Schücking called 'primitive devices'.[48] For it is a general meditation, only broadly appropriate to the immediate circumstances. 'The insolence of office' is hardly a scorn Hamlet has to bear; far from suffering 'pangs of disprised love', he is about to inflict them on Ophelia; and not all the 'thousand natural shocks/ That flesh is heir to' have shocked *him*. The perspective is as general as that of the Gravedigger's cogitation (which similarly extends to a whole community of sinners—lords, lawyers, tanners, ladies, jesters). It is as Everyman, elsewhere, that Hamlet admits to being an arrant knave (although he is complacent in the knowledge of being 'indifferent honest'); it is as Everyman that he shares the universal melancholy anatomized by Burton.[49]

This is not to say, with Edward Burns, that Hamlet's 'To be or not to be' speech is *un*motivated,[50] a *declamatio* or essay like Seneca's, say, or St Augustine's, ordered rhetorically rather than psychologically.[51] Indeed, Hamlet might say with Montaigne, 'I only speak others in order better to speak myself'.[52] For one thing, the speech follows a specific, dichotomizing method: 'To die—to sleep/ No more [sc. no more than a sleep]'; and later 'To die, to sleep;/ To sleep, perchance to

---

[43] Clemen (1987) 133 has to admit that here 'the dovetailing with the dramatic action is less apparent'.

[44] Levin (1959) 70; Jenkins (1982) 152; Stanton (1994) 175.

[45] Edwards (1985) 25–7. On the placing of the speech, see Dodsworth (1985) 109.

[46] Dodsworth (1985) 94 strains to find a single sequence.   [47] Bradbrook (1952) 111.

[48] Cit. Clemen (1964) 26 n. 9. Nuttall (1983) 145 discusses the German tradition Levin Schücking represents. On the actor as rhetorician, cf. Burns (1990) 10. Rose (1985) 111–12 needlessly invokes Freud's idea of plays depending on 'the neurotic in the spectator' and 'crossing over the boundaries between onstage and offstage'.

[49] III. i. 122–30; cf. Alexander (1971) 27, 60. Hamlet may however *think* of himself as suffering all this by a sort of legal fiction: cf. Dodsworth (1985) 158.

[50] Burns (1990) 147.

[51] Clemen (1964) 23 remarks its unusual reflectiveness; cf. Edwards (1985) ('extraordinary'). The soliloquy, and much else in *Hamlet*, owes a debt to St Augustine's study of the infirm will in *Confessions* VIII, ix–x. There may also be an echo of Petrarch's assurance that the 'arrows of fortune' cannot touch the citadel of mind, unless will opens the gates: *Fam. Epist.* XVIII. xv.

[52] Montaigne, *Essays* I. xxvi.

dream.' Levin shrewdly identifies this method as Ramist; one may add that Ramist rhetoric was in England a mark of militant Protestantism.[53] The monologue is apt, then, to a student from Wittenberg, the home of scepticism, reform, Lutheran Protestantism in religion, and 'mixed Ramism' in rhetoric.[54] In its highly theoretic generalizing about humankind, the speech suits Hamlet's youth and his evasion of simple duty.[55] Its extremity may suggest the 'beleaguered sanity' characteristic of stoicism's contained passions.[56] And it is thematically apt, in that it sets out the play's central issue—in the central of seven soliloquies—the choice between responsibility and evasion, between being and not being, between aggressive action and passive submission. (Alternatives developed separately in the perspectives of Laertes and Ophelia, according to the convention of genealogical allegory whereby siblings stand for complementary or contrasting effects.)[57] The malcontent diatribe is also apt, in that it amounts to a *contemplas mundi* removing any justification for ever avoiding a duty, no matter how dangerous. The monologue is on a different scale, however, from the rest of the scene. It dramatizes the *longue durée*, as it were, of Hamlet's consciousness of evasion. Its perspective is more distant, if not exactly detached.[58] Yet, like Pyrrhus's speech, it is indispensable. No less indispensable than, say, Bellini's landscape parergon in the throne of his Pesaro *Coronation of the Virgin*, or insets in the picture-within-a-picture genre, or the play within the play.[59] Nigel Alexander has shown how closely relevant such elements as Pyrrhus's speech are. My aim is to generalize this, arguing that such apparently artificial digressions come within the orbit of Renaissance realism.

Others of Shakespeare's soliloquies similarly disappoint modern expectations of a continuously maintained viewpoint.[60] 'Oh what a rogue and peasant slave am I' (II. ii. 575–673) follows closely enough after the weeping Player's compassion for Hecuba—a compassion Hamlet himself lacks. But then (again convincingly) Hamlet thinks of a plan—'I'll have these players/ Play something like the murder of my father' (590–1)—which is the very plan he put into effect forty lines earlier (at 531–6). The soliloquy thus resembles his stream of consciousness, but not

---

[53] Levin (1959) 69. See Miller (1939); Seaton (1950) xi; Ong (1958); Shuger (1988) Index s.v. Ramism, Puritan, esp. 96; and the Ramist analysis of Sir Philip Sidney's *Apology* by his secretary William Temple: Webster (1984).

[54] Wittenberg was associated with both Martin Luther and Philip Melanchthon. For mixed or Philippo-Ramism, Melanchthon's systematic version of Ramism, see Ong (1958) 298–9; Howell (1956). Jenkins (1982) 436 and Brandes (1902) 358 take the reference as local colour: it was common for Danes to go for education to Wittenberg.

[55] Everett (1989) 22. [56] Cf. Nuttall (1983) 103, 107.

[57] Cf. Alexander (1971) 75, 121; Backman (1991).

[58] For arguments against detachment here, see Dodsworth (1985) 108; elsewhere, however, Hamlet often affects a spurious aristocratic detachment; see ibid. 263.

[59] 'Repetition, discontinuity and excess...run right through the fabric of the play', Rose (1985) 117. Cf. Burns (1990) 145–6 on the difficulty of putting Ophelia's report of Hamlet's 'down-gyved' state into a cause–effect sequence.

[60] Similarly the second soliloquy compresses several states of consciousness: Fowler (1987) 79.

consciousness of the same time when it is voiced. Here Muriel Bradbrook and Wolfgang Clemen fall back on the non-explanation of a special archaic convention, retrospectively explanatory direct address.[61] And there is talk of textual inconsistency. Already in 1935, however, J. Dover Wilson suggested that the soliloquy recapitulates Hamlet's earlier emotions, and is 'a dramatic reflection of what has already taken place'.[62] This gives us our clue. The earlier, external representation shows the putting of the plan in motion; the later voices the vague internal planning that achieved specificity in enactment. Again, two distinct versions of the same action. Such redundancy is sometimes put down to incomplete revision. But this explanation (or explaining away) may often be unnecessary. Multiple, paratactic representations of the same action are normal in Elizabethan drama, as in Renaissance picturing.[63]

III

Questions about mimesis have often centred on Hamlet's problematic character. From the time of William Richardson (1743–1814), those identifying with Hamlet—and who has not done that?—have had difficulties with his cruelty, aggression, and especially his wish to kill Claudius in a state of mortal sin (Dr Johnson called this 'too horrible to be read or to be uttered'). Hazlitt, Levin, George Hunter, Nuttall, and others have followed Richardson in supposing, subtly, that Hamlet's holding back in the prayer scene results from 'amiable sensibility'.[64] The malicious reason he expresses for delay must be rationalization, since 'nothing in the whole character...justifies such savage enormity'. Hamlet deceives himself, since he is ashamed of his moral scruples (his true reason, or excuse, for inaction).[65] Without disagreeing with Hunter that Hamlet's sympathetically hesitating nature is 'fully human',[66] one is struck by how often such rescuing of Hamlet's amiability generates increasingly speculative interiorization.[67] Yet all these idealizing efforts have scarcely irradiated Hamlet's obscure irresolution. (Martin Dodsworth seems nearer the mark in detecting culpable evasion of responsibility.) And psychoanalytic criticism, while admittedly raising more metaphysical questions, has supplied so many answers to them that one concludes they are not answerable. Is Hamlet an Oedipal father-hater perplexed to find his new rival a fellow father-killer? Does Hamlet's femininity identify passively with Gertrude's?[68] (One suspects that family

---

[61] Clemen (1964) 14.   [62] Wilson (1935) 142n.
[63] Cf. Dodsworth (1985) 163–6 on double representation in the dumb show and the Gonzago play.
[64] Richardson: Vickers (1974–81) 5. 159; Hazlitt (1902) 234; Levin (1959) 34; Nuttall (1983) 107. On eighteenth-century censure of Hamlet, see also Prosser (1967) 244 ff.
[65] These 'would expose him...to censure': Richardson, reprinted in Vickers (1974–81) 6, 365–8.
[66] Hunter (1963) 98.   [67] Cf. de Grazia (1991) Afterword, esp. 223 ff.
[68] Jones (1955) 88, 106, cit. Rose (1985) 113.

relations may have been a good deal different in an age when well-born infants seldom saw their mothers.) So many psychological inferences have been invented that fainthearted poststructuralists despair of a coherent protagonist; announcing that there is no reality, no 'essential Hamlet', behind his show.[69] But this capitulation hardly satisfies.[70] Constructive inference needs to be sustained; although hopefully with more thought for relevance to pre-novelistic conditions.

The old question why Hamlet delays is not exclusively one of character; at times, indeed, delay seems a device to allow prolonged analysis of honourable duty.[71] The duty to revenge is seldom questioned very deeply in revenge tragedy; and some critics accept it as par for the Jacobean course.[72] Yet revenge is anything but Christian.[73] And Shakespeare's profound realism examines the call to requite wrong more searchingly than to accept repetition of the wrong as a duty. In particular, a distinction between private revenge and civil retribution emerges as crucial.[74] Not least for a prince, honour itself—the displaced chivalric ethic of an outworn ancestral order—had grown problematic.[75] Hamlet is torn between disagreeable alternatives: on one hand public confrontation, challenge, and perhaps insurrection; on the other, individual heroic agency. Significantly, the Ghost has for Horatio a political explanation, whereas Hamlet avoids any political role.[76] After the inset play (which might have been an opportunity for public initiatives), deutero-Hamlet's thoughts of revenge take on an increasingly private, malicious character.[77] The change is emblemized by the Ghost's third appearance, to Hamlet alone, in a private closet. He appears 'in his nightgown', lacking the moral armour of the public appearances on the Platform, when he was visible to Horatio and the others.[78]

Much turns on the Ghost's authority. The challenge of the dead is that of honour, of duty to an inherited, ancestral ethic. But is the voice of honour to be obeyed without question? Is there a divine commission to revenge—an appointment, even, as 'scourge and minister'? All this is left realistically uncertain. And when Hamlet ceases to question it, when he becomes a 'true believer', a certain moral coarsening sets in. Nevertheless, Shakespeare does so much to make the Ghost's visitations portentous, that they acquire an authoritative significance, perilous to ignore. Honour must be satisfied. The generalizing

---

[69] e.g. de Grazia (1991) 224–5; Belsey (1985) 50.   [70] Cf. Nuttall (1988) 59.
[71] As Alexander (1971) 10. On the ambiguity of the Ghost's 'call to honour', and Hamlet's unpreparedness for it, see Dodsworth (1985) *passim*.
[72] Levin (1959) 35; Cruttwell (1963) 118 ff.; Alexander (1971) 189–90.
[73] As Alexander (1971) rightly stresses. Cf. Montaigne, *Essays* II. xi, 'Of Cruelty'.
[74] Cf. Kirsch (1993) 113–14.
[75] As Mousley (1994) 79 suggests, overstressing Hamlet's conscious scepticism. For the broad sense revenge might have in the sixteenth century, see Dodsworth (1985) 63.
[76] e.g. I. i. 83–4; cf. Robson (1975) 20; Dodsworth (1985) 49; Battenhouse (1969) 246. On Hamlet's eventual choice of private revenge, see Bowers (1989) 96; Nuttall (1988) 61.
[77] *Pace* Bowers (1989); cf. Prosser (1967) 199.
[78] For the doffing of armour as implying a dangerous moral fluidity, cf. Spenser, *The Faerie Queene*, I. vii. 2 (also VI. iii. 7, etc.), discussed in Leslie (1983) 126.

application seems inescapably universal: everyone is given, like Hamlet, an absolute obligation to reform the world ('born to set it right'). In this very broad sense, Hamlet's delaying needs no explanation. He delays as culpably as everyone else, leaving undone those things which he ought to have done. (In 1713, interestingly, Guthrie could still perceive Hamlet as an Everyman, speaking 'the real language of mankind, of its highest to its lowest order'.)

Hamlet's delay is sometimes attributed to mental disturbance. But, as Arthur Kirsch reminds us, 'Hamlet is always conscious of the manic roles he plays and is always lucid with Horatio'.[79] If Hamlet is continuously rational, though, his apologies to Laertes for the distraction with which he is 'punished' invite unpleasant inferences. Assuming he was only ever 'mad in craft' (III. iv. 187), with north-north-west madness, his apologies must be similarly Machiavellian. Patrick Cruttwell shrewdly remarks that Hamlet's madness is most emphasized by those who wish to avoid confessing his faults.[80] Perhaps his protean madness may partly be explicable in terms of multiple perspectives corresponding with different irrational responses to the rational madness of society. His irrationality can be youth's subversive wildness,[81] careful evasiveness ('crafty madness keeps aloof', III. i. 8), licence for aggressive truth-telling (as in Marston's satiric malcontents and the Amleth of Saxo's *Danish History*), or simply a refuge in which to hide from responsibility.[82] And, of course, with continued pressure, there is also the threat of really insane sanity like that of Kohlhaas in Kleist's powerful story. To Polonius, Hamlet is insolent in a way once taboo with seniors, even if socially inferior. To Rosencrantz and Guildenstern he is as deviously manipulative, taking advantage of inconsequentiality, perhaps, to turn a casual question about recorder-playing into sudden accusation. Hamlet is a chameleon. Or, as W. S. Gilbert puts it in his *Rosencrantz and Guildenstern* libretto,

> Some men hold
> That he's the sanest, far, of all sane men—
> Some that he's really sane, but shamming mad—
> Some that he's really mad, but shamming sane—
> Some that he will be mad, some that he *was*—
> Some that he couldn't be. But on the whole
> (As far as I can make out what they mean)
> The favourite theory's somewhat like this:
> Hamlet is idiotically sane
> With lucid intervals of lunacy.[83]

---

[79] Cf. Kirsch (1990) 33.
[80] Cruttwell (1963) 114; cf. Alexander (1971) 27, 'What alienates Hamlet from us is his inhumanity.'
[81] Cf. Everett (1989) 22.   [82] Cf. Dodsworth (1985) 86.
[83] Gilbert (1982) 176.

Undoubtedly 'one man in his time plays many parts'. Nevertheless to regard Hamlet as a walking contradiction would be simplistic. Allowing for subclinical instability and occasional losses of control ('passions'),[84] his moods vary intelligibly enough with his interlocutors.

IV

Consider the nunnery scene, Hamlet and Ophelia's first meeting on stage. The dutiful daughter, who is being used to test Hamlet's disposition, returns his love tokens. But Hamlet says—with the thoughtlessness of recently acquired honesty—'I never gave you aught' (III. i. 96). After a few clever, sharp words, he makes inadequate amends: 'I did love you once' (III. i. 115); yet within four lines he takes even that away: Ophelia should never have believed his vows—'I loved you not'. And he launches defensively into misogynistic diatribe.[85] Faced with these baffling vacillations, some follow Dover Wilson in supposing Hamlet aware of eavesdroppers.[86] Many invent previous erotic passages. Salvador de Madariaga, like some earlier German critics, thought Ophelia was Hamlet's mistress; Kay Stanton imagines Hamlet's visit to Ophelia's closet as a scene of rape—his doublet was not unbraced for nothing; and even Eleanor Prosser visualizes the leave-taking of a lover too sensitive to be a trifler.[87] Harold Goddard, in a way more sceptical, takes the entire visit to be Ophelia's invention; perhaps he remembers Goethe's percipient remark that Hamlet's feeling is 'without conspicuous passion'.[88] Others invent various acceptable emotions explaining Hamlet's cruelty in the nunnery scene. He is ending a relationship that must now lead to suffering.[89] Or, he is voicing disgust at Gertrude: 'I loved you not' means 'there is no such thing as pure love'.[90] Or, Ophelia has taken his love too seriously; he realizes he has never been in love as she is. Faced by honest love, he is guiltily incoherent: his vacillation expresses faltering commitment.[91] Or (a plea of self-defence), he would rather reject than be rejected. Or (applying Felperin's genetic theory), Hamlet falls short of the revenger's role, and turns to

---

[84] On the extent of Hamlet's madness, see Dodsworth (1985), e.g. 156.
[85] This aggressiveness continues, as V. i, 190 ff. shows.
[86] The text counts against this speculation, as the best recent editors, Harold Jenkins and Philip Edwards, agree.
[87] Madariaga (1948) 64; Stanton (1994) 168; Prosser (1967) 130, 146. Everett (1989) 31 more subtly suggests that Ophelia's madness takes the form of *believing* she has been 'brutally seduced'; but see Empson (1986) 108.
[88] Goddard (1946) 462–74; Gervinus (1883) 579.
[89] Hazlitt (1902) 236 obscurely argues that Hamlet could not 'wound her mind by explaining the cause of his alienation'.
[90] Cf. Burns (1990) 145: the diatribe has little to do with Ophelia herself.
[91] Cf. Alexander (1971) 112.

the reformer's—to *sermo*, to the satiric, misogynistic discourse of Wittenberg.[92] But it is useless. We are like eavesdroppers ourselves, unable to make sense of what we hear. Even Bradley, who carried motive-hunting as far as anyone, confesses its futility here: 'What is pretence, and what sincerity, appears to me an insoluble problem.'[93]

Instead of immediately construing motives that exculpate Hamlet, one might consider what other perspectives Shakespeare has given of Hamlet's love. Ophelia, reporting his visit to her closet, describes him as mad with love (II. i. 85–6). But her wishful view is surely undercut by dramatic irony. The audience recognizes Hamlet's 'wildness' as simulated, his disordered dress as antic costume; being prompted to this recognition by an introjected memory of the Ghost in Hamlet's look—Ophelia describes him looking 'As if he had been loosed out of hell/ To speak of horrors'.[94] He is not thinking of her.

Then, there is the love-letter, which to Polonius proves Hamlet to be in love. This letter carries the weight (considerable in that age) of documentary evidence:

> Doubt thou the stars are fire,
> Doubt that the sun doth move,
> Doubt truth to be a liar,
> But never doubt I love. (II. ii. 115–18)

Jenkins is alert to a danger here of insincerity: 'Since each of the poem's first two lines assumes the certainty of what had now begun to be doubted, there is an irony of which Shakespeare (though not, I take it, Hamlet) must have been aware.' But Hamlet must have meant the irony. He cannot for a moment have been unaware of the controversies besetting the sun's motion, for his university was famously in the forefront of astronomical thought. The junior mathematical professor at Wittenberg was George Joachim Rheticus himself; while the senior professor was none other than Erasmus Rheinhold, foremost astronomer of the century after Copernicus.[95] In short, Hamlet's love letter is malapert, as flip as its facile parody of poetic conventions might suggest.[96] Beneath its fri-

---

[92] On the composition of role from fictional ingredients, see Felperin (1977) 55–61, Dodsworth (1985) 252.

[93] Bradley (1920) 157–8. The insolubility has continued to influence acting: Ian McKellen's style consistently seeks to validate indeterminacy: cf. Hodgdon (1994) 263, 270.

[94] II. i. 83. Cf. Alexander (1971) 129.

[95] Rheticus, an enthusiastic disciple of Copernicus, did much to assist the publication of the Copernican hypothesis by his *Narratio Prima* (1540); and Rheinhold compiled the first Copernican tables. Rheticus's edition of Sacrobosco was printed at Wittenberg, as was one of Copernicus's mathematical works. Other scientific luminaries there included Johannes Fleischer (optics and astronomy); and Michael Neander (medicine and astronomy).

[96] Cf. Dodsworth (1985) 155: 'innocently ludicrous sophistication'. Polonius's introduction of his reading ('I will be faithful': II. ii. 114) already introduces the notion of trust.

volity there is a disagreeable suggestion of evasiveness, of casual, patronizing over-confidence. Its only sign of grace is the compunction of its breaking off—unless that, too, is a trick of languid offhandedness. Hamlet and Ophelia, in fact, have very different conceptions of the love that divides them—hers the true nobility of generous, virtuous love, his the lordliness that does honour by loving.[97] Ophelia, we recall, admits Hamlet never promised marriage, but only gave 'countenance' to his love speeches 'With *almost* all the holy vows of heaven'.[98]

There is an additional viewpoint in the nunnery scene itself. Words are heard as well as spoken; and Ophelia *hears* Hamlet say, 'I did love you...I loved you not'. What he means by this *correctio* or reformulation is reserved to his private consciousness (in which, possibly, he never gives Ophelia much thought).[99] What stands out for the audience is the words' painful impact on Ophelia. They are as relevant to her consciousness as to his; conveying, as they do, the contradictory feelings of rejected, 'disprised love'. Poor Ophelia has herself become uncertain about the mutual love her little intrigue was to prove (III. i. 39). The words mime *her* uncertainty, although Hamlet speaks them.

This reflexiveness appears in other ways too. Hamlet and Ophelia are both excessively attached to a parent; and each suffers 'distraction'. It is not exactly that Ophelia's 'real madness punishes the feigned insanity of Hamlet, which gave the first shock to her mind'.[100] In her image, rather, we see the morbid potential of Hamlet's irrationality. Their resemblances have been attributed to a 'multiple focus casting attention on Ophelia' and other characters 'as well as the protagonist'.[101] But the reverse seems nearer the truth: the multiple foci are all on aspects of the protagonist. What they all reflect is Hamlet's experience, and, through his, Everyman's and Everywoman's.[102]

V

The mirroring extends to details. Both Hamlet and Ophelia are given to carrying books, as critics have noticed. Attention to such material viewpoints has led to

---

[97] On the distinction between *vera nobilitas* and merely ancestral nobility, a favourite theme in Jonson, see McCanles (1992).

[98] I. iii. 114 (my italics).

[99] On Hamlet's total silence about Ophelia to others, not to be explained in theatrical terms as concentration of focus, see Bradley (1920) 154, 158; he is not prepared, however, to think of the prince as having taken advantage of his rank.

[100] Gervinus (1883) 581.

[101] French (1992) 109.

[102] But see Showalter (1985) 113, where she objects to Lacan's treating Ophelia as an aspect of Hamlet.

considerable advances in Shakespeare criticism.[103] Previously, exclusive concentration on verbal mimesis induced neglect of indirect, dispersed characterization such as Warren Ginsberg has traced in ancient literature.[104] For one has to imagine, before our spectator realism, a realism more participatory, engaging the emotions in a world less externalized. When Hamlet enters 'reading on a book',[105] the book is not only an appropriate accessory for a scholar: it characterizes him. And when he swears that the Ghost's 'commandment all alone shall live/ Within the book and volume of my brain' (I. v. 102–3), one may guess that the actor carried Hamlet's figurative tablets literally, thus supporting Alexander's connection of Hamlet's 'word' (or motto) with the art of memory.[106] For, as Cesare Ripa explains, a book is Memory's attribute—her memory-prompt.[107] Frances Yates's white magic has rather obscured the fact that artificial memory was a religious discipline, designed to form the soul through meditation.[108] Hamlet's words 'adieu, adieu, remember me', besides referring to the sacred obligation imposed by the Ghost, echoes the Eucharist's memorial, 'do this in remembrance of me'. Yet in the same breath Hamlet speaks of forgetting:

> Remember thee?
> Yea, from the table of my memory
> I'll wipe away all trivial fond [foolish] records,
> All saws of books, all forms, all pressures past
> [impressions on his memory]
> That youth and observation copied there. (I. v. 97–101)

This must have been deeply shocking to a generation for whom the book was a symbol of devout Protestantism, appearing as such in countless sepulchral monuments.[109] In effect Hamlet's soon-broken promise is to forget all religion and tradition: to remember only revenge.[110] He claims to prefer the sword of violence to the political, persuasive book.[111] And the passage may seem still more

---

[103] e.g. Alexander (1971), Doebler (1974), Dessen (1984), Manning (1994).
[104] Ginsberg (1983); cf. Dessen (1984).   [105] II. ii. 167 Folio s. d.
[106] Dessen (1984) 67–8, 171n. 15; Alexander (1971) 47.
[107] Ripa (1976) 335–6. When Polonius accosts Hamlet when reading (II. ii. 168–71), another book emblem may be evoked: Whitney (1586) 171 ('study is useless without practice').
[108] See, e.g., Carruthers (1990).   [109] See Mowl (1993) 31.
[110] Hamlet is not unaware, then, that memory's recollection counts against revenge, as Alexander (1971) 117 asserts. Mousley (1994) 71 sees an act of simplifying; Cruttwell (1963) 118 an act of forgetting.
[111] Since Hamlet's sword is probably unsheathed continuously from I. iv. 85 to I. v. 154, Shakespeare may also allude to a familiar emblem picturing a king (or Hercules his type) with book and sword, to signify that 'the ideal king masters both skill in arms and knowledge of liberal arts' (Wither (1635) I. xxxii), or that 'eloquence is better than strength' (le Fèvre (1536) 93; Alciati (1985) clxxxi).

insistently overdetermined, still sharper in ironic challenges, if one recalls the vindicta divina book emblem.[112] 'Vengeance is mine, saith the Lord.'

In the nunnery scene, Ophelia's book is similarly eloquent. She carries it to 'colour' her 'loneliness...with devotion's visage' (III. i. 45-6): to suggest 'orisons'. Hamlet, perhaps deceived, begs 'in thy orisons/ Be all my sins remembered' (III. i. 89-90). But, beneath its false appearance, Ophelia's book is a book of memory, too—memory of their mutual vows of love. Silently, it puts Hamlet's subsequent moralizing in a bad light.[113]

In such ways, any material object or action may have an aspect to add to the total representation. The most profound example, perhaps, is that of the inset play, brilliantly interpreted by Anne Barton and Nigel Alexander. Hamlet may claim to 'know not "seems" ', and have 'that within which passes show'.[114] But as the plot unfolds, he is increasingly involved with show. He puts on an 'antic disposition'; he dresses for the part of prisoner of love (or of Denmark), with stockings 'down-gyved';[115] he recites a dramatic speech; and he organizes the performance of a show-within-a-show-within-a-show. All these counter-shows have the implicit effect of suggesting that Hamlet knows (or comes to know) 'seems' only too well.[116] Illusion and false appearance are universal in the fallen world. Thus, the broken oaths in *The Murder of Gonzago* are Hamlet's too, to the extent that he spends time on theatricals—only tangentially relevant to his mission—instead of revenging. In the denouement, similarly, the ceremonious duel with its salutes of ordonnance completes the picture of Hamlet's ensnarement within the shows and customs of honour, the repetitive pattern of conflict that makes up fallen history.[117]

These are large perspectives; but lesser details may have their own aspects. When Hamlet stabs Polonius, the arras functions of course as a necessary hiding-place (although not an inevitable one: in Saxo the eavesdropper is under the rushes). And it is a deliberately superfluous detail serving the rhetoric of realism: Hans Knieper's tapestry workshop at Elsinore was famous.[118] Dessen suggests that symbolically the arras is 'a surface that prevents one from seeing the truth,...that epitomises the seeming world of Denmark' (tapestry was often

---

[112] See, e.g., Peacham (1612) 140: the divine wings of the emblem are appropriated at I. v. 29.

[113] On the book as Ophelia's devotion, see Lyons (1977) 61. Alexander (1971) 131 supposes a book of contemplation; but the text's insistence is on memory; the love tokens are 'remembrances' (III. i. 93).

[114] I. i. 76, 85. Often misinterpreted: e.g. Mousley (1994) 70 following Belsey; Potter (1991) 121; Burns (1990) 141, 154. 'That within' has little to do with 'essential subjectivity': Hamlet means he has real grief, not just its show—so Wiggins (1994) 215-16.

[115] Dessen (1984) 37.

[116] Cf. Weimann (1985) 288 ('Hamlet is both a product and, as it were, a producer of mimesis, a character performed in a role and one who himself performs and commissions a performance') and Wiggins (1994) 221 ('Hamlet must maintain an exterior persona that is wholly discontinuous with his inner self'). In *Doctor Faustus*, similarly, the middle scenes mime Faustus's frivolity: all he can think of to do with his powers is tricks.

[117] Hunter (1963) 107.   [118] See Heiberg (1988) 115.

symbolic, from its presenting figures and texts[119]); his Hamlet seeks truth under surface appearances. But a more relevant clue may be found in R. B. Graves's reminder that 'the overall illumination' of the Elizabethan stage encouraged 'a sense of continuity between...the actors and their background'.[120] Perhaps, then, the closet tapestry is to be interiorized. We recall how Spenser's Britomart gazes a long day at Busirane's erotic tapestries, while she orders her own chaste thoughts about love. And Francis Bacon quotes the observation 'that speech was like cloth of Arras, opened, and put abroad; whereby the imagery doth appear in figure; whereas in thoughts, they lie but as in packs'.[121] If tapestries were associated with words and thoughts, Hamlet's killing through one may suggest that his thoughts have indeed become bloody, his words aggressive to a fatal degree. This resonates with his resolution to 'speak daggers' (III. ii. 387) and Gertrude's cry 'these words like daggers enter in my ears' (III. iv. 95); strengthening the idea of a matricidal impulse.[122] Hamlet's emblematic insertion into his self-righteous text is intemperate violence—now the revenger's, now the reformer's, now the satirist's.[123] The incident, however indirect its mimesis may now seem, is plausibly realistic. Recognizing such dispersed aspects of character, far from disintegrating Hamlet as an individual, helps to resynthesize his Renaissance subjectivity.

VI

Most often character was dispersed among personal surrogates. In *Hamlet*, these may be mythological, like the moral Hercules; historical, like the ruler-hero Julius Caesar;[124] or else contemporary, fictional people of Elsinore with characters of their own. Much as real princes were supposed to be mirrored in their courts,[125] Claudius's half-remorseful Machiavellianism is half-reflected in his unwitting *ficelles* Rosencrantz and Guildenstern. And, when Laertes' machismo is perverted by Claudius, his devious plot against Hamlet is a distorted reflection of the devious plots of his politique father. (Polonius makes deviousness so much a principle as to defend the family name by having his son accused of whoring—a tactic effectively revealing honour's double standard.) As for Hamlet himself, he is mirrored in Horatio his mentor, Laertes and Fortinbras his rivals for honour, the

---

[119] Dessen (1984) 151. Cf. *As You Like It*, III. ii. 273.
[120] cit. Dessen (1984) 77.
[121] Bacon (1985) 84, developing Plutarch, *Lives*, 'Themistocles': 'men's words did properly resemble the stories and imagery in a piece of arras: for both in the one and in the other, the goodly images of either of them are seen, when they are unfolded and laid open. Contrarywise they appear not, but are lost, when they are shut up, and close folded.'
[122] Mooted in French (1992) 104.
[123] On emblematic insertions in *Hamlet*, see Manning (1994). Cf. Mousley (1994) 73; and Prosser (1967) 199, on Hamlet's self-righteousness in the closet scene.
[124] On these character-mirrors see Colie (1974) 231–2.
[125] For court as the king's mirror, see Grabes (1982) 79.

Ghost his chivalric self, and the First Player his compassionate self.¹²⁶ (Hamlet's compassion, being fictitious, is displaced onto an actor.) The First Player weeps for Hecuba as Hamlet cannot: a 'monstrous' disparity at which Hamlet exclaims, 'Had he the motive and the cue for passion/ That I have' (II. ii. 555–6). The occasion of the Player's tears is the important point in his speech when even Pyrrhus stops killing, arrested by Hecuba's piteousness; when an alternative to endless revenge is momentarily suggested.¹²⁷

Hamlet's personal mirrors, although usually treated as thematic parallels, are more integral than that—surrogates, rather; 'parts' he plays; sides of his nature; exemplars or descriptions;¹²⁸ selfs or potential selfs of social existence. (Hotspur and Falstaff are comparably selfs of Prince Hal and his father.) One is reminded that St Augustine's analysis of irresolution posits that 'there are as many contrary natures as there are wills in someone beset by indecision'.¹²⁹ Moreover, Hamlet's character-mirrors add independent views of him to the main representation, additional perspectives. Mirrors, we recall, were closely associated with perspective construction, from its origin in Brunelleschi's Florentine Baptistery demonstration, through its application in catoptric or reflected anamorphism, to its apotheosis in Vermeer's use of the camera obscura.¹³⁰ Shakespeare's mirroring can generally be naturalized into modern realism by treating the virtual images as completely separate individuals. But not always. In the closet scene, when Hamlet sees the Ghost, Gertrude sees 'nothing but ourselves' (III. iv. 134 f). To resolve this contradiction, some accept Hamlet's version of reality—confirmed, after all, by the Ghost's presence on stage¹³¹—and reject Gertrude's version. Perhaps Gertrude (innocent of considerations of honour) somehow cannot retrieve Hamlet senior's memory enough to shape the Ghost in her imagination; or perhaps she cannot remember what it was like to be honourable.¹³² Alternatively, Gertrude and her corrupt world may be sane, and the Ghost Hamlet's hallucination—'alas! he's mad' (III. iv. 106). But on the basis of continuous

---

¹²⁶ Alexander (1971) 97; Colie (1974) 223–4.

¹²⁷ Hamlet (or Shakespeare) may allude to Plutarch, *Moralia* 334B, where the tyrant Alexander of Pherae was ashamed to weep for Hecuba in Euripides' *Troades*, when he himself had killed far more people, without emotion. See Jenkins (1982) 481.

¹²⁸ Cf. Hunter (1963) 94: 'figures whose meaning depends on their relationship inside the observing and discriminating mind of Hamlet himself'; Jenkins (1974) 98.

¹²⁹ *Confessions*, VIII. x. 23 (transl. H. Chadwick).

¹³⁰ See Kemp (1990), s.v. *Camera*; *Mirrors*; and especially 189, on use of the camera obscura in the sixteenth century. On distorted cylindrical mirroring, and anamorphic images generally, see Baltrušaitis (1977). Shakespeare had opportunities to see the anamorphic portrait of Edward VI in Whitehall Palace (a *memento mori* double image): see ibid., 18–19. Shakespeare several times uses 'perspective' in the sense of an anamorphic double view: see *Henry V*, V. ii. 338 'you see them perspectively, the cities turned into a maid'; *Richard II*, II. ii. 16–20 'sorrow's eye, glazed with blinding tears,/ Divides one thing entire to many objects,/ Like perspectives, which, rightly gazed upon,/ Show nothing but confusion; eyed awry,/ Distinguish form.' For 'mirror' = true description, see *OED* s.v. *Mirror* 4; for 'mirror' = play, work of art, cf. Alexander (1971) 20–1.

¹³¹ Authorized by the important Q1 s. d., 'enter the ghost in his night gown'. See Potter (1991).

¹³² Cf. Dessen (1984) 141, 153.

spectator realism, neither resolution will work. The Ghost's earlier appearances were seen by all.[133] Here, at least, the alterity of Shakespeare's realism must be admitted. In its own terms, the action of the closet scene is not contradictory.

Without inconsistency, the scene dramatizes defective moral vision twice over, in two character-mirrors.[134] Thus, Hamlet sets a glass for Gertrude; but she is also a glass for him, as frequent verbal repetitions underline.[135] He makes her look at his father's portrait, the 'counterfeit presentment' of honour, to bring home to her the state of her 'inmost part' (III. iv. 19), her sinful soul. He repeatedly directs her to watch the Ghost—'look you, there, look' (III. iv. 136). But all the time Hamlet himself fails to see Polonius's body, to feel remorse for his death, to look into his own soul.[136] (I would have Gertrude, meanwhile, keep looking horrified at the corpse.) It is like the parable of the mote and the beam:[137] Hamlet is oblivious to the dead man he killed, yet impatient with Gertrude's obliviousness to a dead man's ghost, of whose death she is innocent. Similarly, Hamlet calls Polonius 'rash, intruding fool', having just himself committed a 'rash and bloody deed', as Gertrude rightly calls it.[138] He has broken his own vows, yet blames Gertrude for breaking hers. And he says heaven is 'thought-sick' at her act (III. iv. 50), without thinking to repent his own. Dessen treats Gertrude's blindness to the Ghost as a conventional device, adducing many comparable metaphorical failures of vision in contemporary plays. (In *Hamlet* itself, Claudius fails at first to see the dumb show.[139]) But 'convention' hardly seems to fit the immediacy—psychological illusionism, even—of such discrepant perceptions. They are more like the discrepant viewpoints that form much of our experience of moral reality. In Shakespeare's world, Hamlet's and Gertrude's experiences both reflect the same moral failure. T. S. Eliot complains that Gertrude 'is not an adequate equivalent' for Hamlet's disgust; failing to see how adequately she mirrors Hamlet's lack of self-awareness.[140] She constitutes a powerfully diffuse metaphor of his moral insensitivity. For Hamlet the moral accuser displays a positively Pharisaic

---

[133] The same objection counts against Dodsworth (1985) 50, naturalizing the Ghost as a manifestation of Hamlet's own nature. The Ghost is intelligible only as a separate, indirect perspective on Hamlet and other honourable men.

[134] See Dessen (1984) esp. 153 ff.

[135] e.g. III. iv. 8–9: 'Hamlet, thou hast thy father much offended./ Mother, you have my father much offended'—discussed from a different viewpoint in Dodsworth (1985) 130, 185–6, 191, 212. On the Gertrude mirror generally, see ibid. 200 'In attacking his mother, Hamlet attacks the weak and "feminine" part of himself.'

[136] 'The pivotal not-seer is...Hamlet': Dessen (1984) 153. On Hamlet's lack of remorse for killing Polonius, cf. Dodsworth (1985) 253.

[137] Matthew 7:3 f.   [138] Cf. Dodsworth (1985) 259–61.

[139] Prosser (1967); Robson (1975); Hawkes (1985) 325. Wilson (1935) naturalizes Claudius's neglect of the dumb show, against W. W. Greg; so does Robson, more plausibly suggesting a gradual comprehension, reconcilable with the failure-to-see convention.

[140] Eliot (1945) 101, to which Rose (1985) 96 concedes too much. Hypocrisy is already a topic in Saxo: Amleth says to his mother, 'thou shouldst weep for the blemish in thine own mind, not for that in another's': Bullough (1973) 66.

self-righteousness. Far from being exceptional, the closet scene typifies Shakespeare's realism. Dissatisfied with simple, direct representation of experience, he also represents it indirectly through mirroring characters, so adding subliminal complications.

As Gertrude offers a perspective of Hamlet's deficient self-awareness, so Claudius mirrors his heartlessness.[141] Claudius's ruthlessness reflects Hamlet's own potential for Machiavellianism, as his mission degenerates into criminal counter-intrigue. Eventually the 'mighty opposites', never very mighty, are not opposites either. Hamlet, who once shared a compassionate speech with the First Player, now shares with Claudius the responsibility for a death-warrant. The murders of Rosencrantz and Guildenstern have been justified by Hamlet's admirers as self-defence.[142] But they were unnecessary—and not even poetic justice, if, as seems likely, Hamlet's travelling companions were ignorant of the contents of their sealed commission.[143] Would Hamlet senior, whose ring reseals the commission, have judged the forgery honourable? The everlasting 'fixed/ His canon' against slaughtering others; only Hamlet's arrogant divinizing of his rank allows him to eliminate 'baser nature' at will. Whatever else the doctrine of the Unjust Magistrate might legitimize, it hardly extended to murdering fellow students.[144] Significantly, this crime puts Hamlet in the same boat, or rather ship, with pirates, a type of lawless inhumanity.

VII

That Laertes is another character-mirror, Hamlet himself tells us, in curiously recursive, not to say reflexive, syntax: 'by the image of my cause I see/ The portraiture of his [Laertes']' (V. ii. 77–8); and again (addressing Osric): Laertes' 'semblable is his mirror, and who else would trace him, his umbrage [shadow], nothing more' (V. ii. 118–20). To translate this camped-up, ironically encomiastic court-speak: Hamlet cannot emulate Laertes except by becoming Laertes himself. The comparison with painting, implied in 'portraiture', signals a fresh perspective on Hamlet, in which he becomes, or assimilates, Laertes the new man of correct

---

[141] And much else; cf., e.g., Dodsworth (1985) 93.
[142] On the speculation that Hamlet found evidence incriminating them as accomplices: Bowers (1989); Cruttwell (1963).
[143] Cf. Prosser (1967) 203–4; Dodsworth (1985) 180.
[144] On resistance theory, see Frye (1984) 41 ff. Although Calvin himself argued for obedience even to tyrannical magistrates, *Institutes* IV. ii was used to justify ecclesiastical and political disobedience. Belsey (1985) 114–16 imagines that 'orthodoxy' permitted passive disobedience only. Whose orthodoxy?

honour.[145] Contrasts between Laertes and Hamlet are regularly remarked;[146] but the resemblances that emphasize these, and the strikingly similar circumstances, are more numerous. Each loses a father; each loves Ophelia; each gives her moral advice; each is a gambler and a duellist; each, out of filial piety, is bent on revenge. Each is the 'calendar of gentry', 'the glass of fashion and the mould of form'—the latter Ophelia's description of Hamlet, not Osric's of Laertes. Each, moreover, is represented in two phases. As there is a young as well as a mature Hamlet, so there is a callow embarrassed stuffed-shirt Laertes who goes off to Paris to learn French fashions and earn a reputation, to sow wild oats and imitate Lamord; and there is a tougher Laertes who returns, in whom we see 'immaturity harden into forms positively evil'.[147] The young Laertes can set nature above—or at least alongside—honour; the elder reverses this hierarchy. Laertes the honour machine is of course very different from Hamlet the humanly perplexed, hesitating Prince. But in his stereotypical behaviour Laertes reveals the pressure of the time—of the honour code—under which Hamlet also acts, albeit more consciously and reluctantly. The virtual image brings out how Hamlet, confronted by a similar challenge, chose not to respond.[148] For, if the rabble call Laertes lord, Hamlet too is 'loved of the distracted multitude'.[149] Laertes' insurrection shows how Hamlet might have used his own much greater eloquence to enforce retribution publicly.[150] Hamlet's sympathy with Laertes' cause is thus insightful. But it is also inculpatory, since Laertes represents the questionable aspects of honour Hamlet has been drawn to imitate. He is much given to measuring himself against the field of honour—against Laertes, against Fortinbras.

When Hamlet wrestles with Laertes in Ophelia's grave, he thus wrestles with his own image—with the Antaeus of his own 'towering passion', his competitive vying ('emulate pride'). Descending to Laertes' level as a man of earth and invoker of rebellious Titan myths ('o'ertop old Pelion': V. i. 246), Hamlet lowers himself to competitive boasting. He is more bereaved; his honour is more injured. Although he thinks he is like 'Hercules himself' (V. i. 286), Hamlet loses this wrestling: to engage in it at all shows that status matters more to him than anything. He is more passionately resentful of the 'bravery' or magnificence of [Laertes'] grief than passionate with grief himself, or even respectful of poor Ophelia's grave. It hardly seems apropos to speculate whether Hamlet belatedly falls in love.[151] Both wrestlers think they love; but both, thinking they love honour more, trample the loved body. Some say the Folio and Q1 stage direction here must be corrupt: no

---

[145] Cf. Alexander (1971) 120. On shadow ('umbrage') as a painter's term of art (sometimes used for the painting itself), see Gent (1981) and Dundas (1993) Index s.v. *Shadow*.
[146] e.g. Jenkins (1982) on IV. v. 132–5.
[147] Dodsworth (1985) 28.   [148] Cf. Jenkins (1974) 103.
[149] IV. iii. 4; cf. IV. vii. 18. Not merely Claudius' improvisation: Laertes finds the excuse plausible.
[150] Cf. Jenkins (1974) 103. But see Hunter (1963) 97–8; Frye (1984) 132–5.
[151] As Alexander (1971) 127, 131, 149, 159.

sensitive person like Hamlet would ever jump into a grave. But even above ground, wrestling at a funeral is not a very convincing sign of sensitivity. In fact, the struggle shows how brutalizing a single-minded pursuit of honour has been to Hamlet.[152] There is little to choose, at this stage, between his histrionics and Laertes'. The episode is not exactly a psychomachia—allegorizing, say, a struggle against false honour. ('Shakespeare never sacrifices naturalism to symbolism.'[153]) But neither does the doubled image dramatize external behaviour of a brother and a lover, merely for the sake of sociological comparison. The complementary perspectives of bereavement emphasize by repetition how the emulousness of competitive honour is able to displace the natural passion of grief.

Making a triptych with the perspectives of Laertes and Hamlet, there is a third character-mirror, Fortinbras. That 'delicate and tender prince...with divine ambition puffed' (IV. iv. 48–9) is the subject of Hamlet's seventh and last soliloquy, full of admiration of his rival's honourable achievements:

> Rightly to be great
> Is not to stir without great argument,
> But greatly to find quarrel in a straw
> When honour's at the stake. (IV. iv. 53–6)

There is no ironic censure in Hamlet's wonder-struck admiration of this prince's readiness to send 20,000 men to their deaths 'for a fantasy and trick of fame'. Like Hamlet's, Fortinbras' portraiture comes in two perspectives, two very different temporal views. The earlier Fortinbras is an adventurer of 'unimproved mettle, hot and full', who has 'sharked up a list of lawless resolutes'. But the later is a 'tender prince', the ego-ideal of Hamlet's mirror-gazing, who leads a regular, well-disciplined army. The contrast is so extreme that to Jenkins it suggests revision.[154] But it may be that here again we have to do with the before-and-after vignettes of Renaissance compressed narrative.

Fortinbras, unlike Laertes and Hamlet, seems not to suffer moral deterioration. He submits to the King of Norway, and promises not to proceed revengefully against Denmark. He pursues, in fact, a legal course of action, however displeasingly martial this may seem to modern critics. Similarly, he is prepared to submit his 'rights of memory' in Denmark to due election by 'the noblest'; thus again taking an honourable course.[155] Is then Fortinbras' honour superior to Hamlet's, as Hamlet himself thinks? Certainly war was an appropriate context for chivalric honour—was, indeed, its ultimate validation. The symmetry of the

---

[152] Cf. Dessen (1984) 21. Edwards (1985) 27 and Nuttall (1988) 58 reject the leap, the latter describing Hamlet's demeanour as courteous. Empson (1986) 100 is good on this issue.

[153] Colie (1974) 236. Ophelia's 'maimed rites' (V. i. 212) might hint at the Reformation's disfigurement of traditional ceremonies; but only as an enhancing suggestion.

[154] Jenkins (1974) 101–6.   [155] In contrast to Claudius, who 'popped in' (V. ii. 65).

triptych implies a formal distribution of matter between the private honour of Laertes and the monarchic or martial honour of Fortinbras. Hamlet himself is irresolute, divided between ideals of revenge (passionate Laertes) and of public redress (disciplined Fortinbras). The highest honour must, it seems, be Fortinbras'. But Shakespeare with his usual realism complicates this scheme to the point of enigma. For Fortinbras' incessant martial enterprises have an alarmingly Tamburlainian or Cromwellian aspect. Is Fortinbras' efficiency altogether preferable to Hamlet's hesitations and botched attempts? Would the world not be better off without an honour that kills so many thousands? Honour has been one of the cultural forms bringing mankind from the law of the jungle to the order of civil society. And indeed elements of the code continue still to be valuable. Yet, as ever, Shakespeare challenges still more discrimination, more charity.

From the mirror of Hamlet's confidant Horatio (to whom he mostly presents his agreeable side), one might expect a more flattering image. And indeed, in the final scene Horatio projects his own resignation, so that many suppose Hamlet dies well, justifiably comparing himself to the Morality Everyman—'this fell sergeant, Death,/ Is strict in his arrest'.[156] Taking his cue from this, the scholarly Horatio alludes to the Everyman morality in his prayer 'flights of angels sing thee to thy rest'.[157] But, if Hamlet is Everyman, what of Everyman's companion, Good Deeds? Fredson Bowers thinks Hamlet guiltless of murder: his death expiates all.[158] And Roland Mushat Frye, with able special pleading, finds triple 'endorsements' of Hamlet, by his friend, his adversary, and his rival for royal honour.[159] But Laertes' forgiveness of Hamlet ('my father's death come not upon thee': V. ii. 335) partly depends on his believing Hamlet's dubious excuse ('what I have done...was madness': V. ii. 226–8).[160] And Fortinbras' endorsement proceeds from ignorance; he accords Hamlet the 'rite of war' with no more to go on than an impressive head-count ('This quarry cries on havoc': 'what a king is this!'), and, of course, reputation.[161] Hamlet's mission of retribution has come

---

[156] Jenkins (1982) V. ii. 341 Long Note; Felperin (1977) 64. Cf. *Pilgrimage of the Soul* (OED s.v. Sergeant 4b) ('death's sergeant, malady'); Tourneur, *The Transformed Metamorphosis* xli ('sergeant death'); John Knox, *The History of the Reformation in Scotland* IV (OED s.v. Sergeant, 1563) (Death 'laid on his areist'); Sylvester, *Divine Weeks*, I. iv. 818 ('Serjeant Death's sad warrant').

[157] Cf. Felperin (1977) 64. With Horatio's prayer cf. Everyman 891–3, where an angel sings 'come excellent elect spouse'. The detail of the singing angel indicates allusion, as against the commonplace envisaged in Frye (1984) 270–1.

[158] 'There can be no question of Hamlet's death in continuing sin or crime': Bowers (1989) 135. Cf. Everett (1989) 27 on the 'accidental killing of Polonius'; Alexander (1971) 182 (Polonius was killed in self-defence); Cruttwell (1963) 119 on the 'wild justice' of killing Rosencrantz and Guildenstern.

[159] Frye (1984) 135, 256, 259–62.

[160] V. ii. 226–8. Nuttall (1983) 164 compares Agamemnon's excuse in Homer, *Iliad* xix. Another pertinent source is St Augustine's analysis of the infirm will in *Confessions* VIII, ix. 21, asking whether it has an explanation in *latebrae poenarum hominum et tenebrosissimae contritiones filiorum Adam* ('the hidden punishments and secret despondences that befall the sons of Adam').

[161] V. ii. 404. Hawkes (1985) 331 improbably proposes that Fortinbras orders the rite for Claudius.

down to messy slaughter: his 'most royal' martial honour is achieved largely by accident.¹⁶²

But what of the third endorsement, Horatio's? Hamlet's better part can hardly endorse private vengeance. Promising to tell 'How these things came about', Horatio specifies 'casual [chance] slaughters', which must include Polonius's killing, and 'deaths put on by cunning and forced [contrived] cause', which presumably includes Rosencrantz and Guildenstern's. Hamlet may think himself a divine minister (V. II. 48), but Horatio says nothing about that. There remains only his prayer that Hamlet may be sung to rest by angels, which is surely well short of an endorsement. Meanwhile, Hamlet has something other than angels in mind: namely fame's afterlife of honourable remembrance. He forbids his friend's suicide because he wants his own reputation cleared.¹⁶³ Felperin connects the 'multiplicity of responses' to Hamlet's guilt with Shakespeare's repudiating the older 'drama of salvation and damnation'.¹⁶⁴ But, even on the newest Renaissance assumptions, the dying perspective reveals desperate obduracy. There cannot have been many different responses to Hamlet's total lack of remorse, let alone contrition, at this solemn juncture.¹⁶⁵ Claudius voices remorse in the prayer scene; Laertes voices remorse in his dying speech; Hamlet, never. Rosencrantz and Guildenstern are 'not near [his] conscience'.¹⁶⁶ Do we honestly suppose that Hamlet—a man who destroys the entire Polonius family and who murders two former friends—do we suppose that such a man can make a good end without repentance? Yet, if any perspective is privileged in Renaissance tragedy, it is that of the dying scene.

VIII

All the character-mirrors and multiple representations—whether models, foils, contrasts, *repoussoirs*, 'sides' of Hamlet, analogous narrations, or relational images—together compose an astonishingly complex representation. The individual identity, the self, was formed and apprehended—then as now—through relations with others. (Shakespeare anticipated the psychologies of Jung and Fairbairn, quite as much as that of Freud.) I am not suggesting that Shakespeare's magic can be explained as all done by mirrors. But, by assembling

---

¹⁶² Kastan (1982) 27 argues that Fortinbras' command to bear Hamlet 'like a soldier' symbolizes the displacement of humane by martial values. Perhaps, rather, displacement of Christian values by honour.
¹⁶³ Kastan (1982) 90 finds this quite fitting.   ¹⁶⁴ Felperin (1977) 64–5.
¹⁶⁵ For all Hamlet's talk about Gertrude's repentance, his own remorse for Polonius's death is limited to the perfunctory 'For this same lord/ I do repent'—followed by self-exoneration, blaming heaven. Cf. Prosser (1967) 199, 202n. on Gertrude's invention of his weeping; Battenhouse (1969) 251.
¹⁶⁶ V. ii. 58; cf. V. ii. 67. Cf. Prosser (1967) 202 and Dodsworth (1985) 180 on Hamlet's malice towards Rosencrantz and Guildenstern.

the relational images of Hamlet, one can in principle arrive at a full estimate of his character (one not without its vacuities). Defective motives have been taken to betray the absence of inner subjectivity. But often the gaps are defects only on the assumption of continuous spectator realism. In Shakespeare's Renaissance realism, what may seem gaps are really transitions between perspectives. And the separate psychological perspectives can be synthesized, much as a multi-perspectival illusion is formed by a stereoscopic viewer. Whatever it is that Catherine Belsey calls 'essential subjectivity'[167] may not yet have developed; but that does not mean there was no realism, no dramatic illusion. Still less, that 'emergent illusionism' was in 'collision' with an emblematic mode. Realism through relational mirror images seems to have been quite accessible to Renaissance audiences. Direct and indirect mimesis were not conflicting opposites but complementary, mutually supportive perspectives. Shakespearean mimesis could 'suit the action to the words', combining indirect with direct representation, 'external' metaphors with subjective introspection.[168]

Shakespeare's psychological realism may be compared with that of *The Faerie Queene*.[169] In Spenser, he found not only precedents for mixing allegory with direct mimesis, but also examples of multiple character-mirrors. Spenser tells us he represents Queen Elizabeth in Gloriana, 'and yet in some places else' (that is, in Belphoebe and Britomart) 'I do otherwise shadow her'.[170] Perhaps because few Shakespeareans have been avid readers of Spenser, the extent of emblem and allegory in his tragedies—like the frequency of multiple perspectives—is insufficiently recognized. What I have tried to describe is no mere 'residue' of untransmuted archaism 'left behind by the ever-encroaching tide of naturalism',[171] but rather a distinct mode of realism, corresponding to a changed experience of the world itself. Although Shakespeare, like Spenser, was to be a pivotal figure in the development of naturalistic realism, he did not practise it as automatically as we have come to suppose. Indeed, it was a conspicuous mark of his dramatic style to enliven traditional genres, supplementing the new with the old, direct with indirect mimesis.[172] He may have sensed that indirect implication was more richly communicative.

What, then, do the separate perspectives in *Hamlet* combine to represent? Most generally, our inheritance of depravity, the 'vicious mole of nature'[173] in a world like 'an unweeded garden/ That grows to seed', 'rank and gross' (I. ii. 135–6),

---

[167] Belsey (1985) 26.
[168] III. ii. 17–18, related in Weimann (1985) to the discursive/non-discursive polarity.
[169] See Potts (1958); Watkins (1950); Hamilton (1990).   [170] Letter to Raleigh.
[171] Felperin (1977) 58–60.
[172] Cf. Felperin (1977) 58. In the inset play, similarly, 'we watch Shakespeare's play approach and embrace, as it were, its own archaic prototype, only to turn and flee it in an almost choreographic pattern of meeting and parting'.
[173] I. iv. 17–38. The theme is already present in Saxo, whose Amleth mysteriously discerns the inheritance of death in things: e.g. Bullough (1973) 68.

where the legacy from father to son, from Achilles to Pyrrhus, Polonius to Laertes, Hamlet to Hamlet, is evil and the duty to reform it, 'to set it right' (I. v. 197). More particularly, the tragedy of chivalric honour's displacement by unheroic, politique forms of ambition.[174] The change and decay of honour is, indeed, a frequent subject in Shakespeare: one thinks of *Henry IV, Henry V, Troilus and Cressida*. From *Romeo and Juliet* to *As You Like It*, duelling especially is attacked—a practice to which the militant Protestant nobility (Leicester, Sidney, Essex, Raleigh) were prone. And in *Hamlet*, the new honour, although not a central subject, is a principal assumption.[175] Hamlet never swerves from commitment to princely honour: his doubt is only whether it is *nobler* in the mind to suffer or take arms. But he shrinks from the duties of honourable action, and, at least at first, hesitates before the homicidal implications of the honour code. More particularly still, *Hamlet* is the tragedy of an attractive but unstable, idealistic but weak young prince, yearning for true nobility, faced with a moral challenge too formidable for him: the tragedy of the ruin of his better features by the logic of honour. As he matures and his hesitancy disappears, his noble honour hardens into egomaniac self-justification.

The problem of *Hamlet* criticism is not Hamlet's delay, but the delay of the critics. Eleanor Prosser made a case against him already in 1967, and Martin Dodsworth's decisive examination should have clinched the matter in 1985. Yet the enigma of Hamlet is still defended against all their arguments. There is a natural reluctance to admit how unpleasant the Everyman in Hamlet is. Just as Hamlet satirizes many sorts and conditions of people who have motes blinding them, so he himself has many planks; and we, identifying with him, share this denial. But there is also an aesthetic reason for our delay: namely, the difficulty of appreciating Renaissance realism.

The play's hermeneutic task is to discern the corruption of Hamlet's honesty, in face of an eloquence that gilds his words seductively—the seductive charm honour really had for many Elizabethans. After all, 'the right use' of Renaissance tragedy was to show forth 'ulcers that are covered with tissue' and the 'weak foundations gilden roofs are builded' upon[176]—as Hamlet himself is clearly aware when he plans to 'tent [probe] Claudius to the quick' (II. ii. 593) with *The Murder of Gonzago*, or when he warns Gertrude not to ignore his censure, since that 'will but skin and film the ulcerous place'.[177] But in his righteousness he is oblivious of the tragedy designed to tent his own, and our, ulcers. Dr Shakespeare comes with his lancet, and we say, 'No need to operate, doctor! The patient has an amiable sensibility.'

---

[174] Cf. Cruttwell (1963) 121–2 on the muddle of contradictory moralities; Mousley (1994) 72–3, 79.
[175] See Dodsworth (1985) *passim*, esp. ch. 1.   [176] Sidney (1973) 96.
[177] III. iv. 149; cf. IV. iv. 27–28: 'th'impostume of much wealth and pace,/ That inward breaks, and shows no cause without/ Why the man dies.'

Relevance

Is this going to be relevant to your interests? You can only tell by reading it to find out what it has to say. Often writing is condemned as irrelevant before its contents are adequately known. Even literary works are expected to conform to a crudely applied criterion of relevance, and there is talk of all literature of the past being less relevant than modern literature. Used like this, 'relevance' generally implies 'political relevance'. Yet I remember the American feminist Elaine Showalter once saying, 'Surely everything's political?' In reply I mumbled something subversive—some doubt as to whether intimate love passages were really all that political. What I should have said is that although any work can be construed as having a political angle, this needn't be its most interesting aspect. Needn't, in fact, be *relevant*. Some literature has very little directly political interest, yet may be relevant to our concerns as readers or critics. 'Relevance' is turning out to be a slippery word.

For one thing, its meaning has unobtrusively changed. In the Middle Ages and the Early Modern period, 'relevance' meant 'pertinent to a case or argument' or occasionally 'pertinent to the matter in hand'. In 1645 Charles I, for example, wrote a letter proposing 'to make our probations [proofs] and arguments relevant'. By 1800, however, 'relevant' was more often used to mean 'pertinent to the issue'; and after that it altered rapidly, since what was taken to be the current issue kept changing.

In fact, 'relevance' began to imply pertinency to specifically new issues, or the newest issue. An article on student activism in *Time* magazine (30 November 1970, p. 40) refers to 'demands for "relevance", especially for the overdue admission of more minority-group students'. Here a normative shading is unescapable: institutions *ought* to be socially relevant. Already *Harper's Magazine* (November 1969, p. 86) makes this explicit: 'Either we can commit ourselves to changing the institutions of our society...to make them—to use a term which I hate—"relevant"...or we can sit back and try to defend them.' It was a keyword, a watchword, of the time. Yet it does not get into Raymond Williams's *Keywords* (1976). Nor, for that matter, into J. A. Cuddon's *Dictionary of Critical Terms* (1977), or any other glossary of critical terms I have seen. Perhaps in the 1970s 'relevance' did not seem a problematic term. What *else* could it mean but social or political relevance?

In literary criticism, this collectivist assumption had an astonishing influence. Relevance came to be used as an overriding criterion. Considerable and negligible, good and bad, were distinguished simply in terms of this one factor. Was the work socially relevant, relevant to the public? Such a criterion could easily exclude much of literature. And soon it did. A Department of Education and Science report of 1975 remarked, 'we have heard the case for "relevance" carried to the point of excluding fantasy or any stories with settings or characters unfamiliar to the pupils from their first-hand experience'. According to S. Braden (1978) 'relevance is achieved when artists meet the real observations of their public'. Poetry, too, was apt to lack relevance. And when relevancy was equated with recency, it was a small step to considering literature as a whole irrelevant and élitist.

Yet 'formalist' critics seemed to go out of their way to confirm this view, to deny literature's public relevance. In 1949 Allen Tate was said to hold that 'the poem is autonomous, and that the only relevance the subject-ideas have is to each other within the formal meaning of the work itself'. Élitist men of letters seemed to be rejecting the public as much as the public rejected élitist literature.

At this juncture, Theory took a hand, and made literary criticism even more élitist and rebarbative, even less accessible. Something can be said in defence of some of the ideas of structuralism (and post-structuralism), at least when these are developed by a master like Roland Barthes. But there is no disputing that the structuralist doctrine of communication as a process of coding and decoding has relegated questions of pertinency to the sidelines. Once authors and authors' meanings were replaced by 'freeplay of textuality', wild interpretations proliferated, and there was less likelihood that any interpretation would ever be challengeable as irrelevant to the work.

In secondary education, meanwhile, the practice of précis was not surprisingly neglected: until the 1960s, this was a standard exercise which required students to set out a condensed and unambiguous version of the meaning of a given passage. If the sense of 'pertinency' was not totally lost, it became rarer. There was increasing confusion as to which meanings were relevant. Was a critic to focus attention exclusively on politically relevant meanings? Or meanings relevant to women? Or meanings illustrating Theory? Alternatively, were meanings arrived at by actually *reading* a work to be attended to? Was relevance to the experience of reading to count for anything?

In this confusion one response has been to reject Theory altogether. Deconstruction, especially, is felt as too remote from reading to have public relevance. Another response, that of new historicism and cultural studies, is to put the blame on literature. Aesthetic experience becomes the enemy, and the defence against it is sociology, or politics. These can replace appreciation of literature with depreciation of it, as a form of connivance with oppression. Yet, although new historicists profess to accept that criticism has a political responsibility, they still deal in terms remote from the experience of ordinary readers. (That may change, of course, if they are able to produce new cadres of post-structuralist readers and cultural students, as they try to do.)

A more hopeful development, to my mind, is the current rethinking of relevance itself. A seminal work in this direction is Sperber and Wilson's *Relevance*. This constructs a theory of meaning as 'optimal relevance', that is, the most pertinent association that can be inferred from a communication. Many associations may seem more or less relevant; but the reader or hearer will generally infer one of them to be optimally so. It will be the meaning, for that reader. The thrust of modern relevance theory, in short, is to replace decoding with ordinary inference and so to recover the idea of pertinency—albeit pertinency reconceived in linguistic terms.

Perhaps relevance theory may offer a way out of our present critical mess. Certainly, where the goal of pertinency is acknowledged, the implication for fashionable sorts of 'relevance' is dire. A criterion of pertinency can lead to severe judgements on some critics' perception of relevance. Certain political constructions, however exquisitely subtle, are liable to be dismissed as having no bearing on the work's optimally relevant meanings, or on its formal structures. This does not mean, of course, that only overtly political works should be interpreted from a political point of view. Nor will it stop some readers taking up more political associations than other readers: that is what interests them. But relevance theory at least foregrounds the fact that political meanings are not necessarily optimally relevant associations—indeed, that they may not even have public relevance.

It is vitally important not to force political interpretations just because they are specially interesting to the critic. A good example of how counterproductive that can be is offered by Kipling. Much criticism of *Kim* has focused on Kipling's imperialism, or his alleged racialist prejudices. Even Martin Green (1980), although an admirer of Kipling, interprets *Kim* exclusively in terms of the political Great Game: the activity for which Kim is being trained is surveying, which brings together the activities of climbing, observing, native disguise, etc. under the aegis of imperialism. It may seem to the modem reader a euphemism to give this name to the secret service of an imperialist power, but in Kipling's time it was at least a general euphemism.

Indeed, it is a consensus view, now, that the political relevance of *Kim* lies in its illustration of the workings of the British Raj. But that is not how the Burmese democratic leader Aung San Suu Kyi sees it. If anyone knows about political oppression, she does. Yet in an article in *The Sunday Times* (16 June 1996) she explains how *Kim* helped to sustain her during enforced solitude. And what seemed then to her its most relevant feature was not at all its 'less attractive' colonial attitudes, but its representations and expressions of Buddhist *metta*, or loving kindness. It *seems* that when it comes to the test in the fight against tyranny, *Kim*'s relevance lies not in its imperialism but in its freedom from imperialism—in its largeness; in the generosity of its vision of the Great Game and what lies beyond that.

In literature of the past, a work's relevance often turns out to be quite different from what has been supposed. The history that literature relates to seems to be of longer duration than political critics are sometimes willing to admit. Indeed, the point of literature may lie in its otherness—in the challenge it offers the present by its remoteness from current assumptions.

My aim has not been to discourage people from using the term relevance. I hope it will be used more than ever. But it should not be used absolutely, without a modifier. We need to make clear always what the work, or meaning, is relevant *to*.

The Emblem as a Literary Genre

Modern emblem studies may be said to begin with Henry Green's paper of 1865, read to the Architectural, Archaeological, and Historical Society of Chester, calling for a facsimile edition of Geoffrey Whitney's *A Choice of Emblems*.[1] After Mario Praz's learned bibliography of 1947, development was rapid. About two thousand emblem collections have now been rediscovered—twice the number listed in Praz's second edition of 1964. Since the first planting of Green's and Howard Bayley's seminal ideas, sizable forests have been consumed in emblem criticism. Emblems, once dismissed as popular, trivial, and visually second-rate, have become the object of an independent specialism. Yet there is still little agreement as to what constitutes the emblem as a genre.[2] And, now that literary criticism threatens to merge into media studies, the emblem is increasingly treated from a visual viewpoint, with consequent neglect of its literary aspects. This paper discusses how far emblems belong to literature, and constitute, indeed, a literary genre.

I do not mean to renew the search for defining characteristics of the emblem as a fixed class of literary works. To define 'the emblem' is to make a rope of sand.[3] A definition that worked for the late Middle Ages, when *imprese* and rebuses predominated, would hardly fit the sixteenth-century device and contrasting emblem—let alone their conflated form in France the century after. Besides, the emblem's chronological *termini* are elusive. Was its origin ancient, as Claude-François Menestrier thought? Or late fifteenth-century, as Daniel Russell? Or did it originate in 1531? Its decline has been variously dated to the seventeenth, eighteenth, and nineteenth centuries, or denied to have taken place at all. Emblem motifs persisted in baroque and rococo decoration; in Victorian picture books; in Robert Louis Stevenson's *Moral Fables*. And they still figure in conceptual art like Ian Hamilton Finlay's, to say nothing of TV commercials, where slogan, visual, and poetic prose often recapitulate the emblem's classic three-part form. The emblem's own emblem is Proteus. As with any literary genre, we are faced with the diversifications of historical existence. Literary kinds have a diachronic

---

[1] *On the Emblems of Geoffrey Whitney...A Paper Read before the Architectural, Archaeological, and Historical Society of Chester*, 1865 (Bodleian Lib. 21998. e. 10).

[2] See Stegemeier (1946); Praz (1964); Jöns (1966); Heckscher and Wirth (1967); Schöne (1968); Hill (1970); Daly (1972); and the classified bibliography in Dees (1986). For recent discussions of the emblem genre, see Daly (1979a); Russell (1985); Bath (1988) and (1990).

[3] Cf. Russell (1985) 15–16; Hill (1970).

dimension: change discloses, fashion fashions them.⁴ It is precisely innovation, in fact, that makes generic form apparent. And the emblem is no exception. It, too, came about through gradual transformation of earlier genres, and went on changing.

Relation of parts

Pre-Wittgensteinian theorists tried to define the emblem in terms of an essential relation between its picture and epigram. That relation being changeable, conflicting theories inevitably resulted. In one, the picture dominated: emblem history was traced back through *impresa* and *devise* to misunderstood Egyptian hieroglyphics, or those of nature. Were not *imprese* in common (or at least, noble) use, long before Alciato? The dolphin-and-anchor motif appeared on an *aureus* of the Emperor Titus in 80 AD, possibly before a motto was linked with it, whether FESTINA LENTE or SEMPER FESTINA TARDE, or SPEUDE BRADEOS.⁵ Nonverbal *imprese*, fulfilling their heraldic function, helped to elucidate medieval Europe. From the thirteenth century onwards, however, mottos began to appear on seals, crests, and shields. (At least a score of British families share the motto FESTINA LENTE.) When the *impresa* had a text, it was of the briefest. Even so, this had genre characteristics or rules, including special rhetorical features— ellipsis, enigma, and (as in FESTINA LENTE) paradox.⁶ Early theorists restricted the topics, too, of the visual device. Hearts and human figures were out; while Henri Estienne disapproved of the dolphin and anchor as insufficiently natural.⁷ *Imprese* came to resemble emblems in attracting explanatory commentary, as in Paolo Giovio's *Dialogo dell' Imprese* (1555). Works like Girolamo Ruscelli's *Le Imprese Illustri* (1566) go from vignettes and descriptions to explanations and digressions not unlike Claude Mignault's, say, in Andrea Alciato's *Emblemata* beginning in the 1570s.⁸ There are obvious grounds for considering the *impresa* a precursor of the emblem.

Nevertheless the theory of pictorial origin meets with formidable difficulties. Not least of these are the many emblems without pictures. Andrew Willet did not mean his *Sacrorum Emblematum Centuria Una* (1592?) to have any; he was

---

⁴ See Fowler (1985).
⁵ BM cat. II, 234, Pl. 45, Nos. 19, 20 (no motto); Aulus Gellius and Suetonius, *Divus Augustus* II. xxv. 4: 'he thought nothing less becoming in a well-trained leader than haste and rashness, and, accordingly, favourite sayings of his were: "More haste, less speed" [Greek, *speude bradeos*].' There are opposite examples, however, like the golden shield with a verbal inscription listing Octavianus's four virtues (clemency, valour, justice, piety), voted by the Senate in 27 BC; see Syme (1960) 313.
⁶ Cf. Russell (1985) 59.
⁷ Ibid. 53. Cf. Contile's strict rules for the motto: see Fraunce (1991) 25.
⁸ E.g. *Emblemata cum Commentariis Claudii Minois* (Padua, 1621).

content with what he calls 'naked emblems.'⁹ Notice the double articulation Willet's words imply: a conceit clothed in language may be further clothed (or not clothed) in picture, just as soul is clothed in flesh. (John Peacock has admirably shown how, in such contexts, 'soul' and 'body' shifted in meaning, according to which side the writer belonged to, in the *paragone* of literature and visual art.[10]) Jacob Cats's emblems similarly displayed their nudity in Heywood's *Pleasant Dialogues*. Surely the nude emblem printers cannot all have been unable to afford clothing?

According to the other main hypothesis, Hessel Miedema's, emblems are primarily verbal: the *picturae* merely illustrate what can exist perfectly well without illustration. Emblem history is traced to literary origins, in Philostratus's *Imagines* and the ekphrastic or descriptive epigrams of the Greek Anthology. (As it happens, Greek Anthology epigrams are found illustrated at Pompeii; but this was unknown in the Renaissance.[11]) Epigrams undoubtedly made a major contribution to the emblem. And proponents of the literary hypothesis can claim the support of Alciato himself, who from his letter to Francesco Calvi was quite clear that emblems—as he conceived them in 1523—were epigrams.[12] They can make something, too, of the emblem's unrestricted topics; for, alone of genres, epigram enjoyed complete freedom of subject. And they can point, of course, to the nude emblem collections; not forgetting Alciato's Lyons edition of 1548, and perhaps also his ghostly project of 1523.

Yet the theory of a purely literary origin has not carried conviction either. For one thing, it depends heavily on the fortuity of many printers simultaneously opting for catchpenny illustrations. If print was decisive, it can hardly have been so quite in the way Miedema suggests.[13] A more serious objection is that many emblems had pictures, but no early publishing history. I am thinking of such cases as Moritz Tilo's additions to Alciato; and (to mention British examples only) the manuscript collections of Thomas Palmer, Abraham Fraunce, Andrew Willet, and Patrick Cary. Palmer actually bypassed the printer by cannibalizing *picturae* from earlier emblem books. Tilo's sketches may have served some private operation of *inventio*, rather than have been meant for publication. Still, they hardly show the emblemist thinking along lexical lines. The epigram theory thus has its difficulties; although, as we shall see, it has much to tell about the origin, and particularly the chronology, of the emblem vogue.

---

[9] Other examples are listed in Young (1988). See also Fraunce (1991) 21. For a medieval instance of *ekphrasis* by Robert Holcot, see Gent (1981) 31 n. 118.
[10] Peacock (1990) 155.   [11] See Praz (1964) 25, 31.
[12] Miedema (1968) 236. For a meticulous account of Alciato's earliest emblem projects, see Scholz (1991).
[13] Nor is there an adequate explanation on the basis of Fr. Walter Ong's suggestion that allegorical tableaux resulted from the introduction of print; see Praz (1964) 15n.

In the Renaissance, visual and literary theories competed wordily. Ernest Gilman (1989, 63) has suggested that 'logocentric bias' led seventeenth-century critics to prefer voice to the 'ekphrastic structures' of the sixteenth century. But the later emblems were no less pictorially conceived than the earlier. And the conception of the emblem as syllogistic goes back before Dominique Bouhours (1628–1702) and Fr. Pierre Le Moyne (1602–1672) to Henri Estienne's *L'Art de faire des devises* (1645).[14] Confusion is, after all, to be expected in early theories of rapidly developing genres. *Impresa*, epigram, and emblem seem each in turn to have exerted generative pressure. One may venture the hypothesis that the complete emblem first arose as a modal transformation of epigram by *impresa*[15] (unless the imperialistic epigram incorporated the *impresa* as one of its many conquered subjects). Subsequently, the emblem vogue became influential enough for its collective form to be sometimes transferred to the *impresa* and *devise*.

Synchronic relations between structural parts cannot by themselves provide an adequate basis for describing a genre. One has to take into account both diachronic evolutions and social settings. Thus, *imprese* might be wordless (especially when used in ornament); or consist of picture and word (the common two-part form); or be accompanied by explanatory commentary—perhaps even by a short verse. *Imprese* and *devises* appeared at first singly, for the most part outside literature. Only later, after the emblem vogue was well under way, did they congregate in printed collections like Ruscelli's. Emblems, by contrast, from the first came typically in collections, and usually printed collections.[16] Occasionally, they had a two-part format of epigram and *pictura*. More often, they had the familiar three-part format of Alciato's *Emblematum Liber* (Augsburg 1531). That is to say: an epigraphic or allusive motto; a picture; and an epigram—usually ekphrastic, but sometimes independent. Commentary or quotations might be added, to make four or five parts, as in Alciato's *Emblemata cum Commentariis* of 1621.

Labels

Allowance must be made for regional differences. The emblem was popular in early seventeenth-century Britain, but almost out of fashion in France until it fused there with the *devise*—something that happened much less in Britain, where honour was valued differently.[17] Yet national preferences could also be overridden by the traffic of international mannerism—not only exchange of ideas

---

[14] Cf. Russell (1985) 44.
[15] For a fuller explanation of the term 'modal transformation', see Fowler (1985), chaps. 9 and 10.
[16] The earliest collection known seems to be Du Moulin's, in a manuscript of 1515–26. For an account of its three-part emblems with prose *subscriptiones*, see Massing (1987).
[17] Cf. Russell (1985) 74.

and copying of pictures, but polyglot macaronicisms and the ubiquitous Latin *koine*. Everywhere device and emblem overlapped, until they were only distinguished by social function. The same picture might appear in tournament *impresa*, mural decoration, printer's device, or emblem. The Vespasian dolphin and anchor, which was reintroduced in Francesco Colonna's *Hypnerotomachia* (1499) and adopted by the printer Aldo Manuzio as his device, appeared also as an emblem *pictura*, for example in Alciato's *Emblematum Liber* of 1531. In a similar way, virtually every Roman coin reverse was reused in some Renaissance emblem. Considering these multifarious continuities, it is striking that early theorists were so certain about the emblem's being new. The emblem label identified, clearly, what was felt to be a distinct novelty.

Modern genre study starts by clearing away confusions between *res* and *verba*, between actual distinctions of genre and mere variation in labelling. All Renaissance critical terms were ambiguous, if not positively misleading—not least *devise*, which in Marot could mean 'motto'.[18] Moreover, the motto might also be termed 'mot'; 'word'; '*sententia*'; '*inscriptio*'; '*elogium*' or picture label; and 'emblem' (as in *The Shepheardes Calender*). The figure, similarly, could be '*pictura*'; '*eikon*'; '*imago*'; and (of course) 'emblem'.[19] Finally, the epigram answered to 'epigraph'; '*subscriptio*'; 'emblem' again (as in Alciato); and '*elogium*'—the last a usage Richard Lovelace plays on in 'Amyntor's Grove', which he presents as a blown-up inscription for a group portrait of the Endymion Porters.[20] Some termed the epigram a *descriptio* or *explicatio* of the figure; others denied it to be anything of the sort, or referred to figure and epigram together as 'emblem'.[21] Mason Tung's advice to be sceptical about all early emblem terminology is amply justified.

Interpreted sympathetically, however, the early labels contain useful suggestions. 'Emblem' itself, Greek and Latin *emblema*, could refer to mosaic, appliqué, or inlaid ornament—as in Milton's paradise, 'the ground, more coloured than with stone / Of costliest emblem'.[22] Daniello Bartoli (1608-1685), interestingly, likens the emblem to an intarsia of metaphorical analogy.[23] Were an emblem's parts thought of as composing the intarsia? Or were whole emblems collectively inlaid like tesserets? Another interesting label is Palmer's title *Two Hundred Poosees*. The term 'posy' goes back before 1530, when Jehan Palsgrave's French dictionary listed 'poysy, devyse, or worde, devise'.[24] Earlier, the posy was a ring motto; but Palmer clearly intends 'emblem'. His title puns on 'posy' of flowers, and hence of poems with their flowers of rhetoric. His book is an anthology. 'Posy' regularly had this collective implication; as when Andrew Kingsmill called

---

[18] Russell (1985) 34.   [19] Ibid. 80.   [20] See Fowler (1994).
[21] Russell (1985) 81.
[22] *Paradise Lost* iv.703; the reference may be to broderie composed of coloured earth and stones.
[23] Praz (1964) 13, 19.   [24] See *OED*, s. v. Posy.

Comfort in Affliction (1585, written ca. 1569) his 'poor posy.' However vaguely framed, Palmer's title lets one glimpse his sense of a collective form.

Thinking in Emblems

Confusions in the Renaissance terminology imply more than failure to resolve differences of opinion about the emblem. The genre was also bafflingly elusive, because the semiotic relations of words to images were altering profoundly, so that different concepts, old and new, existed simultaneously.[25] Nevertheless, intelligible explanations were constructed. On one model, *picturae* worked syllogistically, like hieroglyphs or rebuses. *Pictura* and epigram combined to function as terms in quasi-logical propositions, or to formulate more complex ideas.[26] Here one needs to recall that rebus discourse, widespread in earlier heraldic devices, was still available in the seventeenth century. A striking example is the 1618 Antwerp painting for the Violieren or Chamber of Rhetoricians, by Jan Brueghel I and others, in which four consecutive complicated phrases can be deciphered by suitably combining the eleven human figures, five animals and birds, and other attributes.[27] Thinking in rebuses and emblems was more feasible when the superstructural *picturae* and ekphrastic epigrams accompanied familiar mental images. Iconographic symbols, in particular, seem to have informed the substrate of dreams, fantasies, and imaginative thought. Bringing this to the theoretical light of day, however, entailed—and still entails—very difficult abstraction.

Renaissance processes of thought will not have been like ours. All the same, scholastic hypotheses like the 'soul' and 'body' of emblems give the impression of awareness of associative processes. One may conjecture an emblematic mind-set, in keeping with the shared analogical world-picture (if not quite with Albrecht Schone's monolithic consensus). An important factor, probably, was the memory-art tradition, with its regular associating of words and mental images. Emblems seem to have had close interconnection with mnemonic images (a link still to be examined); declining as they did when memory-art was generally abandoned in the late seventeenth century.[28]

Medieval memory-art assisted the devout in contemplating interpreted imagery, so as to edify, or construct, their souls.[29] A similar purpose clearly governed the English mural emblem series in Lady Drury's Oratory, a closet for private meditation that has amazingly survived intact (although now removed to Christ Church Mansion, Ipswich).[30] Associative habits can also be inferred in

---

[25] On this aspect of the early development of the emblem, see Russell (1985); Bath (1989).
[26] Russell (1985) 52.
[27] Hendrik van Balen and Frans Francken II; see Filipczak (1987) 25, and Fig. 59.
[28] See Engel (1991). Cf. Russell (1985) 83; Gilman (1989) 66; Carruthers (1990) Index, s. v. Sight.
[29] See Carruthers (1990) chap. 5 and passim.
[30] See Farmer (1984) chap. 7. On emblematic motifs in painted ceilings, see Bath (1994).

Palmer's *Poosees*, from his juxtaposition of emblems with *picturae* sharing the same natural object. Here, as in Tilo, groups of *picturae* with a common element bring together parallels, opposites, qualifications, variations. Alciato already followed the practice when he gave Titus's dolphin and anchor the motto A PRINCE WHO SEEKS HIS SUBJECTS' SAFETY, implying something distinct from FESTINA LENTE.[31] And Palmer gave the same *pictura* religious associations by substituting the motto GOD IS OUR REFUGE IN ADVERSITY.[32] Conversely, FESTINA LENTE was attached to many different *picturae*, copiously varied.[33] This associative play finds modern analogies in manipulative reapplications of political symbols and commercial logos, as well as in travesties of classic images, like Marcel Duchamp's moustached Mona Lisa, and Edvard Munch's *The Scream* as a tie or pop-up doll.

Just as the visual images of memory-art often served to call up associated texts, so did emblem pictures and mottos. It is because the motto signals a relevant context that emblem theorists sometimes call it a *lemma*.[34] Brief mottos can cue verses, chapters, passages—even whole books—and so bring to bear complex ideas.[35] In fact, emblem-art was an art of allusion. Hence, perhaps, the genre's strange label. For Greek *emblema* meant an appliquéd insertion, such as an inset ornament or label motif on a *krater*. And the Renaissance emblem was also an insertion: its ideas, extracted from classical literature, the Bible, or the Fathers, were designed to be reinserted in the modern setting, enhancing, ennobling, reforming. Allusion could substitute for the absent situation of utterance, by cuing a familiar context. As with radio fixes in position-finding, epigram and picture might offer an *embarras de richesses* of meanings separately, but together with the motto they focussed an optimally relevant composite meaning.[36] This is particularly obvious when familiar sayings are involved, as in Cats's proverb emblem collection *Spiegel van de Oude en de Niewe Tyt* (The Hague, 1632).

Not that maxims and *sententiae* were univocal. Desiderius Erasmus's *Adagia* would be enough in itself to prove the contrary. Indeed, it was precisely the complexity of the motto in relation to the other emblem elements that often enabled the ensemble to be a suitable channel for classical ideas. Brief as the mottos were, trifling as the emblems seemed, they constituted nothing less than a conduit for the transfer of ancient wisdom. In this transfer and reassimilation—this *translatio studii*—Erasmus's friend Alciato played a not inconsiderable role.[37] In so vital an enterprise of the Renaissance there was no place for glib obviousness.

---

[31] Andrea Alciato, *Emblemata* (Padua, 1621) Embl. CXLIV. On the associative function of emblems, see Goedde (1989) 134 and passim.
[32] Emblem LXVI; see Palmer (1988) pp. xxiv–xxv: a theme returned to more than once.
[33] Wind (1968) 98.   [34] Miedema (1968); Goedde (1989) 131.
[35] Russell (1985) 81.   [36] Cf. Goedde (1989) 76; Fraunce (1991) 37.   [37] Daly (1979) 11.

THE EMBLEM AS A LITERARY GENRE   153

It called rather for indirection and subtle elusiveness—a depth inviting scholarly commentary, or public elaboration in masques, mural paintings, and the like.

Assembly of the Emblem Elements

Associative manipulation of visual images pervaded Renaissance classicism, but for that very reason cannot explain the emblem's novelty. Yet something was new. If anything is certain about Alciato's 1523 letter to Calvi, it is that he is describing a novelty. He has to explain everything from scratch:

> I give in each separate epigram a description of something, such that it signifies something pleasant taken from history or from nature, after which painters, goldsmiths and founders can fashion objects which we call badges and which we fasten on our hats, or else bear as trade-marks...[38]

Yet *imprese* for shields were as ancient as the hills, and hat badges were old hat. For example, the pelican in her piety (soon to appear in emblems by Whitney, George Wither, and others) had been a charge in medieval heraldry, and went back before that to Philostratus. Could the novelty be the individual, secular application, by contrast with religious medieval images? No; for the fifteenth century abounded in compelling secular images like the imperial iconography, or the countless *imprese* ornamenting the Palazzo Ducale at Urbino, with their challenges to respect, admire, or fear. Alciato's tree and plant emblems may have reflected the voguish interest in conceptual garden-art, which often figured mythologically appropriate trees,[39] but philosophical gardens were hardly new either. As for the motto, it was often indistinguishable from that of an *impresa*, say, or from a *sententia* in a tapestry or mural.[40] In fact, the separate elements of the emblem were ubiquitous, in poetry and masque, painting and graphic art, city signboards and house names, ecclesiastical murals and alchemical treatises. Novelty lay solely in their assembly into a multimedia genre combining epigraph, pictural device, and epigram.

New literary genres seldom (perhaps never) appear out of the blue. Instead, they combine or adapt the formal repertoires of existing genres.[41] One of the contributory repertoires will quite often be extra-literary. A structural armature,

---

[38] Letter to Calvi, cit. Miedema (1968) 236.
[39] E.g. Thorpe Castle, as Mildmay Fane describes it in the 1640s; 'Thorp Palace: A Miracle' 10–12; Fowler (1994) 220. Cf. the garden statue in Philipott (1950) 24, 'On a Nymph', which relates to many emblems of weeping nymphs by Hugo and others.
[40] E.g., in the Munich Antiquarium of Duke Albrecht V of Bavaria: Haskell (1993) 21; and, in Tudor England, Sir Nicholas Bacon's *sententiae*: McCutcheon (1977); Bath (1993) 16n.
[41] See Fowler (1985) 156–8.

perhaps, will be imported: examples might include the literary inventory, the testament, and the interview. Regarding the emblem from this point of view, one can see that its immediate literary antecedent was the ekphrastic epigram, that is to say, a short poem describing, explaining, possibly troping, a natural object or work of art. But it is almost as obvious that, whereas the motto by itself had complex antecedents, the structural idea of combining motto and pictura derived, simply enough, from the earlier *impresa* or *devise*. It was taken over, that is, from an extra-literary genre. And one particular group of devices, I wish to suggest, may well have been decisive: namely, the trademarks of printers. (These are omitted, oddly, from the otherwise full list of emblem applications in Daly [1979].)

In his letter to Calvi linking his projected epigram-emblems to trademarks, Alciato himself instances printers' devices. Many of the early printers used these—perhaps to suggest, if not claim, social status. They were thus in a strict sense *devises*, boasting personal or professional ideals.[42] Alciato's first example is Aldo Manuzio's dolphin and anchor. In the context of printing, one may suppose, its FESTINA LENTE motto implied productivity combined with care—'I can certainly affirm that I have as my constant companions the dolphin and the anchor. I have accomplished much by holding fast and much by pressing on.'[43] In this practical, self-advertising implication, the Aldine anchor resembles the elephant device of another printer, Calvi himself. For, as Alciato teased him, the elephant 'carries its young for a long time and produces nothing'.[44] More seriously, the elephant device would imply unhurried labour combined with impressive output. Many other printers adopted familiar devices, often rebuses: for example Guy Marchant (1483–1502),[45] whose musical notes sol and fa, clasped hands of Faith, and FIDES with FICIT 'underneath'—*sous*, making *sufficit*—together make up SOLA FIDES SUFFICIT. Sometimes printers' devices would incorporate a verse epigram, whether in title-page or colophon: an example is the 1497 *devise* of Felix Balligault.[46] The elements of emblem thus occur all together in fifteenth-century title-pages and colophons. The printer's device seems to have been the prototype of emblem, just as colophon typography was, of shape poetry.[47]

In this, we can see one possible reason why the coming of print was a precondition for the emblem genre, and why the emblem should be so bound up with typographic culture. Another reason, perhaps more fundamental, is that the epigram craze itself depended on print. The epigram's ancient models, the Planudean and Palatine Anthologies, had existed for centuries in manuscript—the former

---

[42] Russell (1985) 65, 66, 67, 70, 71–2.
[43] Bayley (1909) 145; Moseley (1989) 5, 30 n. 10; Wind (1968) 98.
[44] Letter to Calvi, cit. Miedema (1968) 236.   [45] Céard and Margolin (1986) Fig. 73.
[46] De Vinne (1902) 11–12, 26, 44. Johnson (1934) Loggan No. 4 has both verse and emblematic figures.
[47] See Fowler (1995).

since 1300. But only with the *editio princeps* of the Planudean Anthology in 1494, Estienne's edition in 1566, and Salmasius's re-discovery of the Palatine Anthology in 1606, did the vogue of the epigram really take off. Further impetus was given by Latin translations like Alciato's in Jan Cornarius's *Selecta Epigrammata* (Basel, 1529), and especially Hugo Grotius's *Poematum Collecta* (1617),[48] besides such vernacular versions as Timothy Kendall's (1577).

The contribution of print was not only to facilitate rapid dissemination of epigrams and emblems. It also fixed the classic emblem format —motto, *pictura*, epigram, in that order—as manuscript circulation could never have done.[49] From the first, the emblem was a literary genre, primarily realized in book form; whereas the radical of presentation of the extraliterary device was mainly heraldic or decorative. This is not to endorse Clark Hulse's contrast of noble *impresa* and popular emblem.[50] The rules of the *impresa* were designed for mass spectator sport; brevity ensuring visibility in the tournament lists. If the difficulty of the *impresa* held the people at lance length, the emblem was not less élitist, with its Latin epigrams and polyglot mottos—to say nothing of its framing cartouches, which were often strapwork, a type of ornament suggesting equestrian leather and nobility.

Emblem Collections as 'Silvae'

Almost invariably the emblem was a collective genre: a salient feature that has received surprisingly little attention. *Imprese* often occurred singly; but emblems typically came in series, or at least in book-length collections. This, too, accorded with the medium of print; only manuscript items circulated singly or in small groups.

If emblems belonged to collections, one may reasonably ask what sort of collections. Since the Greek Anthology was a model, one answer might be that the early emblem books resembled anthologies. I say early, because the more specialist collections—alchemical, erotic, pious, academic—tended to come later, in the seventeenth century, when systematic or encyclopedic summas were produced, sometimes with prefaces explicitly announcing their method. (A similar tendency is observable in visual art; as witness the gallery paintings of Antwerp.[51]) The earlier collections, on the contrary, usually addressed

---

[48] *Poematum Collecta et Magnam Partem Nunc Primum Edita...*, ed. G. Grotius (Leiden, 1617).
[49] Steyner's Augsburg 1531 Alciato already has the 'classic' sequence; although, to save paper (which accounted for more than sixty per cent of production costs) he did not begin each emblem on a new page. That refinement was added by Wechel in his Paris 1534 edition. See Scholz (1993).
[50] Hulse (1990) 164.
[51] See Filipczak (1987).

miscellaneous topics. Palmer's *Poosees* are mixed bunches—'florilege for all', as it were, 'That have not time for studies general'.[52]

Focussing more specifically on the emblem's epigram component, one can add that miscellanies of epigrams were identified as *silvae*. This ancient kind was treated rather sarcastically by Quintilian, who described a fashion for ostentatiously impromptu, disparate effusions, apparently disordered but really contrived as coherent sequences, varied on purpose. So long as classical concepts of art and nature prevailed, the *silva* genre continued current. Sometimes it was clearly labelled. Statius; Augustino Mascardi (1622); Abraham Cowley (1637); John Dryden (1685): all these and many others composed *silvae*, titled as such.[53] Pierre de Ronsard, moreover, had his *Bocage* (1554); Ben Jonson his *Forest* (1616) and *Underwood* (1640); and Francis Bacon his prose *Sylva Sylvarum* (1627).[54] For exploring the genre's metaphorics naturally led to associated syntagms of *silva* itself. Undoubtedly the emblem–epigram collections also would be regarded as *silvae*.

Emblems characteristically exploited figurative relations between their pictures and epigrams; so that it is unlikely to have been accidental that plant emblems were common in emblem *silvae*. Alciato's collections include many. His *Emblematum Libellus* (Venice, 1546) introduced no less than fourteen tree emblems (a continuous group, CXCIX–CCXII, in the synoptic numbering). Here and in the 1548 Lyons edition these and other plant emblems are seeded throughout, as if to make *silvae* in substance as well as form. And still other emblems include subsidiary representations of shade trees suitable for retired meditation. Palmer's *Two Hundred Poosees*, similarly, has a high proportion of plant emblems—twenty-four; while his *Sprite of Trees and Herbes* concentrates on plants exclusively. Georgette de Montenay's *Emblemes ou Devises Chrestiennes* (1571), an influential book in England, has eleven plant emblems out of a hundred. And an earlier French emblem book recently discovered by John Manning (1993), Charles Jourdain's *Le Blason des Fleurs* (Paris, 1555), draws its diverse moral and therapeutic lessons entirely from plants. Early realizing metaphorical possibilities in the genre label, Jourdain's collection anticipated many later emblem gardens. These include Joachim Camerarius's *Symbolorum et Emblematum ex Re Herbaria* (Nuremberg, 1593), Daniel Stolcius's *Hortulus Hermeticus Flosculis Philosophorum* (Frankfurt, 1627), and Henry Hawkins's *Partheneia Sacra* (Rouen, 1633)—the last a monastery rather than a neo-Stoic garden.

---

[52] Complimentary verses before Thomas Philipott's *Poems* (1646), in Philipott (1950).
[53] E.g. Augustino Mascardi, *Silvarum Libri IV* (Antwerp, 1622).
[54] The term was so fashionable that reference books were called *silvae*; see, e.g., Simon Pelegromius, *Synonymorum Sylva* (1632).

One implication of being *silvae* is that emblem collections may have structural arrangements like those found in non-emblem *silvae*, for example Jonson's *The Forest*.[55] So far, only Quarles's emblems seem to have received much structural analysis.[56] Other collections merit it; not least Alciato's *Emblematum Liber* (Augsburg, 1531) and *Emblematum Libellus* (Paris, 1534). Both are structured according to the pattern of embedded pairs known as ring composition. Such patterns were common in mannerist architecture, and are not unexpected, therefore, in the multimedia emblem, itself an interface between spatial and literary art.[57] In the 1531 edition, the first six and last six emblems correspond in order, each to each. The lineage of Massimiliano Sforza in the first emblem matches *optimus civis* in the last; while both feature Athena, goddess of wisdom and of war. In the second and second last emblems, Massimiliano is addressed (ostensibly, but really the next Duke of Milan, Francesco II): one advises Italian alliances; the other, domination of the moribund nation. The third and third last consider silence: fools' silence passing for wisdom, and silence that refuses to flatter. The fourth and fourth last address rhetoric's power to subdue ferocious political beasts. Next comes a pair on patronage (Emblems V and C); the nurturing stork's reward contrasting with the impositions of harpies. Finally, crows (VI) match pigeons (XCIX), in such a way as to compare the precariousness of prestige gained through consensus government to the fragility of a woman's reputation.[58] The structure seems designed to facilitate discreetly implicit admonition. The ineffectual Massimiliano and his successor Duke Francesco (who tried to dispense with imperial support) are reminded who placed them in power, and counselled to a wiser course. One recalls Fr. Juan Nieremberg's example of Porphyry's encomium with its hidden patterns.[59] An outwardly naive form may be the Silenus mask disguising profundities—like nature (says Nieremberg), the panegyric of God. The comicality of early emblem *picturae*, in the same way, probably had as much to do with the *iocosa seriosa* tradition as with artistic shortcomings.[60]

Earlier and later emblem collections seem to have relied on somewhat different conceptions of 'silva'. Besides meaning 'forest' and implying profuse variety, the word also corresponded to Greek *hyle*, 'stuff', material to be interpreted. The early, humanist collections were conceived rhetorically, as didactic or even monitory

---

[55] See Fowler (1982).
[56] Gilman (1989) 95; Lewalski (1979). Both are now corrected in Holtgen (1993).
[57] Emblems are sometimes found visibly linked in pairs. See an example of 1549, Butsch (1969) No. 131. On the relation between ring composition in architecture and in poetry, see Fowler (1970); Fenoaltea (1990).
[58] In the authorized edition by Wechel (Paris, 1534), the pattern remains unchanged; except that the emblem matching that on silence is omitted—possible in mimetic decorum.
[59] Praz (1964) 19–20.
[60] See Bowen (1985); Barolsky (1978). Thus, the jolly dolphin in *Emblematum Liber* (1531) XXII may not altogether be an effect of the crudity of the woodcut. It contrasts strikingly with Palmer's upright, religiously symbolic dolphin and anchor.

miscellanies, hopefully instructing princes through witty indirection. But the great majority of later collections were religious, and either pursued divine love, or attended to the hidden meanings or 'signatures' of the natural world. Bartoli saw the emblems' intarsia of various woods as analogous to nature's enciphered precepts. The *silva* of nature turned out to be composed of Trees of Life, or of Science—or Porphyrian Trees of ramifying distinctions.[61]

If the emblem collection was partly a literary genre, the individual emblem had a place in literature too. For one thing, emblems were continually quarried for metaphors. Praz hardly exaggerates when he writes that in the seventeenth century 'every poetical image contains a potential emblem'.[62] Obvious instances of inset emblems include the *imprese* in Shakespeare's *Pericles* and Donne's notorious compasses in 'A Valediction: Forbidding Mourning'. Critics have tended to treat such borrowed emblems as intertextualities like any others. But emblems came ready glossed, so that they probably had a special function. From being already interpreted, if not overinterpreted, they could facilitate immediacy of uptake, while promoting complexity and compression.

Emblematic Title-Pages

Emblems contributed differently, according to how completely, and directly, they were realized. One possibility was the emblematic title-page, which historically preceded the emblem collection itself.[63] One might almost think of the frontispiece as an emblem *pictura,* with the title as motto. (For Renaissance authors appear to have discovered the complexity of titles at much the same time as that of fictionality itself.) On the same analogy, an epigraph might supply the epigram, or the text itself be the *explicatio.* The relation of frontispiece to text was consciously considered: George Wither desiderated a title-page 'that's emblematical'; and the emblematic frontispiece was often described as the 'soul' or 'ratio' (meaning) of the book. Or, by a compound ratio, soul was to body as title-page to book as motto to *pictura.*[64] An epigraphic epigram, on the other hand, might be 'the mind, or soul, of the frontispiece', or (as in Walter Raleigh's *History of the World*) 'the mind of the front'. After all, it often summarized the frontispiece's themes, and hence those of the book itself.[65] Alternatively, as Richard Wendorf has observed, a frontispiece portrait might constitute the *pictura* (for portraits sometimes had their mottos), with multiple epigrams to follow.[66]

---

[61] For the Tree of Science, see, e.g., Stephanus's device In Davies (1935) 125; Scholz (1988) 67.
[62] Praz (1964) 15. Much the same is true of Renaissance visual art, as, e.g., E. de Jongh (1967), Lawrence Goedde(1989), and Linda Bauer (1988) have effectively shown.
[63] See Höltgen (1986) chap. 3.
[64] Russell (1985) 41, 43, etc. The latter analogy, however, is rejected in Fraunce (1991) 5–7, 21, 37.
[65] Höltgen (1986) 93.
[66] Wendorf (1990) 48–50, referring to Walton's account of portraits of Donne.

Margery Corbett, R. W. Lightbown and others have discussed many frontispieces presenting emblematic *piciurae* of the book's contents. A good example is Burton's *Anatomy of Melancholy* in early editions, whose much-divided title-page has many little cuts figuring the subdivisions, or *cuts*, of the book itself.[67] And in the 1726 edition of Cats's *Philogami et Sophronisci Dialogus* the crowded title-page anticipates the contents so minutely that interpreting it would take longer than reading the dialogue itself.[68]

Title-pages sometimes incorporated tree emblems or devices. Often these were the printer's device—perhaps a rebus like Grafton's of a tun with a grafted tree.[69] Many printers had tree devices, whether from a connection with woodblock printing (continued later with wooden display type), or from their wooden presses' requiring woodworking skills for maintenance.[70] Some of the devices featured the *arbor scientiae* or Tree of Knowledge—for example, Joannes Theodore's, Abraham Wolfgang's, and Robert Roger's, combining the tree with the fox-and-honey fable to imply the book's wholesome edification; or Robert Estienne's NOLI ALTUM SAPERE device, a wood-cut of cut wood, which was used in England, perhaps under licence.[71] We cannot know how often arboreal frontispieces carried associations of *silva* or *hyle*; but such a decorum would have been anything but foreign to the ethos of Renaissance humanism.

Later frontispieces ran more to architectural frames. These might claim to furnish the 'porch' or entrance,[72] or else to figure the book's 'frame' or structure. This type featured paired columns, pyramids, or obelisks, often surmounted by globes, or symbols of sun and moon, or the Tetragrammaton. Janet Levarie Smarr (1984) has analysed several instances;[73] one may add the frontispiece of Richard Brathwait's *A Survey of History* (1638), with its obelisks, and that of John Gerard's *The Herball or General History of Plants* (1636), combining obelisks and plants.[74] Sometimes obelisks or columns supported a sun and a moon (day and night), as in Richard Haydocke's *Spare Minutes*,[75] symbolizing heaven and Earth, or implying the book's comprehensive coverage. Comprehensiveness and cosmic authority is particularly clear in the frontispiece of Petrus Peña and Matthias de Lonbel's *Stirpium Adversaria Nova* (1570), with its map below and celestial spheres above. Smarr draws on neo-Plato-nism to explain the ubiquitous suns as

---

[67] Corbett and Lightbown (1979); Idol (1980); David H. Radcliffe (private information); Frank (1968) Nos. 71, 76, 124.
[68] *Alle de Wercken* (Amsterdam, 1726).   [69] McKerrow (1949) Nos. 104, 114.
[70] See Moxon (1683). A glance through collections of printers' devices turns up more trees than any other single *motif*: e.g. McKerrow (1949) 29, 36, 38–39, 60, 65, 102, 104, 114, 128, 146, 348–52, etc.; Davies (1935) 58, 63, 69, 77, 82–5, 88, 92a, 93, 94, 96, 97, etc.; de Vinne (1902); Butsch (1969).
[71] E.g. Stephanus's *Maximus Tyrius* of 1557. Cf. Davies (1935) Nos. 84, 125.
[72] The proscenium arch, in the case of printed masques; see Limon (1991).
[73] E.g. de Jode, 1578; Valeriano, 1615.
[74] Johnson (1934) Marshall, No. 48; Payne, No.9. See also Marshall, No. 12, illus. in Farmer (1984) Fig. 34 from Henry Isaacson's *Saturni Ephemerides* (1633).
[75] Höltgen (1986) 132.

enlightening sources of wisdom; later examples combined ascent to heaven with signatures in nature.

By setting out the contents in a visual, memorable form, emblematic title-pages perpetuated mnemonic habits.[76] But their pre-expounded emblems served also to prompt an appropriate mind-set for the text to follow. They might even guide uptake by supplying relevant associations. In *Paradise Lost*, the description of heaven-gate's architectural 'frontispiece' or portico includes a Jacob's ladder: 'The stairs were such as whereon Jacob saw / Angels ascending and descending' (III 510-11). This emblem was so familiar, from its use in frontispieces of books,[77] that Milton was able to use it in a highly compressed way. He contrasts Satan's moral crossroads with that of Jacob (also a fugitive, but repentant), for whom the ladder meant spiritual ascent. And the emblem had further implications, of nature's contemplative value. Here, Milton's inset emblem is complete with its motto, the italicized quotation from Genesis: 'This is the gate of heaven.'

Inset Emblems

One group of poems that came particularly close to being complete emblems were shape or figure poems such as Robert Herrick's 'The Pillar of Fame' and George Herbert's 'The Altar'. Shape poems figured prominently in Renaissance *silvae*: a typical British example is Richard Willes's *Poematum Liber* (1573), designed for imitation by Winchester schoolboys. Useful shapes (column, wings, and the like) were also listed among epigram subtypes in poetics such as Julius Caesar Scaligero's *Poetices Libri Septem* (Lyons, 1561), with examples from Simmias, and George Puttenham's *The Art of English Poesy* (1589).[78] In all such cases, typographic patterning supplied the equivalent of an emblem *pictura*.[79]

These are far from being the only emblematic poems of the Renaissance. As Rosalie Colie and others have shown, a great many epigrams and short lyrics may be regarded as effectually constituting nude emblems. It is hardly necessary to elaborate on how often this is true with George Herbert, Henry Vaughan, and Edward Taylor. Taylor's imagery, in particular, even when it seems perfunctory—'bran, a chaff, a very barley yawn [husk]'[80]—covers a wonderfully rich emblematic

---

[76] On the mnemonic background of columnar title-pages and diagrams, see Doob (1990) 121, Figs. 3, 4, 15; and Index, s. v. Bookcase.

[77] Davies (1970).

[78] Cf. Abraham Fraunce's examples in *The Arcadian Rhetoric* (1588). The pattern poems of Hrabanus Maurus (ca. 780–856) were printed in near-facsimile editions early in the sixteenth century: e.g. *De Laudibus Sancte Crucis Opus Erudicione Versu, Prosaque Mirificium*, ed. J. Wimpheling (Phorcheim, 1600).

[79] For a contrary view, emphasizing the difference between shape poems and emblems, see Westerweel (1992).

[80] Meditation II.xviii: Heb. 13.10, 'We Have an Altar'; Fowler (1991) 734. Alan Howard's criticism of Taylor, that the emblem habit led him to skim the Book of Nature perfunctorily, is rejected in Gilman (1989) 59–60.

pith, copious in biblical and world-picture associations. Emblematic allusiveness was second nature to him. Here, the husks associate and contrast with the equally insignificant seed in the parable, that grows mightily when it dies. In such nude emblems, the title often functions as a motto; especially when it is a biblical quotation. The emblem-inspired George Herbert was the first English poet to use titles imaginatively in an enigmatic or allusive way.[81]

As fully emblematic, and similarly multimedia, was the masque. For, what is the action of a masque but animated emblem *picturae*?[82] The masque as a whole can either be seen as dramatized emblem or as modulation of comedy by emblem. Such ideas may be found in Inigo Jones (who described the masque as 'nothing else but pictures with light and motion').[83] And Jonson writes of pairs of masquers presenting fans on one of which is a 'mute hieroglyphic, expressing their mixed qualities'.[84] Perhaps, on the same analogy, masque dialogue presented hieroglyphics not mute—emblem *subscriptiones*. On the City pageants or 'devices,' Jonson goes into more detail:

> The symbols used are not, neither ought to be, simply hieroglyphics, emblems, or *impreses*, but a mixed character, partaking somewhat of all, and peculiarly apted to these more magnificent inventions, wherein the garments and ensigns [symbolic attributes] deliver the nature of the person, and the word the present office.[85]

The emblem has a yet further, but less obvious, claim on our interest: its implicit contribution to several literary masterpieces. The symbolism of Shakespeare's late romances—to mention one group of instances—could be described as a series of emblems writ large. For the inset masque in *The Tempest* is by no means the only emblematic element. From the initial shipwreck, the action unfolds emblem after emblem of moral shipwreck and spiritual repentance.[86] An even more striking example is *A Winter's Tale*, where the visual focus of the dénouement is an enigmatic emblem figure, Hermione's stony-hearted, softened, moved and moving 'statue'.

Such deeply implicit emblems were possible only after lengthy development. The Hellenistic emblem was revived, after many centuries, in the minute and deeply significant descriptions of the *Hypnerotomachia*. Later, Colonna's

---

[81] On epigraphic and postscriptive procedures in the seventeenth-century religious poem, see Chambers (1992) 43–4. On titles, see Gardner (1966); Levin (1977); Fowler (1982) 92–8.

[82] Emblems are sometimes said to have entered the masque *via* its scenery. A source at least as likely was the title-pages of printed realizations; see, e.g., Corbett and Lightbown (1979) 4–6.

[83] Orgel and Strong (1973) II, 480.

[84] Jonson, *The Masque of Blackness* 267–9. Cf. Russell (1985) 86, and see Young (1992).

[85] Discussing *The King's Entertainment in Passing to His Coronation*. Sec Gilbert (1969) 16.

[86] On Renaissance symbolisms of shipwreck, see Goedde (1989). For an excellent account of the emblematic basis of Shakespeare's earlier plays, see Abraham (1991).

reputation extended to England, and his compelling work exerted a profound influence on Spenser.[87] *The Faerie Queene* is certainly the most emblematic long poem in our literature. Critics debate its characterization in the 'Letter to Ralegh' as 'a continued allegory or dark conceit'. But perhaps Spenser simply means that its *concetti*, like those of emblems, are intended as matter for meditation. And, indeed, many of its descriptive passages can be seen as nude emblems. As for the narrative, it sometimes moves consecutively from virtual emblem to virtual emblem, almost in the manner of Jan Brueghel's continued rebus. The emblematic material of Part I ranges from Ponsonby's anchor device on the 1590 title-page and iconographic descriptions of Redcrosse, Una, and the Monster Errour (I.i.1–27), to the Hermaphrodite emblem (III.xii.45–46)—Holzwart's Emblem XXV, AMOR CONIUGALIS[88] —and the *pictura* of St George and the dragon. This dragon is one of several: earlier, Arthur's dragon crest; the dragon under Lucifera's feet; the one under Cupid's statue; and the Old Dragon defeated by Redcrosse; later, Geryoneo's monster; the crocodile-dragon at Isis Church; and Echidna's hind-quarters.[89] To each of these descriptions, familiar dragon emblems make substantial contributions. And this is but one strand of many. Every sort of emblem imagery is to be found in the poem: religious emblems in Book I; moral emblems and the Tablet of Cebes in II; Petrarchan *trionfi* and chivalric *imprese* in III and IV; and, in V, political emblems like that of Geryon, recalling Thomas Palmer's (nude) Emblem CXLIV, CONCORDE UNVINCIBLE. Most prominent of all, the masque-like dance of the Graces in VI.x effectually sets in motion Alciato's Emblem CLXIII, GRATIAE.

A characteristic instance, surely worth further study, is the powerful image of Amoret in the masque of Cupid at the House of Busyrane, carrying her everted heart in a silver basin:

> At that wide orifice her trembling hart
> Was drawne forth, and in silver basin layd,
> Quite through transfixèd with a deadly dart,
> And in her bloud yet steeming fresh embayd…[90]

—which may at first recall Georgette de Montenay's 1571 Emblem LXXXI, BEATI MUNDO CORDE [Blessed are the pure in heart], with its heart in a chalice or laver. This is surely a relevant association; but is it optimally relevant? The Spenserian episode contains many evocations of jealousy, and also of 'envious

---

[87] The *Hypnerotomachia* was translated by Sir R. Dallington as *The Strife of Love in a Dream* (1592).
[88] Daly (1979a) Fig. 1.
[89] I.vii.31; I.iv.10; III.i.48; I.xi.8–15; V.xi.24; V.vii.15; VI.vi.10. Mercilla's suppressed crocodile had several emblem associations, especially Camerarius's NUSQUAM TUTA TYRANNIS; see Henkel and Schöne, cols. 668, 670, 674, 675.
[90] *The Faerie Queene* III.xii.21.1–4.

desire' (III.xi.26). Perhaps, then, a more appropriate association may be emblems of envy. These sometimes had *picturae* portraying, with horrible literalism, the action of 'eating one's heart out'.[91] Emblem collections are far from being dictionaries of meanings; but they frequently offer relevant fields of association that orient criticism usefully.

We may ask what concealed such emblematic pictorialism, until recently, from all but a few good readers, such as Alexander Pope's mother, John Ruskin, C. S. Lewis, and Rosemond Tuve.[92] Ignorance of emblems is only part of the answer. Another factor may well be that Spenser generally blends or synthesizes emblems into composite descriptions. A single *ekphrasis* is liable to correspond to parts of several emblems; and even a complete nude emblem will finesse on its source.[93] This method has a counterpart in Renaissance visual art, where symbolic images may be composite in extremely subtle ways—as, indeed, iconography exists to explain. Spenser critics have tended to be hesitant in addressing this interface with art history. But fortunately, encouraging progress has recently been made in this direction by John Manning, Ruth Luborsky, and others.

However intuitive a work of Renaissance literature may seem, it should be regarded as challenging the combined resources of emblem scholarship and traditional art history. Between these two approaches, I see no necessary division. After all, as Adrien Delen pointed out, some of the finest graphic artists of the Renaissance—Albrecht Dürer, Hans Holbein II, Arnold Nicolai, Wenceslaus Hollar among them—were happy to practise emblem-art.[94] An emblem's raison d'être, however, lay in its ideas and wit rather than in independent picturing. Indeed, the emblem collections were among other things, as I have argued, collective literary works. On this depended the strategic position of emblem-art as a third Grace between the Sister Arts of *Poesia* and *Disegno*. And on this, too, depended the potential of emblems for rearrangement and reapplication.

---

[91] As in Jan van der Straet's design, engraved by Philip Galle; see Harvey-Lee (1992) No. 10.

[92] Lewis (1967); cf. his study of the emblem source of 'Spenser's Cruel Cupid', Lewis (1966); Tuve (1966) and (1970).

[93] See Fowler and Manning (1976).   [94] Delen (1935) II, 107.

Lord's Space in Seventeenth-Century Britain

By 'Lord's space,' I mean the space (or notional space) round a feudal lord, especially a sovereign prince—or, indeed, space symbolically associated with the Lord God. My focus is on the seventeenth century, partly because my ignorance of that period may be less obvious, partly because it is still not well enough understood how long feudal ceremonies and conceptions endured. They did so even into the Enlightenment.[1] I shall concentrate on literary examples, particularly plays and masques, which were undoubtedly designed in part to assert through their display the prince's greatness, even if they contained specific contents of an advisory or controversial nature. France and Britain in the seventeenth century are apparently to be regarded as 'theatre states', to use Clifford Geertz's all-too-convenient term. That is, the state (like that, we are told, in nineteenth-century Bali), was less concerned with government than with 'spectacle...the public dramatization of...social inequality and status pride'. Geertz argues that royal ritual was not an instrument, still less a fraud, but an end in itself. 'Power served pomp, not pomp power.'[2] This simplistic exaggeration, in the popular mode of facile structuralist dichotomy, nevertheless states an important half-truth. Display was a self-justifying activity, although not quite an end in itself; in July 1633, when the Earl of Newcastle entertained Charles I so lavishly at Welbeck that he damaged his estate, he was not pursuing some absolute pomp, but was recommending his service to his prince. Service was much more than a ritual display of 'social inequality', being frequently offered, indeed, between social equals. Display was factitive of a greatness shared by princes with their retainers and ultimately with all their subjects. Moreover, the element of ceremony involved was regarded as a mystery showing forth transhuman values.[3]

An example of the sense of lord's space outliving the feudal system proper would be the so-called 'King's peace'. Disorder in the sovereign's immediate environment counted as a breach of the King's peace. In the Middle Ages, the conception was local and personal; later, it extended throughout all England, so

---

[1] For the seventeenth century itself, there is valuable evidence of this in the Note Books of John Finet, Master of Ceremonies to Charles I. See Finet 1987.
[2] Burke 1992, 12 citing Geertz 1980, 13. [3] See, e.g., Fraunce 1588 and 1991.

that disorder anywhere might amount to 'a breach of the peace'.[4] After the Restoration, Charles II, although unusually accessible, could be keenly conscious of the dignity due to a prince in this respect. When the Earl of Rochester struck someone in the royal presence, the incident led to much discussion. 'Even to insult another man in front of the king was sufficient to earn banishment from the court'.[5] And when the Earl of Clarendon's son pushed past a porter to see a play at Whitehall after the king had declared the auditorium devoid of free space, he not only lost his court post, but suffered the humiliation of being refused another office, ten years later. He had infringed the king's space. In a famous Shakespearean scene, *2 Henry IV*, IV. v, the dying king thinks his son (Prince Hal, popularly supposed to have lost his place in the Council by quarrelling with the Lord Chief Justice in the King's presence[6]) has now further intruded on his personal space by putting on the crown before its legitimate possessor is dead.

In the late sixteenth and early seventeenth century, the dominant symbol of nature had become the theatre. Then as now, everyone was familiar with the analogy between theatre and cosmos. In Shakespeare's theatre, explicitly called the Globe, an actor might be heard to declare 'all the world's a stage....'.[7] Nature herself was conceived as spectacle, as a visual object of contemplation, something to be looked at, where the enactments of providence taught God's will. The word 'theatre' (derived from Greek thea/omai, 'gaze at, contemplate, wonder at') appeared in countless book titles.[8] Jean Bodin's *Universae naturae theatrum* (1596) conceived nature as a display open to all; Giulio Camillo's memory theatre offered a physical or virtual structure in which to locate mentally the images of the Hermetic system.[9] Guillaume de la Perrière called his book of emblems a *Théâtre des Bons Engins* (1539).[10] And Richard Verstegen's Catholic martyrology must count as the first theatre of cruelty—*Theatrum Crudelitatum Haereticorum Nostri Temporis* (1587). There was a *Théâtre des Instrumens Mathématiques et Méchaniques* (1578) no less than a *Theatrum Florae* (1622). Bodies were anatomized in lecture theatres, and tabular pedagogical theatres of philosophy, mnemonics, and geography appeared on title-pages.[11] And in *Paradise Lost* the cosmic drama of the Fall is enacted in 'a woody theatre/ Of stateliest view' (iv 141–2), until eventually the angelic dramatist Michael tells Adam 'now prepare thee for another scene' of its consequences (xi 637). In the midst of all this

---

[4] Allen 1953.   [5] Hutton 1989, 453.
[6] *I Henry IV* III ii 32, referring to the legendary quarrel recounted in Sir T. Elyot, *The Governour* (1531) ii 6.
[7] *As You Like It* II vii 139. See Blair 1997 ch. 5 *et passim*; Yates 1969 on the correspondence of zodiac to seating in Shakespeare's Globe theatre; Christian 1987.
[8] Blair 1997, 154.
[9] Blair 1997 ch. 5, esp. 154, 160, 283 ns. 21, 22; Bernheimer 1956. On Camillo's *L'Idea del Teatro*, see Yates 1966 chs. 6, 7.
[10] Blair 1997, 169.   [11] See Blair 1997 ch. 5, esp. 172, 174.

significant theatricality, a prince's location, both in the cosmic or intellectual and in the material theatre, must be a matter of moment. The prince required to be the cynosure of all the looking, so that theatres must be constructed accordingly.

That was possible, because in the early seventeenth century court theatres were hardly ever permanent buildings, but rather temporary facilities, usually erected for a single performance, perhaps in a hall of Whitehall Palace that also served many other functions. The details may be worth considering. Seating was provided by *degrees* ('steps', 'bleachers', but also 'ranks') temporarily erected round the walls. The *stage* might be in the centre (early seventeenth century) or at one end, as in John Webb's Hall Theatre of 1660, in Whitehall Palace. But one feature was invariable: the isle or royal state on its footpace or platform.[12] The chair of *state* or of *estate*[13] consisted of a raised chair or throne under a canopy. So Falstaff, role-playing king with Prince Hal, says, 'This chair shall be my state.'[14] The *state* indicated that whoever legitimately sat on it was himself a state, that is, a prince or noble of high degree.[15] So, in *Paradise Lost*, Satan the usurper sits 'high on a throne of royal state' (ii 1). The *state* might also mean specifically the canopy, as in a description by the republican James Harrington: 'at the upper end hangs a rich state overshadowing the greater part of a large throne.'[16] He could be describing any number of portraits by Vandyke and others of the period. Or compare Satan's canopy at his brief triumph: 'his high throne, which under state/ Of richest texture spread.'[17] The chair of state rested on the footpace,[18] a low platform like the high table dais in an Oxford college. Francis Bacon, in his essay 'On Judicature', writes, 'the Place of Justice is an Hallowed Place; and therefore not only the Bench, but the Footpace and Precincts and Pourprise [enclosure] thereof ought to be preserved without Scandal and Corruption.'[19] We should notice that the footpace was not confined to kings and queens. Bulstrode Whitelocke relates how Cromwell used one: 'At the upper end upon a footpace and carpet, stood the Protector with a chair of state behind him.'[20] The *footpace* or *halpace* established a threshold, a *limen* of feudal degree, and so was sometimes called a *grounsel*.

All this still took for granted the hierarchic ordering of objects and people that had long governed the visual imagination of medieval people. Throughout the Middle Ages, depiction of things had relatively little to do with the ordering of

---

[12] Orrell 1985, 3, etc., Index, s. v. *Theatres, component parts of.* See also Thurley 1999; Nicoll 1963, 33–4, where, however, *state* is wrongly taken to mean 'platform'.

[13] OED s. v. *state* 17b, 20, *estate* 4. Hakluyt writes of the 'imperiall throne of estate'.

[14] *1 Henry IV* II iv 373. For the King's chair under a *baldachino* in the Paved Court theatre at Somerset House in 1614, see Orrell 1985, 14.

[15] OED s. v. *state* 24.   [16] *Oceana* 1700, 121.   [17] *Paradise Lost* x 445–6.

[18] OED s. v. *footpace* 2 b.

[19] Bacon 1985, 168. M. Kiernan there calls *footpace* a crux, wrongly supposing the context to imply a 'walking area near the bench'.

[20] *Memoirs* (1682), 609. Cf. Whitelocke 1990, ii 470 (26 June 1657): 'A place being prepared at the Upper end of Westminstre hall, in the midst of it was a rich cloth of Estate set up, and under it a chair of State upon an ascent of two degrees covered with Carpets...'

spatial relations, still less with unifying of space (the terms of Panofsky's essay of 1927). Medieval artists were far more intent on showing objects, people, and things, in their feudal or religious relations. Indeed, this delayed the invention of modern perspective with its logic of proportion. For in medieval pictures, objects were likely to be high or large because more important, or hierarchically superior. So donors tended to be smaller than saints, while the Virgin, Alice-like, might dwarf the church in which she nevertheless somehow stood. In the sixteenth century this was still part of the domain of assumptions—as, for example, in Sidney's 'Ye Goteherd Gods', where mountains are 'stately' or 'lofty', but valleys 'humble' or 'basest', clearly in a social or political sense.[21]

By the seventeenth century, however, objects might be ordered in a different, altogether more modern way. One can see the two conceptions of spatial relations confronting one another in 1605, on the occasion when a theatre was set up in Christ Church, Oxford, for a play to be attended by James I of Britain.[22] This temporary Christ Church theatre, for which a drawing survives, was apparently devised by Simon Basil (Comptroller and Surveyor of the Works) and Inigo Jones, largely on the basis of Sebastiano Serlio's designs for neoclassical theatres. Serlio's 48-foot *orchestra* was scaled down to 24 ft (the area in which nevertheless the isle was to be placed). Governed by Vitruvian proportions[23] and neoclassical or Italian conceptions of staging, it proved far too modern for the court. When the Lord Chamberlain's party inspected the arrangements, they disliked them as unusual, innovative, and unworkable.

They (but especially Suffolk) utterly disliked the stage at Christ Church, and above all, the place appointed for the chair of estate because it was no higher and the king so placed that the auditory could see but his cheek only. This dislike of the Earl of Suffolk much troubled the Vice-Chancellor, and all the workmen, yet they stood in defence of the thing done, and maintained that by the art of perspective the king should behold all better than if he sat higher.[24]

The assumption of a theatrical space based on perspective and sight lines was in confrontation with the hierarchic assumptions of the Lord Chamberlain's party. A compromise had to be worked out by the Privy Council. The isle was moved back from the forestage to the middle of the *cavea* or auditorium, thus displacing the young ladies and the King's servants. These were now accommodated in front of the isle, but lower. (By convention, attractive young ladies were placed next to the *piazza della scena*, as encouragement to the actors of a masque.) It might be thought (if it were not unthinkable) that they would have their backs turned to the King. But they seem to have faced inwards, so that they and the King could

---

[21] Sidney 1962, 111–13.   [22] Johnson 1994, 26; Orrell 1978, Introd. and ch. 1.
[23] On the Vitruvian proportions, see Orrell 1978.
[24] Orrell 1985, 29 citing an anonymous report by a Cambridge visitor; cf. Orgel 1973, i 8.

comfortably gaze at more than one another's cheeks.²⁵ The idea was in short to display the King's status and presence, rather than to give him the best vantage for seeing and hearing the play. Indeed, the King's place was now 'too far from the stage (*videlicet* 28 ft), so that there were many long speeches delivered, which neither the King nor any near him could well hear or understand.' So far as the King was concerned, the *ancien regime* had won a Pyrrhic victory.

By 1634, the King was now Charles I, a prince far more punctilious than his father. Nevertheless, one can sense a somewhat changed attitude regarding arrangements for masques. Perhaps Charles's more cultivated appreciation of aesthetic value had triumphed over the narrowly political approach; perhaps it was Henrietta Maria's keen personal interest in masquing. However that may be, at Shirley's *Triumph of Peace* on 4 Feb. in the Banqueting House, Whitehall, the hundred gentlemen that rode 'bravely mounted' before the masquers through the streets 'were placed all together...on an upper gallery there purposely reserved for them, behind and over, the King's seat'.²⁶

Turning to the *frontispiece* or boundary between the forestage and the scenic stage (precursor of the proscenium arch), one is struck by how closely it resembled a triumphal arch—that is, (in Sigfried Giedion's definition) 'a gateway, torn from its original context as part of the city wall, and given a monumental and symbolic character. The purpose of this isolated sculptural element was to provide a passageway for a solemn procession.'²⁷ The architectural allusion is noticeable in John Webb's design for the Cockpit-in-Court theatre, and still more so in his unidentified theatre plan at Worcester College, Oxford.²⁸ One should recall that masques often concluded with the prince or other noble person making a triumphal descent through the frontispiece to the dancing space, there to transmit sovereign virtues to their subjects. The external façades of permanent theatres might also emphasize a ceremonial entry way; as for example in Wren's Sheldonian Theatre at Oxford, where royal or other formal processions entered through the straight S side. Up to the nineteenth century, indeed, London theatres sometimes had a special door reserved exclusively for royal parties.²⁹

Complete triumphal arches in permanent architecture were almost unknown in the Middle Ages, and even after the Renaissance they were 'hard to introduce into the Christian atmosphere'.³⁰ But it was different with temporary arches designed to represent the city and its qualities. Literally thousands of these wooden arches were erected throughout Europe for royal entries, coronation

---

[25] Orrell 1985, 30; for the royal box faced by all, see also 11.
[26] Finet 1987, 149.
[27] Giedion 1971, 131. For the frontispiece, see Orrell 1985, xiii, 98–9, 162.
[28] Orrell 1985, ch. 9, pl. 28. For a working definition of a triumphal arch, one may rely on Giedion 1971, 131; although for the late medieval period more castellar forms have to be taken into account, on which see Kernodle 1944, 90–3.
[29] See Orrell 1985, 2.   [30] Giedion 1971, 135.

celebrations, and the like.³¹ In 1661 a sizeable moiety of the carpenters of England—600, it was said—were put to work on arches through which Charles II's coronation procession was to pass.³² For James I's coronation in 1604, none other than Ben Jonson wrote the festival book, explaining among other things how the Fenchurch arch was inscribed CAMERA REGIS, to signify Londinium, 'The King's Chamber', and how it 'not only laboured the expression of state [stateliness] and magnificence (as proper to a triumphal Arch) but the very site, fabric, strength, policy, dignity, and affections of the City were all laid down to life'.³³ (The various tableaux showed the harmonious agreement of the guilds and other cadres of the city in their loyalty to the new King.) A. W. Johnson has drawn attention to Jonson's description as the earliest statement of Vitruvian ideas in English; it continues: 'the nature and property of these Devices being, to present always some one entire body, or figure, consisting of distinct members, and each of those expressing itself, in the own active sphere, yet all, with that general harmony so connexed, and disposed, as no one little part can be missing to the illustration of the whole'.³⁴

One source of these Vitruvian ideas is Colonna's *Hypnerotomachia* (1499), from which probably came the triple doorway (itself an allusion to the triumphal arch) used in Jonson's masque *Oberon*.³⁵ It was 'discovered' at the denouement, and from it Oberon (the role taken by Prince Henry) approached the chair of state in a silent chariot.

The *Hypnerotomachia* fascinated the Elizabethan and Jacobean imagination. Motifs, images, narratives were everywhere drawn from it and used to animate masques, architecture, poetry. It would be impossible to list the pyramids and obelisks that appeared in the palaces, country houses, and even churches of the period.³⁶ A triple doorway, perhaps from the same source as that in *Oberon*, appears in Spenser's *The Faerie Queene*, in the Cave of Mammon. It is a travesty of the inscriptions over *Hypnerotomachia* doors: instead of GLORI DEI, MATER AMORIS, and GLORIA MUNDI we have 'Here Sleep, there Richesse, and Hel-gate them both betwext' (II vii 25).

One must not make too much of the *Hypnerotomachia* connection, since other possible sources for the triumphal triple archway abounded, such as the west

---

³¹ See Kernodle 1944, 90, 92: 'To enter Edinburgh in 1503, Queen Margaret went under a triumphal arch resembling a castle, built in the characteristic form of two towers with central opening between. From windows in the towers angels sang, and in the centre niche or window an angel stood to present keys to the queen.' Cf. Giedion 1971, 134 on the wooden triumphal arch of Alphonso I in Naples (built 1451–8) and the triple arch in honour of Pope Julius II for his victory over Bologna (1506). See Kruft and.Malmanger (1975).
³² See Ogilby 1988, 11.
³³ 'The King's Entertainment,' lines 27, 244–6, in Jonson 1925–1952, vii 83, 90. See Johnson 1994, 47–9.
³⁴ The 2 : 1 proportion in the Christ Church theatre plan (not from Serlio) expresses a similar harmony; see Orrell 1985, 28.
³⁵ Johnson 1994, 69 and pls. 18 and 19; Colonna 1499, 1904, sig. h8r.
³⁶ See Kernodle 1944, 76 on pyramids from Italy, 102 on pyramids in the Lisbon entry.

doorways of many cathedrals, and the architectural frontispieces of books. The point I want to make is simply that triumphal arches were heavy with liminal symbolism, much of it political. George Chapman's Bussy D'Ambois seditiously threatens, 'I'll make th'inspirèd thresholds of court / Sweat with the weather of my horrid steps.'[37] As Gordon Kipling's study of civic triumphs makes clear, the royal entry did not merely demonstrate the prince's right to enter at will, but also that prior agreement with the city had been reached.[38] This obtained even with countries and capitals: Charles II would not have had his coronation entertainment, had he not earlier been invited to return to England by Parliament's Commissioners, after reaching agreement on terms. Power over the threshold—like the keys of the city—has continued to be significant. Within living memory, in Scotland, the laird has felt himself entitled to open a tenant's door, invading his privacy and perhaps throwing in a present of game.

Like the frontispiece or porch of a building, the frontispiece of a book had special importance. Indeed, a frontispiece was sometimes considered the 'mind' of the book. And Ben Jonson's anonymous sonnet before Raleigh's *History of the World* (1614) is titled 'The mind of the front,' amended in the 1640 edition of *Underwood* to 'The Mind of the Frontispiece to a Book'—that is, the *ratio* or 'explanation' of the frontispiece, which itself explains the contents of the book to follow.[39] The frontispiece was often architectural in design, as if to create a mental space. This space contained images displaying the main subjects of the book—not only to advertise them (as is too readily assumed to be the sole purpose) but also to image them for memory. So the earlier frontispieces were often divided into three columns—the triumphal motif again—like the columns of shelves of the *columna* or book cupboard of the Middle Ages. The subjects imaged (sometimes inscribed in chapter-titles or topic-lemmas) thus occupied memory *places* in the *columna*.[40]

The iconography of the Renaissance frontispiece confirms these suggestions and adds others. Thus, many frontispieces have a recess, which, Serlio explains, if the plinth is omitted, 'may...serve for an Arch triumphant'.[41] The suggestion of a triumphal arch, already mentioned, becomes explicit in Michael Drayton's verses 'Upon the Frontispiece' to *Poly-Olbion* (1612, 1622):

> Through a Triumphant Arch, see Albion placed,
> In Happy site, in Neptune's armes embraced,
> In Power and Plenty, on her Cleevy Throne
> Circled with Nature's Girlands, being alone

---

[37] *Bussy D'Ambois* 1604 IV ii 184–5.   [38] Kipling 1998 *passim*.
[39] Corbett 1979, 130, 135 on Jonson's 'The Mind of the Front' (for Sir W. Raleigh's *History of the World* 1614) reprinted in *The Underwood* 1640 as 'The Mind of the Frontispiece to a Book'.
[40] Carruthers 1990, Index s. v. *Columna* (bookpress) and *Scrinium* (book chest) as receptacles of memory.
[41] Corbett 1979, 4–5.

Styled th' Ocean's Island. On the Columns been
(As Trophies raised) what Princes Time hath seen
Ambitious of her....[42]

One might think of the frontispiece, then, as an entryway to the book beyond. As Corbett and Lightbown rightly observe, however, more often the plinth is *not* omitted, and one has to look for another building type as model. It may be found in the *pegma* or temporary façade, often with *tableaux vivants* of allegorical personages, used for a royal entry, street theatre, festival, or *landjuweel* (annual contest of rhetoric societies).[43] Intended for political display, the *pegma*'s iconography symbolized the presiding authority, claiming space around it as rightfully the prince's, or Rhetoric's, as the case might be. Hence its tabernacle, heavenly throne, or throne-of-honour.[44] Transferred to the frontispiece, as in Thomas Geminus's *Compendiosa totius Anatomiae Delineatio* (1545), it appears as a scalloped niche suggesting a throne, with putti before it holding the imperial crown.[45] The empty throne (to which we'll return) recalls the denouement of Shakespeare's *Measure for Measure*, where the city gate of Vienna is provided with three thrones, for the Duke, Angelo, and Escalus. The central one of these the providential Duke vacates so that Angelo may occupy it and judge Isabella and himself with borrowed authority. In other frontispieces, a cartouche may make a more implicit claim to authority; the strap-work of the cartouche (probably originating in Rosso Fiorentino's designs for the royal palace of Fontainebleau) always carried associations of nobility. As Corbett and Lightbown notice, the closest models for the frontispiece cartouche are those of the royal imprese in Girolamo Ruscelli's *Le Imprese Illustri*.[46] Inscriptions, similarly, often asserted the prince's authority—perhaps heraldically, like the motto DIEU ET MON DROIT in Geminus' title-page. One might compare the *leges hortorum* on the entryway porch or frontispiece of gardens in the Renaissance,[47] the inscriptions above doorways in the *Hypnerotomachia*, and, in Dante's *Inferno*, the authoritative inscription inscribed above the gate: PER ME SI VA NE LA CITTÀ DOLENTE,...LASCIATE OGNE SPERANZA, VOI CH'INTRATE.[48] The highest of all claims to authority came in the iconography of the frontispieces of religious books, and books with a religious aspect. These often had at the top, instead of the empty niche (or in addition to it), a triangle with the divine tetragrammaton.[49] Thus, in several ways, the frontispiece displayed the lord's or the Lord God's, authority over its space— and hence the space of the book, which might be glimpsed through its arches.

---

[42] See Corbett 1979, 154.   [43] For the *landjuweel,* see Kernodle 1944, 112.
[44] For the throne-of-honour, see Kernodle 1944, 37, 43, 44, 46, etc.; for the triumphal arch, 38.
[45] Hind 1952–1955, i, pl. 17. In the 1559 edition the crown is replaced by a portrait of Queen Elizabeth, Hind pl 18 (a).
[46] Corbett 1979, 13; Ruscelli 1566.   [47] See Morford 1987.   [48] *Inferno* iii 1–11.
[49] See Corbett 1979, 39–40.

So, in *Paradise Lost* iii, Satan comes to the frontispiece of the Book of Nature: he sees

> Ascending by degrees magnificent
> Up to the wall of heaven a structure high,
> At top whereof, but far more rich appeared
> The work as of a kingly palace gate
> With frontispiece of diamond and gold
> Embellished, thick with sparkling orient gems
> The portal shone, inimitable on earth
> By model, or by shading pencil drawn.
> The stairs were such as whereon Jacob saw
> Angels ascending and descending...
>
> (*Paradise Lost* iii 502–11)

If Satan were 'to dare / The...easy ascent' (iii 523–4)—if *per impossibile* he were to ascend the ladder, he would come to where he could humble himself and acknowledge fealty. Instead, he turns down the opportunity, and soon he is on Mount Niphates, suffering agonies of remorse and guilt. The Niphates monologue has often been compared to a tragic soliloquy. I should like to suggest we regard it as indeed a tragedy in miniature enacted on a stage behind the frontispiece in Book iii. The repeated word 'step' in the Niphates passage—'from hell / One step no more than from himself can fly' (iv 22); 'I...thought one step higher / Would set me highest' (iv 50–1)—serve to recall similarly repeated steps in the earlier passage: 'Ascending by degrees magnificent' (iii 502); 'the lower stair / That scaled by steps of gold to heaven gate' (iii 540–1).

Jacob's ladder was generally portrayed with fifteen rungs or steps,[50] to symbolize ascension through meditation to heaven, or approach to the divine throne. The origin of the symbolism seems to have been the fifteen Psalms of Degrees, corresponding to the fifteen ceremonial steps to the Temple in Jerusalem.[51] Subsequently it became a common compositional number, although this may have partly arisen from additional associations. Thus, Du Bellay's fifteen sonnet-visions may allude to the fifteen signs of apocalypse; and Sir John Harington's fifteen emblems suggest the fifteen mysteries of the Virgin and Christ.[52] Jonson himself used the number for *The Forrest* (1616), so arranging the

---

[50] See Davies 1970, 49–52; Kuntz 1987; Climacus 1959.
[51] For the steps to the Temple, see Cassiodorus on Ps. 119; also Bongo 1591, 406–10 giving other pious patristic explanations, e.g. $7 + 8 = 15$; 5×3 of grace; $1, 2, 3...15 = 120$ (perfection; the number of disciples at Pentecost).
[52] Miller 1984, 151.

sequence that fifteen poems lead up to a final prayer 'To Heaven,' before the throne of judgment.[53]

In spatial, Pythagorean terms, fifteen is both a triangular and a pyramidal number. A crucial speech in *The Mask of Queens* (1609), introducing the masque proper, is that of Heroic Virtue, in 78 lines—a triangular number.[54] According to Jonson's own note, in place of the antimasque came a transformation scene,

> a glorious and magnificent building, figuring the House of Fame, in the upper part of which were discovered the twelve masquers sitting upon a throne triumphal, erected in form of a pyramid, and circled with all store of light. From whom, a person, by this time descended, in the furniture of Perseus; and expressing heroical, and masculine Virtue began to speak.[55]
>
> (*Mask of Queens* 354–65)

Jonson and Inigo Jones's use here of the triangular number has to be seen in its historical context. No-one can fail to have been struck by the contemporary prominence of the pyramid as a decorative motif, not only in Italy but throughout Europe, in palace architecture, monumental sculpture, and garden-art. The fame of Pope Sixtus V's achievements in this direction was everywhere trumpeted— 'Thy pyramids built up with newer might' as Shakespeare's Sonnet 123 puts it. Twelve pyramids or obelisks were erected in Rome: Sixtus used them again and again in his city planning, as if to set his princely seal on Rome at focal points. The gesture of the Vatican obelisk was most powerful of all, since it involved a considerable feat of engineering.[56] Sixtus' enduring influence is seen as late as the Arc de Triomphe, which, though incorrectly placed in terms of the antique form, is in the Renaissance spirit of princely assertion.

Besides such historical contexts, the ordering of space in Stuart masques also had a literary context, in the doctrine of *ut architectura poesis*. According to this doctrine, literary works were conceived of as composed, like material buildings, from parts in numerical proportion or arranged symmetrically, or by some other design. After all, Pythagorean and Vitruvian formal relations could be displayed quite as well in literature, or in garden-art, as in expensive masonry. Jonson, son of a mason and one of the finest exponents of the doctrine, theorizes it in *Discoveries* like this:

> in the constitution of a poem, the action is aimed at by the poet, which answers place in a building; and that action hath his largeness, compass, and proportion. But, as a court, or King's palace, requires other dimensions than a private house:

---

[53] Fowler 1982, 173.   [54] See Johnson 1994, 190.   [55] See Johnson 1994, 183.
[56] Described in Fontana 1590, cit. Dibner 1950.

so the epic asks a magnitude, [different] from other poems. Since, what is place in the one, is action in the other, the difference is in space.

(*Discoveries* 2688–95)

The *ut architectura* doctrine lies behind much of the Renaissance numerical composition that has attracted attention in recent decades.[57] Such designs might be described as Vitruvian style at bargain prices. The structure of literary works—lines, stanzas, books, chapters, speeches—could display much the same formal proportions, arrangements, and motifs as architecture. Triumphal motifs, for example, or the solar cult of sovereignty, which everyone is familiar with, from descriptions of the ceremonies of the Sun King himself, Louis XIV.[58] No need to tell how Louis danced the role of Apollo in ballets of the 1650s;[59] how his cosmic role was dramatized in Vincenzo Maria Coronelli's vast globes, more than fifteen feet in diameter, for the Château de Marly;[60] or how Versailles was so oriented that the merely macrocosmic rising sun illuminated the bedchamber of *Sol Oriens* himself.[61] As A. W. Johnson notes, Kepler dedicated his *Harmonice Mundi* (1619) to James I 'with its maintenance of the implied analogy—so central to masque—between monarchy and the solar system, its sun a centre and solitary auditor of the celestial harmony ("*nam quid aliud est Regnum, quam Harmonia*").'[62] Unaccountably, A. W. Johnson supposes that 'the tools of the new astronomy...were too powerful to sustain such a view' and that the Rudolphine Tables meant the end of the old world picture of Ptolemaic analogies.[63]

In actuality, the sun's central place among the planets was not less but more emphatic in the new astronomy. Otherwise, Copernicanism might not have been embraced so enthusiastically by the princes of Europe.[64] Pace A. W. Johnson, Kepler's Rudolphine Tables of 1627 were not (like Reinhold's Prutenic Tables of 1551) based on the Copernican system, but rather took their starting point from Tycho Brahe.[65] As my earlier quotation suggests, Kepler seems to have thought his system quite compatible with the monarchic analogy. In any event, symmetric structures with a central accent are found throughout the literature of the earlier seventeenth century, Catholic and Protestant alike, in poetry, masques, and even prose. Jonson's masque *Love's Triumph through Callipolis* (1631) may serve as a typical example. Its climactic triumph, led in by sea-deities numbering five (the triumphal number) 'consisteth of fifteen lovers, and as many Cupids, who rank

---

[57] See Palme (1959) 95–107; Fowler 1964 and 1970; McFarlane 1986; Røstvig 1963 and 1994; Heninger 1974; Finoaltea 1991; Johnson 1994; Parker 1998.

[58] Burke 1992; Mitford 1966; Macdonald 1984; Fowler 1970.   [59] Macdonald 1984, 141.

[60] Macdonald 1984, 221.   [61] Mitford 1966.

[62] Kepler 1937–, vi 10, cit. Johnson 1994, 229.

[63] Johnson 1994, 241. He thinks of the old centralization of the sun among the planets and the 'centralized placement of Christmas Day between Anne's birthday and Twelfth Night' in the early masques as having 'a specifically Catholic resonance'.

[64] Fowler 1996, 41.   [65] North 1994, 295, 309.

themselves seven and seven on a side, with each a Cupid before him, with a lighted torch, and the middle person (which is his Majesty), placed in the centre.'[66] The King, in the role of Heroic Love, is addressed by Euphemus as 'the centre of proportion' (130).[67] The entire masque has been designed as a circle with the King as its centre—'All which, in varied, intricate turns, and involved mazes, expressed, make the Antimasque: and conclude the exit, in a circle' (46–8).

Such central emphasis was a dominant form in encomiastic works of all kinds. So well-known was it that the centre did not have to be announced loudly, but could be economically signalled by the slightest of hints, or even finessed upon in subtle ways.[68] Thus, the person to be honoured at the centre need not be named, but might be represented instead by a surrogate, or merely by something associated with sovereignty—the *crown*, perhaps, or the *sun*, or (surrogate of a surrogate) a *carbuncle*. So Ben Jonson praises the art of Thomas Palmer the emblematist by likening it to 'the Carbuncle…in Centre';[69] and Margaret Cavendish, Duchess of Newcastle, imagines 'an imperial room with a centred carbuncle 'which representeth the sun'.[70]

Sometimes the finessing of a central accent could be more extreme, even parodic. A good example is Andrew Marvell's *The First Anniversary of the Government under O. C.* (1655). Oliver Cromwell acceded on 16 December 1653; for a representative event of the year, Marvell chooses the coach accident of 29 September 1654, so that the central line of 402 brings not a triumphal ascent, but 'Cromwell falling'. Portrayed throughout as a 'sun-like' ruler among planets (Saturn, Jupiter, Mars) in Ptolemaic order, we expect Cromwell to complete the sequence as Sol. Instead, the coach overturns like Phaethon's: 'It seemed the earth did from the centre tear; / It seemed the sun was fallen out of the sphere' (205–6).[71] Or, consider the subtly finessed central accent in Robert Herrick's 'A Panegeric to Sir Lewis Pemberton', where the central lines, instead of honouring his patron, rise above all such secular considerations. Far from a noble person, the poem's centre brings 'the lower end / Of thy glad table'. This equal sharing of the food, regardless of rank, alludes to the Dominical prophecy of the Kingdom, where 'the last shall be first' (Matt. 19:30).

Numerology may not seem very relevant to my topic of lord's space, so long as it is imagined, in structuralist terms, as coded communication. But that may change if one follows through with the architectural analogy, *ut architectura poesis*. It is not just that this or that literary feature has an architectural equivalent, so that stanza resembles room, or stave resembles column.[72] More broadly,

---

[66] Jonson 1925–1952, vii 738. [67] Johnson 1994, 117.
[68] Some of these are explored in Fowler 1970.
[69] *Ungathered Verse* i 13–16, discussed in Johnson 1994, 80–1. [70] Cavendish 1994, 260.
[71] See Fowler 1970, 81–2.
[72] See Fowler 1970, 18–19, on Drayton's explanation of his choice of stanza. Lindley 1984, 38 reveals a complex substantive number symbolism of dynastic dates in Daniel's *Tethys' Festival*; but my focus is rather on the ordering of the formal space of the masque.

the literary work resembles a building; and the literary space corresponds to a building plot or messuage. In each, the tenancy has its hierarchic implication. Feu duty, as it were, is exacted. So, in *Love's Triumph*, the King is prayed to: 'Deign to receive all lines of love in one…And by reflecting of them fill this space.'[73] The symmetry and harmony of the space, of the groundplot, is thus an expression of loyalty and love.

The doctrine of *ut architectura* found elaborate application in James I's Solomon cult, which was probably devised as a Protestant counterblast to the Solomonic cult of the Catholic Philip II of Spain.[74] Philip built the Escorial in 1563–84, partly as a retrospective allusion to Solomon's Temple. The Temple's tripartite plan, its most prominent feature in Reformation and Counter-Reformation visualizations (like the Geneva Bible illustrations), was imitated in Juan de Herrera's design for the Escorial, the three courts being triply echoed in the Laurentian gridiron plan.[75] As Richard Fanshawe's poem 'The Escurial' puts it, in its combination of convent, college, and court, it 'Hath three proportioned bodies joined in one.'[76] Fanshawe's 186-line poem itself has a tripartite division, signalled unobtrusively by self-referring mentions of partitioning at lines 62 and 124.[77] And at its centre, line 93 of 186, is the 'dreadful presence' of the Lord God, imaged in Titian's painting.

The Temple of Solomon was the great archetype of northern Renaissance architecture.[78] Allusions to its building and its ceremonies throng the literature of the period: think of such poems as George Herbert's 'Aaron' or the much-admired *De Triumpho Christi* (1499) of Macarius Mutius, a 317-line poem whose centre line has the gold of Aaron's breastplate.[79] Mysterious Ophir supplied King Solomon with gold (itself a symbol of sovereignty), so that gold, or Ophir, was often celebrated at the centre of compositional arrays. So was the ephod, the linen-and-gold vestment regularly worn by the high priest but alluded to also in the vestment worn by the priest-king David for his prophetic dance.[80] Its twelve jewels include the solar carbuncle we have already met. A central accent may have seemed particularly appropriate in the Solomon cult, since the Temple was thought to be geographically situated *in meditullio mundi*, at the mid-point of the world.[81]

The twelve-jewelled ephod of the high priest inspired much interpretation. Juan Bautista Villalpando relates it by analogy to the twelve tribes of Israel and

---

[73] Jonson 1925–1952, vii 740.
[74] See Johnson 1994, 241–2; Taylor 1967, 99–102; Parry 1981, 261 n. 31 (citing a sermon by Bishop John Williams); Lee 1990.
[75] Illus. Rosenau 1979, fig. 123; Fowler 1996, fig. 3; Taylor 1967, fig. xvii. 1.
[76] Fowler 1996, line 44.   [77] Fowler 1996, 133.
[78] See Rosenau 1979; Kubler 1982; Taylor 1967.
[79] See Fowler 1970, 66 on Antonio Possevino's praise of the poem, which he reprinted in 1593 as an example to others.
[80] Exo. 28:6; 39:2; II Sam. 6:14.   [81] Giorgio 1545, I vii 33, fol. 158v. See Fowler 1970, 25, 66.

the twelve bastions of the Temple (with the Ark of the Covenant at *its* centre); cosmically, the jewels correspond to the twelve signs of the zodiac. All this is in Villalpando's influential allegorization of Ezekiel,[82] a book that Charles I read at Carisbrooke Castle as he awaited trial and execution.[83] Ben Jonson, as we have seen, had the ephod in mind in his encomiastic verses on Thomas Palmer; at the centre of the 31-line poem, he writes:

> Next, that which rapt me, was: I might behold
> How like the Carbuncle in Aaron's breast
> The sevenfold flower of Art (more rich than gold)
> Did sparkle forth in Centre of the rest.[84]
>
> (*Ungathered Verse* i)

The ephod was understood alchemically, the radiant Urim being identified with the philosopher's stone. Joachim Tancke calls it 'the right, true sun itself...the right Urim and fiery carbuncle'.[85] It is in this tradition that Milton's *Paradise Lost* has, at the midpoint of 10,550 verses, Messiah ascending a sapphire throne on his triumphal chariot: a throne, inlaid with colours of the 'showery arch', on the *machina mundi* itself. 'He in celestial panoply all armed / Of radiant Urim, work divinely wrought' (vi 760–1). By a long-standing typological allegoresis, the ephod with gold of Ophir was regarded as prophetic of Christ. Among relevant texts is Psalm 45:9, 'upon thy right hand did stand the queen in gold of Ophir'.[86] More immediately, Macarius Mutius' neo-Latin Christian epic *De Triumpho Christi* (1499), had had at its mid-point Aaron and his ephod, *magnusque sacerdos / Inscriptas humero gemmas, tunicamque hiacyntho*.[87]

Within these Solomonic contexts, we may be able to make sense of an otherwise obscure passage in *Paradise Lost*, the visions of the world's Asian and African empires shown by Michael to Adam at xi 388–407. The problem is that in the two elaborately symmetrical catalogues of imperial names, the central positions are not occupied, like the others, by a powerful ruler, Mogul, Sultan, or whatever. Clearly the two arrays must belong to the type I mentioned earlier, in which a central accent is finessed.

With the Solomonic image-clusters in mind, it becomes less difficult to interpret Milton's vision of world empire. The two arrays of capitals twice honour

---

[82] Prado 1594–1605.   [83] Johnson 1994, 239–41.
[84] BL Add. MS 18040, composed 1598–9; see Jonson 1925–1952, vii 361, xi 124; Jonson 1975, 283; Johnson 1994, 81.
[85] See Qvarnström 1967, 63; Milton 1998, 26.
[86] *Vulg.* Ps. 46: 9; see, e.g., Lefèvre d'Étaples 1513 and 1979, 71; Milton 1998, 619; Johnson 1994, 241.
[87] See Fowler 1970, 66; Milton 1998, 27; Johnson 1994, 110–11 n. 13, where the passage is quoted *in extenso*.

Ophir, since 'golden Chersonese' (xi 392) was often identified with Ophir, and Sofala too, we are told, was 'thought Ophir'. Yet Solomon is not mentioned as the ruler; and this omission forces a more allegorical interpretation. Keeping in mind the main triumphal chariot image at vi 750–62, the poem's centre—

> The chariot of paternal deity...
> Whereon a sapphire throne...
> He in celestial panoply all armed
> Of radiant Urim, work divinely wrought,
> Ascended...

—we may conclude that the imperial vision in *Paradise Lost* xi enacts the typological prophecy of Psalm 45, and refers to Christ. Yet we are not dealing with realized eschatology either, since the imperial throne is empty. Milton, after all, wrote less than enthusiastically of the tenure of kings, and in 1660 was against 'any single person' ruling the English republic. We may conclude that Milton, who was a Millennarian, refers here to the world emperor of an apocalyptic future. Then Christ the Messiah, antitype of the gold of Ophir, would come, not only as redeemer but as judge and ruler of the world. The millennium would commence.

As we ourselves approach a millennium of a very different sort, it is hard to imagine the intensity of Milton's vision of an empty throne—that highly charged Siege Perilous. We have no great hopes, perhaps, of our millennium. Still, we know what a power vacuum is; and from Milton's arrangement of thrones, we can glimpse something of what it meant for him.

The Formation of Genres in the Renaissance and After

THIS TITLE MAY SEEM TO IMPLY that many genres originated in the Renaissance. And it is true that the early modern historical context made possible the revival of several ancient genres and the fresh invention of new ones. Explorations and new world discoveries, for example, stimulated a return to classical georgic, which appealed to the appetite for practical information on the one hand and on the other for images of exotic places. Again, the development of a print culture was a prerequisite for several important kinds.

For the most part, however, 'formation' may be misleading. The Renaissance was not always characterized by new forms; often it worked by adapting old forms or imparting to them a new spirit. The majority of the principal kinds had already been available in the Middle Ages. Most Renaissance innovations were not totally new, even when they were given new labels. Thus, classical georgic, an instructional or informative genre written *in persona auctoris*, had a shadowy existence in the Middle Ages as one of the three generic realms of the *rota Vergiliana*. It also thrived under the disguise of prologue, a dominant medieval form; and there were georgic sonnets long before Luigi Alamanni's *La Cultivazione* (1546). Fulgore da San Gimignano's *Soneli del Mesi* were composed between 1309 and 1317.[1] Again, comedies and tragedies were common before the Renaissance, although differently conceived, as narrative rather than drama. Comedy in St. Isidore's definition 'begins with sorrowful material, namely Hell, and ends with gladness, namely with Paradise and the divine being'.[2] But, in the new historical or external context, these medieval kinds changed profoundly. The *tractatus* or treatise is a significant example. Galileo's famous *Dialogo* of 1632, a treatise on the Copernican and Ptolemaic world systems, is cast in a dialectic form: this had the great advantage of avoiding dangerous commitments in a repressive, ideological age. So, too, with pendent works presenting pro and con positions or opposite perspectives, like *L'Allegro* and *Il Penseroso*. A key medieval genre was the epistle, used as an instrument of government at a distance. Rut the Renaissance epistle,

---

[1] *Arte della Caccia*, ed. Giuliano Innamorati (Milan, 1965); sec *Renaissance Genres: Essays on Theory, History, and Interpretation*, ed. Barbara Kiefer Lewalski (Cambridge, Mass., 1986); Rosalie L. Colic, *The Resources of Kind: Genre-Theory in the Renaissance* (Berkeley, 1973).

[2] See R. D. S. Jack, *Patterns of Divine Comedy: A Study of Medieval English Drama* (Cambridge, 1989), pp. 1–10.

meeting very different social needs, was often informal, or intimate, or newsy, or given to satiric parody like the *Epistulae Obscurorum Vironim* (1515-16). On 25 July 1625, in one of his *Familiar Letters,* James Howell listed five types of letter: 'letters, though they be capable of any subject, yet commonly they are either narratory, objurgatory, consolatory, monitory, or congratulatory.'[3]

The mention of comedy and tragedy is a reminder that the ancient genres revived in the Renaissance were to be 'pure' forms of what was alleged to have been adulterated in the Middle Ages (that is, modified to counteract their paganism). Paganism was now felt to be no longer a danger, so that ancient rhetorical treatments of genre could be followed freely. This led to some interesting but much dull theoretical debate about genre by Italian Renaissance theorists. Was Ariosto's *Orlando Furioso* true epic or not? The theorists, even the broad-minded Bishop Minturno, tended to take a Scholastic path and to be more concerned with defining vague entities and inventing categories than with describing kinds actually practiced. J. C. Scaliger's great *Poetice* (1561) is a grand exception. It reflects remarkable progress towards useful genre criticism, giving detailed descriptions of kinds, based on rhetorical *dispositio.*

Occasionally, a new genre had no ancient precedent, so that one had to be faked. The 'poetics' genre was invented on the basis of only a very few ancient exemplars, notably Aristotle's. But soon so many Renaissance imitations and commentaries thronged the scene that it became a lively genre. Its social basis was the novel activity of literary criticism.

This new grasp of genre was obviously arrived at through humanistic education, which encouraged closer study of the best ancient authors. Less obviously, what made the difference was the specific method of education: the better grammar schools, like Winchester College, gave instruction in creative writing. That is to say, exercises in Latin verse composition. Every schoolboy learnt the form *silva*, a sequence or gathering of short verse genres such as epitaph, elegy, and especially epigram. Richard Wills meant his *Poematum Liber* (1573) to give Winchester boys models for their composition exercises. The epigram, for example, was of course a common medieval form, but it now came to be practiced with a distinctive precision. The interest of epigram arose from its low status, beneath the notice of ancient theorists. This at first allowed it to be practiced more freely. But that could not be allowed to go unopposed by French theorists, eager as always to regulate and complicate simple matters. Thomas Sébillet professed to pin down the correct structure for epigrams and sonnets; prescribing (to name but one folly) just where the 'points' (witty turns) of an epigram-sonnet should be placed.[4] The *silva* or

---

[3] *Familiar Letters, or Epistolae Ho-Elianae,* ed. O. J. Smeaton, 3 vols. (London, 1902), vol. 1, p. 2; compare *Erasmus Newsletter* (1976), 28, and Claudio Guillén, 'Notes toward the Study of the Renaissance Letter', in *Renaissance Genres,* ed. Lewalski, pp. 71-3, 75-6.

[4] *Art poétique françoyse* (Paris, 1548), fol. 39r-44v.

miscellany became a dominant form in manuscript circulation and later in print too.⁵ A good example is Robert Hayman's *Quodlibets, lately come over from New Britaniola. Epigrams and other small parcels...* (1628). 'Quodlibet'—whatever you like; what you will—adumbrates a critical term, as yet nonexistent, for *silva*; just as 'parcels' is a trope for the non-epigrams in the miscellany. (Almost always a form appears earlier than the critical term for it.) Another collective metaphor was 'posy' or 'nosegay', applicable not only to emblems but to any anthology.

The anthology, a genre we take for granted, depends heavily on the print medium. True, the term was used by Diogenianus in the second century. And the Greek Anthology had existed in manuscript only, from about 900 CE. Its fullest form, the Palatine Anthology (not widely known until after 1606) did not appear in print until the nineteenth century. But a substantial part of it, the Planudean Anthology (gathered in 1301), was printed in 1494 and edited by Henri Estienne in 1556. And it is this printing of the Planudean Anthology, rather than that of the Appendix Vergiliana or the Anthologia Latina,⁶ which marks the flowering of the epigram genre for the majority of Renaissance readers and poets. Soon there were so many anthologies that I can only gesture to bibliographies of early exemplars, such as Arthur Case's *English Poetical Miscellanies* and John Sparrow's 'Renaissance Latin Poetry'.⁷

Surveying the new and the new-old genres of the Renaissance period, one cannot but think that many of them arose from changed social circumstances. Thus, the estate poem (country-house poem) seems to have emerged in response to changes in the character of hospitality. The decline of 'housekeeping' was so critical that satiric comments grew noticeably frequent, and new topoi became recognizable. Dialogue is another instance: informal debate became more common than would have been usual in the Middle Ages. Again, the development of literary coteries and new forms of patronage made possible the seventeenth-century genre of critical elegy, a subgenre distinct from epitaph, epicede, and personal funeral elegy. The occasionality of the critical elegy focussed on a notional, imaginary ceremony mourning the death of an admired poet. But the actual occasion was often the printing of a volume of similar critical elegies, like the *Justa Eduardo*

---

⁵ See Alastair Fowler, 'The Silva Tradition in Jonson's *The Forres*', in *Poetic Traditions of the English Renaissance*, ed. Maynard Mack and George deforest Lord (New Haven, 1982), pp. 163–80.

⁶ Begun perhaps in the early ninth century, frequently modified, and not printed until 1729.

⁷ Arthur E. Case, *A Bibliography of English Poetical Miscellanies 1521–1750* (Oxford, 1935); John Sparrow, 'Renaissance Latin Poetry: Some Sixteenth-Century Latin Anthologies,' in *Cultural Aspects of the Italian Renaissance*, ed. C. H. Clough (Manchester, 1976). Among many epigram anthologies may be mentioned *Delitiae CC. Italorum Poetarum*, 2 vols. (Frankfurt, 1608); *Delitiae C. Poetarum Gallorum*, 3 vols. (Frankfurt, 1609); *Delitiae Poetarum Germanorum*, 6 vols, (Frankfurt, 1612) containing about 250,000 poems; *Delitiae C. Poetarum Belgicorum*, 3 vols. (Frankfurt, 1614) (all ed. by Jean Gruter); *Delitiae Poetarum Scotorum*, ed. Arthur Johnston (Amsterdam, 1637); *Enchiridium Epigrammatum Latino-Anglicum*, ed. Robert Vilvain (London, 1654); *Delitiae Poetarum Danorum*, ed. Friedrich Rostgaard, 2 vols. (Leiden, 1693). See also Hoyt Hopewell Hudson, *The Epigram in the English Renaissance* (New York, 1966), p. 24 n 3.

King Naufrago, ab amicis moerentibus... (Cambridge, 1638) for Edward King, or the similar collection for Donne appended to his 1633 *Poems*; although single critical elegies are of course also found, like Ben Jonson's 'To the Memory of My Beloved...(whose occasion was the printing of the Shakespeare First Folio of 1623). Poets' elegies like Thomas Carew's 'An Elegie upon the Death of the Deane of Pauls, Dr John Donne' not only allude to the poetry of the deceased, but may also use their style, as in the *hommage* or *tombeau*.[8] And sometimes the mourning is for the art of poetry itself, as in Carew's elegy and in William Dunbar's *Lament for the Makaris* (c.1505).

In the formation of kinds, it seems usual for subgenres to emerge before genres. If this appears counterintuitive, one has only to reflect that particulars are identified before generalities. We see trees before we see the wood they are parts of. This is particularly obvious with the genres of visual art. In painting, the flowerpiece, breakfast piece, and so forth, appeared before the category 'still life'; the *doorkijke* appeared before the interior; the journey and the world landscape before the landscape in general; and the brothel scene, the guardroom, the merry company, and the conversation piece before the 'genre' category (a term not used until the nineteenth century).[9] At first there is no name for the broader type, only for the particular 'subject'. The absence of a genre label is of course no argument against the genre's existence; after all, the architectural orders themselves went unnamed for more than 1,500 years.[10] Even the emblem was not at first identified by name; Andrea Alciato himself seems to have thought of it as a special sort of epigram.[11] One can almost see the epigram part of the emblem emerge in an epigrammatic poem by Bonaventura Peeters on his own painting: his associative thought makes the poem virtually a nude emblem.[12] What crystallized the familiar emblem form of *motto, pictura, inscriptio* (epigram), and *descriptio* was probably the print format. Indeed, long before Alciato, it made an almost complete appearance in the printer's device, which sometimes incorporated a motto and a quotation.[13]

---

[8] Thomas Carew, *The Poems*, ed. Rhodes Dunlap (Oxford, 1957), p. 74.

[9] See Judikje Kiers and Fieke Tissink, *The Glory of the Golden Age*, exhibition catalogue (Amsterdam, 2000), p. 169.

[10] See John Onians, *Bearers of Meaning: The Classical Orders in Antiquity, the Middle Ages, and the Renaissance* (Princeton, 1988), p. 3.

[11] Many associated (or confused) emblem and epigram; see, for example, Francis Thynne, *Emblemes and Epigrames* [1600], ed. F. J. Furnivall (London, 1876).

[12] See Lawrence O. Goedde, *Tempest and Shipwreck in Dutch and Flemish Art: Convention, Rhetoric, and Interpretation* (University Park, Penn., 1989), pp. 128–9, quoting Peeters's poem on his own *Ships in a Tempest*. On the naked emblem, see John Manning, *The Emblem* (London, 2002), p. 18.

[13] See Alastair Fowler, 'The Emblem as a Literary Genre,' in *Deviceful Settings: The English Renaissance Emblem and Its Contexts*, ed. Michael Bath and Daniel Russell (New York, 1999), pp. 1–31.

In literature, similarly, poems of country life were commonly named as such long before the terms landscape, or georgic, became usual.[14] Other Renaissance subgenres include the calendar (as in Spenser's *Shepheardes Calender* or *Cantos of Mutabilitie*); and the time-of-day (a sort of almanac, as in Charles Cotton's *Morning Quatrains* or Nicholas Breton's *Fantasticks*). Breton's Preface calls what he is doing 'description of the twelve houres, the twelve monethes, and some speciall dayes in the yere', and (disclaiming originality) tells how his inspiration was 'a peece of paper, in which I found a kind of discourse, set down upon an imagination of midnight', which he wished to emulate.[15] Robert Herrick's country festivals and transshiftings are in a similar vein. All the works just mentioned probably reflect the rethinking of temporality that seems to have preoccupied the age. And all show influence of the visual arts, in which calendrical programmes were extremely common, from the Middle Ages to the eighteenth century.

During the process of conceptualizing a genre, an important part was played by metaphors. Many genres had regular metaphors or synecdoches associated with them. Among these, culinary metaphors were particularly prominent, in view of the highly developed analogy between eating and talking, not only in 'table talk' but in criticism of all sorts.[16] Many literary genres drew their names from the kitchen: *satura; farrago; sal* and *mel* epigram—to mention only the best known. To the many examples in Michel Jeanneret and Gilbert Highet, one might add two: *The Wit's Album, or Pine-apple of Literature*…(1829) and Philofunniculus's *A New Oxford Sausage, Spiced to Suit the Taste of Town and Gown, Dons and Duns* (1844). As their metaphors died, identifying the genres became easier and more conscious.

Claudio Guillén has shown how genres were moulded by composition manuals, for example letter-writing manuals.[17] And another popular source of genre topoi and associations was Paul Aler's *Gradus ad Parnassum*,[18] one of many similar thesauri. From the *Gradus* one learns, for example, that *syrma* and *cothurnus* can be put for tragedy or any poem of high seriousness: that is, the trailing robe and the buskin, used *ad maiestatem*, for dignity. Literary references follow: to Juvenal ('the trailing robe of Thyestes or Antigone') and Martial ('nor does my Muse swell with frenzied tragic strain', *insano syrma*). A particularly interesting citation is Ovid's *Amores*, a work well known to Milton, which personifies several genres:

---

[14] See Jay Appleton, *The Symbolism of Habitat: An Interpretation of Landscape in the Arts* (Seattle, 1991).

[15] Nicholas Breton, *Fantasticks Serving for a perpetuall Prognostication* [1626], in *The Works*, ed. Ursula Kentish-Wright, 2 vols. (London, 1929), vol. 1, p. 4.

[16] See Michel Jeanneret, *A Feast of Words: Banquets and Table Talk in the Renaissance*, tr. Jeremy Whiteley and Emma Hughes (Chicago, 1991); Gilbert Highet, *The Anatomy of Satire* (Princeton, 1962).

[17] See Barbara K. Lewalski, 'Notes toward the Study of the Renaissance Letter,' in *Renaissance Genres*, ed. Lewalski, pp. 70–101.

[18] Thirty-two editions in the British Library, from Cologne 1680 onward.

Whilst I was strolling here enveloped in woodland shadows, asking myself what work my Muse should venture on, came Elegy with coil of odorous locks, and, I think, one foot longer than its mate.[19] She had a comely form: her robe was gauzy light, her face suffused with love, and any fault in her carriage added to her grace. There came, too, raging Tragedy, with mighty stride: her locks o'erhung a darkling brow, her pall trailed on the ground; her left hand swayed wide a kingly sceptre, and on her foot was the high-bound Lydian buskin.[20]

Elegy's coil or knot 'of odorous locks', *odoralos Elegeia nexa capillos*, surely reappears in Milton's elegy for Edward King as 'the tangle of Neaera's hair'. Milton asks, 'What boots it / To...meditate the thankless muse' of serious poetry. 'Were it not better.../ To sport with Amaryllis in the shade, / Or with the tangles of Neaera's hair?'[21] The question is more than a rhetorical one: he himself had ten years earlier written Latin love elegies, and more recently had rejected them in the retraction '*Haec ego mente*' of about 1635.

In such metaphors the mood of a genre is cultivated, meditated, perhaps modified; this can be of value to an interpreter. A good instance is *Aeneid* I 336-7, where Venus tells her son Aeneas, 'Tyrian maids are wont to wear the quiver, and bind their ankles high with the purple buskin.' Very soon after, Dido is named—and so associated with buskined tragedy. In the same book, Aeneas brings Dido the gift of Ilione's *sceptrum* (I 653). The tropic attributes of tragedy—purple buskin and sceptre—thus combine together in a dramatic irony foreshadowing Dido's tragic end.

It is time to look in more detail at how genre works in practice. Consider Meliboeus's lines opening Virgil's First Eclogue: '*Tityre, tu patulae recubans sub tegmine fagi/ silvestrem lenui musam meditaris avena.*'[22] One is to imagine Tityrus as meditating his woodland Muse on slender reed. Such formulas have been described as coded; everyone knows to decode *avena* ('reed') as pastoral song. But weren't early pastoral idyls and eclogues, for Theocritus if not for Virgil, accompanied on actual reed pipes? And, if so, should we not think of the *avena* as a part of the external situation, the context of utterance? Genres are coming to be understood as virtual contexts: as providing for the individual work a context equivalent to the pragmatic context of speech. Abandoning the notion of genres as fixed classes, criticism moved on in the 1980s and 1990s to discussing them as coded structures or matrices for composition and interpretation. Perhaps now it is time to move on again, and to think of genres as fields of association like those in actual situations of utterance.

---

[19] In the elegiac metre, hexameter and pentameter verses alternate.
[20] Ovid, *Amores*, tr. Grant Showerman (Cambridge, Mass., 1963), III.I.I 1–14, p. 445.
[21] Milton, *Lycidas*, in *Complete Shorter Poems*, ed. J. Carey (London, 1997), lines 67–9.
[22] Virgil, *Eclogues*, in *Virgil*, tr. H. Rushton Fairclough (Cambridge, Mass. 1999).

Codes have indeed their parts to play in the reception of every literary work, as I stressed (and probably overstressed) in *Kinds of Literature* (1982). Ordinary speech has its codes too. But, just as in speech itself meanings are taken up through inferences drawn from assumptions shared with the speaker about pragmatic contexts, so too in literature, where the speaker is often absent, the finer meanings need to be inferred from the shared literary (not least generic) contexts. We may be too ready to assume coded signals. The general case is that of an untutored readership with little knowledge of literary codes—an audience, say, that has heard shepherds' pipes and read a few poems but knows little of subgenres and modes.

Genres seem to differentiate, more or less systematically, a combination of features, both formal and substantive, ranging from minute to large, from specific topics to elusive moods.[23] This repertoire may include characteristic diction, favourite rhetorical figures, peculiar meters, principal subjects, and typical themes. Each genre has more or less obligatory topics, for which material has to be found by the writer. The georgic topic of retirement, for example, may lead a poet back to Seneca's *Epistola* XC. Such shared sources draw exemplars of the genre together and adumbrate for a reader the broad field of associations in which the most relevant ones are to be found. One may usefully think of genres as domains of association—specialized, literary equivalents of the fields of association whereby meaning is communicated in ordinary speech. As such, the genres adjust a reader's mental set and help in selecting the optimally relevant associations that amount to a meaning of the literary work.[24]

Genre's associative function can be clearly seen at work in the attributes or conventional tropes of the kind. In the verses from Virgil's First Eclogue, *tenui musam medilaris avena* calls up associations and assumptions (literary and extraliterary) connected with the outside world of shepherds and country song, and with the literary world of pastoral poetry. In the rejected opening of the *Aeneid* ('I who formerly tuned my song on a thin reed...now sing of Mars's bristling arms'), the reed is obviously self-referring, the poet's attribute as much as the shepherd's. It is 'thin' because the lowly mode of pastoral properly requires a *stylus tenuis*. Since Virgil, generations of poets have deployed similar metaphors. Spenser's Cuddy complains, 'I haue pyped erst so long with payne, / That all mine Oten reedes bene rent and wore';[25] and when Spenser wishes to announce that his poem has cracked the mould of pastoral, he writes that Colin (the poet's persona) 'broke his oaten pype'.[26] Shakespeare, too, complains, 'My shepherd's pipe can

---

[23] Alastair Fowler, *Kinds of Literature: An Introduction to the Theory of Genres and Modes* (Cambridge, Mass., 1982), ch. 3.
[24] See Dan Sperber and Deirdre Wilson, *Relevance: Communication and Cognition* (Cambridge, Mass., 1986).
[25] Glossed by E. K. as *avena* to signal the Virgilian allusion.
[26] *Shepheardes Calender* (London, 1579), October, line 8; January, line 72.

sound no deal'; he, too, has shepherds piping on humble 'oaten straws'[27]—just as, in *Lycidas*, 'the rural ditties were not mute / Tempered to the oaten flute'. Milton occasionally makes the genre association explicit: '*pastoral* reed with oaten stops'; 'Arcadian pipe, the *pastoral* reed'.[28] In 1730, James Thomson, both Virgilian and Miltonic, can still claim, 'The Doric reed once more / Well-pleased, I tune.'[29] And, beneath John Greenleaf Whittier's bust, more vaguely, is inscribed 'Making his rustic reed of song / A weapon in the war with wrong'.

This pastoral landscape is well trodden;[30] but it may be less widely known that other genres, too, have metaphoric attributes. Some of the most prominent genre metaphors were already consciously recognized by the ancients; others accrued in the Renaissance (see Fig. 1):

Fig. 1.

GENRE	TROPE	LOCUS CLASSICUS
POETRY	*cicada*	Plato, *Phaedrus* 258E
	cygnus	Mignault on Alciato clxxx
COMEDY	*soccus* (sock)	Horace, *Epistles* II i 174
TRAGEDY	*cothurnus* (buskin)	Horace, *Satires* I v 64
	palla, sceptrum	Ovid, *Amores* III i 11
		Milton, *Il Penseroso* 97–8
	drum, ejaculations	Donne, *Sermons*[30] in 271
PASTORAL	*avena* (reed)	Virgil, *Aeneid* i 1a
GEORGIC	*arvum* (field)	Virgil, *Aeneid* i 1c
EPIC	*tuba* (trumpet)	Martial, VIII iii 22
ODE	*lyra* (lyre)	Horace, *Odes* I vi 10
		Martial, XII xciv 5
EPIGRAM	*mel* (honey), *sal* (salt), *fel* (gall), *acetum* (vinegar)	Scaliger, *Poetice* III cxxii

One notices that *mel, acetum*, and the others are not merely taxonomic labels classifying epigram types. For the imagery of the poem itself is likely to belong to a corresponding register. Katherine Wilson draws attention to Francis Meres's comparison of Shakespeare to Ovid in *Palladis Tamia* (1598): 'the sweet witty soul of Ovid lives in mellifluous and honey-tongued Shakespeare, witness...his sugared

---

[27] *The Passionate Pilgrim* 7.17; *Love's Labour's Lost* 5.2.893. For the 'humility' (*stylus humilis*) of the oaten reed, see Thomas Watson, 'An Eglogue upon the Death of...Walsingham...': 'An humble stile befits a simple Swaine / My Muse shall pipe but on an oaten quill': *Poems*, ed. Edward Arber (London, 1895), p. 163; Arthur Golding, *The XV Bookes of P. Ovidius Naso, Entytuled Metamorphosis, Translated*...(London, 1567), vol. 1, p. 842, 'Oten Reede'.
[28] *Comus* 344; *Paradise Lost* xi 132, in *The Poems of John Milton*, ed. John Carey and Alastair Fowler (Harlow, 1968).
[29] James Thomson, *Autumn* [1730] lines 3–4, in *The Poetical Works of James Thomson*, ed. Bertram Dobell (Cambridge, 1994).
[30] John Donne, *Sermons*, ed. G. R. Potter and Evelyn M. Simpson, 10 vols. (Berkeley, 1953–62).

sonnets.'³¹ As she points out, *sugared* 'was often used by the sonneteers of their love talk': 'sugared speech and siren's song' (Thomas Watson); 'No other sugaring of speech to try' (Philip Sidney); 'Oh sugared talk! Wherewith my thoughts do live' (Giles Fletcher). Wilson defines *sugared* as 'sweetened by artifice', a sung or lyric quality: 'the sugared quality is a sort of wit'. But 'wit' may be misleading; sweetness and honey more probably imply an erotic charge. In Sidney, kisses are sweet, and breath, and ladies. The statistics of *sweet* are surprising. In *Astrophel and Stella*, mostly *mel* epigram-sonnets, *sweet* occurs no fewer than fifty times; if one includes the Other Sonnets, the total rises to sixty-seven. *Sugared* adds a further six occurrences. In Shakespeare's *Sonnets*, similarly, *sweet* occurs fifty-five times.

From an early date, such associations as these fused with the enduring symbolism of the Muses. Clio, for example, Muse of history and sometimes epic, had as attributes the trumpet and the laurel wreath or crown. Chaucer knows the trumpet's association with heroic achievement in *The House of Fame*; his account of 'hem that maken blody soun / In trumpe, beine, and claryoun' contains as many as eight references to the instrument in twelve lines.³² Several other Muses were also assigned musical instruments, which became part of a network of genre symbolism. In the seventeenth century, the system of symbolic modes and its corresponding *instrumentarium* culminated in cosmic summas like Fr. Athanasius Kircher's *Musurgia*.³³

In the Middle Ages, the three major modes were schematized and expanded through genre metaphors in the so-called *rota Vergiliana* (see figures 1 and 2). This enormously influential diagram, popularized by John of Garland, associates pastoral with *otiosus pastor*, sheep, crook, pasture, and beech tree. Georgic is comparably linked with farmer, ox, plough, field, and fruit tree; and epic, with *miles dominans* (knight), horse, sword, city and camp, laurel of victory, and cedar of status. Sophisticated Renaissance poets were able to use the medieval and ancient genre metaphors in allusions of great economy. So, in Milton's 'Then to the well-trod stage anon / If Jonson's learned sock be on', the reference is clear without the word 'comedy'. Similarly with the 'trembling strings' of lyric or hymn.³⁴ And Joseph Hall, whose 'scornful Muse' cannot abide 'with tragic shoes her ankles for to hide', nor to write poems of patronage ('trencher poetry'), nor to 'speak rhymes unto my oaten minstrelsy', announces his preference for satire by rejecting a series of other genre associations: 'Trumpet, and reeds, and socks, and buskins fine / I them bequeath.'³⁵

---

[31] Katherine M. Wilson, *Shakespeare's Sugared Sonnets* (London, 1974), pp. 11–12.

[32] *The House of Fame* lines 1239–50. Compare Ariosto, *Orlando Furioso*, XXXIV xxv.

[33] *Musurgia Universalis sive Ars Magna Consoni el Dissoni* (Rome, 1650). See Emanuel Winternitz, *Musical Instruments and Their Symbolism in Western Art* (London, 1967).

[34] *L'Allegro* 131–2; *Il Penseroso* 106–7. Compare Michael Drayton, 'The Sacrifice to Apollo', line 50, 'Or in the Sock, or in the Buskined Strayne'.

[35] Joseph Hall, 'Satire 1', *Virgidemiae* (London, 1598) lines 9–20. The tropic legacy is itself a satiric topos.

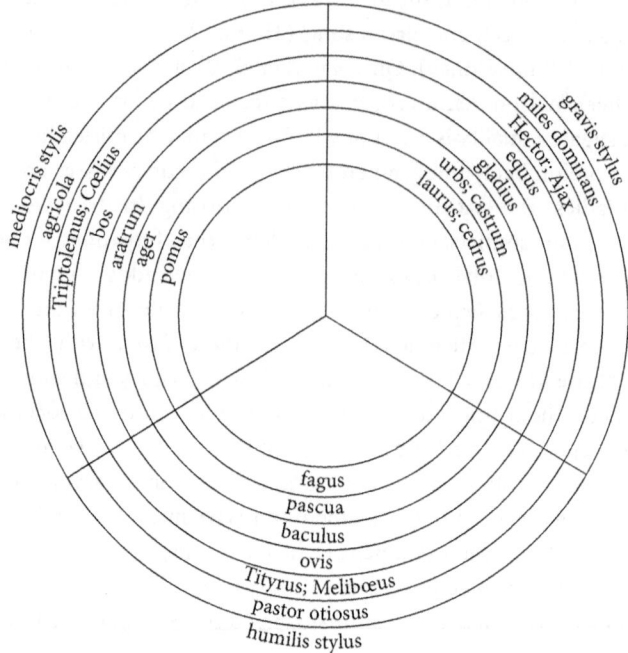

Fig. 2. The Wheel of Virgil. From Edmond Faral, *Les Arts poétiques de 12 et de 13 siècle* (Paris, 1962), p. 87.

Fig. 3. The Wheel of Virgil, expressed in tabular form

	Epic	Pastoral	Georgic
STYLE	gravis stylus	humilis stylus	mediocris stylus
CADRE	miles dominans	pastor otiosus	agricola
NAME	Hector; Ajax	Tityrus; Melibœus	Triptolemus; Cœlius
ANIMAL	equus	ovis	bos
TOOL	gladius	baculus	aratrum
LOCALE	urbs; castrum	pascua	ager
TREE	laurus; cedrus	fagus	pomus

Satire, a genre that called for no invocation, had scarcely an attribute in ancient literature—unless one counts epithets like 'biting', 'piercing', and 'scornful'. But Renaissance satire acquired several tropic attributes: the shaggy satyr from false etymology of *satire* from *satyr* rather than *satura*; the whip of 'corrected' abuses; and, in Marston, the biting dog of *cynic-ism*.[36] The whipping metaphor was

---

[36] W. Kinsayder [that is, gelder of dogs] (John Marston), *The Scourge of Villanie. Three Bookies of Satyres* (London, 1598); John Davies, *The Scourge of Folly. Consisting of Satyricall Epigrams...*(London, 1611); John Taylor, *The Scourge of Baseness* (London, 1624); compare Alexander Pope, 'Epistle to Dr. Arbuthnot' line 303: 'A lash like mine no honest man shall dread.'

particularly common as a disguise around 1600, when satires were being burnt by the hangman. Among many one may mention the anonymous *The Whipper of the Satire* and *The Whipping of the Satire* (both 1601) and Breton's *No Whipping, nor Tipping, But a Kind Friendly Snipping* (also 1601).

Similarly, the georgic farmer's equipment was supplemented in the Renaissance with a goad;[37] as when Michael Drayton boasts about the variety of the Fourteenth Song of *Poly-Olbion*:

> As to the varying Earth the Muse doth her apply,
> Poor Sheep-hook and plain Goad, she many times doth sound:
> Then in a buskined strain she instantly doth bound.[38]

In his elegy on Donne, Henry King associates the funeral elegy genre with a solemn passing bell: 'Oh! Hadst thou in an Elegiac knell / Rung out unto the world thine own Farewell.'[39] And in his 'Elegy Written in a Country Churchyard', Thomas Gray famously develops the same association: 'The curfew tolls the knell of parting day.' He probably complicates it with an echo of Milton's 'I hear the far-off curfew sound / Swinging slow with sullen [melancholy] roar'—the solemn counterpart in *Il Penseroso* of *L'Allegro's* 'merry bells'[40]—and certainly (as he acknowledged to Bedingfield) he follows Dante's *Purgatorio* Canto 8, lines 5-6, where 'from afar a bell...seems to mourn the dying day' (*squilla di lontano / che paia il giorno pianger che si more*). Milton's pendant modes and moods form an emotional and experiential polarity as well as a contrast of genres.

Something of the complexity of association involved in genres may be glimpsed from James Jensen's fine account of the trumpet in baroque literature. It has connections not only with martial and heroic contexts but with musical semiotics, mural painting, contemporary music and musical theory, allegory, prosody, and iconography.[41] All this may suggest that genre metaphors call up an entire world, or at least all of it that is susceptible to representation in a single genre or mode. Doubtless this is so potentially. But the genre ambiences invoked have a limited number of focuses. And it is to these in the first instance that the tropes of invocation gesture.

The pastoral ambience, for example, the genre's mental 'set', may be evoked by a distinct constellation of interrelated metaphoric properties: the oak-pleasance, the sedge-fringed river, the sheep-hook, the occupations of *otium*, and not a great

---

[37] Suggested perhaps by the iconography of the constellations, in which Boötes the Herdsman wielded a *stimulus*.
[38] Michael Drayton, *Poly-Olbion* (London, 1619), song 14, lines 2-4.
[39] Henry King, 'Upon the Death of My Ever Desired Friend Dr. Donne of Paul's', lines 35-6.
[40] *Il Penseroso* 73-5; *L'Allegro* 33-4.
[41] H. James Jensen, *The Muses' Concord: Literature, Music, and the Visual Arts in the Baroque Age* (Bloomington, Ind., 1976), pp. 171-91.

many others.[42] The oasis guarantees that *otium* is unlikely to be interrupted. And the reed raises the subject of poetry itself, the self-referential topic of much pastoral poetry. Naturally, these metaphors soon became autobiographically over-determined. Thus, for his choice of pastoral river, Virgil returns to his own native locality and the river Mincio. In *Eclogues* VII, 'Mincius fringes his green banks with waving reeds', and in the survey of poetic themes that opens *Georgics* III he promises a temple 'beside the water, where great Mincius wanders, in slow windings and fringes his banks with slender reeds' (*et tenera praetexit haurdine ripas*).[43] After Jacopo Sannazaro, the river became a more prominent element in Renaissance pastoral and love poetry: Edmund Spenser makes much of his 'sweet Thames', Michael Drayton of 'sweet Ankor'. In *Lycidas*, Milton alludes to Virgil's river more openly, with a self-conscious, *parados*-like effect: 'thou honoured flood, / Smooth-sliding Mincius, crowned with vocal reeds, / That strain I heard was of a higher mood' (85–7). As often, the tropic pastoral river is the river of poetry, the ever-changing stream that flows now as Alph or Hippocrene, now as Arethuse or Mincius. His 'somewhat loudly sweep the string' (17) prepares for a high lyric or hymnal passage; his 'Mincius' returns to the Latin pastoral mode. This last transition is confirmed in the next verse: 'But now my oat proceeds.' The reeds of the Mincius signal a return after the higher modulation.

This does not mean that *Mincius* is invariably coded as an indicator. It can carry many complex associations—suggesting, for example, Milton's relations with previous pastoral poetry and with Virgil; the latter's life-stream, which sprang from a neighbouring fountain; the waters that ended Edward King's life; and much else besides. In other words, genre metaphors often function as associative contexts rather than mere indicators.

The potential complexity of associations can be glimpsed even in the work of quite minor poets. Probably written in the 1640s, 'The Vote', by the Spenserian Ralph Knevet, draws motifs from Virgil's *Georgics* and from Isaiah 2:4:

> The helmet now an hive for bees becomes,
> And hilts of swords may serve for spiders' looms;
> Sharp pikes may make
> Teeth for a rake;
> And the keen blade, the arch-enemy of life,
> Shall be degraded to a pruning knife;
> The rustic spade,
> Which first was made
> For honest agriculture, shall retake

---

[42] See Rosalie Colie, *Shakespeare's Living Art* (Princeton, 1974), p. 301, where she shows Shakespeare testing the limits of pastoral by introducing extreme instances of antipastoral.

[43] *Eclogues* vii 12–13; *Georgics* iii 15; cf. *Aeneid* x 206.

> Its primitive employment, and forsake
> The ram pires [ramparts] steep
> And trenches deep.⁴⁴

One can see how, in a different poem, the contrast of 'blade' and 'pruning-knife' might have been used simply to signal epic and georgic, or to modulate from the one to the other. But, even then, the extraliterary associations obvious here would surely not have been altogether abstracted into a world of specialized conventions. After the battles of the Civil War, real weapons were dug up by farmers who had not necessarily read Virgil's *Georgics*.

Interaction of politics with the literary world is specially evident with the emblem genre. During the Renaissance emblematic objects and their meanings were at first mostly ancient, like the originally warlike dolphin and anchor from an *aureus* of the Emperor Titus, which became the device of the printer Aldus. But before long they were given modern applications; already Alciato replaced Titus's FESTINA LENTE motto with A PRINCE WHO SEEKS HIS SUBJECTS' SAFETY. In modernized versions of Cupid with his arrow, similarly, the archer might become a crossbowman or a gunner. The French revolution generated a great many novel emblems, notably the bourgeois emblem sabres of 1789 and the revolutionary sabres of the following decade. Mayors, judges, and minor officials all carried a sword then, as a sign of office and symbol of nobility. The revolutionary sabre was often bought privately, and engraved either by private commission or on the maker's initiative. Gérard Sabatier, who has studied the emblem sabres in considerable detail, shows that the armourers used two main sources of imagery.⁴⁵ Sometimes they drew on the human body or heraldic images ultimately derived from the bestiaries; sometimes they used Cesare Ripa's *Iconologia* (Rome, 1593), which was still being enlarged and reprinted in the eighteenth century. Or, new allegories, Masonic or revolutionary, might be invented, involving perhaps the scales of justice, the fasces of unity, or the eye and pyramid, as in the dollar bill. The liberty cap might surmount a helmet, or be raised on a tree of liberty.

Genre metaphors continue to function in modern literature but usually are there deployed less overtly. Particularly in complex, mixed works, they serve to re-establish or maintain a generic ambience. Readers of novels may not think they need genre metaphors to tell them they are reading a novel. But the metaphors are often introduced nevertheless, perhaps to indicate some particular subgenre of novel. Attributes or associations of the novel (suitably literalistic, even transparent) include letters and letter-writing; diaries; notebooks; autobiographical journals; and unfinished drafts, not impossibly of a novel. Again,

---

⁴⁴ Ralph Knevel, *The Shorter Poems*, ed. A. M. Charles (Columbus, 1966), pp. 307–8.
⁴⁵ Gérard Sabatier, 'Aux Armes, Citoyens!' *FMR*, 39 (1989), 65–80.

modern novels are sometimes presented as the diary of someone (a rapist, perhaps, or a nobody).[46] Doubtless, letters sometimes allude to the genre's originary variant, the epistolary novel of Richardson and Smollet. More generally, however, the letter implies intimacy—once, an intimacy greater than that of speech. At critical stages of Richardson's *Pamela* and his *Clarissa*, writing a letter or journal figures prominently in the action. In the romantic, and still in the Victorian novel, the emotional commitment a letter represented was a valuable association; the approach to intimacy in Wilkie Collins's *Basil* actually leads to a concluding section entirely in epistolary form. In realistic novels, it may be the documentary status of letters or official records that is more prominent as a genre indicator. Or, it may be the occupation of writing. Thus, in *The New Grub Street* and in *The Private Papers of Henry Rycroft*, George Gissing writes about what he knows—writing.

Genre metaphors are nowhere more actively explored than in avant-garde novels of the twentieth century. All the associations just mentioned may still be operative, together often with an implication that the pages presented are mere jottings—'papers', 'notes', and the like.[47] Novels may be deprecatingly titled 'Chronicles' or 'A Tale of Such and such', even when they are not actually in chronicle or tale form.[48] Or, an espionage novel will be called something like *The Ipcress File*, where 'file', however, does not merely suggest an early draft or the raw material of Fiction. It is associated specifically with classified information, confidentiality leaks, and the open or closed society.

The writing metaphor is most prominent in self-referring, self-conscious, or 'self-begetting' novels: in 'metafiction'.[49] This genre or subgenre has commonly been related to that seminal antecedent of novel genres, Laurence Sterne's *Tristram Shandy*, a work that itself introduces, more than once, the metaphor of autobiographical writing. Comparable self-references sometimes work their way into the titles; as with James Merrill's *The Diblos Notebook* (1965), Doris Lessing's *Golden Notebook* (1972), and Lawrence Durrell's *Black Book* (1973). The culmination or *reductio* of this tendency may be found in Robert Grudin's thoughtful *Book: A Novel* (1992), where every stage of writing—and of editing, publication, bookselling, and pulping—has been assimilated to the fiction. To regard such genre metaphors as encoding would miss much of their point. What

---

[46] For example, Evan S. Connell, *Diary of a Rapist* (London, 1966); George Grossmith and Weedon Grossmith, *The Diary of a Nobody* (London, 1892).

[47] Evan S. Connell, *Notes from a Bottle Found on the Beach at Carmel* (New York, 1963); Brian Higgins, *Notes while Travelling* (London, 1964); and Robert Lowell, *Notebook 1967-8* (New York, 1969), which is on the model of actual notebooks like Rilke's *The Notebook of Malte Laurids Brigge* (London, 1959). 'Notes' in a title may also indicate autobiographical or confessional writing; and, particularly in Russian literature, it has subversive associations.

[48] For example, Charles Reznikoff, *Family Chronicle* (London, 1969).

[49] See Steven G. Kellman, *The Self-Begetting Novel* (New York, 1980); Patricia Waugh, *Metafiction: The Theory and Practice of Self Conscious Fiction* (London, 1984).

matters is the associations they prompt. Even so, they only indicate more or less relevant fields of association; the optimally relevant associations—the meaning—depends less on codes and conventions than on the individual handling: on what new departures the shared associations and formal shaping allow to be taken up.

Comparing genre metaphors can be instructive. The prominence of the writing metaphor in postmodern metafiction may suggest how far it has turned in on literature itself, or at least on the literary community. By contrast, the trumpet of epic used to refer to the martial music of the outside world: to a city not primarily concerned with literature.

Gavin Douglas: Romantic Humanist

Nevill Coghill tells how once as he went round Addison's Walk he met C. S. Lewis, and asked him why he was looking so pleased. 'I believe,' said Lewis with a modest smile of triumph, 'I *believe* I have proved that the Renaissance never happened in England. *Alternatively* that if it did, *it had no importance*.'[1] ('Never in England', one notices, not 'Britain'.) Besides the joy of intellectual discovery, Lewis would foresee prospects of controversy: of clipping the wings of local humanists, those complacent promoters of their predecessors' glorious Renaissance. Emrys Jones attributes the disparagement of humanism in Lewis's *Oxford History of English Literature* volume to neglect of northern, religious humanists like Erasmus and of their contributions to education.[2] But intellectual politics may have come into it too. The dating and significance of the Renaissance were moot in the 1950s: E. M. W. Tillyard and Rosemond Tuve minimized the significance, while Erwin Panofsky proposed intermittent renaissances going back to the twelfth-century 'renascence' and the School of Chartres.[3] The debate now seems remote, conducted as it was without much historical or political reference—or discussion of the historians' own motivations. Was John MacQueen not influenced, in his hunt for fifteenth-century Scottish humanists and avoidance of the term 'Scottish Chaucerians', by any trace of nationalist enthusiasm? A humanist Gavin Douglas would be that much more independent of English Chaucer. Recent cultural history, however, has supported MacQueen's early dating of the Scottish Renaissance. To mention but one direction of research: evidence has emerged of Renaissance architectural features at Stirling, Linlithgow, and Falkland Palaces, and in country houses of 1540–1590.[4]

Douglas's Humanism

To ask whether Douglas was a true humanist is to try to fix the fluidities of a transitional period. And, besides, 'humanist' covers as many subtexts as its

---

[1] 'The Approach to English', *Light on C. S. Lewis*, ed. J. Gibb (London, 1965), pp. 60–1.
[2] L. Jones, *The Origins of Shakespeare* (Oxford, 1977), pp. 8–11.
[3] E. M. W. Tillyard, *English Renaissance* (London, 1960): R. Tuve, *Allegorical Imagery* (Princeton, NJ, 1966); Panofsky, *Renaissance and Renascences in Western Art*, rev. edn. (London, 1970).
[4] See C. McKean, *The Scottish Chateau: The Country House of Renaissance Scotland* (Stroud, 2001), dis. 1–5, esp. pp. 14, 87, 162; also C. Edington, *Court and Culture in Renaissance Scotland* (East Linton, 1995).

dictionary definitions betray.[5] Assume a fourteenth-to sixteenth-century scholar of Latin and Greek literature, and Douglas qualifies—although classical studies then were not as now. (In sixteenth-century Winchester College, Latin 'dictates' still emphasised the moral lessons of short passages studied without much philological support; in seventeenth-century Cambridge, the syllabus was still largely medieval.[6]) Douglas was no philologist; but if he often submits to Josse Bade's authority, he can also assert his own against Chaucer's or Caxton's. More importantly, as Christopher Baswell and A. E. C. Canitz rightly recognize, Douglas was a brilliant translator.[7] His sensitivity to Virgil's stylistic variations evidences much study of classical Latin. And Lord Sinclair's suggestion that Douglas might translate Homer shows he was at least reputed to know some Greek—possibly as much as one or two of his modern critics. But, take humanism as a movement away from religious to secular concerns, and Douglas's humanism is more doubtful. He was a prelate at a time when religious leaders were not eager, as they often are today, to declare their secularity. Here, the common definitions of humanism can mislead. For Renaissance humanism was largely a movement of reform,[8] and by this more than curricular reform is implied. Lorenzo Valla, an agreed humanist whom Douglas quotes, initiated a new phase of reformation by unmasking the Papal Decretals as forgeries.

One needs to avoid any simplistic sectarian line-up, of Protestant Reformers advocating new doctrines *versus* secular humanists concerned only with textual purity. The instance of Erasmus should be enough to show such a dichotomy inadequate. Many northern humanists believed that learning was religion's handmaid:[9] 'right reason' and 'godly reason' became Reformation watchwords. English humanists, moreover, made vital contributions to the political and educational reforms of Henry VIII and Elizabeth. Many had links with Continental Reformers—like Roger Ascham, who was deeply influenced by the Strasbourg Reformer Johann Sturm. Their overt ideology provides a convenient contrast to

---

[5] Cf. J. K. Cameron, in *Humanism in Renaissance Scotland*, ed. J. MacQueen (Edinburgh, 1990), p. 161.

[6] Only later were assignments such as to allow detailed attention to individual words. See L. P. Wilkinson, *The Georgics of Virgil* (Cambridge, 1969), pp. 295-6; T. W. Baldwin, *William Shakespere's Small Latins & Less Greeke*, 2 vols. (Urbana, IL, 1944), I, 231-2. On Cambridge, see J. A. W Bennett, *The Humane Medievalist*, ed. P. Boitani (Rome, 1982), p. 190. Even in Johann Sturm's pedagogy Virgil's *Bucolics* were explicated at the rate of an eclogue a day; see P. Mesnard, 'The Pedagogy of Johann Sturm', *SR* 13 (1966), 211. The common cause of reform may be gauged from the alliances between 'Protestant' humanists and early Jesuits; see Mesnard, 'Pedagogy', p. 218.

[7] C. Baswell, *Virgil in Medieval England: Figuring the 'Aeneid' from the Twelfth Century to Chaucer* (Cambridge, 1995). A. E. C. Canitz, 'From *Aeneid* to *Eneados*: Theory and Practice of Gavin Douglas's Translation', *M&H* 17 (1991), 81-99.

[8] See P. Bawcutt, *Gavin Douglas* (Edinburgh, 1976), pp. 28-9, 31-2; *The Cambridge Companion to Renaissance Humanism*, ed. J. Kraye (Cambridge, 1996), *passim*; A. Fowler, *Time's Purpled Masquers* (Oxford, 1996), p. 6, n. 22.

[9] On *pietas litterata* and *devotio moderna*, see A. Grafton, *Defenders of the Text* (Cambridge, MA, and London, 1991); R. R. Bolgar, *The Classical Heritage and Its Beneficiaries* (Cambridge, 1954), chs 7 and 8.

Douglas's pre-Reformation position.[10] Ascham famously wrote against Malory's glorification of 'open mans slaughter, and bold bawdrye'; recalling when 'Gods Bible was banished the Court, and *Morte Arthure* received into the Princes chamber'.[11] This stance, easily mistaken for moral puritanism, was fairly typical of Renaissance humanists, who from Erasmus to Milton rejected chivalric honour and war.[12] Ascham, notoriously, detested the culture of 'our forefathers tyme, when Papistrie, as a standyng poole, covered and overflowed all England'[13] (such remarks by Ascham were themselves enough to alienate Lewis, to whom Malory was a favourite author). So far as Scotland is concerned, however, the battle-lines are less distinct. There, partly in response to the Council of Trent, the church introduced many reforms, both educational and ecclesiastical, in the first half of the sixteenth century. Especially in Aberdeen, St Andrews, and the north through Kinloss Abbey, a humanist movement and a 'Catholic' Reformation can be discerned, well before the 'Protestant' Reformation in the ordinary sense.[14]

To tie Douglas down to this or that Protestant sect would require a rope of sand. Kurt Wittig thinks Douglas's Prologue XI 'almost exactly attuned to the innermost principle of the Kirk of Scotland, as defined by a former Moderator G. D. Henderson'; but Priscilla Bawcutt reads the scale of Protestantism better: 'Douglas's remarks about man's salvation do not reveal a new or distinctive concern with divine grace'.[15] Both Bawcutt and Wittig apply a doctrinal criterion. But before 1513 no Protestant theology nor Catholic rebuttal of it existed. Even Luther's theses were nailed up only in 1517. But ecclesiastical reform was a different matter: it was already in the air. Douglas quoted from Valla's attacks on logic-chopping Scholastic speculation, and so aligned himself with those who desired reform through recovery of Biblical, Augustinian Christianity.[16] Even so, Douglas shows no liking for subversion or disorder. He introduced legal reforms

---

[10] Even so, Sturm at first made common cause with the Jesuits on matters of reform. On Sturm's ecclesiastical alignments, see Mesnard, 'Pedagogy'. Ascham was also a close friend of Martin Bucer's, and with Queen Elizabeth read the Greek Testament and the *Common Places* of Melanchthon; see L. V. Ryan, *Roger Ascham* (Stanford, CA, and London, 1963); R. Ascham, *The Scholemaster*, ed. J. E. Mayor (1863), p. 224.

[11] R. Ascham, *English Works*, ed. W. A. Wright (Cambridge, 1904), p. 23 L. Cf. 'A Declaration of the Faith', a tract of 1539, reprinted in J. Collier, *An Ecclesiastical History of Great Britain*..., 2 vols. (London, 1708-14), II, 36: '*Englishmen* have now in hand...the Holy Bible...instead of the old fabulous and phantasticall Books of the *Table round, Launcelot du Lake, Huon de Bourdeux, Bevy of Hampton, Guy of Warwick*, etc. and such other whose unpure Filth and vain Fabulosity, the Light of God has abolished utterly.'

[12] Erasmus, *Querela pacis*, trans. B. Radice, in Erasmus, *Collected Works*, vols. 27-8 (Toronto, 1986), p. 289; J. Milton, *Paradise Lost* IX, 27-42.

[13] Ascham, *English Works*, p. 230.

[14] See *The Renaissance in Scotland: Studies in Literature, Religion, History and Culture Offered to John Durkan*, ed. A. A. MacDonald, M. Lynch, and I. B. Cowan (Leiden, 1994), chs. 7, 10, 13, 16.

[15] K. Wittig, *The Scottish Tradition in Literature* (Edinburgh and London, 1958), pp. 82-3; Bawcutt, *Gavin Douglas*, p. 29.

[16] Cf. Tyndale's attacks on the 'chopological sophisters' in *The Obedience of a Christian Man* (London, 1528), in *Doctrinal Treatises*, ed. H. Walter (Cambridge, 1948), p. 307. See Bawcutt, *Gavin Douglas*, p. 69.

to remove causes of dispute, for example, and his dealings with papal and other authorities were less confrontational than, say, Erasmus's. One may think of Douglas as characterized by fideism rather than doctrinal innovation.

Douglas's cultural orientation has also been elusive. Would his authorship of a romance-like dream-vision, *The Palice of Honour,* make him vulnerable to the condemnation of such as Ascham? And what of his whole-hearted narration of noble war in the *Eneados*? Again, does he deliver a medieval or a Renaissance Virgil—or an Augustinian or Dantean one?[17] But these may not be quite the right questions to ask of a translation so individual. Douglas had no vernacular Virgil to emulate, yet he used with discrimination the sometimes stifling commentaries surrounding the *Aeneid*—those of Servius, Donatus, Cristoforo Landino (1424–1498), Josse Bade (1462–1535), the popular but unfortunate Antonio Mancinelli (1452–1506), and the more conservative Domizio Calderini (1447–1478).[18] Lewis gathers (to defend them) a harvest of quaint instances of 'the general medievalisation' to which, he thinks, Douglas subjects the *Aeneid*—like Camilla's Turkish bow, and that 'holy religious woman clene', the Sibyl.[19] But such apparent anachronisms need not manifest naïve innocence of history; they may illustrate, only, that consistent realism lay in the future. Deliberate anachronism for the sake of immediacy was long to continue; as when Jan Steen dresses his Bathsheba according to seventeenth-century Netherlandish fashion. To take another notorious instance in the *Eneados*: *nun*, meaning 'pagan priestess'—as in 'nuns of Bacchus'—was common usage from King Aelfred (893) to Clarendon (1647), appearing, even, in Surrey's proto-classicist *Aeneid* IV.[20] Douglas seldom Christianizes Virgil; his Book VI, for example, rejects the hell mouth of Sebastian Brant's 1502 illustrations.[21] Bawcutt may plead specially when she distinguishes Purgatory from 'purgatorial experience' and calls the circles of

---

[17] Bawcutt's question. On the romantic element of the *Aeneid,* see C. S. Lewis, *English Literature in the Sixteenth Century* (Oxford, 1954), pp. 291 ff.; Baswell, *Virgil*.

[18] From the 1490s, the *Vergilii Opera* typically appeared *cum commentariis quinque,* i.e. Servius's, Donatus's, Landino's, Mancinelli's, and Calderini's. Bawcutt decisively establishes that Douglas used the Paris 1501 *Opera* edited by Josse Bade (Jodocus Badius Ascensius). Cristoforo Landino has impeccable humanist credentials; yet the method of his neo-Platonic interpretation is allegorical. Bade himself is generally regarded as a Renaissance humanist publisher; but he also wrote a life of Thomas à Kempis and, under the pseudonym of Thomas Waleys, revised Pierre Bersuire's fourfold allegorization of the *Metamorphoses* (1509); see *Medieval Literary Theory and Criticism c.1100–c.1375: The Commentary-Tradition,* ed. A. J. Minnis and A. B. Scott (Oxford, 1988), p. 318. Douglas himself never attempts fourfold interpretation, but only Renaissance moral or 'physical' allegory as practised by Landino, and still by Natale Conti (1520–1582).

[19] Lewis, *Sixteenth Century,* p. 86.

[20] *OED* s. v. Nun 1 b. Add G. Chapman's tide 'Against the Samian Ministresse or Nunne', in *The Lesser Homerica.* Surrey need not have borrowed 'nun' from Douglas, *pace* E. Ridley, 'Surrey's Debt to Gawin Douglas', *PMLA* 76 (1961), 29, 33.

[21] *Publii Vergilii Maronis Opera cum Quinque Vulgatis Commentariis: Expolitissmisque Figuris atque Imaginibus nuper per Sebastianum Brant Superadditis…*(Strasbourg, 1502); illus. in D. Gray, "'As quha the mater beheld tofor thar e'", *A Palace in the Wild,* ed. L. A. J. R. Houwen, A. A. MacDonald, and S. L. Mapstone (Leuven, 2000), pl. 2.

hell 'not a peculiarly medieval idea'.²² But, after all, Douglas's explicit purpose is to show Virgil's anticipation of Christianity.²³ In any case, one can easily be too superior about the medieval Virgil. Douglas alludes to the legend of Aristotle ridden and Virgil left suspended in a basket: 'Men says thou [sc. Love] brydillyt Aristotyll as ane hors,/ And crelyt up the flour of poetry [Virgil]'.²⁴ Embarrassed scholars call these credulous legends. But actually they are symbolic stories, embodying the idea that even great authors can be enslaved by their lower natures.

Mimesis and Ekphrasis

A critical approach to the *Eneados* might begin with the rhetoric of ekphrasis. The term *ekphrasis* (ἔκφρασις) is commonly defined as 'description, particularly description of works of art'. But the term is much richer; the verb ἐκφράζω means 'tell, recount, express ornately'. Michael Baxandall has explained how the Byzantine convention of essays in ekphrasis was introduced to the Italian Renaissance, influencing it profoundly. Hermogenes had set out the aim: 'Ekphrasis...brings before the eyes that which is to be shown. Ekphraseis are of people, actions, times, places, seasons, and many other things...The special virtues of ekphrasis are clarity and visibility; the style must contrive to bring about seeing through hearing'.²⁵ During the last few decades scholars have shown how ekphrasis dominated the entire Renaissance conception of mimesis, literary imitation of experience, indeed, mimesis was generally theorized in terms of ekphrasis.²⁶ Douglas Gray, in an article on the imagery of the *Eneados*, successfully applies the narrower conception of ekphrasis as 'the detailed description that "brings before the eyes that which is to be shown"'.²⁷ And ekphrasis in the broader sense proves equally applicable to Douglas's narration.

Ekphrasis inevitably dominates the *ut pictura poesis* tradition,²⁸ from Callistratus and the Greek Anthology to the narrative poetry of the seventeenth

---

²² Bawcutt, *Gavin Douglas*, pp. 125–6.
²³ VI. Prol., 1–80. Unless otherwise specified, citations of, and quotation from, the text of Douglas's *Eneados* refer to: *Virgil's 'Aeneid' Translated into Scottish Verse*, ed. David E. C. Coldwell, STS, 4 vols. (Edinburgh & London, 1956–64).
²⁴ IV. Prol., 31–2; Bawcutt, *Gavin Douglas*, p. 69.
²⁵ Quoted in M. Baxandall, *Giotto and the Orators* (Oxford, 1986), p. 85.
²⁶ See M. Krieger, *The Play and Place of Criticism* (Baltimore, 1967), ch. 8; '*Ekphrasis*' (Baltimore, MD, and London, 1992); N. E. Land (University Park, PA, 1994); M. Smith, *Literary Realism and the Ekphrastic Tradition* (University Park, PA, 1995).
²⁷ Gray, 'Douglas's Treatment', p. 96. For the narrower interpretation, see also A. Barchiesi, 'Virgilian Narrative: Ekphrasis', *The Cambridge Companion to Virgil*, ed. C. Martindale (Cambridge, 1997), pp. 272–3.
²⁸ On the *ut pictura poesis* tradition, see R. Lee, '*Ut Pictura Poesis*: The Humanistic Theory of Painting', *Art Bulletin* 22 (1940), 197–269; W. Trimpi, 'The Meaning of Horace's *Ut Pictura Poesis*', *Journal of the Warburg and Courtauld Institute* 36 (1973), 1–34; J. H. Hagstrum, *The Sister Arts: The Tradition of Literary Pictorialism and English Poetry from Dryden to Gray* (Chicago and London, 1958); J. Dundas, *Pencils Rhetorique: Renaissance Poets and the Art of Painting* (Newark, DE, 1993).

century. Norman Land traces the tradition's illusionism from Philostratus and the rhetoricians up to the art criticism of Giorgio Vasari.[29] Ekphrastic criticism focuses on the art of making objects and actions lifelike, for example by evoking impressions from several senses. Thus, in the *Purgatorio*, when Dante views marble reliefs, he is moved, as if the images were real.[30] Renaissance theorists discuss realism in terms of *evidentia* or *enargeia*, 'lifelikeness'. And the Tudor poet Nicholas Grimald is advised by his tutor John Airey to make his morality plain through *clavo et illustri spectaculo*—lifelike depiction—rather than through allegory.[31] Sir Philip Sidney similarly, writes of virtues, vices, and passions so in their own natural seats laid to the view, that we seem not to hear of them, but clearly to see through them'.[32] Renaissance literature explores viewers' engagement with ekphrastic images almost obsessively: think of the seductive embroidery in *Hero and Leander*, the aroused spectators in Michael Drayton's *Mortimeriados*, the animated tapestries of Busyrane, and, in the *Arcadia*, Zelmane's jealousy of the River Ladon.[33]

Douglas happily accepts this tradition. When Virgil's Aeneas arrives at Carthage and views murals of the sack of Troy they are so lifelike that tears flood his face.[34] Douglas, who appreciates the *Aeneid* to be 'felable in all degree',[35] intensifies the effect by extending the emotional engagement to poet and reader. Where Virgil has simply *en Priamus* ('lo Priam'), Douglas puts 'Allace, behald, se jonder Kyng Priam'.[36] Gray thinks such elaborations imitate the 'subjective style of Virgil'[37]—a line of Virgilian criticism going back to Brooks Otis. But Otis's view, now seen to be based on too narrow a canon, scarcely merits assent. The subjective manner was not Virgil's only but practised also by rivals such as Callimachus. And Douglas could have found similarly engaged descriptions in Chaucer and others more nearly contemporary. It hardly matters whom Douglas imitated in this respect. For in Douglas's age *all* mimesis was 'subjective' (to use Otis's term).

---

[29] Land, *Viewer as Poet*.   [30] Land, *Viewer as Poet*, p. 58.
[31] N. Grimald, *The Life and Poems*, ed. L. R. Merrill (New Haven, CT, and London, 1925), pp. 106 7.
[32] Sir P. Sidney, *Miscellaneous Prose*, ed. K. Duncan-Jones and J. van Dorsten (Oxford, 1973), p. 86; cf. 117, 'forcibleness or energia', also G. Chapman, *The Poems*, ed. P. B. Bartlett (repr. New York, 1962), p. 43, 'Energia or clearness of representation. *Enargeia* and *energia* were often confused'; see N. Rudenstine, *Sidney's Poetic Development* (Cambridge, MA, 1967), ch. 10; F. Robinson, *The Shape of Things Known: Sidney's Apology in Its Philosophical Tradition* (Cambridge, MA, 1972), pp. 130–1; Dundas, *Pencils Rhetorique*, pp. 16, 125.
[33] Dundas, *Pencils Rhetorique*, p. 112; Sidney, *The Countess of Pembroke's Arcadia (The New Arcadia)*, ed. V. Stretkowicz (Oxford, 1987), pp. 188–9. See A. Fowler, *Renaissance Realism* (Oxford, 2003), p. 79.
[34] *Aeneid* I, 465, *largoque umectat flumine voltum*.
[35] I. Prol., 13: 'affecting to the highest degree', as C. Burrow translates, in 'Virgil in English Translation', *The Cambridge Companion to Virgil*, ed. C. Martindale (Cambridge, 1997), p. 22.
[36] *Aeneid* i, 461; *Eneados* I.vii, 76.
[37] Gray, 'Douglas's Treatment', pp. 97, 98f, 102, 105, citing B. Otis, *Virgil: A Study in Civilized Poetry* (Oxford, 1963) and J. N. Smith, 'Ekphrasis as a Stylistic Element in Douglas's *Palis of Honoure*', *MÆ* 48 (1979), 240–53.

The resemblances most probably result from cognitive affinities rather than rhetorical imitation.

Until the seventeenth century the detached observation that leads to objective, scientific appraisal was rare. Apart from a few scientists—members, usually, of religious orders—those describing nature were emotionally involved with it. They wrote not as spectators but participants. Until a century or more after Douglas, virtually all mimesis was in this sense participatory. One could call certain early Renaissance descriptions realistic; but their realism was participatory realism, not our spectator realism. Participatory realism, indeed, was the only mode available. This broad generalization should be qualified. Since Erich Auerbach's *Mimesis* (1946), literary historians have agreed that fifteenth-century writing is capable of 'graphic portrayal...in the service of earthly events'—of mimesis with the Vigour of the sensory.[38] Emotions, however, tended to be specified perfunctorily. Nuances of inner experience were not portrayed graphically, but explored instead through allegory, a mode still available to John Bunyan. Not until the nascent 'spectator realism' of the novel—foreshadowed in Spenser, Sidney, and other ekphrastic Elizabethan poets—did an observer-subject or narrator-spectator emerge. But surely, it may be objected, Douglas observes landscapes minutely? Yes, of course: in this, as in much else, he is a prescient, anticipatory figure. Indeed, Douglas's transitional position is just what makes his depiction of nature so interesting.

For his poetic description of landscape and seasonal change, Douglas had few models. Chauvinistic English critics refer to a single short passage in *Gawain and the Green Knight*; and doubtless there were hints in French, Italian, and Neo-Latin—from Folgore's *Sonetti dei Mesi* to Polidanus's *Rusticus* (1483).[39] But Bawcutt is surely right: Douglas's primary model is Virgil's *Georgics*.[40] Acceptance of this view has been delayed by widespread scepticism as to the Virgilian character of the *Eneados*. Its alleged prolixity, and Douglas's 'medieval' view of the *Aeneid* as a *preparatio evangelii*, are contrasted with Surrey's concision and secularity.[41] But is Virgil (as compared with Callimachus, say) *concise*, exactly—as distinct from close-textured? Classicists have drawn attention to paratactic features in Virgil's style, such as his fondness for hendiadys and theme-and-

---

[38] E. Auerbach, *Mimesis: The Representation of Reality in Western Literature*, trans. W. R. Trask (Princeton, NJ, 1953), pp. 259, 261.

[39] F. da Sangimignano (G. da Michele, fl. 1305-32); his *Sonetti* may be found in *Arte della Caccia*, ed. G. Innamorati (Milan, 1965). On A. Poliziano (A. Ambrogini, 1454-94) see Wilkinson, *Georgics*, p. 279.

[40] Bawcutt, *Gavin Douglas*, pp. 89, 190; 'The "Library" of Gavin Douglas', in *Bards and Makars*, ed. A. J. Aicken, M. P. McDiarmid, and D. S. Thomson (Glasgow, 1977), p. 117. On Renaissance use of the *Georgics* generally, see Wilkinson, *Georgics*.

[41] For a discussion of the complex matter of Douglas's additions to the length of his original, see Bawcutt, *Gavin Douglas*, ch. 5. In Bk. ii, e.g., Douglas adds 76% as against Surreys 32%. The very different percentages in different Books indicates deliberate change of proportions.

variation patterns.[42] His parataxis often calls for doublets, sometimes involving adventurous syntax: *quo fremitus... et sublaius ad aethera clamor* (*Aeneid* ii, 338); *adytis arisque* (351); *moriamur, et in media arma ruamus* (353).[43] Some of Douglas's own doublets must of course be put down to the usual straddling tactic of early translators; but surely at least *some* may be regarded as imitating Virgil's own repetitions? If Douglas sometimes overdoes this, he may be forgiven. His aim is not to match the proportions of the *Aeneid*, but to suggest its literary qualities.[44] He broadens Virgil's effects, exaggerating them for clarity. Like all the best translations, Douglas's had a political purpose; and his purpose was educational.

Jones rightly hails Surrey's syllabic symmetries as a Virgilian patterning eloquent of a new classicism.[45] But Douglas was quite capable of comparable symmetries.[46] In 1977 I gave a few examples, and I add some more here (see Fig. 1).[47]

Fig. 1.

	1	1 1 1	2	1	1 1	1
II viii 54–6	And first of all, before the porche in ran					
	1	1 1	2 1	2	1 1	1
	Hard to the entre, in schyning plait and maile,					
	2	1	2	2 1	2	
	Pirrus, with wapnis fersly to assaile:					
	1	1 1	2	2	1 1	1
VII i 7–9	Thy tomb and banis, markit with thi name,					
	1 1		3	3	1 1	
	In gret Hesperia witnessing the same,					
	1	1 1	2	2	1 1	1
	Geif that be only glory now to the.					
	1	1 1		5	1 1	1
VIII i 101	Heir is myne habitacioun huge and grete					

---

[42] See J. O'Hara, 'Virgil's Style', pp. 247–8.

[43] Among countless other examples, one may list the following: *gemitu miseroque tumultu* (ii, 486); *auro spoliissque* (504); *auxilio nec defensoribus* (521); *ocalos...et ora* (531); *pro scelere...pro talibus ausis* (535); *grates... et praemia* (537); *referes,..et nuntius ibis* (547); *Troiam...Pergama* (555); *Troiae et patriae* (573); *Spartam...patriasque Mycenas* (577); *ferro...crebrisque bipennibus* (627); *limina...antiquasque domos* (634–5). Longer phrases are doubled at 538–9; 549; 554; and 580. (I give examples from the same passage to show their frequency.)

[44] He may have imitated the proportions in his Prologues, however; their line-total is 2199, close to the 2189 of Virgil's *Georgics* in Ascensius's edition. A medieval touch, perhaps; although Boccaccio similarly matches the line-total of the *Aeneid* in his *Teseida*; and, according to J. A. W. Bennett, *Humane Medievalist*, p. 363, Boccaccio was a sophisticated and 'modern' writer; while to A. C. Spearing, *The Medieval Poet as Voyeur* (Cambridge, 1993), p. 233, the *De Genealogiis* seems 'a manifesto of the Renaissance conception of learned poetry'. Contrast Baswell, *Virgil*, p. 406, n. 21, for whom Boccaccio represents 'medieval material'.

[45] Surrey, *Poems*, ed. E. Jones (Oxford, 1964), Introd., esp. p. xvii; cf. A. C. Spearing, *Medieval to Renaissance in English Poetry* (Cambridge, 1985), p. 312, who agrees with Thomas Warton that Surrey was 'the first English classical poet'.

[46] See A. Fowler, 'Virgil for "every gentil Scot"', *TLS* (22 July 1977), 802–3.

[47] Using John Small's text, based on the Elphinscone MS. Written by a less intelligent scribe, the Cambridge MS often obscures the syllabic patterning; as when it gives 'in ran' as 'inran'.

This feature is hardly one that suggests prolixity.

On occasion, Douglas can be more sensitive than his modern critics to Virgil's style. One example must stand for many. An old but sound critic of Virgil, T. E. Page, notices an apparent confusion as to the materials of the fatal horse—now 'planks of fir', now 'beams of maple', now 'oak timbers'.[48] Page castigates A. Sidgwick for calling this 'natural poetic variation'. It is art, he says, not nature: Virgil 'prefers the particular to the general, and therefore prefers to name some particular tree...but he also loves variety.'[49] How does Douglas render these variations, natural or artful? He translates Virgil's phrases, respectively, as 'sawyn beche'; 'hattyr gestis [shaped joists] beldit up'; and 'statw of tre [wood]'.[50] *OED* takes the extremely rare *hattyr* to mean 'of maple (it renders L. *acernus*)'. But John Small's gloss gives the show away when he writes that *hattyr* 'ought to signify maple'. Why *ought*? Because of the (fallacious) received idea of Douglas's style. 'Explicitness is one of Douglas's most striking qualities as a translator'; 'Douglas has a tendency to nail...words down, make them convey a single, specific concept and so lose the possibility of multiple connotations'.[51] If Virgil had *acernis*, then Douglas must have 'maple'. But Douglas knows the *Aeneid* better than this. And he catches Virgil's spirit not by translating 'word for word' (a method St Gregory forbade[52]) but by discovering an equivalent effect, a correspondent variety: by ringing changes not on the materials but on the stages of construction. So, he moves from sawing and shaped joists to the finished wooden image.[53] Here, as often, the unfamiliar language has hindered appreciation of Douglas's subtlety. Bawcutt valuably suggests that 'some of Douglas's first readers might have said of him, as Ben Jonson said of Spenser, that Douglas "in affecting the Ancients, writ no Language"'[54]—without perhaps intending unqualified praise. But few other twentieth-century critics have grasped that Douglas's Renaissance copiousness (*fouth*) positively belongs with Spenser's, Urquhart's, and Joyce's. (It may be relevant to note that the number of strange words in Small's glossary of Douglas is much the same as in J. C. Smith's glossary of Spenser.[55])

Specific description, pursuing variety and appropriating technical terms, characterizes the georgic genre, a major ingredient of Virgil's *Aeneid*.[56] This genre, now much misunderstood, was once the form of choice for moralizing,

---

[48] *Aeneid* ii, 16; ii, 112; ii, 186.

[49] P. Vergili Maronis Aeneidos Lib. II, ed. T. E. Page, rev. edn. (London, 1959), pp. 41–2. On Virgil's variety, see O'Hara, 'Virgil's Style', p. 246.

[50] II.i, 6; II.ii, 99; II.iii, 80; cf. II.i, 70 ('ionyngis of the thrawyn wame of tre').

[51] Bawcutt, *Gavin Douglas*, p. 115; E. Ridley, 'The Distinctive Character of Douglas's *Eneados*', *SSL* 18 (1983), 113. The notion of Virgil's frequent ambiguity may partly derive from the fashionable deconstructive theories of Stanley Fish and others; see, however, O'Hara, 'Virgil's Style', pp. 249–50.

[52] I.Prol., 395. Yet: Douglas also rejects loose paraphrase, claiming in the 'Direction' 44–6 to match Virgil 'al maste word by word'.

[53] *Sawyn* (II.i, 6); *hattyr gestis* (II.ii, 90); *statw of tree* (II.iii, 80).

[54] Bawcutt, *Gavin Douglas*, p. 145.

[55] About 4,750, as against 4,790.

[56] Bawcutt, *Gavin Douglas*, Index, s. v. *Georgics*.

description, and direct address *in persona auctoris*—an almost inevitable choice, then, for autobiographical prologues.[57] It particularly suited discussion of the writer's own art, a staple topos of georgic up to Alexander Pope's *Essay on Criticism* and beyond. Other topics include work, and natural processes observed in detail; the details often being arranged in catalogues, a form now despised but enjoyed by Douglas himself and by early epigones like John Rolland (1504–c. 1575).[58] Another prominent georgic topic was seasonal change, the main subject of calendrical works like Hesiod's *Works and Days*, Nicholas Breton's *Fantasticks*, or James Thomson's *The Seasons*. In all these characteristics, georgic was the exact antithesis of pastoral, whose shepherds do nothing, know nothing in particular, and experience no season but spring.[59] Ian Ross, otherwise illuminating on the Prologues, gets this badly wrong when he writes of Douglas's 'Winter Eclogue' with its 'close observation' discovering 'the mode of the Virgilian Eclogue'. Pastoral eclogue has no winter, no plough, no 'puyr labouraris' or 'bissy husbandmen'.[60]

Douglas's georgic mode shapes his diction and imagery throughout the *Eneados*. His frequent use of technical terms is particularly striking; they make for a more wide-ranging vocabulary than Chaucer's. Yet the legitimacy of introducing terms of trade into literature could not be taken for granted. Long after Douglas, it continued to be controversial. Ronsard had to defend 'les noms propres des mestiers';[61] and John Dryden vacillated, including them in 1666 but excluding in 1697.[62] Douglas's nautical terms are especially noticeable. As Florence Ridley admirably remarks, additions of sea imagery to his translation are his 'most original literary contribution', giving a 'persistent smack of the sea'.[63] He knows many nautical techniques, noticing, for example, how ships may 'fly', 'sweep', or 'slide'. It is notable how often Douglas's translation yields the earliest literary examples of a nautical word in OED. So with *starboard*;[64] *fang* ('a rope leading from the peak of the gaff of a fore-and-aft sail to the rail on each side');[65] *luff* ('the weather part of a fore-and-aft sail');[66] and *rabandis*

---

[57] See A. Fowler, *Kinds of Literature* (Cambridge, MA, Oxford, 1982), Index, s. v. *Georgic*; A. Fowler, 'The Beginnings of English Georgic', in *Renaissance Genres*, ed. B. K. Lewalski, Harvard English Studies 14 (Cambridge, MA, and London, 1986), pp. 105–25.
[58] On whom see J. Hadley Williams, 'Dunbar and his Immediate Heirs', in *William Dunbar, 'The Nobill Poet'* [Festschrift Bawcutt], ed. S. L. Mapstone (East Linton, 2001), p. 89.
[59] The Contrast is well stated in T. G. Rosenmeyer, *The Green Cabinet* (Berkeley and Los Angeles, 1969), Index, s. v. *Hesiodic tradition*.
[60] I. Ross, '"Proloug" and "Buke" in the *Eneados* of Gavin Douglas', in *Proceedings of the Fourth International Conference on Scottish Language and Literature—Medieval and Renaissance*, ed. D. Strauss and H. W. Drescher (Frankfurt, 1986), pp. 399, 400.
[61] See his *Abbregé de l'Art Poëtique François* (1565), in *Ouvres complètes*, ed. P. Laumonier, I. Silver, and R. Lebègue, 20 vols. (Paris, 1914–75), XIV, 13.
[62] J. Dryden, *The Poems*, ed. P. Hammond, 4 vols. (London and New York, 1995–2000), I, 117; Dryden, Pref. to *Annus Mirabilis*, in *Essays of John Dryden*, ed. W. P. Ker, 2 vols. (Oxford, 1926), I, 13; Dedic. to *Aeneis*, ibid. II, 236. See Bawcutt, *Gavin Douglas*, pp. 129, 160.
[63] Ridley, 'Distinctive Character', pp. 116–19.
[64] *OED*, few examples before 1513; *Eneados* V.iv, 6.
[65] *OED* 7a, first example; *Eneados* V.xiv, 8.
[66] *OED* 4, first example; *Eneados* V.xiv, 7.

(robbins, ropes fastening the sail to the yard).⁶⁷ Similarly technical terms, although not earliest examples, include *ra* (sailyard), *piggeis* (peggy-masts), and *ballyngar*.⁶⁸ *Nommes propres* with a vengeance. Ridley's sensitive account of the nautical passages generally inspires confidence; although *holl rolkis* are surely 'sunken', not 'hollow', rocks.⁶⁹ One may accept her conclusion that Douglas, more than Virgil, 'had heard the sea'.⁷⁰ Indeed, he may well have drawn on experience of voyages round the Scottish coast or even abroad. Did he also imitate Lucan, an author he greatly admired?⁷¹ Lucan's *Pharsalia* was a *locus classicus* for nautical diction as late as Dryden.⁷² Here again Douglas's writing, usually taken to reflect purely local experience, actually belongs to a classical tradition of *imitatio* with its attendant critical controversies. To these, Douglas made both theoretical and practical contributions.

So, too, with Douglas's words specifying weapons and armour. *Basnet*; *byrne*; *curace*; *gorget*; *sallet*: all are un-Chaucerian. Yet they do not belong, as one might expect, to the tournament nomenclature of 1500 Scotland. Instead, they are anachronistic. The *basnet* was a fourteenth- or fifteenth-century helmet; the *gorget* fourteenth century; while the *curace* (breast- and back-plates) and *sallet* were fifteenth century or earlier. As for *byrne*, it 'was no longer an everyday Scottish word' but belonged to the heroic world of alliterative romance.⁷³ The distinction between deliberate archaism and involuntary poetic diction can be unresolvable. But it seems reasonable to compare the similarly archaic armour in the *Orlando Furioso* (1516) of his Renaissance contemporary Ariosto.⁷⁴

Landscape Description

Douglas's greatest original achievement must be his invention of landscape poetry in English.⁷⁵ This element in his work is again georgic in inspiration: indeed, a curiously Latinate quality pervades the landscape Prologues. They sometimes seem almost to be nature poems in a Virgilian mode—*hommages* to Virgil. In Prologue VII, for example, nature is mythologized: 'Eolus schowtis schill' and 'Boreas his bugill blew' causing the deer to hide.⁷⁶ Douglas sustains georgic specificity throughout. Nevertheless, unqualified praise of his close observation can

---

⁶⁷ *OED*, s. v. *Roband*; *Eneados* III.iv, 110. See H. Manwayring, *The Seaman's Dictionary (1644)*, ed. R. C. Alston (Menston, 1972), p. 86: '*Robins*: Are little lines reeved into the Eylot-holes of the saile, and sure to make fast the saile unto the yard'.

⁶⁸ *Eneados* V.xiv, 8; III.vi, 4; II.i, 19; *OED balinger*, a light sloop.

⁶⁹ So Small. For *holl* = deep, sunken, low-lying, see *OED* 2.

⁷⁰ Ridley, 'Distinctive Character', p. 120.   ⁷¹ See Bawcutt, *Gavin Douglas*, pp. 34–5.

⁷² Pref. to *Annus Mirabilis*, p. 117.   ⁷³ See Bawcutt, *Gavin Douglas*, p. 155.

⁷⁴ Ariosto combined such romance features with shocking realism; see M. Murrin, *History and Warfare in Renaissance Epic* (Chicago and London, 1994), pp. 81ff.

⁷⁵ See D. Pearsall and E. Salter, *Landscapes and Seasons of the Medieval World* (London, 1973), pp. 200–4.

⁷⁶ *Eneados* VII.Prol., 67, 85.

mislead. First, it is seldom observation of single moments. David Coldwell mistakenly faults Douglas's Prologue XII because it catalogues flowers of different seasons as if grow[ing] simultaneously in the same place.[77] This is like criticizing Ambrosius Bosschaert for painfully assembling flowers of all seasons into a single flowerpiece. Douglas's Renaissance realism intentionally combines many different times in a single scene, so as to develop and elaborate on the topic they share.

Secondly, 'observation' may mislead by suggesting detachment. Douglas's realism is participatory, not detached. His landscape description goes far beyond lists of sense data. Consider, in Prologue VII, 'The dolly [dowy] dichis war all donk and wait'.[78] Has this not as much feeling as observation? *Dowy* means 'dull, lonely, melancholy, dreary, dismal': a highly emotive word.[79] At any time, Douglas's nature may be animated or anthropomorphized. Is one to regard 'wysnyt mossy hew'[80] as observation of colour, or flora, or an ageing process? Again, he will treat nature as an art work: 'With frostis hair [hoary] ourfret [embroidered] the feldis standis'.[81] His winter landscape can even become 'a symylitude of hell', 'Reducyng [bringing back] to our mynd.../ Gousty schaddois of eild and grisly ded'.[82] Very often Douglas explores empathy with nature, so that one cannot easily accept Ridley's contrast of Virgil's 'ambiguous words whose varied possibilities increase the implications' with Douglas's tendency 'to nail such words down, make them convey a single, specific concept'.[83] In subtle ways Douglas, too, conveys atmosphere, seasonal ethos, and emotional involvement.

But have the Prologues any autonomous coherence such as one would expect in an original work? Opinions about this differ, from Derek Pearsall and Elizabeth Salter's, that Douglas 'achieved a triumph of landscape as an independent art form', to Ridley's, that the Prologues are 'an integral part of Douglas's translation'.[84] Stylistically, as mentioned above, the Prologues are consistently georgic;[85] and the origins of landscape poetry from Hesiod onwards lie also in the georgic tradition. But there were other, extra-literary models. Bawcutt persuasively compares the indoor scene in Prologue VII to 'the vividness of a Flemish genre painting'.[86] And Douglas's numerous *plein air* vignettes, one might add, invite comparison with calendrical illuminations, in which the most innovative landscape depiction was

---

[77] *Virgil's 'Aeneid' Translated into Scottish verse by Gavin Douglas*, ed. Coldwell, I, 93–4.
[78] *Eneados* VII.Prol., 51.
[79] *Dowy* (dowie, dolly), from ME *dol* and OE *dol* = 'dull'. Cf. *Eneados* X iv 73, 'the dolly tonys and lays lamentabill'.
[80] *Eneados* VII.Prol., 56.   [81] *Eneados* VII.Prol., 42.   [82] *Eneados* VII.Prol., 44–6.
[83] Ridley, 'Distinctive Character', p. 113.
[84] L. Ebin, 'The Role of the Narrator in the Prologues to Gavin Douglas's *Eneados*', *Chaucer Review* 14 (1980), 353–65: Pearsall and Salter, *Landscapes*; Ridley, 'Distinctive Character', p. 115.
[85] Bawcutt, *Gavin Douglas*, pp. 87–91, 180, 182, 190.   [86] *Ibid.*, p. 185.

then to be found. Illuminated Books of Hours may not seem an obvious source of naturalistic realism. But many pioneers of Renaissance naturalism worked on illuminating calendars or service books. One thinks of Jan van Eyck's Turin-Milan Hours; Jean Foucquet's *Hours* of Étienne Chevalier; of the *Tres Riches Heures* of the Due de Berry; or of Joris Hoefnaegel's visionary natural history in the *Mira Calligraphiae Monumenta*. As Pearsall and Salter remark, 'no immediate literary precedent can be found' for the Prologues. 'Only Calendar art suggests a model.'[87]

The Calendrical Cycle

Douglas's Prologues not only use calendar art as a model but have themselves the structure of a calendar. Indeed, Douglas assigns explicit dates on four occasions. But what sort of calendar do the Prologues compose? Bawcutt notices 'fleeting but consistent references to the passage of the seasons', yet rejects 'attempts to fit the Prologues into a pre-meditated, over-all scheme, calendric or thematic.'[88] Instead, she reads the calendrical references as literal autobiography: 'we are...given a sense of the work in progress.'[89] But this cannot be the whole story. J. C. Eade, the historian of astrology, conclusively demonstrates that Douglas's *chronographiae* cannot be construed as recording actual observations, since they sometimes refer to states of the heavens that never occurred in his lifetime, or that are impossible *tout court*.[90] As for the dates, the instance of Petrarch's *Rime* is enough to show that autobiographical events can coexist in a single work with calendrical structuring.[91]

Without rejecting the view that Douglas's Prologues manifest 'organic' personal unity,[92] one needs to introduce the idea of schematic structuring in the Renaissance manner. Douglas's calendar has a cosmic armature; it is based, like many long works of the time, on the cyclic progression of the year with its manifold associations.[93] Thus, the Prologues correspond not only to Books of the

---

[87] Pearsall and Salter, *Landscapes*, p. 200.
[88] Bawcutt, *Gavin Douglas*, p. 166; Bawcutt, 'William Dunbar and Gavin Douglas', in *The History of Scottish Literature: Volume I: Origins to 1660 (Medieval and Renaissance)*, ed. R. D. S. Jack (Aberdeen, 1988), p. 85.
[89] Cf. P. S. Starkey, *SSL* 11 (1973), 84, for the notion that the dates and chronographiae indicate times of composition.
[90] J. C. Eade, *The Forgotten Sky: A Guide to Astrology in English Literature* (Oxford, 1984), pp. 164–70.
[91] See T. P. Roche, Jr., *Petrarch and the English Sonnet Sequences* (New York, 1989), ch. 1.
[92] Bawcutt, 'William Dunbar', p. 85.
[93] E. g. M. Palingenio (Pier Angelo Manzolli), *Zodiacus Vitae* (Basel, 1543). See Fowler, *Time's Purpled Masquers*, pp. 69–70, for further examples.

Aeneid but to months of the year.[94] Some months are explicitly announced; others can be inferred from associated events or correspondences (see Fig. 2).

Fig. 2.

Pro-logue	Month	Text	Comment
1	June (Cancer)	16, 'June rose'	
2	July (Leo)	2, 'Melpomene'	Corresponds to Sol;[95] Leo is Sol's house
3	August (Virgo)	1, 'Cynthia' (Diana)	Feast of Diana, 13 August;[96] Centaurus (Sagittarius) visible
4	September (Libra)	1, 'Cytherea' (Venus)	Feast of Venus Genetrix, 26 September;[97] Libra is Venus's house
5	October (Scorpio)	55, 'Bachus'	Wine month
6	November (Sagittarius)	8, 'Sibil'; 148 'Moder of God'	Cumaean Sibyl; Presentation of Mary (Theotokos), 21 November
7	December (Capricorn)	1–8, 'Phebus…was to enryr the third morn…vndre Capricorn'	Implies 9 December, Feast of Abel[98]
8	January (Aquarius)	2, 'Lent' (spring season)	Ursa Major, Orion, Bootes visible[99]
9	February (Pisces)		
10	March (Aries)	Hymn to creator	World created in March[100]
11	April (Taurus)		
12	May (Gemini)	5, 'Cylenyus' (Mercury);[101] 81, 'Ceres'; 268, 'nynt morow';	Gemini is Mercury's house; Ceres was stellified as Gemini;[102] 268 implies 9 May[103]
13	June (Cancer)	2, 'in the Crab Appollo' (Sol); 3, 'June'[104]	Sol in Cancer

---

[94] This has been obscured, partly, by Coldwell's false assumption that Douglas used the modern, Gregorian calendar, which was not introduced in Scotland until 1600. On Coldwell's blunders, see Eade, *Forgotten Sky*, p. 166.

[95] G. Linocier, *Mythologiae…Musarum*, ch. v, appended to Natale Conti, *Mythologiae*, ed. S. Orgel (New York and London, 1979), p. 570; F. Cafori, *Practica Musicae* (Milan, 1496), frontispiece; S. K. Heninger, Jr., *The Cosmographical Glass* (San Marino, CA, 1977), p. 137. The association influenced decorative programmes; see, e.g., P. Morel, 'Villa Medici', trans. B. Stockman, *FMR* 62 (1993), 100–22. Calliope, conspicuously *not* invoked in I.Prol., 460, was the heroic Muse leader of the Nine, and Muse of pagan literature itself; see Linocier, *Mythologiae*, ch. x, in Conti, p. 576, 'vox est ex omnibus…sphaerarum vocibus'.

[96] B. Blackburn and L. Holford-Strevens, *The Oxford Companion to the Year* (Oxford, 1999), 331; H. H. Scullard, *Festivals and Ceremonies of the Roman Republic* (London, 1981), pp. 173–4.

[97] Blackburn and Holford-Strevens, *Year*, p. 388; Scullard, *Festivals*, p. 188.

[98] Eade, *Forgotten Sky*, pp. 166–7; Blackburn and Holford-Strevens, *Year*, p. 492.

[99] Eade, *Forgotten Sky*, pp. 164–5.

[100] Blackburn and Holford-Strevens, *Year*, p. 766; Wilkinson, *Georgics*, pp. 288–9. Cf. Chaucer, *Nun's Priest's Tale*. ll. 4377–8 ('Whan that the month in which the world bigan, / That highte March') and see J. D. North, *Chaucer's Universe* (Oxford, 1988), p. 118.

[101] Chaucer uses Cylenius as a name for Mercury in *The Complaint of Mars*, 113.

[102] Hyginus, *Poeticon Astronomicon* II.xxii.   [103] Eade, *Forgotten Sky*, pp. 166–7.

[104] Eade, *Forgotten Sky*, p. 169.

Here, Prologue II obviously invokes Melpomene, the Muse of tragedy as befits Aeneas's tragic narrative of the Fall of Troy. Less obviously, Melpomene was correlated with Sol, who inhabited his sign Leo in July. Prologue III addresses 'paill Cynthia', or Diana, whose ancient feast was in August. Prologue IV invokes 'Cytherea', or Venus, whose house Libra was entered by Sol in September and whose feast was anciently celebrated in that month. Prologue V invokes 'Bacchus of gladness', associated with the wine month, October. Prologue VI introduces the Cumaean Sibyl, on whose prophecy of Christ's birth Virgil's religious authority largely depended.[105] The associations of the first six Prologue-months are thus mostly pagan, even if one of them prophesies the redemptive history.

In the second half of the year, from the winter to the summer solstice, the calendar becomes overtly Christian. The chronographia in Prologue VII—

> So neir approchit he [Phebus] his wyntir stage;
> Reddy he was to entyr the thrid morn
> In dowdy skyis undre Capricorn

—indicates 9 December,[106] the feast of Abel, first martyr and type of Christ.[107] Moreover, the month of Christ's birth, December, is dignified as the central, sovereign prologue of the thirteen.[108] Prologue VIII, explicitly 'Lent' or spring, is farther dated by the 'nonsense' chronographia, which Eade shows to refer to the constellations Ursa Major, Orion, and Bootes, all visible in January. Prologue X, a lucid hymn to the Creator ('renewar of kynd, that creat all'), is assigned to Aries and March, when the world was supposed in the Middle Ages to have been created.[109] Prologue XII with its unambiguous note 'perle of May' (307), corresponds to May and Gemini, the house of Mercury, invoked as 'Cylenyus'. Through such 'curious casts poetical', Douglas adumbrates a summa of cosmic correspondences, metaphysical as well as natural.

So far, I have assumed a simple schematic assignment of zodiacal signs to months such as were common in visual art programmes and popular literary

---

[105] Cf. the full treatment of the Sibylline prophecies in Sir John Harington's Virgil Commentary. On the similarities and differences between Harington and Douglas, see *The Sixth Book of Virgil's 'Aeneid' Translated and Commented on by Sir John Harington (1604)*, ed. S. Cauchi (Oxford, 1991), p. xli.

[106] See Eade, *Forgotten Sky*, pp. 166–7: 'Reddy he [Sol] was to entyr the third morn/ In dowdy skyes vndre Capricorn' (VII.Prol., 6–8). This makes It clear that the winter solstice is still three days away— i.e. it is 9 December.'

[107] See Blackburn and Holford-Strevens, *Year*, p. 492.

[108] For the central position of the Cumaean Sibyl, corresponding geographically to Rome, see E. Wind, 'Michelangelo's Prophets and Sibyls', *Proceedings of the British Academy* 51 (1960), 47–84, esp. 58, 69. See also Baswell, *Virgil*, p. 17.

[109] According to Ammianus, Bede, and many other authorities; see Blackburn and Holford-Strevens, *Year*, pp. 126, 766; Wilkinson, *Georgics*, 288. On the *thema mundi*, see R. Eisler, *The Royal Art of Astrology* (London 1946), pp. 192, 200.

works of a non-technical sort. But this may be to oversimplify. In its journey round the ecliptic the sun may originally have entered Aries and passed the vernal equinoctial point, on 1 March; but because of precession and trepidation this was no longer the case. In Douglas's time, Sol entered Aries on 11 or 12 March, and other signs similarly.[110] Almanacs and calendars made this plain by signalizing the day on which Sol entered a sign. Under September, for example, the 1503 *Kalendayr of Shyppars* rubricates the 14th as *Sol in Libra*.[111] But one should not assume from this that Prologue X should be thought of as beginning on 11 or 12 March. In the case of Prologue VII, indeed, the date specified in the text is three days before Sol entered Capricorn, just as the 9 May date of Prologue XII, 268, is earlier than the date that Sol entered Gemini in 1513. If Douglas intends more than very broad schematic correlations, on what day of the month does he mean the Prologues to start?

In the ancient and medieval world, many astronomers adopted the eighth degree of Aries as tropic. That is, they generalized the Babylonian observation that the vernal equinox occurred when Sol had completed 8° of Aries.[112] Douglas may incorporate this idea by assuming a hypothetical year, in which, for example, Sol enters Aries on 9 March, so that Prologue X runs from 9 March to 9 April. On this basis, Prologue VII *begins* on the significant date of 9 December. And in Prologue XI, which runs from 9 April to 9 May, a further calendrical reference emerges. 'Michael' (line 12) now appropriately refers to the Feast of the Apparition of Michael, celebrated during the Middle Ages on 8 May.[113]

The calendrical references so far considered are fixed. Turning to moveable feasts, one notes that in 'The tyme, space and dait' Douglas puts Prologues VIII–XIII in the year 1513.[114] Now, in 1513, Easter was early, falling on 27 March, so that Ash Wednesday, the beginning of Lent, fell on 9 February o. s. Consequently, if Prologue VIII runs from 9 January to 9 February it includes Ash Wednesday, so that 'Lent' (line 2) may carry its more specific sense of 'the period from Ash Wednesday to Easter-eve, observed as a time of fasting and penitence'.[115] These additional associations are entered in the modified Fig. 3:

---

[110] See Eade, *Forgotten Sky*, p. II. In *The Kalender of Shepherdes* (London, 1506), ed. H. O. Sommer (London, 1892), derived from the *Le Compost et Kalendrier des bergiers* (Paris, 1493, etc.), the dates when the sun is first in a sign, reckoned at noon, are: Aries, 11 March; Taurus, 12 April; Gemini, 13 May; Cancer, 13 June; Leo, 14 July; Virgo, 16 August; Libra, 14 September; Scorpio, 14 October; Sagittarius, 14 November; Capricorn, 12 December; Aquarius, 11 January; Pisces, 10 February.

[111] *Kalender of Shepherdes*, p. 29.

[112] See Manilius, *Astronomica*, ed. G. P. Goold (Cambridge, MA; London, 1977), 'Introduction', pp. lxxxii–lxxxiv; Vitruvius IX.iii, 1–2; J. North, *Astronomy and Cosmology* (London, 1994), p. 40.

[113] See J. de Voragine, *The Golden Legend*, trans. W. G. Ryan, 2 vols. (Princeton, NJ, 1993), II, 203.

[114] Douglas, ed. Coldwell, IV; 194: 'Fra Crystis byrth, the dait quha lyst to heir,/ A thousand fyve hundreth and thretteyn ȝeir.' See Eade, *Forgotten Sky*, pp. 168–9.

[115] *OED*, sb.1 2. On the obvious association of Aquarius with purification and temperance, see A. Fowler, *Spenser and the Numbers of Time* (London, 1964), pp. 94–5.

Fig. 3.

Pro-logue	Month	Text	Comment
1	9 June–9 July (Cancer)	16, 'June rose'	
2	9 July–9 August (Leo)	2, 'Melpomene'	Corresponds to Sol
3	9 August–9 September (Virgo)	1, 'Cynthia (Diana) 14, 'Minotaur'	Feast of Diana, 13 August; Centaurus (Sagittarius) visible
4	9 September–9 October (Libra)	1, 'Cytherea' (Venus)	Feast of Venus, 26 September; Libra is Venus's house
5	9 October–9 November (Scorpio)	55, 'Bachus';	October was the wine month
6	9 November–9 December (Sagittarius)	8, 'Sibil'	Cumaean Sibyl
7	9 December–9 January (Capricorn)	1–8, 'Phebus...was to entyr the third morn ...vndre Capricorn	Implies 9 December; Feast of Abel
8	9 January–9 February (Aquarius)	2, 'Lent' (ecclesiastical)	Ursa Major, Orion, Bootes, visible; Ash Wednesday 9 February
9	9 February–9 March (Pisces)		
10	9 March–9 April (Aries)	Hymn to creator	World created in March
11	9 April–9 May (Taurus)	12, 'Michael'	Feast of Apparition of Michael, 8 May
12	9 May–9 June (Gemini)	268, 'nynt morow'; 5, 'Cylenyus' (Mercury)	Implies 9 May; Gemini is Mercury's house
13	9 June–9 July (Cancer)	2, 'in the Crab Appollo (Sol)'; 3, 'June'	Sol in Cancer

Steering a course between Bawcutt and Eade, one might call these calendar references experiential, in that they allude to regularities of an organic world picture actually inhabited by Douglas. His astronomy is not simply observational, but takes in schematic associations. The annual cycle is for him not only a natural, astronomical year, but one with mythological and ecclesiastical patterns superimposed.

This is not to disengage Douglas's Prologues altogether from his translation of Virgil. In the view of early commentators, indeed, the *Aeneid* itself had a calendrical structure.[116] Douglas was aware of this commentary tradition, for he cites it in a detached note at his translation's mid-point. In the first six Books, he writes, Virgil follows Homer's *Odyssey*; but in the second six 'follows Homer in his Iliads'.[117] Appropriately, therefore, Douglas's passage on cranes, 'Palamedes byrdis crowpyng in the sky,'[118] derived from *Iliad* III 1–14, appears in Prologue VII, between the epic's two halves, where the wanderings of the *Odyssey* turn to the

---

[116] See R. M. Cummings, 'Two Sixteenth-Century Notices of Numerical Composition in Virgil's *Aeneid*', NQ 204 (1969), 26–7.
[117] Appendix, in Douglas, ed. Coldwell, III, 300. [118] *Eneados* VII Prol., 119.

founding of a city. Palamedes's cranes allude, then, to the two-part structure. But they do more; for when Douglas observes them they are 'Fleand on randon shapyn lik ane Y',[119] and this letter *upsilon*, one of the Greek vowels Palamedes was fabled to have invented, symbolized (according to Pythagoras) the *bivium*, or parting of the ways between virtue and vice. In the medieval commentary tradition, the *bivium* figured as a major Virgilian theme.[120] Aeneas's bifurcating golden bough (itself doubled, being the double of Proserpina's) was interpreted by Servius and others as a variant of the Pythagorean Y.[121]

On such lines, I believe, a case can be made for interpreting the Prologues as a structurally coherent work. We should not let anxiety about Douglas's Renaissance credentials mislead us into inventing a completely free-standing unity for the Prologues. As a transitional poet, Douglas was inclined, like Spenser, to use gothic forms—additive, 'irregular', dependent on extraneous entities. The Prologues are not independent of Virgil, or of Douglas's autobiographical experience, or of the medieval world picture. All the same, they strongly suggest a coherent vision. There is something to be said for Lois Ebin's view of their movement as dramatizing themes of creativity, divine and human. They defend pagan literature as prophetic of Christian doctrine, and then affirm the poet's powers, renewed when the solar creation of spring dispels the hellish darkness of winter. The change from prophecy to realization comes with the Incarnation, in the central Prologue. Then the second half year turns from pagan darkness to the clarity of astronomical events and Christian festivals—the winter solstice, Lent, and the Creation. The culmination in Prologue XII is a hymn to the sun, 'ruler of the year' and 'lord of lycht', who was supposed to stay longer in Gemini than in any other sign.[122]

This pattern of light and dark is the *raison d'être* of what Baswell calls the 'codicological frame' of Douglas's translation.[123] In cultural terms, the sequence from dark to light embodies the very spirit of the Renaissance. One thinks of the repeated imagery of Vasari, for whom 'painting had lain so long in such great darkness... in so great darkness Cimabue could see so great light'.[124]

---

[119] *Eneados* VII Prol., 120.

[120] Dryden's *Aeneis* retains this; see, e.g., vi, 726–9. See Baswell, *Virgil*, pp. 95, 110–12, 114, 116, 325 n. 71 on *Aen*. vi, 540.

[121] 'The Samian branche' in Palingenio, *The Zodiake of Life*, trans. B. Googe, ed. R. Tuve (Delmar, NY, 1976), p. 176. See Baswell, *Virgil*, pp. 68, 342 n. 117.

[122] The idea that the sun slowed at its auge or apogee while in Gemini was no longer true in the sixteenth century, by which time this took place with the sun in Cancer. But as late as George Chapman's translation of Gilles Durant's *Le zodiac amoureux* (1587) as 'The Amorous Zodiac' (London, 1595), poets continued to use the old dating, probably in adherence to the authority of medieval *auctores*. See, e.g., Macrobius, *Commentary on the Dream of Scipio*, tr. W. H. Stahl (New York and London, 1952), p. 110, 'in Gemini...the sun consumes more than thirty-two days in the steep ascent of this sign'; *Martianus Capella and the Seven Liberal Arts*: Vol. II: *The Marriage of Philology and Mercury*, tr. W. H. Stahl and R. Johnson (New York and London, 1977), pp. 330, 336.

[123] Baswell, *Virgil*, p. 277.

[124] G. Vasari, *Lives of the Painters, Sculptors and Architects*, trans. G. du C. de Vere, ed. D. Ekserdjian, 2 vols. (London, 1996), I, 54.

I have tried to suggest some of the ways in which criticism might begin to do justice to Douglas's subtle complexity. For hardly any recent criticism known to me gives much of a hint that his poem carries a freight of ideas. False notions of northern roughness probably have obscured much; and so has an underestimate of Douglas's largeness of mind. Perhaps only C. S. Lewis and Ezra Pound (strange pair!) give a sense of his true calibre. In Douglas we have the inventor of verse translation into English, and one of the first translators of Virgil into any vernacular.[125] In Douglas, effectively, we have the inventor of nature poetry; engaging with nature in a way that looks forward to the Romantic poets. Yet he is seldom discussed furth of Scotland, and has even been neglected in histories and surveys of translation.[126] When are we going to begin discussing again, in appropriate terms, the Chaucer of Scotland?[127]

---

[125] The only rivals are Octovien de Saint-Gelais (1468–1502), whose translation (published 1509) is far less close; an Italian version by Atanagoras Graecus (1476); and a Spanish version by Don Enrique d'Aragon (1428).

[126] The worst offender is H. B. Lathrop, *Translations from the Classics into English—from Caxton to Chapman 1477–1620* (1932, repr. New York 1967).

[127] Early estimates were very different: J. Norden (1548–1625?) groups Douglas with Chaucer and Gower, and Franciscus Junius (1589–1677) puts him on a level with Chaucer. On Douglas's early reputation see Bennett, *Humane Medievalist*, pp. 85–7.

Anagrams

A recent article in *The Times Literary Supplement* by Adele Davidson on acrostics and anagrams redirects attention to a neglected topic. But it also calls for qualification, for George Herbert's patterning was far from unique. When *MacFlecknoe* directs Thomas Shadwell to 'some peaceful Province in Acrostick Land,' it refers not to Herbert alone but rather to the entire mode of patterned verse that disgusted John Dryden's generation. From a rhetoric of schemes and a poetry of structural designs they were turning to more direct (if not exactly overt) forms. Thomas Wyatt had doubtless been pleased with his anagram A WIT, and John Cleveland with HELICONIAN DEW, but Joseph Addison and his contemporaries thought anagrams and acrostics 'false wit,' dull, or frivolous. By the time of Richard Cambridge's *Scribbleriad* (1751) anagrams would seem 'uncouth,' a 'distorted train, / Shifting, in double mazes.' So extreme was the change of taste that a bundle of court anagrams among the manuscripts of Sir Julius Caesar was labeled simply 'trash.' In the Victorian age Lewis Carroll and others renewed interest in both acrostics and anagrams, but only as a relatively trivial pursuit, like crosswords or Sudoku today. Even Ferdinand de Saussure's ludic hypograms now have less interest for critics than for poets like Edwin Morgan and theorists like Julia Kristeva.

The anagram had once a very different status. For despite the efforts of Ronald Knox in *A Book of Acrostics* (1924) and of Christopher Ricks in his British Academy Shakespeare lecture (2002), the anagram's heyday must still be considered the seventeenth or even the sixteenth century. Then, anagrams were 'divine notes' (William Camden) in which providence and destiny might be discovered. Mysterious texts, double like the Sibyl's, they might conceal great matters, *secrets de l'Éternité* (Guy Lefèvre de la Boderie). By far their commonest appearance was in names, especially the names of the great: '*Tourne* NOBLE *au rebours, tu trouvera* LE BON.' The first of the royal anagrams Joshua Sylvester prefaced to *Du Bartas His Divine Weekes and Workes* is JACOBUS STUART: JUSTA SCRUTABO (I shall examine just matters); he comes to the conclusion, 'My liege JAMES STUART A JUST MASTER is.' Similarly, James's mother had been MARIA STEUARTA: VERITAS ARMATA; Elizabeth I had been ELISABETHA REGINA ANGLIAE: ANGLIS AGNA, HIBERIAE LEA (a lamb to the English, a lioness to Spain); and Anne of Denmark, ANNA REGINA: INGANNARE (deception). FRANÇOIS DE VALOYS might be DE FAÇON ROYAL; but to ensure equally favorable transpositions Louis XIII thought it worth appointing his own court *anagrammateur*; Thomas Billon, at a huge salary.

Some sort of apogee was reached with Mary Fage's verse collection *Fames roule: or, the names of our dread soveraigne lord king Charles... with the names of the dukes, marquesses... Anagrammatiz'd and expressed by acrosticke lines on their names* (1637). For those constructing anagrams or palindromes Peter Levins's *Manipulus Vocabulorum* (1570) in alphabetical order of final syllables provided a useful resource.

Different views of the anagram were indeed possible, as came out when Eleanor Davies appeared before the Court of High Commission. Her prophetic calling depended on the anagram ELEANOR DAVIES: REVEAL O DANIEL; but a dean of the Arches hit on the counter-anagram DAME ELEANOR DAVIES: NEVER SO MAD A LADIE! She was abashed and the situation defused. As the thoughtful recognized, anagrams were multiple: a text of sufficient length might have many possible transpositions. On the name of Augustus de Morgan alone, 800 were discovered; Henri Dupuy found 1,022 in a Latin verse by Bauhusius; and AVE MARIA, GRATIA PLENA, DOMINUS TECUM yielded thousands. William Drummond of Hawthornden consequently dismissed anagrams as a 'most idle study; you may of one and the same name make both good and evil.' Their intentionality has always been problematic, as with TONY BLAIR M.P.: I'M TORY, PLAN B. Mr. Blair's parents may not have intended this political flexibility; but he himself could have elected to be known as Anthony.

On the other hand, paradoxically, good anagrams were difficult to find. This may have been in their favour (*difficilia quae pulchra*); but the searching could drive an anagrammatist mad. So licenses became customary: I and IE might be interchanged with Y, and J with I. Even the 'precise,' says Camden, are 'bold with H... in omitting or retaining it,' and those ardent to defend poetic license 'will pardon themselves for doubling or rejecting a letter, if the sence fall aptly, and thinke it no injury to use E for AE, V for W, S for Z, C or K, and contrariwise.' Fage considered E in final position optional; and allowed QU for QV, W for W, CS for X, SS for Z, and contrariwise. Even the rigorous Drummond, who at first thought 'there must not be fewer nor more nor other letters,' later retreated: 'When the same letters occur many times in the name, then the omission of one or more is pardonable.' As for imperfect anagrams, they had the authority, after all, of St. Augustine: they must be admissible.

The anagram passion succeeded an earlier rage for acrostic order (*acrostichis*, extremity of a verse line), which came to be thought much inferior: 'No ingenuity can make an acrostic ingenious' (Isaac Disraeli). Acrostics go back to 1000 BC at least, but achieved their most elaborate forms among Christian authors such as Publilius Optatianus Porfyrius and Hrabanus Mauius, who wove bewilderingly intricate carpets of them. In the Middle Ages and early Renaissance they were ubiquitous, sometimes serving a mnemonic function, as with the acrostic of internal capitals in the quatrain 'Hit is Lawe that sailleth [assails] nother [nowhere]' in MS Harl. 7322, laboriously explained in a preface: 'sunt quatuor litere, scilicet L.O.V.E.' Aldhelm, Bede, Commodian, Eustaches Deschampes, Venantius Fortunatus, and Clément Marot, triflers all in Addison's view, produced undisputable examples. In the *Aenigmata,* St. Boniface has a particularly ingenious example, depending on braided series: CSAARTIITRAASCAIT; letters used in the sequence 1, 3, 5, 7, 9, 11, 13, 14, 12, 10, 8, 6, 4, 2, 15, 16, 17, spell CARITAS, CARITAS, AIT (Charity, charity, he says).

Before the age of title pages, and in anonymous publication, acrostics most often affirmed an author's identity. François Villon is a familiar example; and Pier Angelo Manzolli's *Zodiacus Vitae* has the simple acrostic MARCELLUS PALINGENIUS STELLATUS. Other early instances include Q. ENNIUS FECIT, attested by Cicero; POLIAM FRATER FRANCISCUS COLUMNA PERAMAVIT (Brother Francis Colonna passionately loves Polia); and FRANCISCUS GODWINVVS LANDAVENSIS EPISCOPUS HOS CONSCRIPSIT. Or else the acrostic complimented an addressee, as with John Salesbury's DOROTHY BALSALL, Robert Parry's HELENA OWEN (read upward in both Sonetto 18 and Sonetto 19), Sir John Davies's ELIZABETHA REGINA, and Edgar Allan Poe's FRANCES SARGENT OSGOOD. According to Ethel Seaton, the acrostics in Sir Richard Roos set out a whole social register. And Giovanni Boccaccio, almost in the spirit of OULIPO, constructed a huge, 1,501-letter acrostic in the *Amorosa Visione* spelling out two sonnets and a madrigal (sometimes printed as a gratuitous preface). In the first of the invisible sonnets is inset an inner, quintessential acrostic, the initials of lines 1, 3, 5, 7, and 9 spelling MARIA, in compliment to Maria D'Aquino.

Less often the acrostic conveyed a message, perhaps the work's title or subject (Plautus's TRINUMMUS; Ben Jonson's THE ALCHEMIST), or supplemented the text itself (George Herbert, John Milton). An early instance of such half-explicit comment is the FICTIO acrostic in Robert Henryson's *The Testament of Cresseid,* which Sir Francis Kinaston's 1639 translation shows he noticed. Similarly, Thomas Watson's *Hekatompathia* 52 contains the acrostic AMOR ME PINGIT ET URIT (Love pierces and burns me); as his pedagogic note explains, the line initials, 'being joyned together as they stand, do conteine this posie agreeable to his meaning.' In a very few cases an acrostic or anagram has thematic value, as with chapter 24 of Kingsley Amis's *Take a Girl Like Row* (1960), where Patrick dreams of a mysterious inscription on a classical pediment: MORS / AVT IBI / MORS TIMOR MORS. In the year of publication, taking advantage of the fact that Amis was still alive, I asked him what it meant. Perhaps in an unguarded moment he furnished a clear and irrefutable answer: the anagram TIMOR MORTIS MORBUS AMORIS (fear of death is the disease of love). But since I did not puzzle it out for myself, critical orthodoxy regards this as irrelevant to the novel.

According to whether announcement or concealment was uppermost, various types were available: simple acrostic (reading line initials downwards or upwards), mesostich (last letters before caesuras), letters before and after caesuras, telestich (final letters of lines), double acrostic (first and last letters of lines), triple acrostic (first, last, and medial letters), progressive or diagonal acrostic (as in Poe), mathematically selected line initials (as in Boccaccio), initial letters of metrically selected lines (as in Herbert's 'Vanitie [I]'), initial and final letters of hemistichs or half-lines (as in Desiderio Erasmus's to JOHANNES MERLIBERCH DIEST), initials of first and second words in lines; initial capitals (not necessarily line intials); and acrostics (noticed by John Knox) in which 'each significant letter is separated by the next by uniform number of letters,' as OptAtiAnuS. All these rules might be imperfectly observed, or leave a residue. They might call for the customary licenses. Or they might, more licentiously still, require anagrammatic rearrangement.

Unruly anagram acrostics were a staple of the Baconians, whose enthusiasm tempted them to break the rules of the game or invent others at whim: a main target of William and Elizebeth Friedman's decisive study *The Shakespearean Ciphers Examined* (1957). To mock Walter Conrad Arensberg and others, the Friedmans obeyed the Baconian 'rules' and reached such impossible results as finding their own names in Shakespeare's works. The Friedmans promoted the science of cryptanalysis, demanding that each acrostic follow an unvarying rule. And they informed unscientific scholars that short acrostics occur by chance in any long text. In *A Midsummer Night's Dream*, Act 3, Scene 1, a speech of Titania's contains the simple acrostic TITANIA (taking two letters in the fourth line). Similarly, in *Paradise Lost* seeming acrostics may come and go into the mind of poet or reader without implying any Miltonic intention.

The Friedmans would presumably have rejected as fortuitous the simple acrostic SATAN at *Paradise Lost*, 9.510–14, subsequently discovered by Paul Klemp. John Leonard nevertheless justifies it as coinciding with the Tempter's intrusion into Paradise and his 'affixing of enmity' in the serpent: Lucifer was not called 'Satan' until after the Fall. The context of naming makes the acrostic, short though it is, particularly apt and probably intentional. Most have accepted the Klemp-Leonard hypothesis; the statistics of cryptographic and literary concealment are not quite the same.

This distinction apparently escaped the attention of the Friedmans, focused as they were on combating Baconian delusions. In a 1958 review of Seaton's early work on medieval acrostics they scorned the entire notion of unkeyed anagram acrostics and proscribed even the traditional licenses. They laid down laws for decipherment: 'The anagrammatic process itself must be controlled or guided by some key,' and 'the message that emerges must be semantically and orthographically acceptable.' Seaton, however, used 'diffuse and inexact rules' and took 'the final, fatal step of anagram.' In her 'unkeyed transposition' she 'permitted herself to be led astray...by wishful thinking.'

Seaton, as courageous as she was learned, was not so easily crushed. She raised her game in *Sir Richard Roos* (1961), answering criticisms of her methods in 'A Plea for the Liberty of Anagrammatizing.' Laxities in her practice continued; but she is surely right to reject many of the Friedmans' objections as irrelevant to fifteenth- and sixteenth-century practice. After all, literary acrostics, unlike encrypted messages, were meant to be discovered by fit readers. Seaton's abundant examples establish that imperfect and anagram acrostics were common, and that it was quite usual for a 'residue' or surd to remain after elucidation. Besides, imperfect anagrams have always passed muster in authorial pseudonyms, which are by definition intentional: for example COMES D'ALCINOIS: NICHOLAS DENISOT; CALVINUS: ALCUINUS; VOLTAIRE: AROUET L. J. Even without strict rules and statistical improbability, anagrams need not give free rein to interpreters' whims if aptness to context is considered. Ingenuity—guided by hints, shared associations, and contexts—will in time find out the right acrostic.

An anagram acrostic, apparently unnoticed, may be found in Edmund Spenser's commendatory sonnet to his friend Gabriel Harvey:

> Harvey, the happy above happiest men
> I read: that sitting like a Looker-on
> Of this worldes Stage, does note with critique pen
> The sharpe dislikes of each condition:
> And as one carelesse of suspition,
> Ne fawnest for the favour of the great:
> Ne fearest foolish reprehension
> Of faulty men, which daunger to thee threat.
> But freely does, of what thee list, entreat,
> Like a great Lord of peerelesse liberty:
> Lifting the Good up to high Honours seat,
> And the Evill damning evermore to dy.
> For Life, and Death is in thy doomefull writing:
> So thy renowme lives ever by endighting.

In 1950 Arthur J. Perret wrote to the Spenserian W. L. Renwick claiming that this sonnet contained the acrostic HOBBINOL NATHAN. (Harvey's plain speaking resembled the prophet Nathan's.) HOBBINOL, Harvey's pastoral name, is plausible enough; but it will not do to extract NATHAN from the residue TANLAFS. Renwick took advice but seems to have given Perret little encouragement. Reading Renwick's papers in the 1970s, I was skeptical too. But

Ferret's idea grew on me: as I learned about Boniface's and Boccaccio's mathematical acrostics I came to wonder if Spenser had used a similar device.

Listing the sonnet's line initials—

H	I	O	T	A	N	N	O	B	L	L	A	F	S
1	2	3	4	5	6	7	8	9	10	11	12	13	14

—shows that the series 1, 3, 9 (where each term is multiplied by three to form its successor) produces the arostic HOB. The next term in the series, 27, is too large to correspond to a line number, but its digits, 2 and 7, indicate the line initials I and N. The next term again is 81, whose first digit, 8, indicates O and brings the acrostic to HOBINO. But its second digit, 1, is already assigned; which calls for the license of substituting 10 (on the strength of the arithmological doctrine identifying 10 and 1). Since 10 indicates L, the complete acrostic is HOBINOL.

The following are confirming factors: (a) the acrostic is apt, being Harvey's poetic name; (b) its text begins with the first letter; (c) the letters observe a rule; (d) the rule is the odd-number lambda series, appropriate to Harvey's interest in mathematics. (His Commendatory Verses to *The Faerie Queene* have a line total of 56, the Great Quaternion.) Few, perhaps, will regard the acrostic as fortuitous.

Its interest is twofold. First, it is the earliest public disclosure of Hobbinol's identity. Although Harvey's 'Gallant familiar letter' of 1580 mentions 'Hobbinoll' as one of Immerito's 'olde Companions' and 'Hobbinolus' as one loved *copiose*, the first explicit connection of Hobbinol with Harvey is not made until his Commendatory Verses in 1590 and Spenser's own confirming reference in *Colin Clout's Come Home Again* in the same year.

Second, the acrostic is a short anagram of the type the Friedmans condemned. Worse, it leaves a residue of unused line initials and is imperfect orthographically (the most usual spelling was 'Hobbinoll' or 'Hobbinol' with two Bs). If, then, we accept the acrostic as intentional, there is good reason to sit light to the Friedmanian criteria. This is not to say we should ignore them: where they are relevant they offer useful cautions. But it is time to recognize that the Friedmans' victory over the Baconians gave them a disproportionate influence over criticism: the general distrust of anagrams is unreasonable.

From Alcofribas Nasier to Llareggub and Sir Leigh Teabing, names and pseudonyms have always been a part of literature rich in anagrams, and this is strikingly true of *The Faerie Queene*. Its neglected names are usually treated as romance wallpaper, but they have more varied functions. Besides evoking the atmosphere of romance or serving the allegory, they may, like the names of *Argenis,* refer to historical individuals.

At the tournament for Florimell's spousals Marinell's six co-challengers are probably all identifiable despite their cryptic disguises:

> The first of them was hight [named] Sir Orimont,
> A noble Knight, and tride in hard assayes [trials]:
> The second had to name Sir Bellisont,
> But second unto none in prowesse prayse;
> The third was Brunell, famous in his dayes;
> The fourth Ecastor, of exceeding might;
> The fift Armeddan, skild in louely layes;
> The sixt was Lansack, a redoubted Knight:
> All sixe well seene in armes, and prov'd in many a fight.

Here, 'Orimont' masks Thomas Butler, tenth earl of Ormond and Ossory (1531–1614), recipient of Dedicatory Sonnet VII. The thin disguise consists of an epenthetic or gliding vowel 'i,' and substitution of 't' for 'd,' the same indication of Irishness that Ben Jonson uses in *The Irish Masque* ('ant' for 'and,' line 18, and so on).

For 'Bellisont,' John Draper suggested 'wager of war' (Latin *bellare*), a relevant association. But Seaton's suggestion (in a 1950 letter) takes us further, to Sir Warham St. Leger (1525?–97), in State Papers sometimes given as 'Sentleger,' 'sent' or 'sont' being an archaic form of 'saint.' St. Leger was Provost Marshall of Munster. For 'Brunell,' A. B. Gough proposed 'Little brown man'; the specific reference might be to Sir Valentine Browne (d. 1589), another key player in the settlement of Munster. In 'Ecastor,' John Upton reasonably saw Arthurian and classical associations; but in view of Latin *castor* (beaver), one may also see George Beverley, Victualler of Ireland. Similarly 'Armeddan' may anagram Marmaduke Redmayne. And in 'Lansack,' Seaton was surely right to see Sir Henry Bagnal (*c*.1556–98): 'lan' backwards spells 'nal,' and 'sack' for 'bag' is not difficult. Professor A. C. Hamilton's proposal, 'Lan(d)sacker,' adds an enhancing suggestion.

What sort of men were these? At least four (Ormond, St. Leger, Browne, and Redmayne) were, like Spenser, 'undertakers' in the Munster plantation. Indeed, the '-mont' of 'Orimont' recalls the personalized seignory name of Ormond's land grant, Mount Ormond. All were actors in an Irish, perhaps Munster, scene. Ormond, of old English Catholic descent but reared a Protestant, was a powerful, turbulent grandee: an administrator, not specially friendly to new English like Spenser or Baron Grey of Wilton (to whom he nevertheless on occasion extended the protection of Kilkenny). Ormond's loyalty to his regal cousin was questioned, not only by his enemy St. Leger, and eventually Grey dismissed him from his Lieutenancy of Munster. St. Leger, one of Lodovic Bryskett's friends in *A Treatise of Civill Life*, was an unprincipled adventurer who lacked the resources to realize his ambitions; as custodian of the rebel Fitzgeralds he cheated the earl of Desmond of his daily allowance. Later he helped Sir Walter Ralegh to plunder David Barry. St. Leger's nomination as Lord President of Munster had been opposed by Ormond, under whom he served, however, during the second Desmond rebellion.

Bagnal or Bagenal, another greedy adventurer, was notorious for his scandalous quarrel with the earl of Tyrone (with whom his sister eloped). Marshal of the army, like his father under Grey, Bagnal was often at loggerheads with him. A house divided, then.

Can interpretation be so simple? Apparently not. For alternative possibilities beset the interpretation of anagrams: perhaps the anagrammatists, fearful of repercussions, value escape clauses. Thus, St. Leger had a nephew (d. 1600) of exactly the same name—'Young Capt. Warham St Leger' in a 1586 State Paper—a soldier of less eminence. Similarly Brunell might anagram Henry Burnell, Recorder of Dublin, of old English Catholic descent. Burnell was certainly 'famous in his day': in the 1580s he organized opposition to taxes on recusants and was one of the three lawyers who went to London to negotiate. He was briefly imprisoned in the Tower (an effective bargaining counter); yet the composition reached on the victualing of soldiers was of his framing. He won the grudging respect of Sir Henry Sidney as 'the least unhonest of the three, and yet he trusted to see the English Government withdrawn.' A perfect anagram for Brunell, Burnell would imply a wider Irish setting and political range. But Edward Denny, another candidate for 'Armeddan,' was again a Munster undertaker. And the Great Gogan had a castle called Beaver. In short, anagrams are not immediate solutions; they must take their place among many factors leading to an identification.

All six descriptions are respectful and complimentary but have distinct overtones: 'Second unto none,' for example, is only too apt for the overambitious St. Leger. Marinell and the six 'challenge all in right of Florimell,' the ideal form of the state; and Marinell, at least, shows great prowess. But at last he is taken prisoner and has to be rescued by the sovereign power embodied in Arthegall (5.3.10–11). Together they now defeat the rebel 'crew' opposing Elizabeth's sovereignty. Marinell's knights, inadequate without Arthegall, seem to represent discordant cadres of old and new English. As often in *The Faerie Queene*, the meaning of Marinell himself is hinted through an identifying genealogy: he is the 'warlike sonne unto an earthly peare [peer], / The famous Dumarin.'

Dumarin ('Of the Sea') surely anagrams Raimund, Raymond Fitzgerald (Le Gros) (d. 1182.), in Giraldus Cambrensis a pillar of the Anglo-Norman conquest of Ireland. This makes Marinell of old English descent, unlike some of his six companions. Marinell's earlier overthrow by Britomart on the Rich Stronde (3.4) together with his capture at the tournament (5.3) suggest that independent loyalty is unworkable for the old English without the sovereign power of Elizabeth's representative. For the capture figures captivation, even assimilation: the old English were always liable to blend in with the rebel crew. Even Ormond, with his English upbringing, was suspected of double loyalties; and St. Leger, too, was accused (although probably wrongly) of being Catholic.

Far from being frivolous formalism, Spenser's anagrams may be indispensable in disentangling the complicated historical allegories. They facilitate political identifications more discriminating than those presently current. Instead of broad, speculative generalizations, specific identifications will help to engage with the details of Spenser's historical fiction. For his allegory is no crude line-up of rebels and loyalists.

The anagram route is full of risks. When Perret sees an acrostic of LOBIN in *Ruines of Time*, 561–65, one wonders if he is discussing patterns in Spenser's conscious or unconscious mind—or in his own. Still, no one has made heavy weather about anagrams in Spenser's shorter poems like MORELL: AYLMER, LA MORT: MAROT, and PHILISIDES: PHILIP SIDNEY, imperfect as they are. It may be time now to take a similar route with *The Faerie Queene*, relying on historical and literary contexts, the customs of anagram, and authorial clues.

Ut Architectura Poesis

The analogy between architecture and literature is a subject that Roy Eriksen has made his own;[1] I return to it here only to explore a little further the metaphors of the analogy, and to focus more on British examples.[2]

As early as the Carolingian Abbot Einhar of Fulda (770–840), Vitruvius was known to the medieval world, even if his language often seemed obscure.[3] His approach through proportional numbers was certainly familiar.[4] Throughout the Middle Ages, however, architectural theory and practice were dominated by sacred geometry: by mysterious incommensurables and pious associations.[5] The favoured proportions tended to be those of the New Jerusalem, Biblical and symbolic.[6] Symbolism also attached to columns. The Sainte Chapelle, for example, had twelve columns, each with its apostle statue.[7] In a tradition predating Vitruvius, columns had been anthropomorphized and gendered, their capitals especially being mythicized. Now Christian meanings accrued: unworked, 'unfinished' capitals might signify pristine perfection.[8] And, more generally, what justified architecture (and provided a model for individual churches) was the authoritative precedent of the Biblical Temple of Solomon,[9] a powerful influence throughout the Reformation and Counter-Reformation.[10]

The Renaissance aesthetic, however, became less intricately theological. Vitruvian proportions harmonized every art, as Rudolf Wittkower decisively showed. But Wittkower perhaps overplayed his hand a little in applying the thesis of *Architectural Principles in the Age of Humanism* to the untheoretically minded Andrea Palladio.[11] A more lucid theorist, Leon Battista Alberti (1404–72), was to preside over the next phase of architectural thought, ousting Vitruvius's pagan symbolism and

---

[1] Eriksen 1994; 2001.
[2] Architectural metaphors in French literature are comprehensively treated by Cowling 1998, metaphors in Italian by Bolzoni 2001.
[3] Sandys 1906: 481–2; Reynolds 1983: 441.   [4] Simson 1962: Index s. v. *Vitruvius*.
[5] See Lesser 1957; Simson 1962; Onians 1988: 88; Lawlor 1990.
[6] See Braunfels 1972: 164; March 1998: 119–23.
[7] Onians 1988: 49. For pillars as apostles, see also Bede 1995: 74. On the human metaphor in general, see, e.g., Rykwert 1996: 128ff.
[8] Onians 1988: 88.
[9] Onians 1988: 72, 76, 241; also 200 (precedent for the proportions of the Ospedale) and 127 (cherubs validated by the same precedent). Cf. Reiss 1970:162; Rosenau 1979; van Eck 2003: 106–10, 121, 124.
[10] See Wittkower 1962: 121. E.g. Fuller 1650: Book 3, Chapters 2 and 3; Rosenau 1979: Index, s. v. *Villalpando*.
[11] See Boucher 1994: 239; Palme 1959: 101, note 2. On the rediscovery of Vitruvius in the fifteenth century, see Ackerman 1991: 498.

formulating an architecture fitter for a Christian society.[12] In Christian humanist literature stemming from Alberti the proportions were ethical or musical rather than abstractly mathematical like those of Vitruvius; encomiastic symmetries abounded, and the moral ratios of Neoplatonism. Thus, the invocations in *Paradise Lost* (1974) were so located as to mark out the diapason ratio (1 : 2) of rational integration.[13] Ben Jonson was the most Vitruvian poet of his time; but even Jonson—had he not been an inveterate Ancient—could be called Albertian.[14]

Renaissance architectural theory drew analogies with music, painting, or poetry, and developed these in progressively greater detail. The Horatian doctrine *ut pictura poesis* was restated in terms of architecture; Horace himself, after all, had implied such a metaphor when he boasted *monumentum exegi*.[15] At first the analogy was drawn somewhat broadly, as when Laurentius Valla (*c*.1405–1457) compared restoring Scripture to restoring the Temple of God, or Alberti associated building and writing materials—'the metaphor connects the laying of *tesserae* in a mosaic with the distribution of materials in written work'.[16] These inter-art analogies were not impressionistic and subjective like those of Wylie Sypher,[17] but depended on shared rhetorical conceptions. Indeed, they probably derived from Cicero's *De Oratore*—for example III. xlvi, on the functionality of pediments and columns, products not merely of beauty but of necessity. *Hoc in omnibus item partibus orationis evenit*: 'The same is the case in regard to all the divisions of a speech'.[18] Rhetorical function certainly informs Jonson's imitation of Ludovico Vives describing 'the figure and feature in Language' in architectural terms: 'Whether it be round, and streight, which consists of short and succinct Periods, numerous, and polished; or square and firme, which is to have equall and strong parts, every where answerable, and weighed'.[19] The ideal is well-joined components that fit together strongly: their *compositio* 'rests in the well-joyning, cementing, and coagmentation of words'.[20]

---

[12] See Eriksen 2001; and cf. Alberti 1988: xvii, 228–9.

[13] See Fowler 1968: 851, note to *Paradise Lost* ix 1–47, a pattern noticed (apparently independently) in Morissey 1999: 36; cf. Eriksen 2001: 34 on the diapason proportion in Propertius.

[14] On the later influence of Vitruvius on literature, see Erskine Hill 1979.

[15] *Odes* III. xxx. 1.

[16] Eriksen 2001: 56 and 162, notes 39 and 40. Cf. Cowling 1998: 141 finding the basis of this metaphor in ordering or constructing, i.e. *dispositio*. Others imagine the analogy as between architecture and language: e.g. Clarke and Crossley 2000: 2; cf. Payne 2000: 125. They cite Castelvetro's comparison of poet to architect and words to building materials; but that implies a very different analogy, between the *arts* of poetry and architecture, poems and buildings.

[17] Sypher 1955.

[18] Roland Fréart turned also to *De Oratore* I, on the close relation of architect to orator; see Fréart 1664: 115.

[19] *Discoveries*: Jonson 1925–1952; vol. 8: 626, lines 2062–6. Cf. ibid. 2686–95, where the analogy is between poetic action and architectural space: 'as a Court […] requires other dimensions then a private house: So the Epick askes a magnitude, from other Poems'.

[20] ibid. 2067–8; cf. 1976–80, 'The congruent, and harmonious fitting of parts in a sentence, hath almost the fastning, and force of knitting, and connexion: As in stones well squared, which will rise strong a great way without mortar'—probably from Vitruvius V. xii. 6 but adding the stylistic analogy; see Johnson 1994: 33.

The architectural analogy, as we shall see, was developed in other, equally specific ways. But first we should look at shared number symbolisms, a medieval inheritance but one by no means abandoned in the Renaissance.[21] Alberti dignified number as one of the elements of beauty, and found occasion in the *De re aedificatoria* (1485) to explain several number symbolisms.[22] Numbers shared gave the *ut architectura poesis* doctrine a demonstrable basis.

Symbolic numbers

Earlier I mentioned the symbolic twelve columns of the Sainte Chapelle. In early modern England columns were still counted, as were other architectural features. Sir John Harington (1561–1612) noted the calendrical numbers of Salisbury Cathedral:

> Faire Sarum's Church, beside the stately tower
> Hath many things in number aptly sorted,
> Answering the yeere, the month, weeke, day and houre,
> But above all (as I have heard reported,
> And to the view doth probably appeare)
> A piller for each houre in all the yeere.[23]

And John Evelyn (1620–1706) might think the Cathedral of Notre Dame 'a Clumsy Gotic pile', but knew it was 'sustained by 120 Pillars'.[24] Secular buildings displayed similar number symbolisms: the Sackvilles' Knole House was known to have 365 rooms, 52 staircases, and 7 courts corresponding to days of the week.[25]

Renaissance literature affords many analogous symbolisms, both Biblical and temporal.[26] Spenser's 'monument' *Epithalamion* (1595) famously has 365 long lines;[27] on a larger scale Du Bartas' *La Sepmaine* (1578) and unfinished *Seconds Sepmaine* (1584), translated by Joshua Sylvester as *Divine Weeks* (1598, 1621, etc.),

---

[21] On number symbols in Renaissance architecture, see Hersey 1976; 1976a; 1998; and 2000; March 1998. For Alberti's treatment of symbolic numbers, see Summerson 1963: 36–7 and Alberti 1988: Book ix.

[22] Alberti 1988: 302–6, 388.

[23] Hudson 1966: 136, note 76; probably following Daniel Rogers's Latin epigram quoted in Camden's *Britannia* (Camden 1586: 181). The count of about 8,760 hour-columns must have included colonnets.

[24] Evelyn 1955: vol. 1: 63. For the many significances of the 'admirable' 120, see, e.g., Bongo 1591: 581–9.

[25] Fowler 1964: 240. Chambord also had 365 rooms, according to one account; although others say 440: see Hieatt and Prescott 1992: 314.

[26] See Fowler 1970, Chapter 7.   [27] See Hieatt 1960.

are divided into weeks and days. *Les Sepmaines* belonged to a patristic hexaemeral tradition, but Du Bartas and Sylvester gave the form a new twist by presenting it as architecture. Their paratext includes a 'Corona Dedicatoria' of columnar figure poems.

Astronomical numbers and shapes abound in Renaissance literature and architecture alike.[28] A notable example is Sidney's *Arcadia*, where Basileus retires to a hunting lodge built in the shape of a star. In the real world, Sir Thomas Tresham's Triangular Lodge makes a more elaborate programmatic statement, mingling numbers, shapes, and texts.[29] And throughout the period pyramidal figure poems, like architectural pyramids or obelisks, were fashionable.[30] Perhaps the most elaborately mathematical design of all was that of Caserta, not complete until 1774.[31]

Symmetry

Alberti, careful to distance himself from Vitruvius, comprehensively reinterpreted the ancient idea of *symmetria* according to *Quattrocento* taste. 'Central elements should sit over central ones', he recommends; 'and those equidistant from the centre should be balanced.[32] Similar formal ideas are ubiquitous in Renaissance poetry. A common pattern in both arts is the arrangement of seven items as 3 | 1 | 3, sometimes with astronomical implication, as when Sol occupies the central place of honour among the planetary deities.[33] At first Renaissance façades were often arranged similarly. Later, however, the symmetries become more complicated, as in the palace façades of Androuet du Cerceau (*c.*1505/10–1585), which Doranne Fenoaltea has compared with Ronsard's *Odes*.[34] Fenoaltea distinguishes two patterns, which she terms 'ring composition' and 'interlocking ring': that is, *a b c d d c ba* and *a b c d a b cd*. In the four books of *Odes* of 1550, for example, the individual odes are distributed in the pattern

---

[28] I have discussed some of these in *Time's Purpled Masquers*, Fowler 1996.
[29] See Isham 2003.
[30] For the astronomical significance of the pyramid, see Fowler 1996: 117–21, notes 48, 61, 62, 67.
[31] See Hersey 1976a.
[32] IX ix: Alberti 1988: 314; cf. 310, 'We must therefore take great care to ensure that even the minutest elements are so arranged in their level, alignment, number, shape, and appearance that right matches left, top matches bottom, adjacent matches adjacent, and equal matches equal' and 29, 'Although it was customary to give doors and windows an uneven number, those on one side would be equal to and would match those on the other, while those in the middle would be somewhat larger'. Cf. also Hamberg 1959: 77, 83.
[33] See, e.g., Fowler 1970: 24, 37, 82, 119.
[34] Fenoaltea 1990: figs. 2, 3, and 7. See also Burroughs 2002: 3, 100, comparing the façade structure to *partitio* in rhetoric.

I	II	III	IV
20	29	27	18

where the odd-numbered and even-numbered books both contain forty-seven odes (20 + 27 = 29 + 18 = 47).

In English odes of the seventeenth century, one finds similar patterns. With their strophes obviously varying in length, Pindaric odes are now assumed to be irregular. Already in the eighteenth century, indeed, John Ivory Talbot compared their irregularity to that of gothic façades: 'I would by no means have my Front regular [...] since the Beauty of Gothic Architecture (in my opinion) consists, like that of Pindarick Ode, in the boldness and Irregularity of its Members'.[35] But in fact seventeenth-century Pindarics often had symmetries of the interlaced type, which time and changing fashion have obscured. Abraham Cowley's ode 'The Muse' (1668) is a case in point: its four strophes have 19, 16, 20, and 17 lines, of widely varying metrical length. All seems bold irregularity. Yet the array conceals ring composition: the line-totals of both outer and inner pairs of strophes add to 36, the Great Quaternion.[36] Cowley's 'The Resurrection' (1668), with strophes of 12, 15, 24, and 13 lines, has a comparable pattern: its interlaced pairs add to 36 and 28, triangular numbers on the bases 8 and 7; the 8 of regeneration redeems the mutable, mortal 7. Moreover, 28 is a perfect number, a familiar symbol of perfect virtue:[37] no accident that Cowley's note refers to another 'Perfect Number'. Milton, too, draws attention to the hidden regularity of his ode *Ad Joannem Rousium* (1647), when he hints that the strophes and antistrophes *omnes nec versuum numero* [...] *respondeant*. For, although the line-totals of strophes and antistrophes are not entirely regular (12, 12, 12, 10, 14, 12), the first three and the last three both add to 36, the Great Quaternion. Moreover, Milton's concluding epode is 15 lines, the number immediately preceding 36 in the series of triangular numbers.

Specific analogies

Turning to textual rather than numerical metaphors, one encounters another sort of symmetries in the topomorphic patterns of phrases and sentences studied by

---

[35] Cited McCarthy 1987: 122–3.

[36] i.e. 19 + 17 = 36; 16 + 20 = 36. The Great Quaternion was so called as the sum of the first four odd and the first four even numbers (1 + 3 + 5 + 7) + (2 + 4 + 6 + 8) = 36, a form of the *tetraktys*. It was called Cosmos by Plutarch; see Hopper 2000: 55; Røstvig 1963: 97, citing Henry More; and Bongo 1591: 496–9.

[37] Perfect numbers equal the sum of their factors (e.g. 6 = 1 + 2 + 3). On 28, see Bongo 1591: 464–73. Cowley's subtotals, 16 and 20, are the totals of the first four odd and even numbers respectively, making the allusion to the *tetraktys* doubly clear.

Maren-Sofie Røstvig and Roy Eriksen. These correspond in architecture to the balance of individual features recommended by Alberti and other theorists. Their discourse of symmetry, decorum, and proportion shows the pervasive influence of literary theory, which supplied many of the conceptions found in architectural treatises.[38]

In an early phase of the Renaissance architecture and language were often compared, so that one can imagine an *ut lingua architectura* doctrine.[39] The comparison arose from debates about imitation, or about die use of vernacular language. (We still speak of 'vernacular architecture' and of literary language in contrast to the more mutable language of ordinary life.) This somewhat vague analogy depended on the shared notion of assemblage: the putting together of words in an act of speech and of materials in building.[40] It was useful for a time. But architecture and literature shared many more interests than the language analogy covered: with the efflorescence of poetics and rhetoric, literary and architectural discourses came to overlap more and more.[41] Already in the Middle Ages—and certainly in Ludovico Castelvetro (1506-71)—a more profound analogy was glimpsed, between the *arts* of architecture and literature, between buildings and poems or orations.[42] Literary terms and concepts such as ornament deeply influenced the treatises of such as Sebastiano Serlio (1475–c.1554) and Gherardo Spini.[43] As the vernaculars achieved independence from Latin, the doctrine *ut lingua architectura* lost much of its interest; now *ut architectura poesis* seemed of more moment.[44]

In the latter doctrine, each phase or division of writing or rhetoric was compared to a corresponding stage of building. Thus, *inventio* resembled the quarrying of materials, just as arranging stones in a wall resembled *disposition*[45] and architectural *ornatus* (ornamentation) answered the figures of *elocutio*, with issues in both arts of decorum and style. As for *memoria*, it corresponded to an entire building, imagined as a repository of collective memory or a setting for mnemonic operations.[46]

From the fifteenth century on, the analogy was elaborated in terms of architectural specifics: temple; palace; theatre; house; castle; *tabernaculum*; tower; corner; recess; room (Italian *stanza*); kitchen; façade (frontispiece); gallery;

---

[38] In his *Brief Discourse Concerning the Three Chief Principles of Magnificent Building* (1662), e.g., Sir Balthazar Gerbier writes that architects like writers ought to remember 'how every Particle must have its just Proportion'; see Van Eck 2003: 192.
[39] Payne 1999: 60–5; 2000: 125; Clarke and Crossley 2000: 2.   [40] Payne 1999: 63–4.
[41] E.g. Shute 1912: B iiv. Cf. Payne 1999: 99; Davies and Hemsoll 2000: 102–17.
[42] So already in Filarete (Payne 1999: 64) and Castelvetro (ibid. 30, 62, 64).
[43] Payne 1999: 99, 139, 153.
[44] For a contrary view, see Clarke and Crossley 2000: 2; Payne 2000: 125.
[45] Coulet 1977; Cowling 1998: 141, 152; Eriksen 2001: 56 and 162 notes 39, 40.
[46] Evidence for this last correspondence is gathered in Cowling 1998: 110. On architecture and memory, see Carruthers 1998: Index s. v. *Architecture in mnemotechnic*; *Buildings*.

threshold; monument; staircase; court; storeroom; library; altar; square; pyramid.[47] Each particular metaphor turns out to have had a distinct content and application. Some belonged to allegories of the poet's mind as a building, others to allegories of the text itself.[48] An extreme case of the analogy is figure poems, which combined textual with spatial existence.[49] Julius Caesar Scaliger, Richard Willes, George Puttenham, Mario Bettini, and many others treat square, column, pyramid, and altar shape poems—all architectural types.[50] Were these different realizations of the analogy merely for variety? Or were they meant to modernize and Christianize a pagan inheritance?

Column

The column figured prominently in medieval allegory, and was almost as popular in the seventeenth century. A. W. Johnson has given a full account of Ben Jonson's 'pillar poems', treating them as poems of praise (the column being an emblem of fortitude).[51] As Johnson shows, the encomiastic epigrams are centred. Most, however, are not columnar shape poems, since they do nothing to represent bases and capitals. Epigram XXVII on John Roe is a true column, with interlaced rhyme in the shaft but couplets in the base and the capital. But most of the encomiastic epigrams are simply rectangular or square, and a few, with *triumph* as a centred word, belong to a distinct, celebratory genre.[52]

Citing Puttenham on 'The Roundell or sphere', Johnson introduces the 'idea of circularity as a moral emblem':[53] is Jonson, he asks, 'squaring' his circle? This needs further explanation. Geometrically, Puttenham's *roundel* denoted a circle or cylinder;[54] architecturally, a round ornament or turret.[55] Both were centred structures. Several of Jonson's epigrams correspond outwardly to the rectangular side elevation of a cylinder, inwardly to its plan, a circle. Puttenham's illustrations of 'The Pillaster or Cillinder' show either an elongated rectangle or a fully differentiated column with capital and base ('a pedestall or base, and a chapter or head'),[56] the body being the shaft: 'By this figure is signified stay, support, rest, state and magnificence, your dittie then being reduced into the form of a Piller,

---

[47] See Eriksen 2001: xiii–xiv; Bolzoni 2001: 212; Cowling 1998: 124, 126.
[48] See, e.g., Mann 1994; Cowling 1998.
[49] On shape or figure poems, see Church 1946; Higgins 1977; Higgins 1987; Westerweel 1984.
[50] Scaliger 1964: 69; Willes 1973: 4; Puttenham 1936: 92–100; Bettini 1614: 60. For other examples see Massin 1970: 159; Higgins 1987.
[51] Johnson 1994: 79–111, 221.   [52] On the triumphal tradition, see Fowler 1970.
[53] Puttenham 1936: 98–100. Pierio Valeriano, however, takes a circular poem to be one 'whose end is the same as its beginning': *Hieroglyphica* xxxix. 12.
[54] *OED* 1, 7.   [55] *OED* 8 a.
[56] Puttenham 1936: 98. For the head as capital of a column, cf. Scaglia 1992: fig. 131.

his base will require to beare the breadth of a meetre of six or seven or eight sillables: the shaft of foure: the chapter egall with the base'.[57]

The column metaphor is most fully elaborated in Michael Drayton's Epistle 'To the Reader' before *The Barons Warres* (1619), where he defends the proportions of his stanza on architectural grounds. His ottava rima stanza of eight lines (abababcc) is 'of all other the most complete and best proportioned, consisting of eight lines, six interwoven, and a couplet in base'. Stanzas of four, five, and six lines are unsuitable for epic, but 'this of eight both holds the tune cleane thorow to the Base of the Columne (which is the couplet, the foote or bottome), and closeth not but with a full satisfaction to the eare for so long detention'.[58] He even specifies the order of column: 'this sort of Stanza hath in it, Majestie, Perfection, and Solidity, resembling the Pillar which in Architecture is called the Tuscan, whose Shaft is of six Diameters, and Bases of two'.[59] Here he probably follows Serlio, whose Tuscan column is also six diameters;[60] although Alberti praises the enduring character of Doric similarly, the order usually likened to epic. Perhaps Drayton's 'Tuscan' is a mistake for 'Doric'.

In the epic comparison we glimpse the possibility of far-reaching analogies between literary genres and architectural orders. But Drayton never follows it up; nor for that matter does Serlio, despite his mention of Tuscan as a rustic order.[61] Serlio is content to compare literature and architecture in a broad way, likening his Introduction to the prologues of the 'comedians'.[62] Henry Wotton is similarly tantalizing when, following Vitruvius, he calls the Tuscan 'a plain, massie, rurall Pillar, resembling some sturdy well-limbed Labourer'.[63] Nowhere does one find any systematic mapping of genres and orders: almost the only definite pairings seem to have been Tuscan with rustic (pastoral? georgic?), Doric with epic, and Corinthian with triumph. More often the orders are assigned either to the storeys (degrees) of a palace, or else to a particular sort of building (Gombrich's 'building type'); as when Corinthian is said to be decorous for a triumphal arch.

Robert Herrick's column metaphors return to a Biblical simplicity. 'A Panegyric to Sir Lewis Pemberton' sustains an architectural allegory (house, building, gates,

---

[57] Puttenham 1936: 97. Base and capital are to be trimeter or tetrameter, the shaft dimeter. In a few instances, the column has a simulated abacus, in the form of a solitary final line: e.g., Bettini's double column, illus. Higgins 1987: 43.

[58] Drayton 1941: vol. 2: 4. For the foot as the base of a column, cf. Shute 1912: sig. Bivv. Cf. Tasso 1973: 201–2, cit. Eriksen 2001; 168, note 13. Tasso's thinking is less architectural than Drayton, more concerned with number symbolism: 'the eight-line stanza is the best, since the number eight, according to mathematicians, is the first of the solid or cubic numbers, the ones that have fulness and weight. It is moreover perfect and fittest for action because it is composed of twos, duality being the first moved or *primum mobile*'.

[59] For the proportions of the Tuscan order, see Onians 1988: 271; Shute 1912: 11.

[60] Van Eck 2000: 75; Serlio 1982: Book IV. 3r.   [61] Serlio 1611: Book IV, sig. A2r.

[62] Book IV, sig. A2v.   [63] Wotton 1651: 228–9.

threshold, columns) that recalls late medieval building poems and *The Faerie Queene*. A pair of genii–columns support the roof:

> Goodness and greatness, not the oaken piles;
> For these, and marbles, have their whiles
> To last, but not their ever: virtue's hand
> It is, which builds,'gainst fate to stand.

(Lines 99–100)

These enduring moral supports recall the two columns of Solomon's Temple,[64] and contrast with the jet columns avaricious lordship might have purchased.[65] Herrick's 'The Pillar of Fame', which concludes *Hesperides* (1648), is a shape poem with capital and base distinguished by different line lengths. Couplets run throughout, except for triplets at the transition from capital to shaft and shaft to base.

The paratext of Sylvester's *Devine Weekes*, like that of Du Bartas' *Sepmaines*, includes a sequence of twelve columnar poems, or at least typographical shapes. Bart Westerweel calls these 'altar-shaped poems' and 'altars of praise'.[66] But they are clearly columns: their shafts are girdled, in the French mannerist fashion, with bands bearing dedicatees' names (King and Queen; Mnemosyne; Phoenix; the Muses). The sequence thus constitutes an extended prostyle or portico of encomium.

Altars

Column and altar shapes were often indistinguishable, as for example the figure poems by William Browne, Samuel Speed, Francis Davison, Edward Benlowes, and Robert Herrick.[67] Historically this was appropriate enough, since in early churches the capitals of pagan columns were often converted to Christian altars.[68] Only occasionally was the altar shape capped by a shorter line or couplet representing the sacrificial slab, as in Porfirius' unambiguous altar of 100 AD and Richard Willes's of 1573.[69] The finest of all Renaissance shape poems is probably George Herbert's 'The Altar', in which the broken, penitent heart is wrought upon by Christ until self-sacrifice is internalized. Almost a process poem, 'The Altar'

---

[64] I Kings 7:21 and Ezekiel 40:49.   [65] Fowler 1994: 100, 112, notes 96–100.
[66] Westerweel 1984: 79.
[67] Discussed and illus. Westerweel 1984: 58–9, 66, 68–73, 79–84; cf. Browne 1894: vol. 2: 142; Benlowes, *Theophila, or Loves Sacrifice* (1652) (Saintsbury 1905: vol. 1: 345).
[68] Fowler 1995: 48.   [69] Illus. Westerweel 1984: 72, 78, figs. 10, 12.

symbolizes this transformation through metrical and numerological structures as well as a pattern of capitalized words.[70]

Secular poems, too, could be conceived as offerings of love or praise, and so as virtual sacrifices, Richard Carew entitles a love poem 'A New-Year's Sacrifice: To Lucinda',[71] claiming to follow the ceremonies of Egyptian priests and 'her pure Altars dresse / With gums and spices of humble Thankfulnesse'.

The altar subgenre could hardly remain unaffected by the Reformation, which often led to altars being moved or transformed into memorial communion tables.[72] Subsidiary altars were largely eliminated—and not only in Protestant churches. Alberti, for example, advocates a single altar, and considers its best position to be central, before the tribune or apse.[73] In Britain the altar's position was highly controversial, becoming after 1620 a major subject of contention between Puritan and Laudian Anglicans. Communion tables were brought into the middle of the nave, and then (in High Church reaction) moved to the centre of the chancel or even to the east end.[74]

These changes were reflected in Elizabethan poetry, where centred altars abound. Psalm translations, again, offered seminal models: in Sir Philip Sidney's version of Psalm XXVI (Vulgate XXV), for example, 'And with those hands about Thy Altar waite' comes in the sixth verse of twelve.[75] Probably in imitation of the Psalms, centred altars became common in offerings of praise generally.[76] Thus, in Spenser's *Hymnes*, the lines 'Then her they crowne their Goddesse and their Queene, / And decke with floures thy altars well beseene' come near the end of *An Hymne in Honour of Love*. But if this hymn and the following *An Hymne in Honour of Beautie* are treated as a single entity, the altars are at its centre. The three central stanzas contain the altars and a prayer to Love:

41 | 3 || 41
AN HYMNE IN HONOUR. OF LOVE || AN HYMNE IN HONOUR OF BEAUTIE

This framing pattern may be referred to in a deceptively artless line of the prayer: 'This simple song, thus framed in praise of thee'.

---

[70] See further in Fowler 1995. It may be mentioned that the patterned words are not signalized by capitalizing in the Williams MS, perhaps showing that uptake was thought possible without it.
[71] See Fowler 1996: 29–31, esp. notes 95, 100. Cf. the common figure of 'hecatombs' of praise.
[72] See Duffy 1992; Yates 2000. [73] Alberti 1988: 228–9.
[74] Yates 1991: 30–3. The issue was so sensitive that the central location of altars in poems could hardly escape notice.
[75] Sidney 1962: 305, translating Vulgate *circum dabo altare tuum domine*. Similarly in Sidney 1962: 336, Psalm xliii (Vulg. xlii), line 19 of 36. In both cases, the altar was interpreted as Christ in the Quincuplex. For Ariosto's centred altar *nel mezzo* in *Orlando Furioso* iii. 7, see Eriksen 2001: 132–3.
[76] For a centred altar of praise, see *Jonsonus Virbius* in Jonson 1925–1952: vol. 11: 437.

Frontispieces and façades

The metaphor of the frontispiece, which once held great significance, has become obscured. We think of a frontispiece as an illustration facing a title-page. But the Renaissance frontispiece might be the title-page itself, besides serving as a contents page introducing through its words and images the substance of the; book to follow. In architecture, the *frontispiece* (from medieval Latin *frontispicium* 'forehead, face, or façade') was a porch or portico; an entrance.[77] So an architectural title-page might offer entry or initiation into the book's space, or be designed to indicate an appropriate mindset for readers.[78] Care was lavished on it: the frontispiece was an expensive item. It was sometimes designed by the author, as with Thomas Hobbes's famous title-page for *Leviathan* (1651).

Title-pages often listed a book's contents or symbolized them visually. To us, an abstract of contents is at best an informative summary. But abstract generalities were formerly considered more real than concrete particulars. Consequently a frontispiece could be thought of as the 'soul of the book' (as Jonson called the title-page of Walter Ralegh's *History of the World*). And the title-page is similarly conceived by Adolph Mekerch, George Wither, Hubert Goltzius, and John Guillim.[79] In Ralegh's case, the theme of the frontispiece is the monumental endurance of historical writing. Elsewhere, it may be initiation. George Herbert's 'Superliminare' precedes the turning of the page that takes the reader of *The Temple* into 'The Church'.[80] Initiation is similarly the theme of the frontispiece in *Paradise Lost* III: Satan, about to enter our universe, sees stairs leading

> Up to the wall of heaven a structure high,
> At top whereof, but far more rich appeared
> The work as of a kingly palace gate
> With *frontispiece* of diamond and gold
> Embellished. (III. 503–7)

Here, *gold* suggests sovereign supremacy, *diamond* sincere faith. Remembering the joys of heaven behind 'the doors of bliss'—the contents symbolized by the frontispiece—Satan has a chance to repent, submit, ascend the steps, and be reinitiated into the fellowship of the blessed.

---

[77] OED 1, 2. [78] On reading as entering, see McLeod 1997: 3–4.
[79] Mekerch on Abraham Ortelius's *Theatrum in Orbis Terrarum* (1606): the reader enters 'the first page of the doorway'; Goltzius in *Fasti Magistratuum* (Bruges 1561), see Corbett 1979: 47; Guillim, 'An epigram explaining the frontispiece of this worke' in *A Display of Heraldry* (1610). Cf. also the liminal epigram '*Mens Authoris*' before Benlowes, *Theophila* (Saintsbury 1905: 315), translated as 'The Author's Design'.
[80] See McLeod 1997: 3–4 *et passim*.

Book frontispieces often incorporated architectural motifs or even a complete façade. In the late sixteenth and seventeenth centuries, indeed, this was a dominant form, familiar from Donne's *LXXX Sermons* (1640).[81] Usually the façade had paired columns, often supporting an arch or trabeation, as in William Rogers's title-page for Hugh Broughton's *A Concent of Scripture* (1590). Sometimes the columns alluded to Solomon's Temple, sometimes to Philip II's PLUS ULTRA *impresa* with the Pillars of Hercules. Such frontispieces imply monumentality: like monuments they were to last in memory. Indeed, they probably originated in the medieval columnar motif used in Canon Tables and elsewhere to mark off memory groups.[82] (Canon Tables listed Biblical chapters or books: they were the first things memorized in learning the Bible.[83]) But the idea was ancient too: in the *Rhetorica ad Herennium* items to be remembered were to be placed in a mental *intercolumnium*.[84] Renaissance frontispieces often resembled architectural (especially theatrical) façades; and here again there is a link with memory, since buildings (especially theatres) afforded spaces for exercising artificial memory. Philander Colutius's *Theatrum Naturae* (Speyer 1611), to mention only one, presents epitomes of ancient thought against an apsidal façade: its arches accommodate Aristotelian sentences amounting to hundreds of words—an astonishing fusion of literature and architecture.[85]

Real façades, conversely, offered metaphors for literature:[86] Lina Bolzoni gathers such comparisons from Pico della Mirandola (1463–94), Giuseppe Betussi (*c*.1512–*c*.1573), Anton Francesco Doni (1513–74), Francesco Sansovino (1521–86), and Paolo Arese (1574–1644).[87] For Sansovino, to begin reading a text was like entering a palace: 'The preface of an oration is like the beautiful and rich entrance hall of a well-planned palace: as soon as it presents itself to viewers, they begin to discuss it', thinking the palace inside 'must be [...] composed with perfect architecture, each part appropriate to the whole' (Bolzoni 2001: 193). Writers advised against regarding prefaces as self-sufficient: those who imagine they can take in the entire contents from a preface, writes Arese, 'are like those who arrive before a royal palace and stop at the door to gaze at its frontispiece' and, amazed by 'what is seen to be beautiful and elegant in the first encounter [...] believe there is nothing else to see'—and he lists the features they miss (Bolzoni 2001:

---

[81] See Corbett and Lightbown 1979: 6–9; Corbett 1964.
[82] See Carruthers 1990: Index s. v. *Canon tables*. On the shared idea of monumentality, see Baker 2001.
[83] See Carruthers 1990: Index, s. v. *Canon Tables; Columnia; Eusebius*; and *Intercolumnia*, also her Fig. 4. An early printed example is Werner Rolewinck, *Fasciculus Temporum* (Venice 1481), in which topics are distributed about a single arch. For the use of columns in memory art, see Bolzoni 2001: 195 (the seven pillars of Solomon's house of wisdom, Prov. 9:1); also John Willis, *Mnemonica* (1661), in Van Eck 2000: 17–19.
[84] Carruthers 1990: Index s. v. *Intercolumnia*.
[85] See Blair 1997: 172 and Fig. 5; Rossi 2000: 61 ff.
[86] For the façade as metaphor for the opening stanza, see Eriksen 2001: xv citing Tasso.
[87] Bolzoni 2001: 193–8.

195). The analogy throws unexpected light on reading practices: who would have suspected so superficial a reliance on prefaces and even frontispieces for a smattering of the contents?

Solomon's Temple

The temple-poem metaphor was Virgilian: *Georgics* III. 13-16 promises a marble temple, literally a poem, dedicated to Augustus (*in medio mihi Caesarerit templumque tenebit*). This passage (itself imitating Pindar) gave rise to a whole *via sacra* of literary temples and temples of memory.[88] The main informing idea, as Virgil makes clear, is dedication.

The most important and most imitated temple was unquestionably the Temple of Solomon, From patristic times the Psalter was imagined architecturally (Jerome called Psalm I the 'grand entrance' to the 'great house' of the Psalter[89]); and the tripartite division of the Psalter came to be compared to that of Solomon's Temple. For the Temple reflected for believers the cosmic order, and served as a type of the Church and of the City of God.[90] From Francesco Georgi (Zorzi) (1467-1540) and Philibert Delorme (1514-1570) to Juan Bautista Villalpando (1552-1608) and Isaac Newton (1642-1727), the Temple was a paradigm of architectural creation.[91] Throughout this tradition of Temple descriptions—1 Kings 5-8, Ezekiel 40-8, Philo, Josephus, Eusebius, Bede's *De Templo*, and Villalpando's commentary—the division into *cella* (temple), *aula* (court), and *vestibulum* (porch) remained a constant feature. Thus, in his *De Templis* (1638), R. T. cites Bellarmine to the effect that 'Christian Temples are built with three parts, after the Fashion of Salomon's Temple.'[92]

In their literary architecture writers followed this tradition of triple division, familiar both from the Biblical texts and from illustrations in the Geneva and other versions. They in turn ordered their own works—words, stanzas, chapters, or larger units—in three parts.[93] It may seem overconfident to say this. (Might not tripartite division have other sources, such as Aristotelian structural ideas?) But, as it happens, the influence of this Biblical model is unusually well attested.

---

[88] On the Virgilian passage, see Virgil 1990: 181; on the later tradition, Cowling 1998; Bolzoni 2001; 195. McFarlane 1984: 3 draws attention to J.-B. Pigna's 'De Templo, Poemate', epitomizing the metaphor on the scale of epigram.

[89] *Tractatus in Librum Psalmorum*, Jerome 1958: 3; cf. Isidore, Pat. Lat. 83, 179-200, and see Kuczynski 1995: 193.

[90] See Bongo 1591: 502-3, 648; Rosenau 1979; Simson 1962: 36-8; McClung 1983: Index s. v. Temple; Temple of Solomon; Psalms; Biermann 2003: 366-77, 389, 576; Goldhill 2004.

[91] See Wittkower 1962: 121-2, 155 (Giorgio on the proportions of the Temple); Simson 1962: 38; Rosenau 1979: 97. On Jesuit interest in Solomonic proportions, see Taylor 1967; 1972.

[92] Van Eck 2003: 124.

[93] The illustration to 1 Kings 6 in the Geneva Bible of 1560 brings out the division particularly clearly.

John Foxe (1516–1587) explicitly compares his own dedication of the *Actes and Monuments* with Solomon's dedication of the Temple. Foxe modestly disclaims any comparison of the two works—then compares their reception histories at paragraph length.[94]

Court masques gave the Temple metaphor further currency, as A. W. Johnson has shown in his study of their contributions to James I's Solomon cult.[95] And Ben Jonson used the same tripartite plan for the structure of 'To Penshurst', which he divided into three parts of seventeen couplets each. The equal parts are marked off by self-referring images: 'the second draught' and 'tells my cups' (lines 34, 67). For *draught* is an architectural pun, meaning both a measure of sawyer's work and a passage of text.[96] Richard Fanshawe, emulating the device in his division of 'The Escuriall' (another Temple anti-type) into parts each of thirty-one couplets, similarly marks the division with self-references: 'wall' in the line ending the first part, and 'The painter shifts his scene' in the line beginning the third part.[97]

Rivalling Jonson as an architectural poet is George Herbert, whose major work is explicitly entitled *The Temple*. The latter is not only architectural in a loose, general sense (as was once thought), but specifically alludes to Solomon's Temple, being divided (again) into three parts. These are widely agreed to be 'The Church-Porch' (*Perirrheterium*); 'The Church'; and 'The Church Militant'.[98] Moreover, individual poems in 'The Church' correspond to topics of Eusebius' description of the Temple: notably 'The Altar'; 'The Church-Floor'; 'Church Monuments'; 'Dedication'; and 'The Windows'.[99]

The placement of 'The Altar' has attracted attention, since (at least according to Esther Gilman Richey) Herbert 'does not place it 'in the middest' of the Temple as his patristic author [Eusebius] does, choosing rather to rear it at the door'.[100] The reason for this she sees as ecclesiastical politics: 'Rejecting the Laudian tendency to move the altar into the recesses of the church—away from the people and closer to the priesthood—Herbert makes his altar immediately accessible to 'all the faithful". Herbert's 'The Altar' may not be centred in 'The Church'; but it is nevertheless located 'in the middest' of a remarkable numerical structure. For

---

[94] Foxe 1610: i sig. 3r: 'Solomon the peaceable prince of Israel [...] after he had finished the building of the Lord's Temple [...] made his petition to the Lord for all that should pray in the said Temple [...] Upon the like trust in Gods gracious goodnesse [...] not comparing with the building of that Temple, but following the zeale of the builder [...] most humbly would crave of almighty God to bestow his blessing [...]'.

[95] Cf. Johnson 1994, Appendix; Onians 1988: 241. Probably James himself ensured that the Chapel Royal at Stirling Castle had the proportions of Solomon's Temple and appropriate iconography; see McKean 2001: 124.

[96] See Fowler 1975: 127 note 46; Johnson 1994: 28.

[97] See Fowler 1994: 135. On the Escorial plan as a lattice pattern, see Hersey 2000; 114–17; March 1998: 121.

[98] See Watson 1962: 356; Richey 1998: 115–16; Williams MS Introd. x, xxxi.

[99] See Richey 1998: 120.

[100] Richey 1998: 121. On centring of altars, see also Yates 2000: 15, 17, 28, 30–3.

'The Church-Porch', long treated as a single stanzaic poem, is actually a sequence of epigrams: it comprises a dedication; a liminal address to the reader; and 78 further epigrams (the last two being headed *Superliminare* in the 1633 edition). 'The Altar' follows, just into the second part, the central court or *aula*, titled 'The Church'.[101] 'The Church' thus consists of 'The Altar' and 162 further poems, ending with *finis*. In numerical terms,

$$2 \mid 76 \mid 2 \mid\mid \text{'The Altar'} \mid 162$$
$$\text{PORCH} \mid\mid \text{CHURCH}$$

Together with the Porch poems, 'The Altar' brings their total to 81, a number in 'one harmony' with the 162 remaining poems. For 81 : 162 or 1 : 2 is the diapason ratio, symbolizing rational control of concupiscence.[102]

Galleries of memory

Among metaphors from secular architecture, one finds unexpected prominence given to the gallery, a room for exercise, conversation, and display of art.[103] Ariosto's *Orlando Furioso*, for example, was more than once compared specifically to a gallery. An explanation may lie in the literature of artificial memory.

Lina Bolzoni shows how allegorical interpreters of the *Furioso* transformed the text into a series of images, readily available to arts of memory.[104] In his commentary, Orazio Toscanella actually refers to images from a manuscript of Giulio Camillo's memory art treatise *L'Idea del Theatro* (1550),[105] as well as to others from Francis I's wardrobe and gallery at Fontainebleau. By the 1580s Camillo Pellegrino (1527–1603) and Galileo Galilei (1564–1642) evidently considered the gallery metaphor familiar enough to use it in literary criticism. Thus, Pellegrino compares the *Gerusalemme Liberata* (1581) to a building with the 'measures and proportions of architecture' but criticizes the *Furioso* as *un palagio [...] falso di modello.*[106] Galileo, however, prefers the *Furioso*, and contrasts Tasso's disordered Wunderkammer of a poem 'made of different scraps gathered from a thousand ruins' with Ariosto's orderly gallery: 'When I enter the *Furioso* I see an open wardrobe, a tribune, a royal gallery adorned by a hundred ancient

---

[101] Temple sacrifices were performed in the *aula* or outer court.
[102] For the use of numerical proportion between parts of a work, see Scaliger, *Poetics* III. xli. 124: Scaliger 1964: 124 (*Repetimus etiam per proportionem*) and cf. Eriksen 2001: 34. Hutchinson gives the poem total of 'The Church' as 164, not 163: several are divided into parts in a way that renders the arithmetic ambiguous.
[103] Cf. North 1981: 135–6, where the gallery is for 'pastime and health' or 'conversation'.
[104] Bolzoni 2001: 205–7.   [105] Giulio Camillo Delminio (1480–1544).
[106] Pellegrino, *Il Carrafa overo dell' epica poesia* (Florence 1584); see Bolzoni 2001: 210; Eriksen 2001: 117 and Chap. 5 *passim*.

statues by the most famous sculptors, with countless complete stories'.[107] Bolzoni reasonably connects these statues, orderly in their niches, with the images in a memory theatre (Bolzoni 2001: 212-13).

By the mid-seventeenth century the architectural metaphor was so familiar in Britain that Sir Thomas Urquhart could apparently take it for granted in arranging the lexicon of his universal language: 'I have before my lexicon set down the division thereof, making use of another allegory, into so many cities which are subdivided into streets, they againe into lanes, those into houses, these into stories whereof each room standeth for a word; and all these so methodically, that who observeth my precepts thereanent shall at the first hearing of a word know to what city it belongeth [...]'[108]

It becomes more and more likely that the *ut architectura poesis* doctrine was bound up with methods of artificial memory. As Bolzoni puts it, those practising the memory art both used and augmented modes of perception formed on the architectural model. But was it a working model in general use? A conclusive answer has proved elusive, and is only now beginning to emerge.

There is abundant evidence that building metaphors were used to organize knowledge: diagrams showing text distributed among the parts of façades, theatres, or castles make that reasonably certain.[109] In the sixteenth century and earlier, rhetoric was a major subject in university education, and in rhetoric memory was a major part.[110] The local or Ciceronian method of *ars memorativa* recommended that things to be memorized should be linked with images positioned in places of a familiar building, real or imagined.[111] For this a range of architectural types and spaces might be used: towns, palaces, temples, theatres, galleries, kitchens, storerooms, *piazze, aulae, bibliotecae, capellae*, and stages.[112] The method called for large and small divisions within which the associated images could be positioned. Thus, Guillaume Lelièvre writes in *Ars Memorativa* (Toulouse 1523) of ten *loca minima*, as does Guglielmo Grataroli; while John Willis prefers twenty. These had to be clearly distinct, dissimilar sites in definite spatial relations to each other.[113] Corners and centre lines of a room or memory stage, for example, were good locations for the images.[114]

For memorizing a large text, many *niches* or subdivisions might be needed— even 150 (Bruno) or 360 (Metrodorus's zodiac).[115] Camillo considered but

---

[107] Bolzoni 2001: 209; cf. Thornton 1997: 123-125. On the gallery at Fontainebleau as a setting for emblems, see Fenoatea 1982: 67.
[108] Urquhart 1983: 73; the version in *Logopandecteision* (1953) I. lxxiii is virtually identical.
[109] E.g. Romberch 1533, illus. Bolzoni 2001: 252; see also Yates 1966, Blair 1997, etc.
[110] The five parts of classical rhetoric were *inventio, dispositio, elocutio, memoria*, and *pronuntiatio*.
[111] See Rossi 2000: 57.   [112] Draaisma 2000: 40.
[113] For Lelièvre, see Cowling 1998: 124; for Grataroli and Willis, van Eck 2003: 17-19.
[114] See Willis in van Eck 2003: 18-19 and fig. 1; cf. Grataroli, ibid. 17.
[115] Yates 1966: 107-108, 212-215. Cf. Bolzoni 2001: 213 on 12 images corresponding to parts of the life of St. Margaret of Antioch.

rejected the zodiac; it is hardly coincidental that Marcellus Palingenius's encyclopedia *Zodiacus Vitae* (1535–6) comprises twelve parts each designated by a zodiacal sign.[116] Above all, the memory 'theatre' was ubiquitous. Its theoretical importance for the Renaissance world has recently been put beyond doubt by the efforts of Frances Yates, Anne Blair, Lina Bolzoni, and others.[117] And, as for the practical value of memory treatises, that is open to verification. There is still debate, however, about how generally the memory art was actually practised, and for what purpose.

Any amount of text, from brief *imprese* to Boethius's entire *Consolatio Philosophiae*, might in principle be placed in a memory theatre for invention or memorizing.[118] Sometimes, indeed, a frontispiece was evidently designed with this in mind: the title-page of Hobbes's *Leviathan* has a panel with images from Johannes Romberch's memory manual *Congestorium Artificiosa Memorie* (1533).[119] Frances Yates and Lina Bolzoni reasonably assume that artificial memory was widely practised. But others are much more cautious. David Cowling's study of architectural metaphors from the Middle Ages to the fifteenth century amply demonstrates their wide currency; yet time and again he mistrusts the evidence of memorial practices.[120] Are we to conclude that no-one, or only a very few, practised memory art?

We can go a little further, perhaps, by taking a more diachronic view of the great cultural changes of the time. The memory art was put under pressure by the vast increase, and increasing complexity, of new knowledge, to say nothing of the difficulty of organizing it on traditional lines. At this critical juncture the invention of printing arrived in the west. Proliferation of books changed reading and writing habits, so that the older memory treatises may well have come to seem ponderous or unnecessary.[121] The invention of printing, however, seems also to have greatly enhanced the status of memory and memory art.[122] It is as if memorial grasp seemed at last more feasible. Thus, in the history of *ut architectura poesis* the coming of the book clearly marks a decisive new phase. Later, as the growth and classification of knowledge developed into scientific method and as rhetoric declined in the eighteenth century, the importance of the architectural metaphor (which as we saw had a rhetorical *raison d'être*) naturally dwindled. Where it survived, its application was altogether broader, vaguer, more subjective.

Later writers, suggests Ellen Eve Frank, 'dematerialize the more material art, architecture, that they may materialize the more immaterial art, literature. In this

[116] Trans. Barnabe Googe as *The Zodiake of Life* (1560). On the question of authorship, see Googe 1976: vi.
[117] Blair 1997; Bolzoni 2001; Yates 1966: 117, 129; and Yates 1969: Index, s. v. *Memory, art of*.
[118] Bolzoni 2001: 196–7; Draaisma 2000: 40.
[119] In Hobbes's literary theory, fancy and memory work together; see van Eck 2003: 27–8.
[120] Cowling 1998: 129. The extreme scepticism of Newton de Molina 1970 is now untenable, although his warning against totalizing historicism was timely.
[121] Cf. Yates 1966: 124.   [122] See Salmon 1972: II 1–112.

way, architecture and literature relinquish an analogical relationship to marry as literary architecture'.[123] Frank rightly distinguishes the classical theory of 'architecture as an artificial memory model' from Walter Pater's patterns of association.[124] In Pater and many other Victorian writers the metaphorical order subsisted in mental associations, not architectural structures. Only Ruskin, perhaps, had enough historical grasp to see that 'architecture, like poetry, was a "conqueror of forgetfulness"'.[125]

---

[123] Frank 1979: 7.   [124] Frank 1979: 41–2.   [125] Frank 1979: 36.

Perspective and Realism in the Renaissance

Those wishing to follow the movements of sensibility accompanying the shift from the Ptolemaic to the modern world (through the medieval, Copernican, and eventually Newtonian universes) naturally have recourse to comparing contemporary literary representations of the world. But in this they meet a great difficulty: namely that methods of mimesis, or representation of life, did not meanwhile stand still. These too suffered, from the fourteenth to the eighteenth centuries, a series of radical metamorphoses. In particular, ideas of realism changed almost beyond recognition.

Spectator Realism

Many will think the development of realism a familiar story—so familiar that it can almost be taken for granted. But this seems to me a misconception. Of the true story of realism, less than half has ever been told. For there are at least two, distinct realisms, of which only one has been much discussed. The familiar realism is the one that became 'classic realism,' the realism of Samuel Richardson or Anthony Trollope or Graham Greene—and of William Congreve, Arthur Pinero, and Terence Rattigan. In this realism action is shown as it appears to an observer. I shall lump together the variants of classic realism, calling them all 'spectator realism.'

Spectators of the action were indeed often enough portrayed in pre-novelistic fiction and in drama before the dramatists named in the last paragraph. Think of the stage audiences of Jacobean drama: Andrea's ghost in *The Spanish Tragedy*, for example, sitting down with Revenge to watch the play that follows: 'Here sit we down to see the mystery, / And serve for Chorus in this tragedy' (1.1.90–1). Or Christopher Sly and a lord's hunting party watching a company of travelling players acting *The Taming of the Shrew*. Or, a more striking example still, Claudius and his court watching *The Murder of Gonzago*, themselves watched by young Hamlet and Horatio, who in turn are watched by the 'real' audience in the Globe. In drama dominated by the Renaissance 'idea of the play,'[1] watching and deliberating spectator-gods were common enough. Shakespeare's characters often refer to such gods: 'Look down, you gods' (*The Tempest* 5.1.201); 'you gods, look

---

[1] Righter 1967.

down' (*The Winter's Tale* 5.3.121); 'sir, gods, upon your thrones, and smile at Troy' (*Troilus and Cressida* 5.10.13); 'The gods look down, and this unnatural scene / They laugh at' (*Coriolanus* 5.3.184–5); 'eyes of heaven' (*Hamlet* 2.2.518); 'You see me here, you gods' (*King Lear* 2.4.274). Such deities, like Bishop Berkeley's observing God, were omnipresent, keeping things under their moral judgment—keeping them, almost, in existence.

In a somewhat earlier period (but lingering on in Shakespeare's) the medieval dream-vision genre typically depended on a spectator who was a dreamer—sometimes a naïve one like the Chaucer of *The House of Fame*—who (conveniently for the reader) needed to have everything explained to him by a guide or presenter. Great differences, however, separate these medieval or early Renaissance observers from those our own spectator realism implies. One obvious difference is that in Renaissance plays and narratives the spectators (Chaucer; Christopher Sly in *The Taming of the Shrew*) may themselves be represented as actually engaged in spectating. They exist visibly, if only at the edge of the reader's attention. Secondly, and less obviously, the early spectators are not always entirely passive. They participate. At the very least they may ask questions—sometimes very frequent questions—and receive answers from a guide or presenter. Occasionally they even involve themselves in the action, perhaps joining in conversation with other characters, as in *The Assemblie of Ladies* (anon., c.1470–80) or Thomas Clanvowe's *The Cuckoo and the Nightingale* (late fourteenth century).[2] This is hardly surprising, since it is the spectator's experience, and the spectator s emotions, that the dream-vision usually portrays. Its narrative is after all the dreamer's own vision.

In the accepted model, medieval dream-vision figures as the anticipation or fore-shadowing of later, more sophisticated, forms of fiction. This model is thoroughly teleological, with classic realism as its telos: The naïve dreamers of dream-vision are determined by the primitive character of the form itself. When literature becomes less uncouth, when the realistic illusion is achieved, dreamers and their allegories can be eliminated—dismantled like scaffolding no longer needed. With the advent of Ian Watt's 'formal realism,'[3] in other words, the spectator-god becomes an invisible *deus absconditus*. This model has appeared to work reasonably well for much fiction and drama of the nineteenth and twentieth centuries—for much of William Thackeray and Henry James, as for Pinero and Rattigan. But it has serious defects, among them the patronizing assumption that medieval and Renaissance mimesis was no more than fumbling experimentation. Besides, it gives no account of the dreamer's or spectator's participation in the action of medieval and Renaissance works. What about the substance of those sophisticated allegories? What of all their emotional content?

---

[2] Spearing 1976: 179.   [3] Watt 1957.

Participative Realism

In short, one may think of realism as composed of two distinct strands. The first, as we saw, developed from medieval allegory into spectator realism and has been much discussed. But another strand (let us call it participatory or empathic realism) is largely ignored and little understood. It is nevertheless a vital component in Victorian literature, and still more so in modernist and more recent fiction and drama. The novels of Henry Fielding, Trollope, and George Meredith, the dramas of Henrik Ibsen, James Barrie, and Luigi Pirandello—to say nothing of absurdist drama—are obviously not cast in the mould of spectator realism.

A Spenserian passage on the border between the two narrative modes may exemplify how they interacted during the Renaissance. In *The Faerie Queene* 2.4.3–15 the knight Sir Guyon 'saw from far, or seemed for to see' an affray which he hoped to 'agree' (settle). A madman was dragging a youth by the hair and cruelly mistreating him. At first Guyon and his guide, the Palmer, are simply spectators viewing a scene of violence described in emblematic detail: the youth in the grip of a madman encouraged by a lame hag. But Guyon is no passive, apathetic spectator: 'moved with great remorse' (Stanza 6) he intervenes, grappling with the madman, only to be himself overcome. Now enraged— 'emboyling in his haughtie hart' (Stanza 9)—he draws his sword. But the Palmer, offering an *explicatio* of the complex emblems of Furor and Occasion, tells him the madman cannot be subdued by main force (so to say, will-power). Guyon must first restrain Furor's mother, the hag 'Occasion, the root of all wrath and despight' (Stanza 10). As in the traditional emblem of *Occasio*, she must be seized by the forelock: Once things have gone too far, there is no holding the smooth back of her head, since 'all behind was bald, and worne away, / That none thereof could ever taken hold' (Stanza 4). The passage is generalizing, allegorical and emblematic, but Guyon and the Palmer are real spectators, not mere *fictiones*. All the same, the mode is not that of our spectator realism: It is more participatory. For Guyon, too, is in the grip of passion: He is involved in the struggle, which becomes in some sense his own. And the Palmer interprets Guyon's own experience, rather than expounding universal generalities the youth's suffering exemplifies.

The narrative now turns to the youth Phedon, who has taken no part in Guyon's encounter with Furor. And for Phedon's story, Spenser shifts into a different narrative mode. As if illustrating the preceding discourse, or unfolding its emblems, Phedon's tale is not allegorical, but a simple exemplum. It is even in a tragic genre: the most realistic form then available.

In Phedon's tale (Stanzas 17–33), his false friend Philemon deceives him by getting the maid Pryene to impersonate her mistress Claribell, Phedon's love. As

Phedon puts it, he himself is made 'the sad spectatour of my Tragedie' (Stanza 27). He sees what he takes to be Claribell betraying him with a 'groom of base degree'. Although a spectator, Phedon is passionately involved: so passionately that he kills the supposedly unfaithful Claribell. The tale continues in this tragic mode, quite as realistically as Ariosto's or François de Belleforest's treatments of the story. That is, up to the point when Phedon, having poisoned Philemon, pursues Pryene to kill her too. But now Phedon finds himself totally possessed by rage. In a characteristically Spenserian *peripeteia* (or sudden reversal), the figure who meets and overcomes him is 'this madman' (Stanza 32): the personification of his own *furor*. And here the narrative returns to internalized experience and to Guyon's adventure, the tempering of passion. Having heard Phedon's terrible story, the temperate Guyon didactically comments, 'Squire, sore have ye beene diseasd; / But all your hurts may soone through temperance be easd' (Stanza 33). Readers and critics understandably take against this advice as priggish. It implies superiority to Phedon's suffering or at least a disagreeable overconfidence. Temperance will not bring back Philemon or Claribell. Taking the passage as reversion to allegory hardly improves matters: The overconfidence is then authorial, and Guyon's later downfall at the Cave of Mammon becomes problematic.

Just as Phedon, although at first a spectator of Claribell's supposed unfaithfulness, is aroused to jealous rage and becomes intensely involved, so with Guyon. He too is at first a compassionate spectator of Phedon's suffering at the hands of the madman. And when Guyon himself participates—struggling with the same madman—he too fails to subdue Furor until he follows the Palmer's advice. Occasion of fury must be dealt with first: 'first her restrain' (2.4.11); 'the sparke soone.quench' (2.4.35). Phedon's tale illustrates this by negative example: Instead of quenching jealousy's sparks he embraces the occasion of wrath by arranging with Philemon to witness what he takes to be Claribell's disloyalty. Similarly Guyon accepts Mammon's invitation to see over the Cave, and in doing so embraces its occasion of worldliness and avarice. Thus, Guyon's glib advice to Phedon, far from showing the triteness of Spenser's morality, is actually a shrewd touch of realism. Guyon, not Spenser, is overconfidently didactic. The reader is surely meant to receive Guyon's advice much as Phedon may be supposed to do; feeling that Guyon makes temperance sound much too easy. As often, Spenser is blamed for his success.

One has to accept that Renaissance readers felt no incompatibility between naturalistic representation of shaded characters and allegorical representation of black-and-white ones. And in visual art similarly, from Jan van Eyck to Jan Steen, it was not thought incongruous that genre scenes or realistic portraits like *The*

Great Picture of Lady Anne Clifford should have emblematic details or attributes.[4] This became more difficult with the advent of formal realism and the gradual development of consistent perspective construction. From the eighteenth century, objects in pictures tended to be plausibly naturalistic—or else the whole picture had to be visionary or symbolic. In the sixteenth and seventeenth centuries, however, it was different, partly because the real world was then itself allegorical and emblematic (even house- and shop-signs were emblems). In literary realism, characters like the human Phedon, the heroic Guyon, and the personification Furor all belong to the same fictive world, part naturalistic and part allegorical.

Realistic effects of such a sort are by no means peculiar to Spenser: Sidney's *Arcadia* and Shakespeare's tragedies are full of them, and so is Milton's *Paradise Lost*. All continue to explore and develop representational devices common in medieval fiction: for example, the dispersal of character among objects, places, and animals.[5] After all, each allegorical *fictio* in a dream-vision is dreamt by the protagonist–dreamer, and so generated as an identification of subjective experience. The medieval allegorise does not narrate events in the external world as if viewed by a notional spectator, but rather presents aspects of subjective experience, encountered when the 'character' (as we say) of an emotion is recognized. In dream-visions of the Middle Ages the dreamer's participation was not often explored in much detail: For the readers or audience to be edified it was only necessary that they should identify broadly with the dreamer's encounters. In general, they were to apply the vision to themselves, appropriating all the *fictiones*.

Viewpoints

Unlike Renaissance fiction, where perspectives perpetually change, medieval allegory shifted viewpoint less often. Exceptions include a few devotional works like the *Arca Noe* of Hugh of St Victor[6] and—far greater exceptions—certain bold narratives of genius. In *Piers Plowman* (c.1360–87), William Langland constructs multiple perspectives on a grand scale, switching the eye-point (and I-point) of his mimesis again and again. When the action is imagined from a supernal viewpoint, in the debate of the Four Daughters of God (B, *passus* 18), no creature can truly have a spectatorial role, since the arguments are between *fictiones* of God. Then, abruptly, Langland turns to Piers's joust: to action performed, at least on one level, by human agencies. In such passages of *Piers Plowman*, in Dante's exchanges with his guides Virgil and Beatrice in the *Commedia Divina* (?1307–20), in the kaleidoscopic narrative of Francesco Colonna's

---

[4] Fowler 2003: 32–6.   [5] Ginsberg 1983.   [6] Carruthers 1990.

Hypnerotomachia (1499), and in late medieval allegorical fiction and drama generally, we may find models for the shifting viewpoints of Renaissance realism.

That this stage of realism had a basis in perception, or in the configuration of the imagination, is strongly suggested by the fact that visual art presents analogous forms. There, too, in manuscript illuminations, biblical dreamers like Jacob and Joseph are often pictured together with the contents of their vision. This motif, termed *Assistenzporträt*, continued into the seventeenth century, and can be seen again in the *Rückenfigur* (or 'back figure') of the nineteenth. Today, spectators in fiction ate discussed in terms of the 'male gaze' or the 'female gaze'; but in sixteenth-and seventeenth-century Dutch art theory, an altogether different range of types of beholders were distinguished. There was the *beschouwer*, for example, who by mime or action interpreted the action; the *sprecher*, who explained the work, much like the presenter of a masque; and the gesturing maidservant eavesdropping through the open door of a *doorkijkje*. The *beschouwer* was often physically involved in the action, as in countless realizations of the myth of Actaeon's discovery of Diana.[7]

Literary historians have been accustomed to think of Renaissance realism as anticipating later forms. Looking forward rather than back, they have eagerly shown how, after Spenser, the conventions of spectator realism displaced those of allegory and participatory realism in a decisive, almost inexorable way. This did not happen, however, so rapidly as has been assumed. So far as Elizabethan and Jacobean drama is concerned, Shakespeare is almost unique in presenting more or less consistent characters, capable of developing through the action of an entire play—through phases imaginable by modern audiences as a single, continuous, organic process. And even so, even in Shakespeare, there are many disconcerting interruptions of the almost modern, illusionistic mode. Inconsistencies and departures from our sort of realism break in more often than we pretend—whole scenes, sometimes, like *I Henry VI* 2.4, the Temple Garden scene. Some characters (Cordelia; Hermione) disappear altogether for long stretches of a play; others, like the Duke in *Measure for Measure*, act unaccountably, without obvious motivation: without, even, motivation subsequently explained.

Here and there, of course, Jacobean tragedy made great 'advances' towards consistent spectator realism. And a similarly modern mode appears in short non-dramatic passages, for example in Donne's satiric monologues. There is no question that Thomas Middleton's *Women Beware Women*, say, seems to belong to a different literary world altogether from Spenser's. Throughout the scene of Isabella's seduction by Livia, Middleton sustains an unbroken sequence of naturalistic, psychologically realized details that can be taken as spectator realism; although early audiences may have referred them to stages of temptation: to

---

[7] Fowler 2003: 66–76.

schemes in the moral theology of the time. Still, modern audiences have no difficulty in understanding most of the scene in terms of classic realism. But that cannot be said of Middleton's play as a whole—least of all its conclusion. It ends with an inset masque of revenge that now seems improbably contrived to maximize the spectacular carnage. In fact, one might describe much Jacobean and Caroline drama as characterized by *discontinuous* realism—or realism at most continuous throughout an individual scene (the unit of organization).

This is strikingly true of Beaumont and Fletcher's tragedies and tragicomedies. *The Maid's Tragedy*, for example, has been treated as a realistic play with protean characters—that is, as defective spectator realism. But the play is more coherent than that suggests. It consists of a structured sequence of scenes during which characters consistently alter according to the requirements of a now unfamiliar mimesis: namely, participatory realism. Thus, the scene of Evadne's prenuptial undressing (2.1) may be regarded as consistently realistic within its perspective. It imitates the world shared by the servant Dula (Greek δούλη, bondwoman) and the ladies in waiting. The Evadne known to them is proper, even severe. But when the ladies have exited (2.1.126) and Evadne is alone with Amintor, in the passage beginning with the shock of 'A maidenhead Amintor / At my years?' (2.1.193–4), she expresses a cynicism that reveals the perspective of Dula and the ladies to be seriously incomplete. This discovery, of which there has been no previous hint, is a sensational *coup de théâtre*. It suddenly puts the audience in a state something like that of the bridegroom Amintor. Such is the surprise that they participate in his experience rather than merely view it: They see things from his viewpoint. Incorrigible spectators as we are, however, we expect to be able to read the new 'reality' back into earlier scenes of the play. And when we fail to find earlier signs of Evadne's hypocrisy, we fault the play for its inconsistent or 'protean' characters.

The realism of Shakespeare and Jonson is sometimes closer than this to classic realism. But it is sometimes further from it than we suppose. Critics are prone to pass over Shakespearean passages that do not accord with the assumptions of spectator realism. They treat these as inset 'spectacles', or interludes, or even (as with the knocking at the gate in *Macbeth*) as interpolations. Yet scenes like the triumph in *Pericles* 2.2, a procession of knights bearing shields with *imprese* that are presented to Thaisa and described by her, surely have a claim to be considered as valid perspectives in a different mimetic mode from ours. As King Simonides says of Pericles' rusty armour, 'Opinion's but a fool, that makes us scan / The outward habit by the inward man' (2.2.55–6). Even in Shakespeare's tragedies, spectator realism is quite often interrupted, notably in the soliloquies. These do not merely express moments of 'stream of consciousness' (which would be interruption enough). For they constitute summarizing, stocktaking retrospects and prospects over mental events, emotions, and realizations that belong to a much longer lapse of time than that of the scene they interrupt. Thus they let an audience share the protagonist's inward viewpoint and even in part the dramatist's.

In many other ways, too, Shakespeare's spectator realism is discontinuous. Some of the most recalcitrant problems his interpreter encounters, indeed, have arisen from inappropriate attempts to discover unbroken spectator realism. Hamlet's character, for example, has often been described as 'protean' in the same way as Evadne's. The godlike spectator-critic pronounces on how far the clouding of Hamlet's intellect has progressed in this scene and in that, as if Shakespeare were a modern novelist. But the nunnery scene, to take only one instance, may not contain information on that point at all. Its perspective may be constructed from Ophelia's viewpoint: meant, perhaps, to involve audiences in her pain and bewilderment at the alteration she meets in her lover. Again, Hamlet seems mad from the viewpoint of certain characters and not from others—not, for example, from Horatio's, or the players'. Until recently, however, such distinctions of viewpoint have largely been ignored. With few exceptions critics have taken for granted the large anachronism of Shakespeare's instant creation of continuous spectator realism.[8]

Scenery

As with 'legitimate perspective' in visual art, so with realism in literature. It is difficult to escape the dominant conventions of one's own time: difficult, even, to suspend belief in them temporarily. The conventions of spectator realism pervade our culture. But in the seventeenth century they were being newly formulated—as we can occasionally glimpse. At first even the coherent perspective of the acting area was grasped only tentatively. It called for a new act of imagination to view the stage and stage sets as part of a unified fictive space. A stage direction in John Shirley's *The Triumph of Peace*, performed at Court on February 3, 1634 at the Banqueting House suggests how far the realistic illusion was from being taken for granted. The scene changes at line 300 to 'a tavern, with a flaming red lattice, several drinking-rooms, and a back door, but especially a conceited sign and an eminent bush'.[9] Far from there being an immediate illusionistic effect, the scene—almost the stage direction itself—is puzzled over by the characters: 'ADMIRATION: Wonderful, here was none within two minutes.' Scenery could not yet be tacitly accepted as part of a continuous illusion; it was still a novelty worth remarking. It was gradually introduced in masques and at private venues such as Christ Church, Oxford (William Strode's *The Floating Island*, 1636); but a realistic illusion was by no means immediate.

[8] Fowler 1995. [9] Spencer and Wells 1967: 290.

Similar adjustments were called for when the proscenium arch was introduced: To begin with, the space beyond the proscenium plane was not consistently ordered. (Even today sets implying inconsistent perspectives are not unknown.) Andrea Palladio's and Vincenzo Scamozzi's Teatro Olimpico at Vicenza (1580–5), with its five *portae* (openings) showing glimpses of fictive streets in perspectival recession, did much to establish the idea of a realistic acting space.[10] But its incompatible perspectives still implied multiple viewpoints. Not until the tragic scene of Sebastiano Serlio (1475–1554) had exerted a century of influence was the unified stage perspective assimilated. Even then, the sight lines and perspectives of the English masques continued to be related to the viewpoint of the noblest persons present. Only they were the godlike spectators of a more or less consistently realistic spatial illusion.[11] A long, slow development in theory and practice was required before the spectator realism of the Edwardian, three-walled stage was achieved.

Survivals of Renaissance Realism

In fiction, elements of Renaissance realism persisted long after the emergence of the novel. At first, however, this was disguised by the dominance of the epistolary genre. In epistolary novels such as Richardson's the perspective of each letter has usually a single viewpoint, that of the letter writer; so that by a curious ambiguity modern readers can receive each letter—and so the entire novel—as if all were spectator realism. The reader becomes an *alter deus* transcending the viewpoints of the novel's various correspondents, except when sympathizing with this character or that. The ambiguity may pass unnoticed because each correspondent is uncontested creator of his own epistolary world, and may have no occasion to become much involved with the other perspectives. So Richardson's fictive mode, although it entailed many narrators, paradoxically promoted single-perspective realism.

Even so, Richardson's formal realism, astonishingly modern as it often seems, is not always entirely consistent with spectator realism. His novels often lack, for example, a coherent topography of outdoor locations. Nor are they always compatible with any single temporal sequence. The amount of time Pamela and Clarissa spend in letter writing is hardly plausible realistically—as can be seen from the strenuous efforts made to account for it. This has been criticized as a failure of Richardson's art. But in terms of participatory realism it is justifiable to represent Pamela as largely occupied in letter writing. In her reduced life,

---

[10] Fowler 2003: 14–16.   [11] Fowler 2001.

correspondence actually is her principal emotional outlet. Moreover, its perspective is one the reader can share.

Spectator realism so dominated Victorian novels that it became the norm it has since remained. Yet the alternative fictive mode was never eliminated altogether. Indeed, some of the finest novels of the period—one thinks of *Our Mutual Friend* and *Vanity Fair*—make extensive use of the older, participatory mode. And whenever critics speak of 'identifying' with a character, or classify a narrator as 'unreliable,' they tacitly acknowledge the existence of a mimesis other than spectator realism. Today, both fictive modes remain viable, so that in theorizing narrative the double origin of modern realism needs to be kept in mind. Theorists tend to link the classic realist novel and its presumptuously godlike author with the social class system at a specific stage of political development; but in doing so they perhaps fail to take sufficient account of long-term interactions with the older, sibling mode.

Interplay of spectator and participatory realisms extended over several centuries, and long antedated nineteenth-century class structures. If political connections are desired, the two modes are probably better linked with older polarities such as that of centralized monarchy and feudal decentralization of power. Or, more broadly still, they may be associated with competing cosmologies. Is it reaching too far to suggest a connection between the profound changes in the Renaissance world picture and the transition from participatory to spectator realism? Copernicanism, the conscious basis of the emergent world picture, was certainly linked in manifold ways with the theory of single-point perspective. It is not a matter, simply, of the obvious analogy between the single view-point of 'legitimate perspective' on the one hand, on the other the undivided centrality of the heliocentric universe. Crucial to the Copernican hypothesis were advances in optics that went back to Robert Grosseteste and Roger Bacon—to medieval approaches to natural science 'that sought explanations of natural species and phenomena in perspective and the mathematics of light rays'.[12] In the Renaissance, moreover, new technological and artisan traditions emerged, bringing revaluation of older mechanical doctrines: 'developments in painting and the fine arts led to renewed interest in optics or *perspectiva*, and Copernicus' proposal of a Pythagorean as opposed to a Ptolemaic, universe gave new life to astronomy'.[13]

The Copernican, Keplerian, and other planetary systems of the Renaissance were bound up with a new consciousness already thought of as modern: consciousness of the Cartesian subject confronting a universe without predetermined meaning. The virtuous cosmos of medieval Aristotelianism was gradually laid aside, not without regrets and controversies. Thus, Bernard le

---

[12] North 1994: 331.   [13] Wallace 1991: 204.

Bovier de Fontenelle (1657–1757) makes his mechanistic Molière say to Paracelsus:

> If most people saw the order of the universe as it really is, so that they noticed neither characteristic virtues in numbers, nor influences of planets, nor fates that are attached to certain times or certain revolutions [periods], they would not be able to prevent themselves from saying, about this admirable order, 'What! Is it nothing more than that?' (*Dialogues of the Dead*[14])

Literary protagonists were now often portrayed as making sense of their worlds—endowing the disappointing 'admirable order' with meaning, emotion, and mystery. Some were naturalized narrators, even novelists within the novel. And in putting their fictive worlds together the causes they traced were efficient rather than final—like the fateful window that determines the shape of Tristram Shandy's biography. Significantly, too, that window is a sash window: a modern, even a recent, item of technology. Tristram's composing of material causes into a consistent narrative represents a stage of mimesis that was by no means arrived at (still less generated) all at once. It emerged piecemeal, tentatively and gradually, in much the same way as time and effort over a long period were required before perspective was assimilated to the western mental set. In 1754, Hogarth's frontispiece to 'Kirby's Perspective' still had to ridicule common absurdities resulting from false extrapolation of perspective constructions.[15] Participatory realism, too, came to seem absurd at times. In Sidney's *Arcadia*, Zelmane's bathing in the river Ladon and empathizing with every object in contact with his lover now seems to belong to a former age—shrouded, even, in quaint alterity. As a spectator, Zelmane is so involved as to be comically unable to think of the material world objectively. What was once the river's participatory arousal at the touch of Philoclea and Pamela—'when cold Ladon had once fully embraced them, himself was no more so cold to those ladies; but as if his cold complexion had been heated with love, so seemed he to play about every part he could touch'[16]—has shrunk to Ruskin's 'pathetic fallacy.'

Spectatorial empathy did not quickly disappear from fiction. It lingered long, and indeed made partial returns in genres out of the mainstream. One such was gothic romance. The many landscape vistas in Mrs Radcliffe's *The Mysteries of Udolpho* (1794) cannot be adequately characterized as descriptive. Journeying towards Rousillon, for example, Emily finds the precipitous terrain so frightening that she is 'terrified almost to fainting'.[17] And later the veiled picture engages her feelings until she is 'somewhat agitated': Even the discussion of it 'excited a faint degree of terror. But a terror of this nature, as it occupies and expands the mind,

---

[14] Cit. Blumenberg 1987: 39. [15] Fowler 2003: 10. [16] Fowler 2003: 73–80.
[17] Radcliffe 1966: 30.

and elevates it to high expectation, is purely sublime, and leads us, by a kind of fascination, to seek even the object, from which we appear to shrink'.[18] Nevertheless, her feelings towards the picture are so strong that she cannot look at it.[19] Throughout the novel, nature—wild, desolate or sublime—is never merely viewed as in spectator realism, but demands emotional, sometimes even physical, engagement. Thus, Emily stops at a neglected avenue where 'the road was yet broken, and the trees overloaded with their own luxuriance... she stood surveying it, and remembering the emotions, which she had formerly suffered there'.[20]

In science fiction, too, objects sometimes compel emotional engagement, whether by their strangeness to a space- or time-traveller, or through their nightmare horror. Alfred Bester's *The Demolished Man* (1953) opens with Ben Reich's nightmare of 'the Man with No Face', from which he is awakened by his own screams. One might consider this nightmarish image, too, as crossing the boundary of spectator realism.

---

[18] Radcliffe 1966: 248.   [19] Radcliffe 1966: 278.   [20] Radcliffe 1966: 501.

Penshurst Revisited

Ben Jonson's 'To Penshurst,' a seminal English estate poem, has been extensively but sketchily annotated, with key passages treated as mere commonplaces. One such describes the Mount which probably gave the estate its name (a 'hurst,' OE *hyrst*, was a wooded hill or mount: 'Penshurst' or Peveneshurste most likely derived from 'Peven's hurst'):[1]

> Thy Mount, to which the Dryads doe resort,
> Where Pan, and Bacchvs their high feasts have made,
> Beneath the broad beech, and the chest-nut shade;
> That taller tree, which of a nut was set,
> At his great birth, where all the Muses met.
> There, in the writhed barke, are cut the names
> Of many a Sylvane, taken with his flames.
>
> (Jonson, 'To Penshurst', ll.10–16)

The estate poem may have originated from the Netherlandish *hofdicht* or court-piece (perambulation of a country-house estate),[2] but Jonson saw possibilities in the genre more far-reaching that his predecessors had done.

Writing on trees

Few have asked what pastoral 'commonplaces' are doing in a georgic poem. These anomalies present no problem of course to Raymond Williams and his followers, who write of country-house poems as simply pastoral (as if no work were ever done in the country), and favour dichotomies of town and country.[3] Most estate poems, however, belong to georgic rather than pastoral. In this, 'To Penshurst' is

---

[1] As in 'Pevensey', etc. See *OED*; Eilert Ekwall, *The Concise Oxford Dictionary of English Place-Names* (Oxford: Clarendon Press, 1951) 345; A. D. Mills, *Oxford Dictionary of British Place Names* (Oxford University Press, 2003) 366. William Camden describes Penshurst as anciently the seat of Sir Stephen de Penherst, 'a famous Warden of the Cinque Ports'; see his *Britannia* (1695) 191 n. 27.

[2] See P. A. F. van Veen, *De Soeticheydt des Buyten-Levens, Vergheselschapt met de Boucken* (The Hague: Van Goor Zonen, 1960); Alastair Fowler, *The Country House Poem* (Edinburgh University Press, 1994) 12.

[3] James Turner sees the matter is not so simple; see *The Politics of Landscape* (Harvard University Press, 1979) 164.

typical—did much indeed to establish the type. Pastoral knows nothing of hunting 'season'd deere' (1. 20); the pastoral fauna includes neither 'bullocks, kine, and calves' (1. 23) nor 'mares, and horses' (1. 24); while 'orchard fruit' and 'garden flowers' (ll. 39-44) are the responsibility of farmers (l. 48) or gardeners, not shepherds.

Yet writing names on trees has been understandably seen as a pastoral activity. It appears (perhaps its first occurrence in Latin) in that quintessential pastoral, Vergil's fifth Eclogue. There, Mopsus carves verses in *viridi...cortice fagi*, 'in the green beech-bark' (5.13-15). And Gallus later speaks of carving his loves on young trees: *tenerisque meos incidens amores / arboribus* (10. 53-4). These and other amorous shepherds prefer the shady beech (*fagus*) for its smooth writing surface, and young trees for their capacity to grow with the loves inscribed on them.[4] The more the trunks grow, 'the greater grow my names' (Ovid, *Heroides* 5. 25). In the early Renaissance Jacopo Sannazaro (*c*.1458-1530) amplifies the ancient topos when he has the solitary Galicio

> ...write and carve
> On the beeches in every wood;
> So that now there is not a tree
> That does not call out 'Amaranth'.[5]

Pastoral is sometimes specifically announced: in *The Shepherd's Garland* (1597), Michael Drayton's shepherd Motto remembers chanting in unbridled youth 'sweete straines of heavenly pastoral' (2. 4); and his Wynken recalls how Rowland 'Upon the Beechen tree.../Carved this rime of loves Idolatrie' (2. 67-9). In the Vergilian *rota* of modes, *fagus* (beech) is assigned to pastoral.[6]

Even so, the writing of names on trees is not generically so simple. Other trees might be written on: in Helen's epithalamium 'I am Helen's' is cut into the platan tree (Theocritus, *Idylls* 18.47); Ovid's Paris scribbles 'Oenone' on the poplar. And the trees inscribed had different genre associations. Some species need work: others, self-seeding, spring up *sponte sua*, of their own free will.[7] Oak leaves, for example, were the garland of heroic honour.[8] In late antiquity, Longus's *Daphne and Chloe* modulated the names on trees topos into the romance mode; and in

---

[4] Cf. Propertius, *Elegies* 1.18.1-4, 19-22, where the grieving lover calls on the beech and pine to bear witness 'how often my passionate words echo beneath your delicate shades, how often Cynthia's name is carved upon your bark'; or Calpurnius *Eclogues* 6, where Ornytus finds a prophecy carved by Faunus on the bark of a beech tree. See W. Leonard Grant, *Neo-Latin Literature and the Pastoral* (Chapel Hill, NC: University of North Carolina Press, 1965) 73.

[5] Jacopo Sannazaro, *Arcadia and Piscatorial Eclogues*, tr. Ralph Nash (Wayne State University Press, 1966) 48, 57.

[6] See Edmond Faral, *Les Arts poétique du 12ᵉ du 13ᵉ* (Paris: Bibliothèque de l'école des hautes études, 1962) 87.

[7] *Georgics* 2.11: an iconic phrase in georgic, epitomizing nature's response to prudent cultivation.

[8] The *rota Vergiliana* assigns fruit trees to georgic, laurel and cedar to epic. Julius Caesar Scaliger regarded forester eclogues as distinct from pastoral; see *Poetice* (Lyons, 1561) 3.99 and 1.4.

the Renaissance this led by way of Ariosto and Honoré d'Urfé to Orlando's sylvan writing in Shakespeare's *As You Like It*. Names appeared on so many trees in Ariosto and Tasso that they provide material for a fine monograph by Rensselaer Lee.[9] And the topos found both epitome and finesse in an emblem by Jacob Cats, where the inscription appears on a gourd—a writing surface selected for its exceptionally rapid growth.[10]

The motive of inscription ranged far from pastoral amours. In ancient Greek literature, for example, it often seems to be admiration or commemoration. Sometimes it was political, as in Aristophanes (*Acharnians* 143). It has been attributed to a primitive impulse.[11] If so, it was an impulse the sophisticated Callimachus could share: in *Aetia* 73 he adjures a tree 'on your bark may you bear so many letters as might say "Cydippe is beautiful."' Still more sophisticated is *Greek Anthology* 12. 130, where the anonymous epigrammatist anticipates Petrarch's internalizations, reiterating that Dositheus is fair, and adding 'These words were engraved on no oak or pine, no, nor on a wall, but Love burnt them into my heart.'[12] Love and commemoration combine in an epithalamium for Helen and Menelaus. And they combine again in an early sixteenth-century ode where Jean Salmon carves his bride's name Gelonis on every tree he comes to.[13] Another motive altogether is prophecy, as in the first of Calpurnius' courtly *Eclogues*, in which Ornytus discovers a tree carved by Faunus himself. The inscription foretells that 'wars shall cease, peace shall return, bringing with it a new age of Saturn.'[14]

Sannazaro, who reshaped several genres for the Renaissance, was keenly aware of the generic hybridity of the topos, with its interweaving of art and nature. In the Prologue to *Arcadia* (1504), he contrasts the Book of Nature with the gilded pages of art: 'woodland songs carved on the rugged barks of beeches no less delight the one who reads them than do learned verses written on the smooth pages of gilded books.' He pretends, however, to prefer 'the lowly pipe of Corydon' to 'the sounding flute of Pallas' with its dangerous, Marsyas-like ambitions.[15] Mixture of art and nature, pastoral and georgic and even epic, is never far from writing on the topos. Simply to carve required an edged tool, entailing technology foreign to pastoral.

---

[9] See Rensselaer W. Lee, *Names on Trees: Ariosto into Art* (Princeton, NJ: Princeton University Press, 1977), 13, 41, and Index, s. v. *Ariosto*; cf. *FMR* 38 (1988) 23. See also Eugene R. Cunnar, 'Names on Trees, the Hermaphrodite, and "The Garden",' in *Celebrated and Neglected Poems of Andrew Marvell*, ed. Claude J, Summers and Ted-Larry Pebworth (Columbia, MO and London: University of Missouri Press, 1992) 122–9.

[10] Jacob Cats, *Proteus* (Rotterdam: van Waesberge, 1627) Fig.35 and n. 3; see Kahren Jones Hellerstedt, *Gardens of Earthly Delight* (Pittsburgh, PA: Frick Art Museum, 1986) 59.

[11] E.g. by Lee, *Names on Trees* 9 and C. G. Osgood in *Variorum Spenser* 4.210 suggest.

[12] Cf. Andrew Marvell, 'Upon the Hill and Grove at Bill-borow,' lines 43–8.

[13] Lee, *Names on Trees* 101 n. 88.   [14] Grant, *Neo-Latin Literature* 73.

[15] Sannazaro, *Arcadia* 30; see Lee, *Names on Trees* 9–11.

The prophetic oak

Jonson's 'To Penshurst', too, offers a mixture of genres. As Harris Friedberg puts it,

> the poem's concern with the natural world, and especially with man's relations with nature, forces it into a complex relationship with the more fictive poetic genres of pastoral and georgic. In 'Penshurst' Jonson describes a landscape in which real and ideal meet. The poem reveals him drawing on different generic resources to link that ideality to the real world.[16]

The first trees Jonson names, 'the broad beech and the chestnut shade' (11–12), recall Sannazaro's first chapter—the *locus amoenus* of a mount shaded by 'a dozen or fifteen trees of special beauty' including beech and chestnut—and suggest pastoral idyll. At Penshurst's Mount (viewing-mount cum local Parnassus) dryads resort 'taken with...flames' of love, and 'many a sylvan' has cut her name. However, the 'writhed bark' in which they inscribe their names is neither beech nor chestnut, but 'that taller tree,' the oak. This oak was set 'at his great birth, where all the Muses met': it is Sidney's Oak, or the Bear's Oak, grown from an acorn planted on 30 November 1554.[17]

The loves of the sylvans (dwellers on the estate) are elevated above ordinary pastoral amours by association with Sir Philip Sidney, the celebrated lover of Stella. Sidney continued to be an amorous *genius loci* for a later generation, when in 1645 Edmund Waller disbelieved his cruel mistress Dorothea could be sprung from the same noble strain

> ...that could so far exalt the name
> Of love, and warm our nation with his flame;
> That all we can of love, or high desire,
> Seems but the smoke of amorous Sidney's fire.[18]
>
> (Waller, 'At Penshurst [II]' 11–14)

'That taller tree', which will be 'the sacred mark of Sidney's birth' to Waller, already in Jonson's poem has a prophetic significance. Like the *magni Caesaris arbor*, the

---

[16] Harris Friedberg, 'Ben Jonson's Poetry: Pastoral, Georgic, Epigram,' *English Literary Renaissance*, 4 (1974) 127. Barbara Lewalski finds 'pastoral *otium* happily associated with georgic cultivation' in Penshurst; see her 'Literature and the Household' in *The Cambridge History of Early Modern English Literature*, ed. David Loewenstein and Janel Mueller (Cambridge University Press, 2002), 603.

[17] For the bear and ragged staff as a badge of the Dudleys, see *Ben Jonson*, ed. C. H. Herford and Percy Simpson, 11 vols. (Oxford: Clarendon Press, [1925–52] 1965) 11.33.

[18] Edmund Waller, *The Poems*, ed. G. Thorn Drury (London and New York, 1893) 64; cf. 46–7. Fowler, *The Country House Poem* 184; cf. 181–2.

plane tree planted by Julius Caesar, it emblemizes greatness in its aspiration to heaven: *viret et ramis sidera celsa petit*.[19] In the brilliant translation of Martial's epigram by Thomas May (1595–1650),

> In midst of th'house, her gods o'ershadowing,
> Does Caesar's plane tree prosperously spring,
> Planted by that victorious guest from whose
> Imperial hand the tender twig arose;
> Which now it seems her lord and founder knows,
> She spreads so fast her sky-aspiring boughs.
> Under that shade the rustic dryads
> And wanton fauns themselves with sporting please...[20]
>
> (May, *Epigrams* 9. 62, ll. 5–12)

Sidney's oak functions as a family tree. Such emblematic trees were a feature of estate poems,[21] just as in many actual country-houses a genealogical tree figured in murals or panel paintings. Identified with the Sidneys, the oak prophesizes their greatness. Such landmark trees, identified with a notable individual or a family's destiny and growing with them in fame, include the Hartshorn tree in Whinfell Forest;[22] Captain Shenton's tree (a wych elm); the Stanhope cedar; the Abbot's oak; the Major oak at Edwinstone; Shakespeare's crabtree; and the Queen's oak at Yardley Gobion.[23]

Had the Sidney tree truly grown taller in Robert? Taller than in Philip, the icon of chivalric honour? In terms of hierarchic nobility, it had. The hot-tempered and quarrelsome Philip lacked advancement beyond a knighthood and the Governorship of Flushing.[24] For Robert, however, the Flushing Governorship was only a beginning. Under Elizabeth, the Cecil and Cobham faction played on suspicions of the Sidneys' militant Protestantism and their involvement in Leicester's dangerous independence, and denied Robert the Wardenship of the

---

[19] Martial 9.61.5–14; see Fowler, *The Country House Poem*, 104. Cf. Vergil's poplar in Suetonius, *Vita Vergilii* 5; Cicero, *De Legibus* 1: 'no tree nourished by a farmer's care can be so long lived as one planted by a poet's verses.'

[20] *Selected Epigrams of Martial* (1629), Sigs D6r–v.

[21] E.g. Richard Fanshawe, 'Upon Occasion of His Majesty's Proclamation' 129–30, 'Plant trees you may, and see them shoot / Up with your children'; see Fowler, *The Country House Poem* 126; also Andrew Marvell, 'Upon Appleton House' 737–44.

[22] Mentioned in Camden, *Britannia* and in Anne Clifford, *Memoirs* (1658). For other examples see Keith Thomas, *Man and the Natural World: Changing Attitudes in England 1500–1800* (Penguin [1983] 1984) 217.

[23] See Jennifer Westwood and Jacqueline Simpson, *The Lore of the Land* (Penguin, 2005) Index, s. v. *Trees*; John Ayto, ed. *Brewer's Dictionary* ([1870] 2005) Index, s. v. *Oaks*; Lee, *Names on Trees* 109–10.

[24] See Katherine Duncan-Jones, *Sir Philip Sidney: Courtier Poet* (New Haven, CT, & London: Yale University Press, 1991) p. xii.

Cinque Ports (which an earlier Sidney had held).²⁵ But after James's accession things were different. Robert's statesmanship and faithful service won promotion after promotion: Baron Sidney and Chamberlain to Queen Anne in 1603, Viscount Lisle in 1605, Knight of the Garter in 1616, and Earl of Leicester in 1618.

Besides, Robert represented nobility of another sort, valued more highly by Jonson, who was unimpressed by his older brother Philip. In his encomium, Jonson praises no mere careerist or carpet knight. Knighted for bravery at Zutphen, and having succeeded his brother at Flushing, Robert fought alongside the Netherlanders in their struggle for freedom (as Jonson himself had done). In a difficult situation with responsibilities for which he was often denied adequate resources, he continued to carry out his dull office despite the false accusations of envious detractors. Robert was wounded at the siege of Steenwyck (1592) and personally engaged the Spanish with distinction at the battle of Turnhout (1598). In England, too, Robert served his country without financial gain to himself. MP for Glamorgan in 1584 and 1593, he was elected Senior Knight of the Shire for Kent in 1597. Most directly, his promotion rewarded successful diplomatic missions to Spain and France as well as Scotland—expensive embassies that cost him dear. Such statesmanship reflected a maturity and moral stature beyond anything his brother displayed. At Flushing he even managed to cooperate with Burghley and Cecil in the national interest. Robert's advancement was earned many times over.

Praise and blame

Several critics, from Richard Newton to William Cain and Victoria Moul, have seized on the frequently negative diction of 'To Penshurst,' inferring ambivalence on Jonson's part, and insecure relations with his patron. This line of criticism has been decisively countered by Richard Peterson, Michael McCanles, and Robert Evans, who characterize Jonson's encomiastic method more persuasively. Their analyses show how Jonson praises role models by contrasting other, opposite types. He sets exemplars of *vera nobilitas*, true nobility or 'ancient virtue,' against opposing, empty figures possessed of only the outward trappings of nobility.²⁶ Because of this, Jonson's encomia are generally mixed with blame. His models

---

²⁵ See Hay, *Life of Robert Sidney* 26–7, 36, 138–9, 155. On Lisle's relations with Burghley, Cecil, and Cobham, see pp. 156, 163.

²⁶ Richard S. Peterson, *Imitation and Praise in the Poems of Ben Jonson* (New Haven, CT, & London: Yale University Press, 1981; 2nd edn., Ashgate, 2011) ch. 2; Michael McCanles, *Jonsonian Discriminations: The Humanist Poet and the Praise of True Nobility* (University of Toronto Press, 1992); Robert C. Evans, 'The Politics of Jonson's house Poems' in *Ben Jonson and the Politics of Genre*, ed. A. D. Cousins and Alison V. Scott (Cambridge University Press, 2009); Blair Worden, *The Sound of Virtue: Philip Sidney's Arcadia and Elizabethan Politics* (New Haven, CT, & London: Yale University Press, 1996) 69–78 on 'ancient nobility'.

shine—as Lord Lisle does here—against the foil of obnoxious figures such as Cecil or Inigo Jones. Lisle 'dwells' in his noble pile Penshurst, unlike certain others (Cobham?) who merely accumulate 'heaps.'[27] Or again, Jonson will contrast types of hospitality. At Penshurst 'all come in,' whereas Cecil's ostentatious show of hospitality kept Jonson 'at the end of my Lord Salisburie's table with Inigo Jones.' Jonson complained that he was not given the same food as his host.[28]

Critical approaches to the estate poem have not always been appreciative. They comes up against the alterity of great house life, the strangeness of the early modern household.[29] Baffled by a type of community with few modern analogues, critics have tended to rely on ideology and anachronism. Williams is so sure of the iniquity of the landowning classes (and therefore of Lisle) that he misreads 'To Penshurst' as attempting to undo the curse of labour 'by a simple extraction of the existence of labourers'. James Turner, a deeper scholar, sees this to be wrong: 'waiters and cheese-makers are not abstracted...nor are sturdy farm girls and grateful farmers.'[30] (And he might have added that Jonson includes the occupations of huntsman, herdsman, groom, gamekeeper, shepherd, fisherman, gardener, countryman, brewer, baker, vine-grower, butcher, stable-boy, butler, and of course mason.) Unfortunately, Turner tries to save the appearances of Williams's interpretation by distinguishing two sorts of country activities. He believes Jonson selects activities 'innocent' of fire and excludes those requiring 'guilty' technology. However, 'guilty' activities are far from absent. Time and again Penhurst life calls for metal-working and other technology. How else is heating (1. 73) provided? How else, walls of country stone reared (1. 45)? And how are sylvans' names cut (1. 15)? Jonson's Penshurst is no unreal paradise. He expects us to recognize 'the presence of an Edenic reciprocity between man and nature, a natural fecundity so overwhelming that it justifies the sense of the hyperbole.'[31] Much of the poem, however, praises and amplifies the contributions of workers.[32]

Other critics, equally reluctant to envisage a virtuous landowner, have taken Jonson's negative rhetoric as a guide to the whole poem. Victoria Moul, for example, detects underlying satire everywhere: beneath the 'apparent idyll' of

---

[27] See Alastair Fowler, 'The Better Marks of Jonson's "To Penshurst"', *Review of English Studies*, 24 (1973) 266–82; Peterson, *Imitation and Praise* 80; McCanles, *Jonsonian Discriminations*.

[28] Food differentials were a common complaint of ancient satirists; see Lucian, *Saturnalia* 17; Juvenal v. 30–2; Martial 3.60.1–9. In the early seventeenth century poets were usually seated with the chaplain and the women, or else at the lord's table, not below the salt as is sometimes said.

[29] On the great household, see Gladys Scott Thomson, *Life in a Noble Household 1641–1700* (Cape, 1937); Kate Mertes, *The English Noble Household 1250–1600* (Oxford: Blackwell, 1988); Felicity Heal, *Hospitality in Early Modern England* (Oxford: Clarendon Press, 1990); C. M. Woolgar, *The Great Household in Late Medieval England*. (New Haven, CT, and London: Yale University Press, 1999); Kari Boyd McBride, *Country House Discourse in Early Modern England* (Aldershot: Ashgate, 2001); R. C. Richardson, *Household Servants in Early Modern England* (Manchester and New York: Manchester University Press, 2010).

[30] Turner, *Politics of Landscape* 164.   [31] Friedberg, 'Jonson's Poetry' 127.

[32] Williams, *The Country and the City* (London: Chatto & Windus, 1973) 32.

Penshurst is 'deepening satiric scene-setting'. She finds Jonson's allusion to the 'reign of terror' under Domitian 'unsettling' and 'discomfiting'. Jonson must have introduced Juvenal's 'gross turbot' to imply that with Lisle too 'there is nothing...godlike power won't believe of itself when it comes to being praised.'[33] She shares William Cain's 'anxiety' at the 'uncomfortable evocation of tribute, predation and even cannibalism within the animal kingdom'.[34]

Cain and Moul seem to have in mind a full-blown version of the feudal system, as if that still existed in Jonson's England. Actually it lay in the past, replaced now by a flexible structure of individual agreements, whereby a lord could stop annuities and a retainer could transfer his services.[35] Even the relationships in so-called 'bastard feudalism' had been greatly modified since the fifteenth century. 'Any one lord's control over a tenant, who might hold parcels of land of several other lords besides himself, had been eroded.'[36] Hierarchy, no longer military, was now a matter of domestic relationships between lords and their *familiares* and annuitants.[37] The parliaments of 1604 and 1610 showed the system of feudal tenures to be obsolete, even in its fiscal embodiment: the king's honour no longer depended on landlordship. As Bacon argued, 'James would lose nothing by relinquishing his claim to landlordship. The real hierarchy of tenure was based instead on merits.'[38] Against this, Cecil took a great magnate's view, cautioning 'that if the king do depart and lose those forms, then both myself and the rest of your Lordships shall lose your tenures and wardships that do depend of you.'[39] Jonson admired Bacon, and in 'To Penshurst' takes his side on this against Cecil's.[40]

So Penshurst presents 'an ideal image of the king's commonwealth,' and Lisle's ideal lordship. Questions of tenure never arise, since the entire estate offers itself in service. Lisle becomes simply 'housekeeper' or host: his are the Penates, the household gods 'set on flame' (1. 79) with zeal to entertain the king and others. In a peaceful kingdom the Penates signify habitation and hospitality, while the king is a welcome guest. The crown poses no threat to the country.[41] Jonson's politics here are both constitutional and factional. He praises Lisle and all those who

---

[33] Victoria Moul, *Jonson, Horace and the Classical Tradition* (Cambridge University Press, 2010) 127–8.
[34] Wiliam E. Cain, 'The Place of the Poet in Jonson's "To Penshurst" and "To My Muse"', *Criticism*, 21 (1979) 37; Moul, *Jonson, Horace* 128.
[35] See Maurice Keen, *English Society in the later Middle Ages 1348–1500* (Allen Lane, 1990) 17–23.
[36] Keen, *English Society* 20.   [37] See Keen, *English Society* 21 n.
[38] See Martin Elsky, 'Ben Jonson's Poems of Place and the Culture of Land: From the Military to the Domestic', *English Literary Renaissance*, 31 (2001) 392–411.
[39] Elsky 'Jonson's Poems of Place' 402–3. See also Elsky, 'The mixed Genre of Ben Jonson's *To Penshurst* and the Perilous Springs of Netherlandish Landscape', *Ben Jonson Journal*, 9 (2002) 1–35.
[40] Cf. Elsky, 'Jonson's Poems of Place' 403–9.
[41] Ibid. 410; Michael G. Brennan, *The Sidneys of Penshurst and the Monarchy, 1500–1700* (Aldershot: Ashgate, 2006).

practice good lordship: he satirizes Cecil and all addicted to display, who are devoid of ancient virtue and service and true hospitality.[42]

Patronage

That 'To Penshurst' is a poem of patronage presents further difficulties to critics. They recall perhaps Dr Johnson's definition of a patron as 'commonly a wretch who supports with insolence, and is paid with flattery.' Cain, for example, regards patronage in a wholly negative light: 'For nearly all poets in the Renaissance, the patronage system was a grim fact of life, and Jonson was no exception.'[43] Moul writes of Jonson as responding to 'the problem of freedom in a climate of patronage'; and R. V. Young takes it for granted that 'Jonson is flattering a patron.'[44] How can such views be reconciled with Jonson's declaration that 'he would not flatter though he saw Death'?[45]

Studies of patronage have come a long way in recent decades and now show it in a mostly favourable light.[46] We are now inclined to recall Dr Johnson's other definition of a patron as 'one who countenances, supports, or protects.'[47] Early modern literature would have been impossible without patrons. They had a role not much unlike that of modern arts councils, universities, and other funding agencies. Renaissance patrons (often themselves writers) supported likely beginners, acknowledging affinities of distant kinship and geographical proximity alike. Patronage could even transcend factional and ideological limits. To some extent

---

[42] Cecil's house Theobalds was so grand that King James exchanged it for the manor of Hatfield; in 1607 the ownership was transferred to Queen Anne; see Jonson's *An Entertainment of King James and Quene Anne, at Theobalds*; Ian Donaldson, *Ben Jonson: A Life* (Oxford University Press, 2012) 362.

[43] Cain, 'The Place of the Poet' 40.

[44] Moul, *Jonson, Horace* 12; R. V. Young, 'Ben Jonson and Learning', in *The Cambridge Companion to Ben Jonson*, ed. Richard Harp and Stanley Stewart (Cambridge University Press, 2000) 55.

[45] *Conversations with Drummond*, in *Ben Jonson*, ed. Herford and Simpson 1.141, 1.332.

[46] See e.g. Ronald D. S. Jack, 'James VI and I as Patron', in *Europäische Hofkultur im 16. und 17. Jahrhundert*, ed. August Buck et al. (Hamburg: Hauswedell, 1979) 179–85; Mary Ellen Lamb, 'The Countess of Pembroke's Patronage', *English Literary Renaissance*, 12 (1982); French R. Fogle and Louis A. Knafla, *Patronage in Late Renaissance England* (Los Angeles: Clark Library, 1983); Margaret P. Hannay, ed. *Silent but for the Word: Tudor Women as Patrons, Translators, and Writers of Religious Works* (Kent, OH: Kent State University Press, 1985); David Loades, *The Tudor Court* (New York: Barnes & Noble, 1986); Coburn Freer, 'Mary Sidney: Countess of Pembroke' in *Women Writers of the Renaissance and Reformation*, ed. Katharina M. Wilson (Athens, GA: University of Georgia Press, 1987) 481–521; R. Malcolm Smuts, *Court Culture and the Origins of the Royalist Tradition in Early Stuart England* (University of Pennsylvania Press, 1987); Michael G. Brennan, *The Sidneys of Penshurst and the Monarchy, 1500–1700* (Aldershot: Ashgate, 2006); Linda Levy Peck, *Court Patronage and Corruption in Early Stuart England* (London: Unwin Hyman, 1990); M. D. Jardine, 'New Historicism for Old: New Conservatism for Old: The Politics of Patronage in the Renaissance', *Year's Work in English Studies*, 21 (1991) 286–304; Sharon Kettering, *Patronage in Sixteenth- and Seventeenth-Century France* (Aldershot: Ashgate, 2002); David Howarth, ed., *Art and Patronage in the Caroline Courts* (Cambridge University Press, 1993).

[47] Samuel Johnson, *A Dictionary of the English Language*, s. v. *Patron*, 1.

this is true of the project of Psalm translations closely associated with the Sidney family. Philip Sidney himself translated some Psalms, which according to Jonson 'went abroad under the name of the Countesse of Pembrock.'[48] After his death, the countess continued their work, and her relation with her niece Mary Wroth, too, was as much collaboration as patronage.[49] The Sidneys' patronage of Psalm translation and paraphrase explains the structure of 'To Penshurst', for it is structured like the book of Psalms as 3 × 17 couplets.[50] A turbot willing to sacrifice itself features prominently in the central passage, in witty allusion to the sacred acrostic of Jesus as Ichthus (fish): I$_5$HTP, *Iesos Christos Theos Huios Soter*, Jesus Christ God, Son, Saviour. In exegetic tradition the miraculous catch in John 21 was connected with the symbolism of 17.[51]

As a patron Lisle had other clients besides Jonson—was in fact a generous patron of letters. Considering the magnitude of his debts, he did well to have dedicated to him nearly forty works, far more than his famous brother Philip. (Lady Lisle received five more dedications, Mary Wroth ten, and the Countess of Pembroke more than twenty.[52]) The dedications to Robert range widely in character, from Abraham Fraunce's *Symbolicae Philosophia* to Simon Robson's *The Choice of Change* (1585) and an edition of Tacitus' Life of Agricola (1585). Poetic dedications include George Wither's *Elegies* (1612) upon Prince Henry and Joshua Sylvester's *Lachrimae lachrimarum* (1613), Thomas Powell's, Thomas Moffet, Sir John Davies, Robert Jones, John Dowland, George Chapman (the *Iliads*), and Sir Thomas Wroth's translation of *Aeneid* 3.[53] Dedications to Barbara have a narrower range: Sylvester twice (1613 and 1614) and a translation from Jean Taffin's *The Marks of the Children of God* (1608). Wealthier magnates, of course, could exercise patronage on a grander scale: the first Earl of Leicester received almost twice as many dedications as Philip and Robert Sidney together.

Jonson for his part had other patrons besides Robert Sidney, notably Esmé Stuart, Lord Aubigny, William Herbert, Earl of Pembroke. As Lord Chamberlain Pembroke knew Jonson well, and annually made him a generous book allowance. Then, Jonson received a court pension from King James, and another from William Cavendish, Earl of Newcastle.[54] But Jonson's relationship with Robert Sidney was closer. They seem to have been on a footing of friendship, enjoying

---

[48] *Conversations with Drummond*, in *Ben Jonson*, ed. Herford and Simpson 1.138.
[49] See Mary Sidney Herbert, Countess of Pembroke, *The Collected Works*, ed. Margaret P. Hannay, Noel J. Kinnamon, and Michael G. Brennan (Oxford: Clarendon Press, 1998) 1.47–9.
[50] See Alastair Fowler, *Conceitful Thought* (Edinburgh University Press, 1971) 126–7. 'Meridianis', Michael Drayton's anagram for Mari Sidnei appears in Amour 51, *Ideas Mirrour* (1594); see Mary Sidney Herbert, *Works* 1.27.
[51] Fowler, *Conceitful Thought* 126; Bungus, *Mysteria Numerorum* (Bergamo, 1591) 594–5.
[52] On the improbable notion that Lady Lisle was illiterate, see Robert Sidney, *Poems*, ed. P. J. Croft (Oxford: Clarendon Press, 1984) 77–8. She may have been ashamed of her bad handwriting.
[53] See Hay, *Life of Robert Sidney*, 206–7; W. David Kay, *Ben Jonson: A Literary Life* (Basingstoke: Macmillan, 1995) 114–35.
[54] See Ian Donaldson's *ODNB* entry; Jonson, ed. Herford and Simpson 1.55.

the mutual respect of poets and men of letters. Some have supposed them sundered by the distance of rank, and even speculated that Jonson only visited Penshurst on a single occasion. But Rathmell's important article of 1971, based on contemporary correspondence and other papers in the Sidney archive, show Jonson's account of the estate and the household to be based on intimate knowledge.[55] The closeness of his connection with the family is reflected in the many poems he addressed to its members—Robert's daughters Philippa and Mary Sidney (Lady Wroth); his neice, Elizabeth Countess of Rutland; his nephew, William, Earl of Pembroke; and his son-in-law, Sir Robert Wroth—who were all at Penshurst in the summer of 1611.[56] 'To Penshurst' is 'grounded in Jonson's intimate knowledge of the Sidney family.'[57]

Lisle's familiars freely counselled him—as his estate agent Thomas Golding did, against the meditated extravagance of enlarging Penshurst park.[58] Similarly Jonson discourages Lisle from other extravagances that evidently tempt him despite his debts, by focussing the poem on the 'better marks' of Penshurst itself, its natural resources and moral worth.[59] He dwells on the trees (but not their value as a realizable asset) and on the orchard Lisle took great pride in, ordering fruit trees from as far as Brabant.[60] In 1611 they had cherries, plums, melicotons, peaches, pears, apples, and apricots. (Lady Lisle made frequent use of the fruit as generous presents to friends at court.) Cultivating the orchard was more commensurate with Lisle's precarious finances than building projects like those at neighbouring Knole. Less prudently, Jonson praises Lisle's traditionally unlimited hospitality, housekeeping that was greatly increasing his mountainous debts. Lisle was not one of those housekeepers who charged guests for fire, stabling, and the like.[61]

Lisle's rank—viscount and soon to be earl—may have obscured the facts of his intimacy with Jonson. Not until the contextual studies initiated by Rathmell expanded by Millicent Hay in her wonderfully detailed biography was it clear how much Jonson and Lisle had in common.[62] Both were poets and both engaged in mounting theatrical entertainments. They shared political independence and

---

[55] See J. C. A. Rathmell, 'Jonson, Lord Lisle, and Penshurst', *English Literary Renaissance*, 1 (1971) 259–60 *et passim*; Don E. Wayne, *Penshurst: The Semiotics of Place and the Poetics of History* (London: Methuen, 1984) 70–3.

[56] See Hannay, *Mary Sidney* 153; Rathmell, 'Jonson, Lord Lisle, and Penshurst' 250.

[57] Ibid. 259–60.

[58] Cf. his steward's comment that painting the columns of Lady Lisle's Banqueting House with fashionable marbling would be 'very chargeable'; see Rathmell, 'Jonson, Lord Lisle, and Penshurst' 257.

[59] See Lawrence Stone, *The Crisis of the Aristocracy 1558–1641* (Oxford: Clarendon Press, 1965) 564 on Robert's large expenditure on masque and court outfits, necessary equipment for an ambitious courtier.

[60] See Rathmell, 'Jonson, Lord Lisle, and Penshurst' 253.

[61] Ibid. 250, 255, 257; cf. Turner, *Politics of Landscape* 143.

[62] See Rathmell, 'Jonson, Lord Lisle, and Penshurst'; Wayne, *Penshurst*; Croft's Introduction to Robert Sidney's *Poems*; and Margaret P. Hannay et al., eds. *Domestic Politics and Family Absence* (Aldershot: Ashgate, 2005).

unswerving loyalty to their sovereign. And they shared responsibility for educating his sons. (Jonson clearly had a tutorial relation with William, and in all likelihood acted formally as his tutor.[63]) These common interests would naturally foster intimacy. Jonson praised Lisle because he thought him to merit praise: why should he flatter such a friend?

Jonson's praise of Lady Lisle as 'noble, fruitful, chaste withal' is equally appropriate. She bore two sons and eight daughters, and was so attached to her sons as to be reluctant to let them leave to keep term at Oxford.[64] As for Jonson's praise of her chastity, it reminds Moul 'almost to the point of scepticism…of the everyday (satirical) reality of avarice and dishonesty'.[65] It was certainly far from gratuitous in an age thought dissolute by more than satirists. But Jonson's formulation is proverbial rather than satiric.[66]

Objects of satire

What then of Jonson's allusion to Juvenal's satire of Domitian in the 'mock-epic turbot' wanting to be caught? Moul infers satire of a desire for flattery: "it wanted to be caught.' What could be more blatant? But still his comb rose with pleasure. There is nothing at all that godlike power won't believe of itself when it comes to being praised."[67] Juvenal denounced Domitian's appetite for flattery, so Jonson must similarly be denouncing Lisle's appetite for flattery. Jonson certainly knew the passage in Juvenal's fourth satire: he mentioned it to Drummond. But Cain and Moul, intent on the hermeneutics of suspicion, miss the pragmatic situation. Far from proving their point, Jonson's insincere flattery disproves it. 'All he says could be dismissed as flattery of the grossest kind'. Yes, he fairly piles it on: that is how you praise a friend—with jokey, over-the-top flattery. Jonson's self-sacrificial pike (not turbot) cannot be a serious allusion to Juvenal. For the difficulty of taking large fish at Penshurst was notorious.[68] What Moul takes to be Jonson 'labouring the point' is Jonson not making a point at all, but a joke. Every creature on the Penshurst estate serves its lord—even the pikes. He signals his facetious tone by the terrible piscine pun 'oFISHously…themselves betray' (line 36).

---

[63] See Rathmell, 'Jonson, Lord Lisle, and Penshurst' 251. [64] Ibid. 253-4.
[65] Moul, *Jonson, Horace* 130-1.
[66] E.g. John Donne, *The Sermons*, ed. George R. Potter and Evelyn M. Simpson, 10 vols. (Berkeley: University of California Press, [1953] 1984) 2.101 line 245. Indeed, there were examples near at hand in the open adultery of William Herbert and William Sidney's seduction of a Maid of Honour; see Mary Sidney Herbert, *Works* 1.10, 18.
[67] Juvenal, *Satires* 4.39, 68-71.
[68] On 20 May 1612 two of Sir Robert Wroth's men, fishing for large fish, 'have not met with a carp, bream, or pike. They now confess that our river is hard to be fished, the great fish keeping the deep still waters, and those so full of old wood as they cannot devise how to use…their…nets in those holds' (Historical MSS Commission, Lisle 77.5.56); see Fowler, *Country House Poem* 60.

Penshurst hospitality extends to all who dwell about the walls, both tenant farmer and 'clown' (countryman). Yet when 'all come in' at Penshurst, 'no one empty-handed', critics' hackles rise: the gifts must be denied. Why should the gifts not be brought, as Jonson says, 'to salute' the Lisles and express their love? Would this be so very different from the modern courtesy of hostess gifts?

The question arises *when* it is that all come in. On some festive occasion? Or do they come in separately, on separate occasions? Don Wayne and Rhonda Lemke Sanford are in no doubt the occasion is rent day: 'What all of this seems to be referring to in actuality is the payment of *rent in kind* by peasants on the Sidney lands.'[69] But feudal 'rents' in kind had long gone out in Kent, where the rural economy was monetarized from the twelfth century. (Much later, landlords in the north and west still received rents in commodities.[70]) The visitors give presents to express love (57)—hardly how one talks of paying the rent.[71] These presents are chosen at discretion, not stipulated by a 'contractual arrangement'. When sixteenth-century inflation made the rights of overlordship over freeholders 'financially almost valueless', large landowners sometimes took rent from substantial tenant farmers 'in the form of a fixed quantity of foodstuffs'.[72] But this was done by contracts, entered into for mutual benefit. It could hardly be the case with bringers of nuts. Besides, Jonson specifically denies that Lisle is dependent on these gifts (line 59). A cheese-maker's pride would hardly be aroused by obligatory rent, and '*better* cheeses' implies that not all the cheese-makers pay this tribute. This hospitality is free to all, not only rent-payers. A thorough article by Robert Evans has demolished the demystifiers' arguments.[73] No-one familiar with Lisle's biography (with his popularity, with his compassion for the needy, his care even for the poor Dutch merchants of Flushing) could suppose for a moment that Jonson is satirizing his friend and patron.

If there is any satire of the entertainment, it is Jonson's self-satire. 'Vindicative...at himself,'[74] he almost boastfully confesses to being a greedy guest:

---

[69] Wayne, Penshurst 67; Rhonda Lemke Sanford, *Maps and Memory in Early Modern England: A Sense of Place* (New York: Palgrave, 2002) 85. Cf. Moul, *Jonson, Horace* 126 ('overtones of tribute'); Michael C. Schoenfeld, 'To Penshurst' in *The Muses Common-Weale*, ed. Claude J. Summers and Ted-Larry Pebworth (Columbia, MO: University of Missouri Press, 1988) 75, condemning the exaction of rent from those who 'have no suit'.

[70] See R. W. Hoyle, 'Rural Economy and Society' in *Trade and Economic Developments, 1450–1550: the Experience of Kent, Surrey, and Sussex*, ed. Mavis E. Mate (Woodbridge: Boydell, 2006); R. W. Hoyle, *A Companion to Tudor Britain* (Oxford: Wiley-Blackwell, 2004) ch. 19; R. W. Hoyle, *Economic History Review*, 60.1 (2007) 190. See also Eric Kerridge, *Agrarian Problems in the sixteenth century and after* ([1967] Taylor and Francis, 2006); Mark Overton, *Agricultural Revolution in England*, Cambridge Studies in Historical Geography (Cambridge University Press, 1996). Fowler, *Country House Poem* 11, 58.

[71] See Heal, *Hospitality*, Index, 'Gifts exchanged and reciprocity'.

[72] Stone, *Crisis of the Aristocracy* 144, 301.

[73] Robert C. Evans, *Ben Jonson and the Poetics of Patronage* (Lewisburg, PA: Bucknell University Press, 1989) 77–8.

[74] *Conversations with Drummond* in Jonson, ed. Herford and Simpson 1.151, lines 688–9.

> Here no man tells my cups, nor, standing by,
> A waiter, doth my gluttony envy...
>
> ('To Penshurst' 67-8)

He was well known to be a big eater and drinker. Drink, says Drummond, 'is one of the Elements in which he liveth.'⁷⁵ Indeed, gluttony was a pervasive feature of Jonson's public self, as Bruce Boehrer shows.⁷⁶

Jonson's gift

When all come to salute the Lisles and no-one is empty-handed, what does Jonson himself bring? Not a capon or a cake but his poem. Just as some thought they made 'the better cheeses' Jonson thought he made the better poems; he boasted to Drummond that he was 'better Versed and knew more in Greek and Latin, than all the Poets in England and quintessence[th] their braines'.⁷⁷ Appropriately, his gift is finely cast in the classical mould—more finely perhaps than is now appreciated. For it adopts the habit of the ancient poets, in their most polished verses, of interweaving covert designs: embedded anagrams, acrostics, numerical patterns, and other subtextual devices.

Gifts commonly bear the recipients' names; and so it is with 'To Penshurst'. The sylvans wrote the names of their loves on Sidney's oak: Jonson inscribes his on the leaves of his poem. 'Thy copse,' he writes, 'named of Gamage, thou hast there' (l. 19). Editors note the reference here to Lady Gamage's Bower. But the line warrants further attention; for its juxtaposing of 'Gamage' and 'thy copse' signals inscription of Barbara's family name.

Names were not always cut in a tree: they might be written on bark or paper, and hung from a branch as they were by Fronimo (Sannazaro's most accomplished of shepherds) and by Shakespeare's Orlando.⁷⁸ Renaissance artists, too, sometimes put their monogram on a classical tablet hung on a tree.⁷⁹ In this classical, Renaissance fashion, Jonson has placed Barbara Gamage's name on the Penshurst trees⁸⁰ not indeed in the poem's surface text but in the silent language of its covert subtext:

---

⁷⁵ *Conversations with Drummond* in Jonson, ed. Herford and Simpson, 1.151, lines 683–4.
⁷⁶ Bruce Boehrer, *The Fury of Men's Gullets* (Philadelphia, PA: University of Pennsylvania, 1997).
⁷⁷ *Conversations with Drummond* in Jonson, ed. Herford and Simpson 1.149, lines 622–3.
⁷⁸ Sannazaro, *Arcadia* ch. 6, p. 63; Shakespeare, *AYLI* 3.2.1–10, 124–37.
⁷⁹ E.g. Albrecht Dürer, *Adam and Eve* (1504); cf. the names hung on trees in Holbein, *The Selling of Indulgences* (1522–3). In modern times the practice continues: e.g. Leger, *Tree-Trunk on a Yellow Ground*. At the Japanese festival of Tanabata poems are tied to trees.
⁸⁰ Cf. Friedberg, 'Jonson's Poetry' 127: 'Jonson's title, and his turning to Martial for so many...details, stress the poem's origin in inscription'. Cf. p. 119 where Friedberg writes of Jonson's 'reduction of the epigram to the act of naming'.

And though thy walls [Be of the countrey stone,	B
They' Are rear'd with no mans Ruine, no mans grone,	AR
There's none, that dwell about them, wish them downe;	
But All come in, the farmeR, A]nd the clowne;	BARA
Some brin[G A capon, some a rurall cake,	GA
Some nuts, some apples; some that thinke they MAke	MA
The better cheeses, brinG 'hem; or elsE] send	GE

As usual with such embedded anagrams, only initial or final letters or letter groups are available. For the rules of embedded anagrams, see William Bellamy, *Shakespeare's Verbal Art* (2015). In this anagram the letters are in correct spelling order, but dispersed. There is another, condensed anagram in line 51, with the letters in random order and the G used twice: 'Some brinG A capon, soME A rural cake': GAMEA = GAMAGE.

Near the centre of the poem, the place of honour, Jonson embeds Latin anagrams of his patron's name. In lines 50–5, a dispersed anagram with letters in natural order will be found—SVTREBOR SVTENDIS, that is, ROBERTVS SIDNEIVS (reading upwards or backwards):[81]

Thy lord, and lady, though they haue no [SVTe.	SVT
Some bring a capon, some a Rurall cake,	R
SomE nuts, some apples; some that thinke they make	E
The Better cheeses, bring 'hem; OR] else send	BOR
By their ripe daughterS, Vvhom theI would commEND	SVIEND
ThIS] way to husbands; and whose baskets beare	IS

Among several condensed anagrams (with letters in random order) in lines 53–4 may be found

The better cheeses, [BRIng 'hem; OR ElSE SeND
BY Their ripe daughterS, VV]hom they would commend
BRIORESESNDYTSVV = ROBERTVS SIDNEIVS

In these embedded anagrams following ancient convention, Jonson honours the Lisles in a way he elsewhere honours the sovereign himself. In *The Speeches at Prince Henries Barriers* (1610) he famously embeds the anagram CHARLES IAMES STEVVART = CLAIMES ARTHVRS SEATE: 'Wise, temperate, iust, and stout, claimes ARTHVRS seat' (line 20).[82] The Lisles must have appreciated receiving an honour equal to that Jonson not long before had paid the King.

---

[81] By convention using only initial and final letters or letter groups.
[82] *Prince Henries Barriers* in *Jonson*, ed. Herford and Simpson 7.325.

Some have thought that, applied to the Lisles, amorous writing on trees becomes embellishment of the sordid political reality of a mercenary arranged marriage, to be deplored by every right-minded romantic. But Barbara Gamage was not left by her father's death 'a very young daughter and heiress.'[83] As P. J. Croft shows, she was twenty-two: older than Robert. In all probability she had already formed an attachment to him, in preference to her other suitors. A great scramble to solemnize their wedding against Sir Walter Raleigh's objections left only an hour to spare before the Queen's messenger arrived, too late to forbid the marriage.[84] Everything suggests that Robert and Barbara remained a devoted couple throughout their life.[85]

Later inscriptions

In succeeding generations, the Sidney tree continued to flourish. Edmund Waller (1606–87) wrote poems of love and patronage to another Robert Sidney, second Earl of Leicester, and to his daughter Dorothy, among them 'At Penshurst [I]', 'At Penshurst [II]', and 'To my Lord of Leicester'.[86] The last of these petitions Leicester to prefer him to Dorothy's other suitors, and was written during Leicester's embassy to the French court in 1636–9. The 'great cause' that requires his presence is not impending war but the 'domestic care' of his daughter:

For one bright nymph our youth contends,
And on your prudent choice depends.
('To My Lord of Leicester' ll. 17–18).

In lines 14–15 of the central stanza of five, dispersed and condensed anagrams of SIDNEY are presented. They read upwards like Jonson s in 'To Penshurst':

...[Your presence herE,
WhereiN there meet the DIverS] laws

And

Wher[EIN there meet the DIverS] laws
EINDIS = SIDNEY.

In 'At Penshurst [I]' Waller orders his passion to be carved on Sidney's Oak, 'the monument and pledge of humble love,' where Philip Sidney's name was already

---

[83] Lawrence Stone, *Crisis of the Aristocracy* 660.
[84] See Robert Sidney, *Poems* ed. Croft 72–81; Hay, *Life of Robert Sidney* 171.
[85] See Hay, *Life of Robert Sidney* 173 *et passim*. For inscriptions of the Lisles' initials at Penshurst, in the Long Gallery (1607) and on the postern of the main doors, see Robert Sidney, *Poems* ed. Croft 78–9.
[86] Waller, *The Poems*, ed. Thorn Drury 46–7, 64–5, 47–8.

carved by the sylvans. (If further authority was wanted, Pamela provides it in *Old Arcadia* III: 'in this growing barke [of pine] growe verses myne.'[87] And in 'At Penshurst [II],' as we saw, Waller reproaches Dorothea-Sacharissa for an unkindness (l. 20) unworthy of the daughter of a Sidney, or of her mother (another Dorothy), 'Who so well does prove / One breast may hold both chastity and love' (ll. 15–16). Apollo hears his complaint and advises 'On yon aged tree / Hang up thy lute, and hie thee to the sea.'

The apparent moral exaltation of the Sidneian love poems[88] contrasts with the sensuality of some other writing on trees. Waller refers to this when he writes 'all we can of love, or high desire, / Seems but the smoke of amorous Sidney's fire.'[89] The smoke of lust was supposed to obscure the mind, whereas fire clarified it, aspiring upward.

Perhaps Waller had in mind the erotic poetry of Thomas Carew (?1595–?1639). In 'The Rapture' (1640) Carew depicts the unrestrained, 'natural' sexuality of a Lucrece who 'reads the divine / Lectures of Loves great master, Aretine' and learns 'to move / Her plyant body in the act of love.' The inscriptions here follow Aretine's notorious *Postures*:[90] to 'quench' the rapist, Lucrece

> ...hurles
> Her limbs into a thousand winding curies,
> And studies artfull postures, such as be
> Carv'd on the barke of every neighbouring tree
> By learned hands, that so adorn'd the rinde
> Of those faire Plants, which as they lay entwined,
> Have fann'd their glowing fires.
>
> (Carew, 'The Rapture' ll. 115–25)

Confessions of love have descended here into obscene graffiti. Instead of names, the trees are defaced with diagrams of anonymous lust: what John Kerrigan calls 'erotically articulate windings.'[91]

Chaster sentiments prompt William Habington (1605–54) to ask his friend Endymion Porter to climb the forked hill of Parnassus

> ...and see if there
> Ith' barke of every Daphne, not appeare

---

[87] Waller, *The Poems*, 47 and 48; Sir Philip Sidney, *The Poems*, ed. William A. Ringler (Oxford: Clarendon Press, 1962) 77.

[88] In the popular view. For a more correct reading of *Astrophel and Stella* see Thomas P. Roche, *Petrarch and the English Sonnet Sequences* (New York: AMS, 1989) 193–242 *et passim*.

[89] Penshurst [II] 13–14, Waller, *The Poems* 64.

[90] For Aretino's *Modi*, see *Philological Quarterly*, 47.4 (1994) Books Received.

[91] 'Thomas Carew', *Proceedings of the British Academy*, 74 (1988) 333. See Leah Knight, 'Writing on Early Modern Trees', *ELR* 41.3 (2011) 462–84.

> *Castara* written; and so markt by me
> How great a Prophet growes each Virgin tree?
>
> ('To my honoured Friend, Mr. E. P.,' ll. 15–18)

With so many trees written on, one can see why the penitent Habington wonders, in another poem, where to find a 'darke silent grove' unprofaned by secular love,

> Where witty melancholy ne'er
> Did carve the trees or wound the ayre,
> Shall I religious leasure winne
> To weepe away my sinne?[92]
>
> (*Cogitabo pro peccato meo*, ll. 3–6)

His impulse is to turn to retirement.

The novelist Francis Coventry (1725–1754) revisited the Sidney trees in 'Penshurst. Inscribed to William Perry, Esq. and the Honourable Mrs Elizabeth Perry', a long poem published in Dodsley's Miscellany in 1750.[93] Addressing the 'Genius of Penshurst old,' Coventry refreshes several of the topics traced above. Here are 'sacred' trees in a landscape long associated with literary production:

> …thy tenants of yon turrets bold,
> Inspir'st to arts or arms;
> Where Sidney his Arcadian landscape drew,
>
> ('Penshurst,' ll. 4–6)

Here too is 'yonder oak' (l. 87), Sidney's oak, as Coventry's note citing Jonson's 'To Penshurst' makes clear. And here are references to Waller and Saccharissa (ll. 10, 78), the smoke and the fire:

> Here mighty Dudly once wou'd rove,
> To plan his triumphs in the grove:
> There looser Waller, every gay,
> With Sacchariss in dalliance lay;
> And Philip, side-long yonder spring,
> His lavish carols wont to sing.
>
> (Coventry, 'Penshurst,' ll. 75–80)

But oh how changed. Gone are the names carved on trees. Coventry's like Habington's is a poem of retirement. It meditates on the amours and the history

---

[92] William Habington, Poems, ed. Kenneth Allott (Liverpool University Press, 1948) 145.
[93] *A Collection of Poems*, ed. Robert Dodsley, vol. 4 (1763) 50.

enacted at Penshurst, 'where ancient bards retirement chose' (l. 85). Since Philip's time, 'patriot Algernon' has intervened—Algernon Sidney, son of the second Earl of Leicester and a prominent republican. Coventry's meditative, 'thoughtful-walking' Liberty remembers the former freedom of nobles' manners,

> Ere yet they grew refin'd to hate
> The hospitable rural seat,
> The spacious hall with tenants stor'd,
> Where Mirth and Plenty crown'd the board...
>
> (Coventry, 'Penshurst,' ll. 55–8)

The politics of the new century set liberty in opposition to 'court-idolatry' (l. 64) and 'Thraldom' against 'the genuine British look.' We are in a world not so very far from that of Raymond Williams and Don Wayne. Coventry dismantles Jonson's complex structure of implications and suggestions, and substitutes overt political abstractions. It is the sort of alteration T. S. Eliot may have had in mind when he wrote about dissociation of sensibility.

Bibliography

Alciati, Andrea, *Emblematum liber* (Augsburg: Steyner, 1531)
Alciati, Andrea, *Emblemata cum commentariis* (Padua: Pietro Paolo Tozzi, 1621; facsimile edn, New York and London: Garland, 1976)
Ariosto, Ludovico, *Ludovico Ariosto's* Orlando Furioso *Translated into English Heroical Verse by Sir John Harington (1591)*, ed. Robert McNulty (Oxford: Clarendon Press, 1972)
Auerbach, Eric, *Mimesis: The Representation of Reality in Western Literature*, trans. Willard Trask (Princeton, NJ: Princeton University Press, 1953)
Barolsky, Paul, *Infinite Jest: Wit and Humor in Italian Renaissance Art* (Columbia: University of Missouri Press, 1978)
Bacon, Francis, *Sylva sylvarum: Or a Natural Historie. In Ten Centuries* (London: W. Rawley, 1627)
Bath, Michael, Manning, John, and Young, Alan R., *The Art of the Emblem: Essays in Honor of Karl Josef Höltgen* (New York: AMS Press, 1993)
Bath, Michael, and Russell, Daniel S. (eds), *Deviceful Settings: The English Renaissance Emblem and its Contexts*, Selected Papers from the Third International Emblem Conference, Pittsburgh, 1993 (New York: AMS, 1999)
Blair, Ann, *The Theater of Nature: Jean Bodin and Renaissance Science* (Princeton, NJ: Princeton University Press, 1997)
Blayney, Peter W. M., *The Stationers' Company and the Printers of London 1501–1557*, i: *1501–1546*; ii: *1547–1557* (Cambridge: Cambridge University Press, 2013)
Boccaccio, Giovanni, *Genealogy of the Pagan Gods*, trans. Jon Solomon, I Tatti Renaissance Library (Cambridge, MA: Harvard University Press, 2011), i
Bongo, Pietro (Petrus Bungus), *Numerorum Mysteria*... (Bergamo, 1591)
Brown, Keith, 'Visualizing Hobbes', in Erik Tonning (ed.), Sightings: Selected Literary Essays (New York: Peter Lang, 2008), 177–81
Burton, Robert, *The Anatomy of Melancholy*, ed. J. B. Bamborough, Thomas C. Faulkener, et al., 6 vols (Oxford: Clarendon Press, 1989–2000)
Camden, William, *Britannia* (1607; Hildesheim and New York: Anglistica & Americana, 1970)
Campbell, Gordon, *Bible: The Story of the King James Version 1611–2011* (Oxford: Oxford University Press, 2010)
Carruthers, Mary, *The Book of Memory: A Study of Memory in Medieval Culture* (Cambridge: Cambridge University Press, 1990)
Cartari, Vincenzo, *Imagini delli dei de gl'antichi* (1556; facsimile edn, ed. Walter Koschatzky, Graz: Akademische Druck, 1963)
Cave, Terence, and Wilson, Deirdre (eds), *Reading beyond the Code: Literature and Relevance Theory* (Oxford: Oxford University Press, 2018)
Cheshire, Paul, '"I lay too many Eggs": Coleridge's "Ostrich Carelessness" and the Problem of Publication', Coleridge Bulletin, NS 23 (2004), 1–25
Christian, Lynda G., *Theatrum Mundi: The History of an Idea* (New York: Garland, 1987)
Cloud, Random, 'From Tranceformations in the Text of *Orlando Furioso*', Library Chronicle of the University of Texas at Austin, 20 (1990), 60–85
Cohen, Jane Rabb, *Dickens and his Original Illustrators* (Cambridge, MA: Harvard University Press, 1968)

Colie, Rosalie, *The Resources of Kind: Genre-Theory in the Renaissance* (Berkeley and Los Angeles: University of California Press, 1973)
Colie, Rosalie, *Shakespeare's Living Art* (Princeton, NJ: Princeton University Press, 1974)
Conti, Natale, *Mythologiae* [...] (Padua, 1616; facsimile edn, ed. Stephen Orgel, New York: Garland, 1979)
Corbett, Margery, and Lightbown, Ronald, *The Comely Frontispiece: The Emblematic Title-Page in England 1550–1560* (London: Routledge and Kegan Paul, 1979)
Daly, Peter M., *Literature in the Light of the Emblem* (Toronto: University of Toronto Press, 1979)
Daly, Peter M. (ed.), *The English Emblem and the Continental Tradition* (New York: AMS Press, 1988)
Empson, William, *Some Versions of Pastoral* (London: Chatto & Windus, 1935)
Fowler, Alastair, *Spenser and the Numbers of Time* (London: Routledge & Kegan Paul, 1964)
Fowler, Alastair, *Triumphal Forms: Structural Patterns in Elizabethan Poetry* (Cambridge: Cambridge University Press, 1970)
Fowler, Alastair, *Kinds of Literature: An Introduction to the Theory of Genres and Modes* (Cambridge, Mass.: Harvard University Press, 1982; Oxford: Oxford University Press, 1985)
Fraunce, A., *Symbolicae Philosophiae Liber Quartus et Ultimus*, ed. J. Manning; tr. E. Haan (New York, AMS Press, 1991)
Frye, Northrop, *Anatomy of Criticism: Four Essays* (Princeton, NJ: Princeton University Press, 1957)
Giovio, Paolo, *A Discourse of Rare Inventions, Called* Imprese, trans. Samuel Daniel (S. Waterson, 1585); repr. edn A. B. Grosart for private circulation (1896; repr. Hardpress, n.d.)
Golz, Hubert, *Thesaurus antiquariae huberrimus, ex antiquis tam numismatum quam marmorum inscriptionibus* [...] (Antwerp, 1579)
Grafton, Anthony, *The Culture of Correction in Renaissance Europe*. Pannizi Lecture, 2009 (British Library, 2011)
Groom, Nick, *The Gothic: A Very Short Introduction* (Oxford: Oxford University Press, 2012)
Hagstrum, Jean, *The Sister Arts: The Tradition of Literary Pictorialism and English Poetry from Dryden to Gray* (1958; Chicago: University of Chicago Press, 1968)
Hamel, Christopher de, *A History of Illuminated Manuscripts* (1996; rev. edn, Phaidon, 1997)
Hamel, Christopher de, *Bibles: An Illustrated History from Papyrus to Print* (Oxford: Bodleian Library 2011)
Harington, John, *Nugae Antiquae: Being a Miscellaneous Collection of Original Papers in Prose and Verse*, collected by Henry Harington, ed. Thomas Park, 2 vols (1804; repr. New York, 1966)
Harp, Richard, and Stewart, Stanley (eds), *The Cambridge Companion to Ben Jonson* (Cambridge: Cambridge University Press, 2000)
Harvey, John R., *Victorian Novelists and their Illustrators* (Sidgwick & Jackson, 1970)
Heninger, S. K., *Touches of Sweet Harmony: Pythagorean Cosmology and Renaissance Poetics* (San Marino, CA: Huntington Library, 1974)
Herrick, Robert, *The Complete Poetry*, ed. Tom Cain and Ruth Connolly (Oxford: Clarendon Press, 2013)
Hilton, James, *Chronograms Continued and Concluded* [...] *A Supplement Volume* (Elliot Stock, 1885)
Hind, A. M., *Engraving in England in the Sixteenth and Seventeenth Centuries*, 3 vols (Cambridge: Cambridge University Press, 1952–55)

Hobbes, Thomas, *Leviathan*, ed. Noel Malcolm, 3 vols (Oxford: Clarendon Press, 2012)
Hodnett, Edward, *English Woodcuts 1480–1535* (rev. edn, Oxford: Oxford University Press, 1975)
Horapollo, *The Hieroglyphics of Horapollo*, trans. and ed. George Boas (New York: Pantheon, 1950)
Johnson, Alfred Forbes, *A Catalogue of Engraved and Etched English Title-Pages down to [...] 1691* (Oxford: Bibliographical Society and Oxford University Press, 1934)
Jonson, Ben, *Ben Jonson*, ed. C. H. Herford, Percy Simpson, and Evelyn Simpson, 11 vols (Oxford: Clarendon Press, 1925–1952)
Jonson, Ben, *The Cambridge Edition of the Works of Ben Jonson*, ed. David Bevington et al., 7 vols (Cambridge: Cambridge University Press, 2012)
Kernodle, George R., *From Art to Theatre: Form and Convention in the Renaissance* (Chicago and London: University of Chicago Press, 1944)
Levin, Harry, 'The Title as a Literary Genre', *Modern Language Review*, 72 (1977), xxiii–xxxvi
Love, Harold, 'Scribal Publication in Seventeenth-Century England', *Transactions of the Cambridge Bibliographical Society*, 9 (1987), 130–54
Luborsky, Ruth Samson, and Ingram, Elizabeth Morley, *A Guide to English Illustrated Books 1536–1603*, 2 vols (Tempe, AZ: MRTS, 1998)
Mack, Maynard (ed.), *The Last and Greatest Art: Some Unpublished Poetical Manuscripts of Alexander Pope* (Newark: University of Delaware Press; London and Toronto: Associated University Presses, 1984)
McKerrow, R. B., *An Introduction to Bibliography for Literary Students* (Oxford: Clarendon Press, 1927)
McKerrow, R. B., *Printers' and Publishers' Devices in England and Scotland, 1485–1640* (1913; rev. edn, Oxford: Oxford University Press for The Bibliographical Society, 1949)
McKerrow, R. B., and Ferguson, P. S., *Title-Page Borders Used in England and Scotland 1485 to 1640* (Oxford: Bibliographical Society and Oxford University Press, 1932)
Manning, John, *The Emblem* (London: Reaktion, 2002)
Marcus, Leah S., *Unediting the Renaissance: Shakespeare, Marlowe, Milton*, rev. edn (London: Routledge, 1996)
Meehan, Bernard (ed.), *The Book of Kells* (London: Thames & Hudson, 2012)
Miedema, Hessel, 'The Term *Emblema* in Alciati', *Journal of the Warburg and Courtauld Institutes*, 31 (1968), 234–50
Milton, J., *Paradise Lost*, ed. A. Fowler (Harlow: Pearson, 1998)
Morison, Stanley, and Day, Kenneth, *The Typographic Book 1450–1935* (London: Ernest Benn, 1963)
Mortimer, Ruth (ed.), *French Sixteenth-Century Books*, 2 vols (Cambridge, MA: Belknap, 1964)
Mortimer, Ruth (ed.), *Italian Sixteenth-Century Books*, 2 vols (Cambridge, MA: Belknap, 1974)
Nesbitt, Alexander (ed.), *200 Decorative Title-Pages* (New York: Dover, 1964)
Newdigate, Bernard H., *Michael Drayton and his Circle* (Oxford: Blackwell for the Shakespeare Head Press, 1961)
Nuttall, A. D., *A New Mimesis: Shakespeare and the Representation of Reality* (London and New York: Methuen, 1983)
Onians, John, *Bearers of Meaning: The Classical Orders in Antiquity, the Middle Ages, and the Renaissance* (Princeton: Princeton University Press, 1988)
Palme, P., 'Ut Architectura Poesis', in *Idea and Form*, ed. N. G. Sandblad, *Acta Universitatis Upsaliensis*, Figura Nova Series 1 (Stockholm, 1959)
Parry, Graham, *The Golden Age Restored: The Culture of the Stuart Court, 1603–42* (Manchester: Manchester University Press, 1981)

Peterson, William S., *The Kelmscott Press: A History of William Morris's Typographical Adventure* (Berkeley and Los Angeles: University of California Press, 1991)

Piper, David, *The Image of the Poet: British Poets and their Portraits* (Oxford: Clarendon Press, 1982)

Praz, Mario, *The Flaming Heart* (New York: Doubleday, 1958)

Praz, Mario, *Studies in Seventeenth-Century Imagery* (rev. edn, Rome: Edizione di Storia e Letteratura, 1964)

Puttenham, George, *The Art of English Poetry*, ed. Frank Wigham and Wayne A. Rebhorn (Ithaca, NY: Cornell University Press, 2007)

Ray, Gordon N., *The Illustrator and the Book in England from 1791 to 1914* (Oxford: Pierpont Morgan Library and Oxford University Press, 1976)

Ripa, Cesare, *Iconologia* (Padua, 1611; facsimile edn, New York and London: Garland, 1976)

Rosso, Fiorentino, *Drawings, Prints, and Decorative Arts*, ed. Eugene A. Carroll (Washington: National Gallery of Art, 1987)

Røstvig, M.-S., *Configurations: A Topomorphical Approach to Renaissance Poetry* (Oslo, Copenhagen, and Stockholm: Aschehoug, 1994)

Russell, Daniel, *The Emblem and Device in France* (Lexington, KY: French Forum, 1985)

Scher, Stephen K. (ed.), *The Currency of Fame: Portrait Medals of the Renaissance* (New York: Abrams and the Frick Collection, 1994)

Scholz, Bernhard F., 'The 1531 Augsburg Edition of Alciato's *Emblemata*: A Survey of Research', *Emblematica*, 5 (1991), 213–54

Scholz, Bernhard F., 'From Illustrated Epigram to Emblem: The Canonization of a Typographical Arrangement', in W. Speed Hill (ed.), *New Ways of Looking at Old Texts: Papers of the Renaissance English Text Society 1895–1991* (Binghampton, NY: Renaissance English Text Society, 1993), pp. 149–57

Shevlin, Eleanor F., '"To Reconcile Book and Title and Make 'em Kin to One Another": The Evolution of the Title's Contractual Functions', *Book History*, 2 (1999), 42–77

Smith, Margaret M., *The Title-Page: Its Early Development 1460–1510* (London: British Library; New Castle, DE: Oak Knoll Press, 2000)

Sperber, Dan, and Wilson, Deirdre, *Relevance: Communication and Cognition* (Cambridge, MA: Harvard University Press, 1986)

Suarez, Michael F., SJ, and Woudhuysen, H. R., *The Oxford Companion to the Book*, 2 vols (Oxford: Oxford University Press, 2010)

Tuve, Rosemond, *Allegorical Imagery: Some Medieval Books and their Posterity*, ed. Thomas P. Roche, Jr (Princeton: Princeton University Press, 1966)

Vinne, Theodore Low de, *A Treatise on Title-Pages* (New York: Century, 1902)

Whitney, Geoffrey, *A Choice of Emblems* (Leiden: Plantin, 1586); facsimile edn, ed. Henry Green (London: Lowell Green, 1866; repr. Hildesheim: Olms, 1971)

Wilson, F. P. (ed.), *Oxford Dictionary of English Proverbs*, 3rd edn (Oxford: Oxford University Press, 1970)

Wilson, Deirdre and Sperber, Dan, *Meaning and Relevance* (Cambridge: Cambridge University Press, 2012)

Wind, Edgar, *Pagan Mysteries in the Renaissance* (rev. edn, London: Faber, 1968)

Wright, David H., The Roman Vergil and the Origins of Medieval Book Design (London: British Library, 2001)

Yates, Frances A., *The Art of Memory* (London: Routledge & Kegan Paul, 1966)

Yates, Frances A., *Theatre of the World* (London: Routledge & Kegan Paul, 1969)

Yates, Frances A., *Astraea: The Imperial Theme in the Sixteenth Century* (London: Routledge & Kegan Paul, 1975)

Index

abstraction 2, 21, 23–4, 37, 40, 67, 87, 98–9, 151, 191, 223, 232, 258, 270
Achelous 5
Acis 5
Acrasia (*The Faerie Queene*) 6–10
Acratia 7, 10
acrostics 108, 213–18, 221, 261, 265
Adam 6, 38 n. 47, 138 n. 160, 165, 177
Adam (*As You Like It*) 45, 50–1
Addison, Joseph 74, 77, 82, 87, 89, 91 n. 19, 213, 215
adventures/adventurers 4, 22–5, 137, 219–20, 243
Aeneas 51, 184, 199, 208, 211
aerial 82
  spirits 66, 69, 72, 79
aesthetic 222
  pleasure 41
  preferences 106
  strategy 82
Ages of Man 50–2
Ages of the World 50
Agrippa, Heinrich Cornelius 68 n. 14
Airey, John 199
Alamanni, Luigi 89
  La Cultivazione 179
Albanese, Giovanni 116 n. 6
Alberti, Leon Battista 222–3, 225, 227, 229, 231
  De re aedificatoria 224
Alciato, Andrea 8, 148, 152–5, 162, 182, 186, 191
  Emblemata 7 n. 12, 109, 147, 149
  Emblematum Libellus 156, 157
  Emblematum Liber 149–50, 157
Aler, Paul:
  Gradus ad Parnassum 183
Alexander of Pherae 133 n. 127
Alexander, Nigel 123, 130–1
almanacs 183, 209
altars 105, 110–15, 160, 228, 230–1, 235–6
Amalthea 42 n. 68, 42 n. 70
Amavia (*The Faerie Queene*) 4–6, 9
Ambrose 7–8
American journals 3
American mystery 18
Amis, Kingsley
  Take a Girl Like Row 215

Amleth (*Danish History*) 126, 134 n. 140, 140 n. 173
anagrams 1, 97 n. 19, 213–21, 261 n. 50, 265–7
Ancient Theology 95–6, 101, 117
Andrewes, Lancelot 95–6, 98
androgyne 48, 101
Androuet du Cerceau, Jacques 225
Angelo (*Measure for Measure*) 171
Anima (human soul) 5
animals/birds/creatures 7, 24, 34–6, 46, 50, 62, 151, 188, 244, 259, 263
Anne (of Denmark), Queen 213, 257, 260 n. 42
Anthologia Latina 181
antipastoral 44, 50, 190 n. 42
Antonio (*The Merchant of Venice*) 117–18
Antonio (*Twelfth Night*) 93, 103
Apollo 68, 112 n. 30, 174, 268
Appendix Vergiliana 181
Aquarius 102, 207, 209 n. 110, 210
archetypes 13–14, 21, 101, 176
architecture 4 n. 1, 32, 38, 112, 114, 157, 169, 173–4, 176, 224 n. 21, 225, 234, 236
Arden (*As You Like It*) 44–7, 50, 54
Arensberg, Walter Conrad 216
Arese, Paolo 233
Ariel (*The Rape of the Lock*) 66–7, 69–70, 72–3, 75, 77, 79–82
Aries 207–10
Ariosto, Ludovico 24, 39 n. 52, 243, 254
  Orlando Furioso 5 n. 4, 180, 204, 236
aristocracy/aristocrats 40, 46, 89, 123 n. 58
Aristotle 19, 180, 198
  Poetics 19 n. 25
art/arts 5, 17, 25, 32, 35, 37, 41, 60, 77–8, 83, 87, 92, 109, 112–16, 119, 121, 130, 136 n. 145, 146, 148, 154, 156–7, 167, 173, 175, 198–9, 202–3, 205–6, 222–3, 225, 227, 237, 249, 254, 260; *see also* graphic art, memory art; visual arts
Ascham, Roger 195–7
Assemblie of Ladies 241
Aston Hall 29
astrology 103, 206
astronomers 128, 209

astronomical:
  events 211
  manuscripts 108
  numbers 225
  thought 128
  twins 101
  works 89
  year 210
astronomy 31, 174, 210, 249
Atanagoras Graecus 212 n. 125
Athene 68
Auden, W. H. 118
Audrey (*As You Like It*) 45
Auerbach, Erich:
  The Representation of Reality in Western Literature 21, 200
Augustine, St 53 n. 31, 122, 133, 138 n. 160, 214
Augustinian:
  Ages of the World 50
  Christianity 196
  theology 9
Ausonius 32
  De Mosella 27
Austen, Jane:
  Emma 23, 25
authorial:
  clues 221
  decisions 22
  intentions 2
  overconfidence 243
  pseudonyms 217
autobiographical:
  events 206
  experience 211
  journals 191
  overdetermination 190
  prologues 203
  writing 192
  see also biographical
avant-garde experiments 12
avant-garde novels 192

Bachus 6–9, 39, 41–2, 197, 208
  Bacchic imagery/images 7, 9 n. 16
Bacon, Francis 132, 259
  'On Judicature' 166
  Sylva Sylvarum 156
Bacon, Sir Nicholas 153 n. 40
Bade, Josse 195, 197
Bagnal, Sir Henry 219–20
Baian villa 39 n. 50, 41
Barber, Cesar L. 93, 99 n. 24, 101, 102 n. 31
Baron (*The Rape of the Lock*) 68, 70, 76, 78, 81, 83
Bartoli, Daniello 150, 158

Barton, Anne 94 n. 7, 103 n. 35, 131
Basil, Simon 167
Basileus (*Arcadia*) 225
Bassanio (*The Merchant of Venice*) 118
Bassus 41
Baswell, Christopher 195, 197 n. 17, 201 n. 44, 208 n. 108, 211
Bateson, Frederick W. 11 n. 2, 57
Bath, Michael 146 n. 2, 151 n. 30, 153 n. 40
bath/bathing 5–6, 8–9, 250
Bawcutt, Priscilla 196–7, 200, 202, 205–6, 210
Bear's Oak 34–5, 255
Beaumont, Francis 121 n. 38
  The Maid's Tragedy 246
Beaurline, Lester 33 n. 29, 36
Beaver Castle 220
Bede 208 n. 109, 215, 222 n. 7
  De Templo 234
Belinda (*The Rape of the Lock*) 67–8, 70–83
Bellagio conference 1
Bellarmine 234
Belleforest, François de 243
Bellegambe, Jehan 8
Bellini, Giovanni:
  Coronation of the Virgin 123
Belsey, Catherine 125 n. 69, 131 n. 114, 135 n. 144, 140
Benlowes, Edward 230, 232 n. 79
Beowulf 22
Berkeley, Bishop 241
Bersuire, Pierre 7 n. 10, 197 n. 18
  Reductorium morale 8–9
Besson, Jacques:
  Théâtre des Instrumens Mathématiques et Méchaniques 165
Bester, Alfred:
  The Demolished Man 251
better marks 27, 31, 262
Bettini, Mario 109 n. 20, 228, 229 n. 57
Bible 57, 152, 176, 196, 233–4
Biblical:
  allusions 37
  associations 161
  commentaries 107 n. 6
  dreamers 245
  parables 35
  publicans 118
  symbolisms 224
Biblis 5
Billon, Thomas 213
biographical:
  contexts 1–2
  speculation 58
  see also autobiographical

INDEX 277

biography 45, 250, 262, 264
Boccaccio, Giovanni 215–16, 218
  Amorosa Visione 215
  Il Teseida 103, 201 n. 44
Bodin, Jean:
  Universae naturae theatrum 165
Bodleian Library 92
Boehrer, Bruce 265
Boethius:
  Consolatio Philosophiae 238
Boileau 71 n. 27, 86
Boire, Gary A. 70, 72–3, 78 n. 59
Bolzoni, Lina 222 n. 2, 228 n. 47, 233,
  234 n. 88, 236–8
Bongo, Pietro 37, 53, 172 n. 51, 224 n. 24,
  226 n. 36, 234 n. 90
Book of Nature 160 n. 80, 172, 254
Bower of Bliss 7–9
Bradley, Andrew C. 119, 128, 129 n. 99
Bradshaw, Graham 120
Braggadocchio (*The Faerie Queene*) 4
Brant, Sebastian 197
Braudel, Fernand 2
Breton, Nicholas:
  Fantasticks 87, 183, 203
  No Whipping, nor Tipping, But a Kind Friendly Snipping 189
brief epic 56, 59–60
Bright, Timothy 102
Britomart (*The Faerie Queene*) 132, 140, 220
Brooks-Davies, Douglas 81, 113 n. 33
Broughton, Hugh:
  A Concent of Scripture 233
Browne, William 230
  Britannia's Pastorals 88
Brueghel, Jan 151, 162
Brunetière, Ferdinand 17
Bryskett, Lodowick:
  A Treatise of Civill Life 219
Bucer, Martin 196 n. 10
Buchan, John 25
Buddhist *metta* 144
Buffon, Comte de 11
Bunyan, John 200
Burgess, Anthony 25
  Tremor of Intent 15
Burghley, Baron, *see* Cecil
Burghley House 29
burlesque 15, 23–5
Burnell, Henry 220
Burnet, Gilbert:
  Exposition of the Thirty-Nine Articles 9
Burns, Edward 122, 123 n. 59, 127 n. 90,
  131 n. 114

Burton, Robert 78, 122
  The Anatomy of Melancholy 70, 73 n. 34,
  78 n. 59, 119 n. 29, 159
Busyrane (*The Faerie Queene*) 162, 199
Butler, Samuel:
  Hudibras 76 n. 42
Butler, Thomas 219
Butsch, Albert F. 111 n. 25, 157 n. 57, 159 n. 70

Cain, William, E. 257, 259–60, 263
calendar 49, 94, 101 n. 29, 136, 183, 206,
  207 n. 94, 208
calendrical:
  cycle 206
  numbers 224
  references 206, 209–10
  variety 87
Callimachus 76 n. 42, 199–200
Calpurnius 254
  Eclogues 253 n. 4
Calvi, Francesco 148, 153–4
Calvin, John 6, 135 n. 144
Cambridge, Richard
  Scribbleriad 213
Camden, William 27, 213–14
  Britannia 224 n. 23, 252 n. 1, 256 n. 22
Camerarius, Joachim 114 n. 37, 162 n. 89
  Symbolorum et Emblematum ex Re Herbaria 156
Camillo, Giulio 237
  L'Idea del Theatro 165, 236
Capricorn 102, 207–10
Carew, Thomas 28–9, 42 n. 68, 42 n. 70,
  109, 182
  'A New-Year's Sacrifice: To Lucinda' 231
  'A Rapture' 39 n. 52, 268
  'An Elegie upon the Death of the Deane of Pauls, Dr John Donne' 182
  'To Saxham' 27, 32, 35 n. 38
Carey, John 29, 58–9, 61
Carruthers, Mary 106, 130 n. 108, 151 nn. 28–9,
  170 n. 40, 227 n. 46, 233 nn. 82–4, 244 n. 6
Cartari, Vicenzo:
  Imagini De I Dei 36 n. 39
Carthage 199
Cary, Patrick 111, 148
Case, Arthur, E.:
  A Bibliography of English Poetical Miscellanies 181
Caserta 225
Cassiodorus 172 n. 51
Castelvetro, Ludovico 223 n. 16, 227
castles 4, 28 n. 5, 31, 36 n. 40, 153 n. 39,
  169 n. 31, 177, 220, 227, 235 n. 95, 237

Catholic 69, 80, 176
  Church 69
  literature 174
  martyrology 165
  Reformation 196
Cats, Jacob 148
  Philogami et Sophronisci Dialogus 159
  Proteus 39 n. 53, 254
  Spiegel van de Oude en de Niewe Tijd 152
Catullus 42, 76
Cecil, William (Baron Burghley) 28, 29, 256–60
celestial:
  harmony 174
  spheres 159
Celia (*As You Like It*) 44, 48, 50, 53, 55
Cesario (*Twelfth Night*) 93, 94 n. 7, 95, 98–103, 117 n. 11
Chalker, John 27 n. 3, 89 n. 13
Chandler, Raymond 18
Chanson de Roland 21
Chapman, George 197 n. 20, 199 n. 32, 211 n. 122
  Bussy D'Ambois 170
  Georgics 90
  Iliad 261
Charles (*As You Like It*) 50
Charles I, King 142, 164, 168, 177
Charles II, King 165, 169–70
Chaucer, Geoffrey 103, 194–5, 199, 203, 212 n. 127
  The Complaint of Mars 207 n. 101
  The House of Fame 187, 241
  'The Knight's Tale' 103
  'The Nun's Priest's Tale' 207 n. 100
children 34–5, 37, 40, 43, 102
chivalric 4 n. 3
  ethic 125
  honour 137, 141, 196, 256
  imprese 162
  romance 25
Christ 5–8, 57, 61–3, 95–6, 107, 110–13, 115, 172, 177–8, 208, 230, 231 n. 75, 261
Christ Church theatre (Oxford) 167, 169 n. 34, 246
Christian:
  altars 105, 230
  authors 113, 214
  calendar 49
  church 110
  deification 42
  doctrine 211
  epic 65, 177
  faith 21
  festivals 211

ideals 71
literature 9
number symbolism 107
poets 110
temples 234
Christianity 119, 196, 198
Christopher Sly (*The Taming of the Shrew*) 240–1
Church, Margaret 108 n. 14
Cicero 215
  De Legibus 256 n. 19
  De Oratore 223
Civil War 89, 191
Clanvowe, Thomas:
  The Cuckoo and the Nightingale 241
Clarendon, Earl of 165, 197
Claribell (*The Faerie Queene*) 242–3
Clarissa (*The Rape of the Lock*) 71–2, 79, 82–3
Clark, D. L. 57
Clark, J. Kent 69 n. 21
Clark, Sir Kenneth 18
Clarke, John:
  Paroemiologia anglo-latina 39 n. 54
classic realism 240–1, 246
Claudius (*Hamlet*) 122, 124, 132, 134–5, 136 n. 149, 137 n. 155, 138 n. 161, 139, 151, 240
Clemen, Wolfgang 122 n. 43, 122 n. 48, 122 n. 51, 124
Cleveland, John 213
Clifford, Anne:
  Memoirs 256 n. 22
Cockpit-in-Court theatre 168
Coldwell, David 205, 207 n. 94
Colie, Rosalie, L. 44 n. 1, 44 n. 6, 50, 51 n. 24, 111 n. 25, 119 n. 29, 120 n. 30, 132 n. 124, 133 n. 126, 137 n. 153, 160, 190 n. 42
Collins, Wilkie:
  Basil 192
Colonna, Francesco 215
  Hypnerotomachia 150, 161, 169, 244–5
columns 109–14, 159, 160, 170–1, 175, 222–5, 228–30, 233, 262 n. 58, *see also* obelisks
Colutius, Philander:
  Theatrum Naturae 233
comedies 54, 84, 93, 117, 119, 179
comedy 20, 46–7, 99, 104, 117, 119, 161, 179, 180, 186–7
concupiscence 6, 7 n. 10, 9–10, 236
Congreve, William 240
Constable, Henry:
  Sonnets 11

INDEX 279

Conti, Natale 7 n. 12, 54 n. 33, 197 n. 18, 207 n. 95
Copernican hypothesis/system 128 n. 95, 174, 179, 249
Copernicus, Nicolaus 128, 249
Corbett, Margery 159, 161 n. 82, 170 n. 39, 171, 232 n. 79, 233 n. 81
Corin (*As You Like It*) 44–5, 50
Cornarius, Jan
  Selecta Epigrammata 155
Coronelli, Vincenzo Maria 174
cosmic:
  chariot 106
  drama 165
  order 234
  proportions 19, 32
  sovereignty 75
  strife 82
  summas 187, 208
  unity 98, 101
Cotton, Charles:
  'Her Hair' 74 n. 37, 76 n. 42, 78 n. 58
  Morning Quatrains 183
Counter-Reformation 176, 222
country-house poems 27, 34–5, 38, 40–1, 90, 181, 252
Coventry, Francis:
  'Penshurst' 269–70
Cowley, Abraham 83, 156
  Essays in Verse and in Prose 87
  Sylva 87, 90
  'The Chronicle' 79
  'The Muse' 226
  'The Resurrection' 226
Cowling, David 45–6, 222 n. 2, 223 n. 16, 228 nn. 47–8, 234 n. 88, 237 n. 113, 238
Craik, T. W. 93
Cramer, Daniel:
  Emblemata Sacra 111
Crispinus 109
Crispissa (The Rape of the Lock) 66
Cromwell, Oliver 166, 175
crown 36, 111, 165, 171, 175, 187, 259
Cruttwell, Patrick 125 n. 72, 126, 130 n. 110, 135 n. 142, 138 n. 158, 141 n. 174
cryptanalysis 216
Cubeta, Paul M. 27 n. 2, 33, 36 nn. 39–40, 39 nn. 49–50, 41, 42 n. 66
Cuddon, J. A.:
  Dictionary of Critical Terms 142
Cuddy (*The Shepheardes Calender*) 185
Cult of the Precious Blood 5
Cupid 42, 162, 174–5, 191
Curio (*Twelfth Night*) 93
Cybele 36

cyclical theory 20–1
Cymochles (*The Faerie Queene*) 7

d'Urfé, Honoré 254
Dallington, Sir R.:
  The Strife of Love in a Dream 162 n. 87
Daly, Peter, M. 146 n. 2, 152 n. 37, 154, 162 n. 88
Dante:
  Commedia Divina 244
  Inferno 171
  Purgatorio 189, 199
Davies, Sir John 86, 215, 261
  'In Claium' 80 n. 64
  The Scourge of Folly 188 n. 36
Davison, Francis 110, 113, 230
De Vinne, Theodore Low 108 n. 16, 154 n. 46, 159 n. 70
deconstruction 2, 143, 202 n. 51
deities 51, 65, 68, 174, 178, 225, 241
Dennis, John 66–7, 69, 72–5, 81 n. 70, 83
  Remarks on Mr Pope's The Rape of the Lock 65, 71, 76 n. 46, 80
detective stories 18, 24
devils 73, 83, 92, 117
dialogues 22, 56, 84, 116 n. 5, 159, 161, 181
Dickens, Charles:
  Our Mutual Friend 249
Dido (*Aeneid*) 184
Dinesen, Isak 24
Dionysius Ronsfertus 109
Discord 65
Disraeli, Isaac 214
Dodsley, Robert:
  A Collection of Poems 269
Dodsworth, Martin 119 n. 29, 121 n. 37, 121 n. 41, 122 nn. 45–6, 122 n. 49, 123 n. 58, 124, 125 n. 71, 125 nn. 75–6, 126 n. 82, 127 n. 84, 128 n. 92, 128 n. 96, 134 n. 133, 134 n. 135–6, 135 n. 141, 136 n. 147, 139 n. 166, 141
dolphin and anchor 147, 150, 152, 154, 157 n. 60, 191
Donne, John 27, 189, 245
  'A Valediction: Forbidding Mourning' 158
  LXXX Sermons 233
  Poems 182
  Sermons 186, 263 n. 66
Dos Passos, John:
  U.S.A. 118
Dosiadas 110
Douglas, Gavin 194–212
  Eneados 197–8, 200, 203
  The Palice of Honour 197
  'Winter Eclogue' 203

drama 24, 33 n. 29, 44–5, 92, 116–17, 124, 139, 165, 179, 240–2, 245–6
dramatic:
　action 122 n. 43
　context 51
　forms 19 n. 25
　illusion 140
　innovation 91
　irony 128, 184
　possibilities 49
　reflection 124
　speech 131
　style 140
Drayton, Michael 76 n. 42, 88, 175 n. 72, 189–90, 253, 261 n. 50
　Idea's Mirror 86
　Mortimeriados 199
　Poly-Olbion 170, 189
　The Barons Warres 229
　'The Sacrifice to Apollo' 187 n. 34
Drummond, William 214, 263, 265
Dryden, John 24, 83, 86–7, 156, 203–4, 213
　Absalom and Achitophel 14
　Aeneis 14, 211 n. 120
　Aureng-Zebe 14
　Georgics 89
　MacFlecknoe 213
Du Bartas, Guillaume de Salluste:
　La Sepmaine 224–5, 230
　Seconds Sepmaine 224
Du Bellay, Joachim 172
　Vision 30
Duke Frederick (*As You Like It*) 44, 46–8, 53, 55
Duke of Venice (*The Merchant of Venice*) 119
Duke of Vienna (*Measure for Measure*) 171, 245
Duke Senior (*As You Like It*) 44, 46–7, 50, 52
Dumas, Alexandre 23
Dunbar, William:
　Lament for the Makaris 182
Dunster, Charles 58
Dupuy, Henri 214
Durant, Gilles:
　Le zodiac amoureux 211 n. 122
Dürer, Albrecht 163
　Adam and Eve 265 n. 79
Durrell, Lawrence:
　Black Book 192

Eade, J. C. 206, 207 n. 94, 208, 209 n. 114, 210
Eagleton, Terry 118–19
ecclesiastical:
　murals 153
　politics 235
　reforms 196
　satire 45
eclogues 13–14, 18, 22, 24, 44, 84, 184, 195 n. 6, 203, 253 n. 8
Edwards, Philip 122, 127 n. 86, 137 n. 152
Egypt/Egyptian 8, 96
　darkness of sin 117
　fountain of avarice 7 n. 10
　hieroglyphics 147
　priests 231
ekphrasis 148 n. 9, 163, 198
ekphrastic:
　criticism 199
　epigrams 148–9, 151, 154
　images 199
elegies 17, 23, 180–2, 184, 189
elements 32, 33 n. 30, 66 n. 7, 70–1, 82, 97–8
Eliot, T. S. 1, 134, 270
　Tradition and the Individual Talent 19
Elizabeth I, Queen 46, 140, 171 n. 45, 195, 196 n. 10, 213, 220, 256
Elizabeth, Countess of Rutland 28 n. 4, 76 n. 41, 262
Elizabethan:
　audiences 48, 103
　comedy 117
　drama 92, 116, 124, 245
　imagination 169
　literature 14 n. 9
　poetry 231
　poets 200
　portraits 116 n. 2
　satires 80
　stage 132
　Twelfth Night customs 93
　wedding masques 53
Elizabethans 103, 118–19, 121, 141
elves 66
Elyot, Sir Thomas:
　The Governour 165 n. 6
emblematic:
　details 242, 244
　figures 154 n. 46
　fountains 5
　frontispieces 158–9
　houses 27
　mode 39, 140
　motifs 151 n. 30
　pictorialism 163
　poems 3, 160, 162
　title-pages 158, 160
　trees 256
emotions 78, 124, 127, 130, 133 n. 127, 200, 241, 244, 246, 250–1
Empson, William 1, 25, 87, 121 n. 41, 127 n. 87, 137 n. 152

INDEX   281

England 18, 84, 88, 119, 123, 153 n. 40, 156, 159,
  162, 164, 169–70, 194, 196, 224, 257, 259, 265
English:
  aristocracy 89
  critics 200
  culture 80
  estate 41, 252
  georgic 89–90
  humanists 195
  journals 3
  literature 87
  masques 248
  odes 226
  pastoral 88–9, 91
  poetry 62, 204, 252
  republic 178
Enlightenment 66–7, 69, 99, 105, 164
ephod 176–7
epicists 14, 16
epics 11, 13–16, 19 n. 25, 20–5, 56–7, 59–60, 62,
  65–6, 80–1, 91, 174, 177, 180, 186–8, 191,
  193, 210, 229, 253 n. 8, 254, 263
epigrammatists 84, 254
epigrams 5, 42, 84–7, 97, 147–56, 158, 160,
  180–3, 186–7, 224 n. 23, 228, 232 n. 79,
  234 n. 88, 256, 265 n. 80
Epiphany 92–6, 101–2, 104, 117
epistles 179, 229
epistolary:
  genre 22
  novels 192, 248
  species 84
Epistulae Obscurorum Vironim 180
Erasmus, Desiderius 194–7, 216
  Adagia 152
Eriksen, Roy 222, 223 nn. 12–13, 223 n. 16, 227,
  228 n. 47, 229 n. 58, 231 n. 75, 233 n. 86,
  236 n. 102
erotic:
  associations 81
  motif 103
  passages 127
  passions 102
  poetry 268
  symbolism 101 n. 26
  tapestries 132
  works 76
Erskine-Hill, Howard 80, 81 n. 73, 223 n. 14
Escalus (*Measure for Measure*) 171
Escorial 176, 235 n. 97
essays 1–3, 18, 21, 74, 87, 109, 122, 166–7, 198
Estienne, Henri 147, 155, 159, 181
  L'Art de faire des devises 149
Euphemus 175

Euripides:
  Troades 133 n. 127
Evadne (*Hamlet*) 246–7
Evans, Robert 257, 264
Everett, Barbara 93 n. 5, 101, 120, 123 n. 55,
  126 n. 81, 127 n. 87, 138 n. 158
Everyman (*Hamlet*) 122, 126, 129,
  138, 141
evolution 17–18, 19 n. 25, 24, 149

Fabian (*Twelfth Night*) 93–4, 103–4
façades 36, 168, 171, 225–7, 232–3, 237
Fage, Mary:
  Fames roule 214
fairies 65–7, 69, 82
Falstaff 120, 133, 166
Fanshawe, Richard:
  'The Escurial' 176, 235
  'Upon Occasion of His Majesty's
    Proclamation' 256 n. 21
Faral, Edmond:
  Les Art poétiques de 12ᵉ et de 13ᵉ siècle 188,
    253 n. 6
Faustinus 32, 41
Felperin, Howard 120, 121 n. 38–9, 127,
  128 n. 92, 138 n. 156–7, 139, 140 nn. 171–2
  trivia 83
  twins 101
  types 67
  vanity 72, 82
  see also women
Fenoaltea, Doranne 157 n. 57, 225
Ferber, Michael 118, 119 nn. 23–4
Feste (*Twelfth Night*) 93, 95–7, 99, 102, 104, 117
festivals/festive occasions 92–4, 171, 183, 211,
  264, 265 n. 79
feudal:
  decentralization 249
  degree 165
  relations 167
  rents 264
  system 164, 259
fiction 14, 15, 18–21, 24, 67, 93, 104,
  122 n. 49, 192, 221, 240–2, 244–5,
  248, 250–1
fictiones 103, 242, 244
Fielding, Henry 119, 242
figure-poetry 108–9
Fletcher, John 121 n. 38
  The Maid's Tragedy 246
Florimell (*The Faerie Queene*) 218, 220
Folgóre da San Gimignano
  Sonetti dei Mesi 200
Fontainebleau 171, 236, 237 n. 107

Fontenelle, Bernard le Bovier de
　　Dialogues of the Dead 249–50
formal realism 241, 244, 248
Fortinbras (*Hamlet*) 132, 136–8, 139 n. 162
Foster, John Wilson 27 n. 3, 40
Fountain of Life 5–6, 8, 10 n. 18
fountains 7, 9–10, 29 n. 10, 107, 190
Fouquet, Jean
　　Hours of Étienne Chevalier 206
Fowler, Alastair 53 nn. 31–2, 117 n. 12,
　　121 n. 41, 123 n. 60, 147 n. 4, 149 n. 15,
　　150 n. 20, 153 n. 39, 154 n. 47, 157 n. 57,
　　160 n. 80, 161 n. 81, 163 n. 93, 173 n. 53,
　　174 n. 57, 175 n. 68, 176 n. 79, 177 n. 87,
　　223 n. 13, 224 nn. 25–6, 228 n. 52, 230 n. 65,
　　231 nn. 70–1, 235 nn. 96–7, 244 n. 4, 245 n. 7,
　　247 n. 8, 248 nn. 10–11, 250 nn. 15–16
　　Conceitful Thought 261 nn. 50–1
　　Kinds of Literature 85, 185, 203 n. 57
　　'Maria's Riddle' 97 n. 19
　　Renaissance Realism 199 n. 33
　　Spenser and the Numbers of Time 53 n. 31,
　　　　98 n. 22, 113 n. 36, 209 n. 115
　　'The Beginnings of English Georgic' 90 n. 16
　　'The Better Marks of Jonson's "To
　　　　Penshurst"' 258 n. 27
　　The Country House Poem 252 n. 2, 255 n. 18,
　　　　256 n. 19, 263 n. 68, 264 n. 70
　　'The Emblem as a Literary Genre'
　　　　182 n. 13
　　'The Image of Mortality' 51 n. 24
　　'The Silva Tradition in Jonson's *The
　　　　Forrest*' 181 n. 5
　　'The Structure of Dryden's Song for St Cecilia's
　　　　Day, 1687' 113 n. 33
　　Time's Purpled Masquers 195 n. 8, 206 n. 93,
　　　　225 n. 28
　　Triumphal Forms 53 n. 32, 81 n. 74
　　'Virgil for "every gentil Scot"' 201 n. 46
Foxe, John:
　　Actes and Monuments 235
France 2–3, 18, 146, 149, 164, 257
Fraunce, Abraham 147 n. 7, 148, 152 n. 36,
　　158 n. 64, 164 n. 3
　　Symbolicae Philosophia 261
　　The Arcadian Rhetoric 160 n. 78
French:
　　court 267
　　dictionary 150
　　fashions 136, 230
　　literature 222 n. 2
　　theorists 180
　　tragedy/tragedies 17
　　see also France

Freud, Sigmund 93, 119, 122 n. 48, 139
　　Freudian assumptions 122
　　Freudian terms 102
Friedberg, Harris 255
　　'Jonson's Poetry' 258 n. 31, 265 n. 80
Friedman, Alan 15
Friedman, William and Elizebeth 217–18
　　The Shakespearean Ciphers Examined 216
frontispieces 158–60, 168, 170–2, 207 n. 95, 227,
　　232–4, 238, 250
Frye, Northrop 13, 19
　　Anatomy of Criticism 14 n. 10, 20–1
Frye, Roland Mushat 138
Fulgore da San Gimignano
　　Soneli del Mesi 179
Furor (*The Faerie Queene*) 242–4

Galilei, Galileo 236
　　Dialogo 179
Galle, Philip 163 n. 91
Gamage, Barbara 265, 267
gardens 33, 140, 153, 156, 171, 173, 253; *see also*
　　plants
Gash, Anthony 96, 101
Gawain and the Green Knight 200
Gay, John 89
　　'The Toilette' 67 n. 8
　　Trivia 87
Gemini 101, 207–11
Geminus, Thomas:
　　*Compendiosa totius Anatomiae
　　　　Delineatio* 171
generic:
　　ambience 191
　　blending 45
　　classification 27 n. 3
　　complex 14–15
　　contradictions 52
　　conventions 57
　　development 22
　　forms 12–13, 16, 20, 24, 147
　　hierarchies 20–1, 88, 91
　　hybridity 254
　　identification 15, 42
　　mixture 49
　　modulation 62
　　realms 179
　　relations 86
　　resources 255
　　rules 12
　　types 14–15, 17
　　variations 25
Geneva Bible 176, 234
Georgi (Zorzi), Francesco 234

georgic 45, 48–50, 52, 54 n. 33, 62–4, 84–91, 179, 183, 185–6, 189, 191, 202–5, 229, 252, 253 nn. 7–8, 254–5
Gertrude (*Hamlet*) 121, 124, 127, 132–5, 139 n. 165, 141
Gervinus, Georg Gottfried 99
Geryon 162
Ghost (*Hamlet*) 120–1, 125, 128, 130, 133–4
Giedion, Sigfried 168, 169 n. 31
Gilbert, W. S. 126
Gillespie, Stuart:
  Shakespeare's Books 2
Gilman, Ernest 149
Ginsberg, Warren 130
Giorgio, Francesco:
  Harmonia Totius Mundi 107 n. 6
Giovio, Paolo:
  Dialogo dell' Imprese 147
Giraldus Cambrensis 220
Gissing, George:
  The New Grub Street 192
  The Private Papers of Henry Rycroft 192
Globe theatre 165, 240
globes 159, 174
gnomes 65, 70–3, 79
God 10, 35, 55, 63, 107, 111–12, 114, 152, 157, 164–5, 171, 176, 196, 223, 234, 235 n. 94, 244, 261
Goddard, Harold 127
gods/goddesses 5, 7–8, 20, 34, 36, 42, 51, 53, 66, 68, 77, 98, 102–3, 157, 231, 240–1, 259; *see also* deities
Goedde, Lawrence Otto 101 n. 26, 152 n. 31, 158 n. 62, 161 n. 86, 182 n. 12
Golden Age 14, 34, 41, 44, 50, 90
Golding, Thomas 262
  Pincher Martin 23
Goltzius, Hubert 232
  'Satisfactio Christi' 10 n. 18
Googe, Barnabe:
  Eclogues 11
Gordon, D. J. 53 n. 32
Gospels 36–7, 95, 118
gothic 15, 24, 72, 92, 211
  façades 226
  novel/romance 24, 250
Grabes, Herbert 78 n. 55, 121 n. 39, 132 n. 125
graphic art 5 n. 4, 8, 109, 153, 163
Gray, Douglas 197 n. 21, 198–9
Great Chain of Being 30 n. 16, 35, 37
Great Game 144–5
Greek:
  emblema 150, 152
  hyle 157

literature 195, 254
myths 13
Testament 196 n. 10
vowels 211
Greek Anthology 8, 85 n. 3, 108–10, 148, 155, 181, 198, 265
Greenblatt, Steven 2, 101, 119 n. 23
  Will in the World 2
Greene, Graham 18, 240
Gregory the Great (St Gregory) 37 n. 44, 202
Grey of Wilton, Baron 219–20
Grimald, Nicholas 199
Grosseteste, Robert 249
Grotius, Hugo:
  Poematum Collecta 155
Grove, Robin 72, 75, 77 n. 47, 78, 81 n. 67, 83
Grudin, Robert:
  Book: A Novel 192
Guildenstern (*Hamlet*) 121, 126, 132, 135, 138 n. 158, 139
Guillén, Claudio 180 n. 3, 183
Guthrie, William 119, 126
Guyart des Moulins:
  Compendium 108
Guyon (*The Faerie Queene*) 4, 6–7, 8–10, 242–4

Habington, William 268–9
hair 5, 67, 70, 74 n. 37, 75–6, 77 n. 54, 184, 205
Hamlet 119–41, 240, 247
Harington, Sir John 5 n. 4, 30 n. 18, 97, 172, 208 n. 105, 224
Hassel, Chris 92, 95
Hatfield House 29, 31, 260 n. 42
Hatton, Christopher 28
Hawkins, Henry:
  Partheneia Sacra 156
Hay, Millicent 257 n. 25, 261 n. 53, 262, 267 n. 84–5
Haydocke, Richard:
  Spare Minutes 159
Hayman, Robert 93 n. 5
  Quodlibets 181
Hazlitt, William 124, 127 n. 89
Hecuba 123, 133
Heine, Heinrich 117
Hellenistic emblem 161
Hellenistic tradition 109
Heller, Joseph:
  Catch-22 24
Henderson, G. D. 196
Henrietta Maria, Queen 167
Henry VIII, King 195
Henryson, Robert:
  The Testament of Cresseid 215

Henschenius, Godefridus 93 n. 6
heraldry 147, 151, 153, 155, 171, 191
Herbert, George 3, 28, 105, 109–12, 161,
    213, 215
  'Aaron' 114, 176
  'The Altar' 113–15, 160, 230, 235–6
  The Temple 232, 235
  'Vanitie' 216
Herbert, William (Third Earl of Pembroke)
    28 n. 4, 261–2, 263 n. 66
Hercules 130 n. 111, 132, 136
Herford, C. H. 29, 30 n. 21, 34 n. 34,
    39 n. 51, 41 n. 63, 42 n. 69, 255 n. 17,
    260 n. 45, 261 n. 48, 264 n. 74, 265 n. 75,
    266 n. 82
heroes 13, 20–1, 73, 91, 118, 132, 244
heroism/heroics 23, 66, 76, 84, 125, 173, 187, 189,
    204, 253
Herrick, Robert 90, 95, 110, 183
  'A Country-life: to His Brother Mr. Thomas
    Herrick' 27
  'A Panegyric to Sir Lewis Pemberton' 27,
    175, 229
  Hesperides 86, 230
  'The Hock-cart' 36 n. 39
  'The Pillar of Fame' 160, 230
Hesiod 205
  Works and Days 90, 203
Hesiodic elements 45
Hesiodic georgic 90
Hesse, Hermann:
  Das Glasperlenspiel/Magister Ludi 18
Heywood, Thomas
  Pleasant Dialogues 148
Hibbard, G. R. 27 n. 2, 28 n. 5, 34 n. 36, 35, 40,
    41 n. 64
Hieatt, Charles W. 44 n. 6, 224 n. 25
hierarchies 20, 35, 36 n. 39, 90–1, 166–7,
    176, 256
hieroglyphics 147, 151, 161
Highet, Gilbert 183
  The Anatomy of Satire 85 n. 3, 183 n. 16
Highsmith, Pat
  They Who Walk Away 15
Hillis Miller, J. 2
Hindu world image 78
Hirsch, E. Donald 1–2, 11 n. 2, 12, 13 n. 8, 15–16,
    17 n. 16
Hobbes, Thomas 19
  'Answer to Davenant's' Preface to
    Gondibert' 20 n. 26
  Leviathan 232, 238
Hobbinol (*The Shepheardes Calendar*) 218
Hoefnagel, Joris:
  Mira Calligraphiae Monumenta 206

Holbein the Younger, Hans 163
  The Ambassadors 116
  The Selling of Indulgences 265 n. 79
Holdenby House 28–9
Hollander, John 97 n. 16, 97 n. 19, 100 n. 25,
    177 n. 11
Holovitreum 30–1
Homer 16, 21–4, 56, 66, 195
  Iliad 75 n. 39, 138 n. 160, 210
  Odyssey 19, 210
Horace 24, 223
  Beatus Ille 27
  Epistles 186
  Odes 186
  Satires 186
Horatio (*Hamlet*) 125–6, 132, 138–9, 240, 247
horses 4, 5 n. 4, 34, 36, 187, 202, 253
hospitality 28, 32–5, 39–40, 42, 90, 181, 258–60,
    262, 264
Hotson, Leslie 93, 97 n. 19
Hotspur 133
Howard, Alan 160 n. 80
Howell, James 123 n. 54
  Familiar Letters 180
Hrabanus Maurius (Hraban Maur) 108,
    160 n. 78, 214
Hugh of St Victor:
  Arca Noe 244
Hugo, Herman 5, 153 n. 39
humanism/humanists 18, 46, 157, 159, 180,
    194–6, 197 n. 18, 223
Hunter, George 124, 131 n. 117, 133 n. 128,
    136 n. 150
hunting 46, 90, 225, 240, 253
Hyginus, Julius 108
  Poeticon Astronomicon 207 n. 102
hyle 157, 159
Hymen (*As You Like It*) 53
hymns 18, 187, 190, 207–8, 210–11, 231
hypograms 108, 213

iconography 5, 77 n. 49, 151, 153, 162–3, 170–1,
    189, 235 n. 95
ideal and real 28, 41–2, 50
idealism/idealists 11, 40, 47, 141
identification 12–13, 15, 42, 110, 220–1, 244
imagery 3–4, 9 n. 16, 13, 81, 92, 95, 112 n. 27,
    132, 151, 160, 162, 186, 191, 198,
    203, 211
imitation 22–3, 25, 27, 29, 32, 42 n. 70, 57, 88, 90,
    160, 180, 198, 200, 223, 227, 231
immortality 42, 73, 101
imperialism 80, 86, 144, 145, 149
imprese 110, 146–7, 149–50, 153–5, 158, 161–2,
    171, 233, 238, 246

INDEX

inscriptions 97 n. 19, 147 n. 5, 150, 169, 171, 215, 254, 265, 267–8
interpretation 7–8, 12–13, 15–16, 17 n. 16, 27 n. 2, 77 n. 49, 79, 81–2, 85, 93 n. 5, 94, 103, 118, 119 n. 23, 143–4, 176, 178, 184, 197 n. 18, 220, 258
Italy 3, 89, 108, 116, 169 n. 36, 173

Jacobean drama 125, 240, 245–6
James I, King 30–1, 35–6, 41, 109, 167, 169, 174, 176, 235, 257, 260 n. 42, 261
  Essayes of a Prentise 109
Jaques (*As You Like It*) 46–53
Jaques de Boys (*As You Like It*) 52
Jauss, Hans Robert 1
Jeanneret, Michel 183
Jenkins, Harold 44 n. 3, 47 n. 16, 51 n. 25, 52, 120 n. 34, 121 n. 41, 122, 123 n. 54, 127 n. 86, 128, 133 n. 127–8, 136 nn. 146–7, 137, 138 n. 156
Jesuits 69, 112, 195 n. 6, 196 n. 10, 234 n. 91
Johnson, A. W. 169, 174, 228, 235
Johnson, Samuel 13, 64, 65 n. 3, 66–7, 72, 83, 87, 99, 124, 260
  Life of Pope 63
  The Rambler 63
Jones, Emrys 67, 69, 92, 119, 194, 201
Jones, Inigo 161, 167, 173, 258
Jonson, Ben 29–30, 33–4, 38–9, 42, 46, 76, 97, 129 n. 97, 161, 175, 177, 202, 223, 228, 232, 246, 263–4, 266, 270
  Discoveries 173–4, 223 n. 19
  Love's Triumph through Callipolis 174, 176
  Oberon 169
  'Sir Robert Wroth' 27
  The Alchemist 215
  The Forest 27, 86, 156–7, 172
  The Irish Masque 219
  The Mask of Queens 173
  The Underwood 156, 170
  'To Penshurst' 27–8, 31–2, 36 n. 39, 37, 40–1, 43, 235, 252, 255, 257–62, 265, 267, 269
  'To the Memory of My Beloved' 182
Jung, Carl 69 n. 19, 78 n. 55, 102 n. 34, 139
Juno 53, 66 n. 7
Jupiter (deity/planet) 53–4, 68, 83, 106, 175
Justa Eduardo King Naufrago 181–2
Juvenal 24, 35, 183, 258 n. 28, 259, 263
  Satires 263 n. 67

Kalendayr of Shyppars 52, 209, 209 nn. 110–11
Katzenellenbogen, A. 5 nn. 4–5
Keats, John 21

Kendall, Timothy 155
Kepler, Johannes:
  Harmonice Mundi 174
  Rudolphine Tables 174
Keplerian system 249
Kermode, Frank 1
Kerrigan, John 109, 268
King, Edward 182, 184, 190
Kingsmill, Andrew
  Comfort in Affliction 150–1
Kinloss Abbey 196
Kipling, Gordon 170
Kipling, Rudyard 18
  'With the Night Mail' 19
  Kim 144
Kirby Hall 29, 250
Kircher, Athanasius:
  Musurgia 187
Kirsch, Arthur 120, 126
Klibansky, Raymond 51 n. 26, 52 nn. 28–9, 66 n. 7, 70 n. 25, 72 n. 28, 102 n. 33
Knole House 29, 31, 224, 262
Knox, John 138 n. 156, 216
Knox, Ronald:
  A Book of Acrostics 213
Kristeva, Julia 213
Kyd, Thomas:
  The Spanish Tragedy 240

labels/labelling 24, 42, 60, 87, 149–50, 152, 156, 179, 182, 186, 213
Laertes (*Hamlet*) 123, 126, 132, 135–9, 141
landscape 21–2, 42, 45, 87, 90, 123, 182–3, 186, 200, 204–5, 250, 255, 269
landscape poetry 18 n. 20, 204–5
Langland, William:
  Piers Plowman 244
langue 11, 13 n. 8
Lascelles, Mary 15 n. 11
Lathrop, H. B. 212 n. 126
Latin 150, 200, 219, 227, 232, 253, 265
  anagrams 266
  epigrams 155, 224 n. 23
  literature 195
  love elegies 184
  pastoral mode 190
  translations 155
  verse 27, 180, 214
laws of genre 84–5, 88, 90
le Carré, John 25
Le Moyne, Pierre 149
Lee, Rensselaer W. 44 n. 2, 254
Lefèvre de la Boderie, Guy:
  L'Encyclie des secrets de l'Eternité 213
legends 4, 19, 198

Lelièvre, Guillaume
    Ars Memorativa 237
Lemmi, C. W. 6 n. 9, 9 n. 16
Leonard, John 216
Leviathan 62, 108
Levin, Harry 121–4
Levins, Peter:
    Manipulus Vocabulorum 214
Lewalski, Barbara 57, 61, 94–5, 117, 255 n. 16
    Milton's Brief Epic 56
Lewis, C. S. 1, 22, 93 n. 2, 163, 196–7, 212
    Oxford History of English Literature 194
    The Discarded Image 18
Lightbown, R. W. 159, 171
Lindheim, Nancy R. 51 n. 24
Linlithgow Palace 194
Lipomanus, Aloysius:
    Sanctorum priscorum patrum vitae 93 n. 5
Lisle, Lady 261–3
Lisle, Viscount (Robert Sidney) 27, 34, 256–9, 261–6, 267 n. 85
Lodge, Thomas 107 n. 6
    Rosalynde 48
Lonbel, Matthias de:
    Stirpium Adversaria Nova 159
Longford Castle 31
Longus:
    Daphne and Chloe 253
Lord's space 164, 175
Louis XIII, King 213
Louis XIV, King 174
Lovelace, Richard:
    'Amyntor's Grove' 150
    'On Sannazar' 76 n. 42
Luborsky, Ruth 163
Lucan:
    Pharsalia 204
Lucian 19
    Saturnalia 258 n. 28
Lucifera (*The Faerie Queene*) 30, 162
Luther, Martin 118 n. 20, 123 n. 54, 196

Macarius Mutius:
    De Triumpho Christi 176–7
Mack, Maynard 71 n. 27, 76 n. 46, 78 n. 57, 81 n. 70
    Alexander Pope: A Life 69
    The Garden and the City 27 n. 3
Macrobius 9 n. 15, 53 n. 31, 98
    Commentary on the Dream of Scipio 98 n. 20, 211 n. 122
Magi 93 n. 4, 95–6, 117
magic 48, 53, 66, 68–9, 77, 81, 96, 101, 130, 139
Maier, Michael:
    Atalanta Fugiens 106

Mailer, Norman:
    Barbary Shore 15
Malory, Sir Thomas 196
Malvolio (*Twelfth Night*) 39, 93, 95–7, 102–4, 117
Mancinelli, Antonio 197
Mann, Thomas:
    Doktor Faustus 15
Manning, John 132 n. 123, 156, 163, 182 n. 12
Mantuan 44–5, 89
Manzolli, Pier Angelo (Marcellus Palingenius)
    Zodiacus Vitae (*The Zodiake of Life*) 206 n. 93, 211 n. 121, 215, 237–8
Maria (*Twelfth Night*) 93, 97 n. 19, 117 n. 11
Marinell (*The Faerie Queene*) 218, 220
Marlowe, Christopher:
    Doctor Faustus 131 n. 116
Marmion, Shakerly 3
Marot, Clément 150, 215, 221
Mars (deity/planet) 51, 66 n. 7, 68, 175
Marston, John 126, 188
Martial 27, 32, 39 n. 50, 41–2, 183, 186, 256, 258 n. 28, 265 n. 80
Martz, Louis 62
Marvell, Andrew:
    The First Anniversary of the Government under O. C. 175
    'Upon Appleton House' 27, 256 n. 21
    'Upon the Hill and Grove at Billborow' 254 n. 12
Mary, Countess of Pembroke 28 n. 4, 261
Mascardi, Augustino:
    Silvarum Libri IV 156
masques 31, 53–4, 153, 159 n. 72, 161–2, 164, 167–9, 173–5, 235, 245–8, 262 n. 59
mathematics 1, 4, 31, 93 n. 6, 105, 128, 216, 218, 223, 225, 229 n. 58, 249
May, Thomas:
    Epigrams 256
McCanles, Michael 129 n. 97, 257, 258 n. 27
McCutcheon, Elizabeth 37 n. 45, 153 n. 40
medicine 1, 70, 128 n. 95
    syllabus 195
    thought 71
    world 209, 211, 222, 240
    see also Middle Ages
Medway 32, 39, 42
melancholy 45, 51–2, 70–3, 78, 90, 94, 99, 102–3, 119–20, 122, 159, 189, 205, 269
memorials 84, 116, 130, 231, 238
memory 20, 34, 42, 81, 85, 106, 128, 130–1, 133, 137, 151, 165, 170, 227, 233–4, 236–9
memory art 106, 151–2, 233 n. 83, 236–8
Mercury (deity) 51, 68, 207–8, 210

mercury (metal) 78 n. 55
Meredith, George 242
Meres, Francis:
  Palladis Tamia 186
Merrill, James:
  The Diblos Notebook 192
metaphors 6, 39 n. 52, 61, 77, 107, 112, 114–15,
  118, 134, 140, 150, 156, 158, 181, 183–93,
  222–3, 226, 228–9, 232–9
Middle Ages 12, 103, 108, 142, 146, 164, 166, 168,
  170, 179–81, 183, 187, 208–9, 214, 222, 227,
  238, 244; *see also* medieval
  allegory 228, 242, 244–5
  art 5, 116 n. 1, 167
  genres 18, 179, 187, 241
  romances 23, 80
Middleton, Thomas 246
  Women Beware Women 245
Midgeley, Graham 117
Miedema, Hessel 148
Miège, Guy 92
Milton, John 1, 16, 30, 61, 107–8, 118 n. 15, 150,
  183–4, 187, 196, 215, 226
  Il Penseroso 90, 179, 186, 189
  L'Allegro 90, 179, 189
  Lycidas 13, 17, 23, 186, 190
  Of Reformation 57
  Paradise Lost 13, 14 n. 9, 23, 56–9, 62,
    97 n. 19, 106, 160, 165–6, 172, 177–8, 216,
    223, 232, 244
  Paradise Regained 56–60, 62–4, 73
  Samson Agonistes 13, 39 n. 49
  The Reason of Church-government 56
mimesis 20–1, 60, 62–3, 116 n. 1, 117 n. 7, 119,
  121, 124, 130, 131 n. 116, 132, 140,
  157 n. 58, 198–200, 240–1, 244, 246,
  249–50
Mirabilia urbis Romae 30, 31 n. 22
modern realism 116, 133, 249
Molesworth, Charles 18 n. 20, 34, 38,
  40 n. 55, 42–3
  'Property and Virtue' 18 n. 20, 27 nn. 2–3
Montaigne, Michel de 78 n. 57, 122, 125 n. 73
Montenay, Georgette de 162
  Emblemes ou Devises Chrestiennes 5 n. 7, 156
Montfaucon de Villars, Henri de:
  The Count of Gabalis 66, 69
morals/morality 4, 10, 15, 30, 38, 40, 43–5, 47, 49,
  54, 60, 63, 66–7, 71, 73, 77, 79–80, 83, 98,
  103, 114, 117–18, 120–1, 124–5, 131–2, 134,
  136–8, 141, 156, 160–2, 195, 196, 199, 202,
  223, 228, 230, 241, 243, 246, 257, 262, 268
Mordant (*The Faerie Queene*) 4–9
More, Sir Thomas 46

Morgan, Edwin 213
mortality 52–3
Morte Arthure 196
motifs 5, 8, 11, 14–15, 22–4, 36, 39 n. 50, 41, 44,
  100, 103, 114, 146–7, 151 n. 30, 152,
  159 n. 70, 169–70, 173–4, 190, 233, 245
mottos 130, 147, 149–50, 152–5, 158, 160–1, 171,
  182, 191, 253
Moul, Victoria 257–60, 263
Munch, Edvard:
  The Scream 152
murals 150–1, 153, 189, 199, 256
Murder of Gonzago (*Hamlet*) 122, 131,
  141, 240
music/singing 14, 22, 53, 93 n. 5, 97 n. 16,
  105, 113, 138, 154, 185, 187, 189, 193,
  223, 269
mysteries 18, 23, 37, 40, 48, 53, 79, 96, 99, 101,
  104–5, 164, 172, 213, 215, 222, 240, 250
myths/mythology 5, 9, 13, 20–1, 34, 37, 41–2, 53,
  65, 75, 132, 136, 210, 245
mythographers 9 n. 15, 101

naturalistic realism 119, 140, 206
nature 32, 41, 45, 47, 66, 68, 105, 120–1, 124,
  136, 140, 147, 153, 156–8, 160, 165, 170,
  172, 200, 202, 204–5, 212, 251, 253 n. 7,
  254–5, 258
Neoplatonism 159, 223
New Criticism 1–2
New Historicism 2, 143
Newton, Isaac 19, 234, 240
novels 3, 15–16, 22, 24, 57, 85, 88, 93, 120, 191–2,
  200, 215, 242, 248–51
number symbolism/symbols 36, 107, 175 n. 72,
  224, 229 n. 58
numerical/numerological:
  associations 108
  centre 81, 106
  composition 19, 105, 174
  organization 36–7, 106
  patterns 1, 265
  proportion 173, 236 n. 102
  structure 36, 115, 231, 235
numerology 1, 81, 105–6, 175
Nuttall, A. D. 116 n. 1, 118, 120, 121 n. 38,
  122 n. 48, 123 n. 56, 124, 125 n. 69,
  137 n. 152, 138 n. 160
nymphs 5, 7–8, 70–3, 82, 153 n. 39, 267

obelisks 159, 169, 173, 225; *see also* columns
odes 186, 225–6, 254
Oliver (*As You Like It*) 48–9, 55
Olivia (*Twelfth Night*) 93, 95, 98–104, 117

INDEX

Onians, John 222 nn. 7–9, 229 n. 59, 235 n. 95
   Bearers of Meaning 110, 111 n. 23, 182 n. 10
Ophelia (*Hamlet*) 121–3, 127–9, 131, 136,
   137 n. 153, 247
Orlando (*As You Like It*) 45, 48–54, 254, 265
Orsino (*Twelfth Night*) 93, 95, 98–103, 117
Orsino, Don Virgilio 93
Ortelius, Abraham:
   Theatrum in Orbis Terrarum 232 n. 79
Osgood, Frances Sargent 215
Osric (*Hamlet*) 121, 135–6
Otis, Brooks 23, 199
otium 54, 189–90, 255 n. 16
Ovid:
   Amores 183, 184 n. 20, 186
   Heroides 253
   Metamorphoses 5, 42 n. 68, 97 n. 19, 197 n. 18

paganism 96, 180
   altars 110, 111 n. 25, 112 n. 30
   wisdom 96, 117
painting/paintings 8, 15, 93 n. 5, 135, 136 n. 145,
   151, 153, 155, 176, 182, 189, 205, 211, 223,
   248, 256, 262 n. 58
Palatine Anthology 154–5, 181
Palingenius, *see* Manzolli
Palladio, Andrea 116 n. 6, 222, 248
Palmer (*The Faerie Queene*) 10, 242–3
Palmer, Thomas 148, 151, 157 n. 60, 162, 175
   Sprite of Trees and Herbes 156
   Two Hundred Poosees 150, 152, 156
   Ungathered Verse 177
Pan 39, 41, 252
Pandemonium (*Paradise Lost*) 30
panegyric 35, 37, 40, 157
Panofsky, Erwin 51 n. 26, 167, 194
Panthea (*The Faerie Queene*) 30
Pantheon 30
Papal Decretals 195
Paracelsus 68 n. 14, 78 n. 55, 250
Parkin, Rebecca 70 n. 23, 74 n. 37, 77
Parliamentary Survey 29
Parnell, Thomas 73
paroles 11–13
Parry, Robert 215
participatory realism 3, 200, 242–6, 248–50
pastoral 11, 25, 27 n. 3, 41, 51, 54, 57, 84–91,
   186–9, 217, 229, 252–5
   comedy 20 n. 26
   drama 24, 44–5
   eclogues 13–14, 18, 24, 44, 184, 203
   elegies 17, 23
   instruction 44, 48
   plays 45, 46, 50

   poetry 185, 190
   romance 24, 44, 46–7
   world 45, 49–50
patronage/patrons 27–8, 34–5, 38, 40, 75, 90,
   153, 157, 175, 181, 187, 241, 257,
   260–1, 266–7
pattern poems 108–9, 114, 160 n. 78
Patterson, Annabel 89
Pattison, Mark 56
Paved Court theatre 166 n. 14
Peacock, John 148
Peake, Mervyn:
   Titus Groan 24
Pearsall, Derek 204 n. 75, 205–6
Peeters, Bonaventura 182
Pelegromius, Simon
   Synonymorum Sylva 156 n. 54
Pellegrino, Camillo 117 n. 9, 236
Peña, Petrus:
   Stirpium Adversaria Nova 159
Penshurst Place 27–9, 31–8, 40–2, 252 n. 1, 255,
   258–9, 262–5
Perret, Arthur J. 217, 221
Perrière, Guillaume de la:
   Théâtre des Bons Engins 165
perspective 34, 71, 79, 116–17, 119–23, 126, 128,
   131, 133, 134 n. 133, 135, 137, 139–40, 167,
   179, 240, 244, 246–50
Petrarch 88, 108, 122 n. 51, 254
   Eclogues 45
   Rime 206
Phebe (*As You Like It*) 48, 54
Phedon (*The Faerie Queene*) 242–4
Philemon (*The Faerie Queene*) 242–3
Philip II, King 176
Philipott, Thomas 153 n. 39
   Poems 156 n. 52
Phillips, Edward 58
Philo 7–8, 234
Philofunniculus
   A New Oxford Sausage 183
Philostratus 153, 199
   Imagines 148
Pico della Mirandola, Giovanni 96,
   113 n. 34, 233
   Heptaplus 36 n. 39
picturae 148–52, 154–5, 157–8, 160–3, 182
Pillars of Hercules 110, 233
planets 29, 51, 52 n. 28, 66, 68, 82, 174–5, 249–50
plants 54 n. 33, 156, 159, 268; *see also* gardens
Planudean Anthology 154–5, 181
Plato 8, 96
   Phaedo 9 n. 15
   Phaedrus 186

INDEX 289

Symposium 101
Timaeus 98
Platonic horse 4
Platonic myth 9 n. 15
Plautus:
  Trinummus 215
Pliny 93 n. 6
Plotinus 9 n. 15
Plutarch 226 n. 36
  Lives 132 n. 121
  Moralia 133 n. 127
Poe, Edgar Allan 215
  The Narrative of A. Gordon Pym 24
Polidanus
  Rusticus 200
Pollux 101
Polonius (*Hamlet*) 121, 126, 128, 130 n. 107,
  131–2, 134, 138 n. 158, 139, 141
Pope, Alexander 3, 27 n. 3, 40, 49, 63, 67–8, 71–3,
  75, 78, 89, 163
  A Key to the Lock 80, 81 n. 71
  'Epistle to Dr. Arbuthnot' 188 n. 36
  Essay on Criticism 203
  Pastorals 88
  The Rape of the Lock 11, 24, 65–6, 69–70, 74,
    76–7, 79–83
  Windsor Forest 27
Porphyrian Trees 158
Porphyry 9 n. 15, 157
Porter, Endymion 150, 268
Portia (*The Merchant of Venice*) 118
Possevino, Antonio 176 n. 79
postmodern critics 116
postmodern metafiction 193
poststructuralism 116 n. 1, 125, 143
Pound, Ezra 212
Powell, Thomas 261
Praz, Mario 5 nn. 6–7, 146, 148 n. 13, 150 n. 23,
  157 n. 59, 158
Prince Hal (*2 Henry IV*) 133, 165–6
printers 148, 154, 159
printers' devices 109, 154, 159 n. 70
prodigy houses 28, 30–1, 38, 42 n. 70
Propertius 223 n. 13
  Elegies 253 n. 4
Proserpina 211
Prosser, Eleanor 124 n. 64, 125 n. 77, 127,
  132 n. 123, 134 n. 139, 135 n. 143,
  139 n. 166, 141
Protestants/Protestantism 112, 123, 130, 141,
  174, 176, 195–6, 219, 231, 256
Psalms 37, 177–8, 231, 234, 261
psychology 22, 92, 102
  psychological realism 93, 140

Ptolemaic:
  analogies 174
  planetary order 51, 175
  universe 249
  world system 179, 240
Ptolemy:
  Tetrabiblos 102–3
Publilius Optatianus Porfirius 112, 214
Puttenham, George 18 n. 20, 44–5, 112–13, 228,
  229 n. 57
Puttenham, George:
  The Arte of English Poesie 14 n. 9, 44 n. 4, 109,
    113 n. 31, 160
pyramids 109, 159, 169, 173, 191, 225, 228
Pyrene (*The Faerie Queene*) 242–3
Pyrrhus (*Hamlet*) 123, 133, 141
Pythagoras 96–8, 117, 211
Pythagorean:
  doctrine 117
  ideas of cosmic unity 101
  musical theory 97 n. 16
  number symbolism 107
  sacred tetraktys 107
  triangle 114

R. T.:
  De Templis 234
Rabel, Daniel:
  Theatrum Florae 165
Racine, Jean:
  Phèdre 17
Radcliffe, Ann:
  The Mysteries of Udolpho 250
Radcliffe, David Hill 87 n. 8, 90 n. 18
Raleigh, Sir Walter 58, 140 n. 170, 141,
  219, 267
  History of the World 158, 170, 232
Rathborne, Isabel E. 30 n. 19, 31 n. 22
realism 2, 20, 45, 86, 88, 99, 116 n. 1, 118, 120–1,
  125, 131, 135, 138, 197, 243; *see also* formal
  realism, modern realism, naturalistic realism,
  participatory realism, psychological
  realism, Renaissance realism,
  spectator realism
Reformation 5, 137 n. 153, 176, 195–6, 222, 231
Reinhold, Erasmus:
  Prutenic Tables 174
relevance 85, 93 n. 5, 125, 142–5
religion 35, 65–6, 77, 123, 130, 195
religious:
  associations 152
  books 171
  collections 158
  content 93 n. 5

religious: (*cont.*)
  discipline 130
  emblems 162
  humanists 194
  interpretation 94
  life 47
  medieval images 153
  orders 200
  poems 43
  relations 167
  subjects 21
  truth 63, 161 n. 81
Renaissance realism 3, 116–17, 123, 141, 199, 205, 240, 245, 248
representation 3, 20, 30, 87, 99, 101, 109, 116–17, 120, 124, 131, 133, 135, 139–40, 144, 156, 189, 240, 243–4
rhetoric 11, 33, 53, 68, 86, 123, 131, 150, 157, 171, 184, 198, 227, 237–8, 258
  conceptions 223 division 38
  figures 185
  imitation 200
  proportions 14
  schemes 15, 213
  texturing 14
  topos 71
  treatments 180
  tropes 16
Rhetorica ad Herennium 233
Richardson, Samuel 240, 248
  Clarissa 192
  Pamela 192
riches/wealth 28, 31, 32 n. 27, 43, 60, 62, 79, 261
Ricks, Christopher 3, 61, 213
Ridley, Florence 203–5
Rilke, Rainer Maria:
  The Notebooks of Malte Laurids Brigge 192 n. 47
ring composition 157, 225–6
Ripa, Cesare 130
  Iconologia 4 n. 3, 8, 68 n. 15, 191
rivers 5, 7–8, 27 n. 2, 33, 107, 189–90, 199, 250, 263 n. 68
Robson, Simon:
  The Choice of Change 261
Robson, Wallace 3, 56–7, 125 n. 76, 134 n. 139
Rochester, Earl of 165
Roe, John 228
Rogers, Daniel 224 n. 23
Rogers, Robert 159
Rogers, William 233
Rolewinck, Werner:
  Fasciculus Temporum 233 n. 83

Rollenhagen, Gabriel:
  Nucleus Emblematum 114
Roman circus 110
Roman coin 150
romance 19–21, 23–5, 44, 46–7, 65 n. 1, 80, 85, 117, 161, 197, 204, 218, 250, 253
Romantic poets/poems 13, 114, 212
Rome 30, 31 n. 22, 173, 208 n. 108
Ronsard, Pierre de 203
  Bocage 156
  Odes 225
Roos, Sir Richard 215
Rosalind/Ganymede (*As You Like It*) 48–55
Rosencrantz (*Hamlet*) 121, 126, 132, 135, 138 n. 158, 139
Rosenmeyer, Thomas G. 45 n. 11, 203 n. 59
Rosicrucian:
  Chemical Wedding 81
  movement 69
  mythology 65
  spirits 66, 72
Røstvig, Maren-Sofie 49 n. 21, 174 n. 57, 226 n. 36, 227
Ruddymane (*The Faerie Queene*) 5–6, 8
Ruscelli, Girolamo 149
  Le Imprese Illustri 147, 171
Ruskin, John 163, 239, 250
Russell, Daniel 146, 151 n. 25
Russian literature 192 n. 47
Rutter, Tom:
  Shakespeare and the Admiral's Men 2

Sainte Chapelle 111, 222, 224
saints 42, 92–4, 104, 167, 219
Salter, Elizabeth 205–6
San Pedro, Diego de:
  Carcel de Amor 103
Sannazaro, Jacopo 190, 253–5
Satan 13, 57, 59–63, 160, 166, 172, 216, 232
satire 20 n. 26, 44–5, 67, 78, 80, 82, 141, 187–9, 258, 260, 263–4
satiric:
  comments 181
  malcontents 126
  mock-epic 14, 24
  models 76
  parody 180
  topos 187 n. 35
Saturn (deity/planet) 41, 66 n. 7, 102–3, 175, 254
Saussure, Ferdinand de 2, 11, 84, 213
Saxl, Fritz 51 n. 26
Saxo Grammaticus:
  Danish History 126
Scaliger, Julius Caesar 19, 24, 109, 228

Poetices Libri Septem 109 n. 20, 160, 180, 186, 236 n. 102, 253 n. 8
scenery 116, 161 n. 82, 247
science 1, 90, 105, 158, 216, 249
science fiction 18–20, 24, 251
Scotland 170, 196, 204, 207 n. 94, 212, 257
Seaton, Ethel 215–16, 219
   Sir Richard Roos 217
Sebastian (*Twelfth Night*) 93, 94 n. 7, 98–101, 103–4
Sebastian, St 94
Sébillet, Thomas 180
Seneca 122
   Epistola 185
Serlio, Sebastiano 167, 169 n. 34, 170, 227, 229, 248
Servius 197, 211
sexual:
   appetite 98
   basis 70
   doubles entendres 76
   identity 103
   innuendos 75
   irregularity 9
   politics 82
   taboos 69
   see also concupiscence
Shakespeare, William 2, 45–6, 48–9, 51, 116, 118 n. 16, 123, 125, 128, 130, 133, 135, 137–9, 185–6, 190 n. 42, 244, 247, 256, 265
   A Midsummer Night's Dream 92 n. 1, 216
   As You Like It 44, 47, 50, 52–5, 141, 165 n. 7, 254
   Coriolanus 241
   First Folio 182
   Hamlet 13, 119–21, 134, 140–1, 241
   Henry IV 106 n. 2, 141, 165, 166 n. 14
   Henry V 116 n. 3, 120 n. 35, 133 n. 130, 141
   Henry VI 245
   King Lear 241
   Macbeth 119, 246
   Measure for Measure 15, 171, 245
   Othello 92, 119–20
   Pericles 158, 246
   Richard II 133 n. 130
   Richard III 92
   Romeo and Juliet 141
   Sonnets 173, 187
   The Merchant of Venice 117
   The Taming of the Shrew 240–1
   The Tempest 161, 240
   The Winter's Tale 161, 241
   Troilus and Cressida 141, 241
   Twelfth Night 92–9, 101–4, 117

Shirley, John:
   The Triumph of Peace 116 n. 5, 168, 247
Showalter, Elaine 129 n. 102, 142
Shrewsbury, Earl of 29
Shylock (*The Merchant of Venice*) 117–19
Sidney, Robert (Viscount Lisle) 27, 34, 256–9, 261–6, 267 n. 85
Sidney, Sir Philip 28 n. 4, 31, 34, 36, 38, 40–2, 87, 89, 141, 167, 200, 221, 231, 255, 261, 267
   Apology 123 n. 53
   Arcadia 24, 199, 225, 244, 250
   Astrophel and Stella 48, 86, 187, 268 n. 88
Sidney's Oak 32, 255–6, 265, 267, 269
signals 12–14, 16, 61, 135, 152, 185, 190–1, 263, 265
silvae 155–60, 180–1
Silvius (*As You Like It*) 45, 48, 50
Simmias 160
Simpson, Percy 29, 30 n. 21, 34 n. 34, 39 n. 51, 41 n. 63, 42 n. 69, 255 n. 17, 260 n. 45, 261 n. 48, 264 n. 74, 265 n. 75, 266 n. 82
Sinclair, Lord 195
Sir Andrew (*Twelfth Night*) 93, 97
Sir Clyomon and Clamydes 45
Sir Oliver Martext (*As You Like It*) 45
Sir Plume (*The Rape of the Lock*) 68, 80, 82
Sir Rowland (*As You Like It*) 48, 50
Sir Toby (*Twelfth Night*) 39, 93–5, 97, 117
Sister Arts 3, 163
Sixtus V, Pope 173
Small, John 201 n. 47, 202
Smarr, Janet Levarie 159
Smart, Christopher 89
Smith, J. C. 202
Smith, Marion Bodwell 95
Smollett, Tobias 21
Solinus:
   Polyhistor 8–9
Solomon, King 38 n. 46, 176, 178, 233 n. 83, 235
Solomon's Temple 30, 176, 222, 230, 233–5
sonnets 11, 21, 86, 170, 172, 179–80, 187, 215, 217–18
Sophocles:
   Oedipus Tyrannus 13
soul 5, 9, 61, 113, 122, 130, 134, 148, 151, 158, 186
spectator realism 3, 116, 130, 134, 140, 200, 240–2, 245–9, 251
Speed, Samuel 113, 230
Spence, Joseph:
   Anecdotes 76 n. 44
   Polymetis 68 nn. 12–13

Spenser, Edmund 5–8, 10, 16, 27, 30, 34, 42, 44, 62, 75, 132, 163, 185, 190, 200, 202, 211, 217, 219, 243–5
   An Hymne in Honour of Beautie 231
   An Hymne in Honour of Love 231
   Cantos of Mutabilitie 183
   Colin Clout's Come Home Again 218
   Epithalamion 224
   The Faerie Queene 1, 4, 14 n. 9, 23, 31 n. 22, 65–6, 68 n. 14, 92, 98, 113 n. 33, 125 n. 78, 140, 162, 169, 218, 220–1, 230, 242
   The Ruines of Time 221
   The Shepheardes Calender 45, 49, 88–9, 150, 183, 185 n. 26
Sperber, Dan 85
   Relevance 85 n. 2, 144, 185 n. 24
spirit/spirits 10, 37–8, 55–6, 66–9, 70, 71–4, 79–80, 81 n. 70, 82, 107, 173, 179, 202, 211, 215
Statius 108, 156
Steen, Jan 77 n. 49, 97, 243
Sterne, Laurence:
   Tristram Shandy 192, 250
Stevenson, Robert Louis:
   Ebb-Tide 23
   Kidnapped 23
   Moral Fables 146
   Prince Otto 25
   The Dynamiter 23
   Treasure Island 22–3
stoicism 45, 47, 62, 123
Stolcius, Daniel:
   Hortulus Hermeticus Flosculis Philosophorum 156
Strode, William:
   'Melancholy' 90
   'Opposite to Melancholy' 90
   The Floating Island 116 n. 5, 247
Sturm, Johann 195, 196 n. 10
Suetonius:
   Divus Augustus 147 n. 5
   Vita Vergilii 256 n. 19
Summers, Joseph H. 112
Summerson, Sir John 28, 29 nn. 10–12, 31, 42 n. 70
Sun/Sol 51, 74–5, 89, 128, 159, 174–5, 177, 207–11, 225
Surius, Lawrence 93 n. 5
Surrey, Earl of 200–1
   Aeneid 197
Swift, Jonathan:
   Gulliver's Travels 17, 24
sylphs 65–7, 69–74, 77, 79, 81–3

Sylvester, Joshua 111, 225
   Du Bartas His Divine Weekes and Workes 110, 138 n. 156, 213, 224, 230
   Lachrimae lachrimarum 261
symbols/symbolism 4–9, 23–5, 28–32, 36–9, 42, 48, 53–5, 67, 74, 76–7, 81, 99–101, 106–8, 111, 113, 116–17, 130–2, 137, 151–2, 156, 157 n. 60, 159, 161, 163–5, 168, 170–2, 176, 187, 191, 198, 211, 222, 224, 226, 231–2, 236, 244, 261

Tablet of Cebes 162
Tacitus:
   Life of Agricola 261
Taffin, Jean:
   The Marks of the Children of God 261
Taffrail (H. Taprell Dorling):
   Pincher Martin 23
Tasso, Torquato 7, 24, 229 n. 58, 254
   Gerusalemme Liberata 65, 236
Taylor, John 107 n. 6, 188 n. 36
temperance 1, 4–5, 7–10, 209 n. 115, 243
Temple, William 123 n. 53
Thackeray, William Makepeace 241
   Vanity Fair 249
Thalestris (*The Rape of the Lock*) 68, 70–1, 73, 75, 82
Thames 42, 75, 79, 190
theatre 104, 116, 120–1, 164–6, 171, 227, 237–8
theatres 104, 165–8, 233, 237
Theobalds House 28–31, 42 n. 70, 260 n. 42
Theocritus 22–3, 46, 184
   Idylls 253
Thomson, Gladys Scott 258 n. 29
Thomson, James 185
   Autumn 186 n. 29
   The Seasons 203
title-pages 154, 158–60, 161 n. 82, 162, 165, 171, 215, 232–3, 238
Titus (*Twelfth Night*) 93
Titus, Emperor 147, 152, 191
Touchstone (*As You Like It*) 44, 47–9, 52–3
tragedy 13–14, 17, 19 n. 25, 20, 24, 84, 119, 121, 125, 139–41, 172, 179–80, 183–4, 186, 208, 240, 243–6
trees 29, 34–5, 37, 39, 41–2, 44, 47, 52–3, 54 n. 33, 106–7, 153, 156, 159, 168, 182, 187–8, 202, 251–6, 262, 265, 267–8
Trees of Life 158
Tres Riches Heures du Duc de Berry 206
Tresham, Sir Thomas 225
Triangular Lodge 225
triangular numbers 37, 173, 226

INDEX 293

Trilling, Lionel 25
Trissino, Gian Giorgio 7
  L'Italia Liberata da Gotti 6, 10
Trithemius, Johannes 108
Trollope, Anthony 240, 242
Tuve, Rosemond 52 n. 28, 163, 194
Twelfth Night 93–4, 97, 174 n. 63

Uhlig, Claus 46
Umbriel (*The Rape of the Lock*) 70, 72–3
Underwood, P. A. 5 n. 7, 8 n. 13
Urquhart, Sir Thomas 202, 237
ut architectura poesis 105, 173–6, 222, 224, 227, 237–8
ut pictura poesis 109, 198, 223

Valentine (*Twelfth Night*) 93, 99
Valeriano, Pierio 9 n. 15, 9 n. 17, 159 n. 73
  Hieroglyphica 5 n. 4, 8, 228 n. 53
Valla, Lorenzo 195–6, 223
van Belcamp, Jan:
  Great Picture of Lady Anne Clifford 243–4
van der Straet, Jan 163 n. 91
van Dyke, Anthony 166
van Es, Bart:
  Shakespeare in Company 2
van Eyck, Jan:
  Turin–Milan Hours 206
van Haeften, Benedict:
  Schola Cordis 111
Vasari, Giorgio 199, 211
Vaughan, Henry 30 n. 16, 112 n. 27, 160
Venus (deity) 39 n. 53, 51, 66 n. 7, 68, 75, 207–8, 210
Verne, Jules 18–19
Versailles 174
Verstegen, Richard:
  Theatrum Crudelitatum Haereticorum Nostri Temporis 165
Vestinus 110
Victorian:
  age 213
  literature 242
  novels 192, 249
  realism 99
  writers 239
  writing 105
Villalpando, Juan Bautista 176–7, 234
Villon, François 215
Vincentio (*Measure for Measure*) 15
Viola (*Twelfth Night*) 93 n. 6, 94 n. 7, 95, 98–103, 117
Virgil 16, 19 n. 25, 22–4, 36, 56, 188, 190, 195, 197–8, 204–5, 208, 211–12

Aeneid 23, 184–6, 197, 199–202, 207, 210, 261
Bucolics 195 n. 6
Eclogues 22, 88, 90, 96, 184–5, 253
Georgics 62–3, 87, 89–90, 190–1, 200, 201 n. 44, 234, 253 n. 7
Opera 7 n. 10, 197 n. 18
virtue 1, 4, 7–8, 10, 33 n. 30, 38, 40–3, 45, 61–2, 70, 75, 111, 121, 168, 173, 198–9, 211, 226, 230, 250, 257, 260
visual arts 2–3, 21, 42, 148, 155, 158 n. 62, 163, 182–3, 208, 243, 245, 247
Vitruvian:
  formal relations 173
  ideas 169
  proportions 167, 222
  style 174
Vitruvius 209 n. 112, 222–3, 225, 229

Waller, Edmund 269
  'At Penshurst' 32 n. 26, 255, 267–8
Warton, Thomas 4 n. 3, 31 n. 22, 201 n. 45
Wasserman, Earl R. 67, 70, 72–3, 76–8
Watson, Thomas 186 n. 27, 187
  Hekatompathia 215
Wellek, René 11 n. 1, 17–19, 24 n. 38, 25–6
Westerweel, Bart 108 nn. 14–15, 109 n. 18, 110–11, 112 n. 29, 114 n. 39, 160 n. 79, 228 n. 49, 230
Westfall, Suzanne 92
Wharton, Goodwin 69
Wheel of Virgil 188
Whipper of the Satire 189
Whipping of the Satire 189
Whitehall 165, 168
Whitney, Geoffrey 130 n. 107, 153
  A Choice of Emblems 146
Willes, Richard 109, 110 n. 22, 113, 228, 230
  Poematum Liber 112, 160, 180
Willet, Andrew 148
  Sacrorum Emblematum Centuria
  Una 147
William (*As You Like It*) 47, 53
William, Earl of Pembroke 28 n. 4, 261–2
Williams, Raymond 27 n. 3, 31, 36 n. 39, 252, 258, 270
  Keywords 142
Willingham, Calder:
  Eternal Fire 15
Willis, John 237
  Mnemonica 233 n. 83
Willoughby, Sir Francis 28
Wilson, Deirdre 2 n. 2, 85, 185 n. 24
  Relevance 144
Wilson, Gayle E. 30, 35, 37, 39, 42

Wimsatt, W. K. 1, 13 nn. 6–7, 82
   'Belinda Ludens' 81
Winchester College 160, 180, 195
Wind, Edgar 42 n. 67, 48 n. 18, 68 n. 14, 68 n. 12, 208 n. 108
Wither, George 90, 109, 114 n. 37, 130 n. 111, 153, 158, 232
   Elegies 261
Wit's Album, or Pine-apple of Literature 183
Wittenberg 123, 128
Wittkower, Rudolf:
   Architectural Principles in the Age of Humanism 4 n. 2, 222

women 3, 48, 50, 67, 69, 74–6, 82–3, 101–2, 121, 143, 157, 197, 246
Wroth, Lady Mary 28 n. 4, 261–2
Wroth, Sir Robert 262, 263 n. 68
Wroth, Sir Thomas:
   Aeneid 261
Wyatt, Thomas 213

Yates, Frances 67 n. 9, 69 n. 17, 106, 130, 238

Zelmane (*Arcadia*) 199, 250
zodiac 29, 31, 165 n. 7, 177, 208, 237–8